Jane's

Ⱳ

Recog **ɩde**

Fourth edition published in 2006 by Collins
Fourth Edition © HarperCollins*Publishers*

HarperCollins*Publishers*
77-85 Fulham Palace Road
Hammersmith
London W6 8JB
UK

www.collins.co.uk

HarperCollins*Publishers* Inc
10 East 53rd Street
New York
NY 10022
USA

www.harpercollins.com

www.janes.com

ISBN-13 978-0-00-718327-2
ISBN-10 0-00-718327-5

Design: Susie Bell
Proofreading: Keith Faulkner
Editorial: Louise Stanley

Printed and bound by Printing Express, Hong Kong

Warship
Recognition Guide

Revised and edited by

Anthony J. Watts

Collins

Contents

Submarines

Patrol Forces

9

Amphibious Forces

Mine Warfare Forces

Foreword

Yet again the international situation has undergone a major change since the Foreword to the last edition was written. The latest challenge to face the world's navies is the global threat of asymmetric terrorism.

The collapse of Soviet communism brought about a radical change which forced many navies to re-assess their strategic position and future requirements. For some of the larger ones the effects of this rethink regarding priorities, commitments and requirements are still being thought through. This is having a major impact on programmes and orders of battle. With plans and programmes having to be defined so far ahead it is inevitable that a number of navies now deploy various classes of warship not really suited to meet current requirements. Many smaller navies too have had to restructure and new designs, unfettered by Cold War thinking, reflect much of the new technology and tactical requirements now pervading the current naval scene. Foremost among these is the requirement for stealth, and this is clearly evident not only in the latest frigate and corvette designs, but even in FACs and more humble patrol and OPV designs.

Events during 2004–05 have highlighted to an unprecedented degree the new global asymmetric terrorist threat. This is now beginning to have an impact not only on general naval requirements, but more specifically on types of vessel and armaments designed to counter the threat. Allied with this is the increasing frequency of acts of piracy on the high seas – and some of this may well be linked to terrorism.

As many commentators are now signalling, we are entering uncharted waters, particularly where naval defence is concerned, and the role and structure of the world's navies may well have to undergo yet another radical change in order to meet this new and developing threat.

United States

The asymmetric terrorist threat, combined with the change to the littoral warfare scenario in the wake of the demise of Soviet communism, has caused the United States Navy to undergo a change that will alter its structure, platform and equipment requirements profoundly.

The ending of the Cold War has led to a major review of the submarine force. Four of the SSBN fleet are currently being modified to deploy up to 54 land attack Tomahawk cruise missiles in place of their ballistic missiles. The SSN fleet is also being reshaped and the 'Seawolf' class project on which so much seemed to depend has now been terminated at three boats, to be replaced by the smaller 'Virginia' class. Rancorous debate continues even over the wisdom of continuing construction of the 'Virginia' class, which although smaller and only slightly less expensive than the 'Seawolf' class still has much Cold War thinking embedded in its design. With submarines continuing to form the core platform of the US Navy's expeditionary concept in littoral warfare, their role has now been considerably widened to embrace a much more comprehensive intelligence gathering and reconnaissance capability, which in the concept of network-centric warfare allows all the information so gathered to be immediately available to all the units of the Task Force, of which the submarine now forms an integral part. To meet the expanded role, a whole new raft of equipment is being developed providing the submarine with the capability to deploy offboard unmanned vehicles for reconnaissance and intelligence gathering missions, surveying for potential minefields in the path of the Task Force and the possibility of deploying AUVs for reconnaissance and targeting as well as other as yet undefined technologies. All these concepts may well dictate that a new and radical type of underwater platform be developed to deploy them.

The surface fleet too is undergoing major changes. The escort fleet will soon undergo a radical one. The last of the Cold War-designed 'Spruance' class destroyers will shortly be withdrawn from service and replaced by the 'Arleigh Burke' class. Construction of the last of the latter is due to start in 2008. Likewise the 'Ticonderoga' class cruisers, having reached their life expectancy, are also beginning to be retired. In the last few years, large numbers of frigates have been handed over to friendly navies, in particular to navies in the Middle East and Gulf.

To replace these units a new, radical design for a family of warship variants is planned that will encompass a land attack version, a cruiser and littoral warfare combat ship. The order for the first of these was placed in 2005 with completion scheduled for 2013. The design features a wave-piercing tumblehome configuration designed to improve stealth and provide a more stable platform. The composite superstructure is totally enclosed and will house all the sensors and antennas. A completely new approach is being adopted for the propulsion system, which will combine electric drive and an integrated power management system. This could lead to the inclusion in the armament of an electromagnetic rail gun and directed energy weapons, but the programme has come in for much criticism, not least because of a cost that will severely curtail any other construction.

The French nuclear-powered carrier Charles De Gaulle while exhibiting numerous stealth features still retains the classic lines of an aircraft carrier. (*Michael Nitz*)

The US 'Arleigh Burke' class destroyer *Paul Hamilton* clearly shows a design prepared for a Cold War scenario, with its massive size, split towering superstructures, large array of electronics and huge missile arsenal. (*Michael Nitz*)

Russia

The Russian Navy appears at last to be receiving some welcome boost to its funding. This has led to a new range of warship designs being undertaken, as well as sufficient funds being made available to purchase fuel and to develop basic training. This has enabled a number of large-scale exercises to be undertaken during the last few years.

Recent tragic accidents and incidents are, perhaps, symptomatic of a Navy that has to a large degree lain unmaintained and idle in port due to lack of funds. Not only have ships been allowed to rust away at their moorings, but so too have their crews who have been given little or no opportunity for ongoing training during the last ten years of the last century.

These problems are now being addressed, but for many vessels far too late, for they are now so rusty and unkempt that it would be dangerous to take them to sea and they must be scrapped. This is not as dire as it may sound for the vast majority were designed and built for Cold War scenarios and are no longer capable of meeting the requirements of a changed world. In addition much of their equipment is outmoded and obsolete. The outcome has been that the Navy is retaining the best units and has begun to replace redundant units with new designs much more suited to the new strategic requirements.

However, some vestiges of Cold War thinking remain, and it may be another ten years or so before the Russian Navy receives more suitable and modern units. Likewise, a new generation of sailors from the most senior admirals to the most junior of ratings will have to be trained in new ways of thinking and using the new systems and ships that will eventually emerge from the chaos of the demise of Soviet Communism.

China

After prodigious efforts at upgrading and modernising her fleet, China is now well on the way to becoming a first class world naval power. China's long-term strategic objective is undoubtedly to project sea power right across the Pacific and down into the Indian Ocean (a possibility of which the Indian Navy is all too aware). Naval units are beginning to regularly exercise right throughout the region, projecting sea power across many areas where ownership of small strategically placed islands are situated.

Japan feels threatened by the new Chinese naval posture and early in 2005 a Chinese 'Han' class submarine was tracked in Japanese waters. Other nations too in South-East Asia, right down to Australia, have noted an increasing Chinese naval presence in their areas, and are bolstering their naval forces to meet this challenge. That China is able to project naval power so far away from home is due largely to the build up of a very modern navy, indigenous new construction being bolstered by modern destroyers and submarines acquired from Russia.

While the surface fleet appears to be developing apace with much use of reverse engineering of German machinery and French and Russian electronics, the submarine fleet has not developed quite so well. Realising that to support global naval operations requires a modern submarine fleet, China has made tremendous efforts to develop new generations of submarines, together with a nuclear deterrent comparable in capability to that of other nuclear powers. The development of this indigenous submarine fleet has been beset by problems both technological and human, and some severe losses both in boats and personnel have been suffered. Because the submarine construction programme has seriously lagged behind surface vessel construction, China has had to resort to the acquisition of Russian 'Kilo' class submarines as a stop-gap measure, pending development of new generations of attack and patrol submarine.

Construction of both the 'Han' ssn and 'Ming' ssk classes has been beset by major problems and construction of both has now ended. They will be replaced by the Type 093 ssn, construction of which is underway, and the 'Song' class ssk, eight units of which are now operational with another two under construction.

A new, totally unexpected, design, the 'Yuan', made its appearance in 2004 and will be commissioned in the near future. It has been conjectured that the 'Yuan' may be fitted with an aip system which would enable it to operate much further afield in support of blue water fleet operations. There is considerable speculation concerning the purpose behind the construction of the 'Yuan', especially as construction of the 'Song' class, which appears to be a satisfactory design, is continuing. If the 'Yuan' does prove to have an aip system, might this indicate that China is having problems with the Type 093 ssn, whose construction may be seriously delayed? The first unit of this class was originally laid down in 1994, well over ten years ago.

The Chinese strategic deterrent has also faced many problems in its

Stealth features can clearly be seen in the South African frigate *Mendi*. Not only are all side surfaces sloped, but all deck fittings are concealed. (*Michael Nitz*)

development. In spite of having commissioned her first SSBN in 1987, China has built no further units and is now engaged in developing both a new missile (the JL-2) and a new submarine (the Type 094) to deploy it. Work on developing both the submarine and the new missile has taken much longer than anticipated with the result that the programme has been seriously delayed.

The one category of warship requirement, which now seems to have been moved down the immediate priority list, is the acquisition of an aircraft carrier. However, the Chinese will have gained much valuable knowledge concerning carrier design and construction from the ex-Soviet vessel Varyag, and doubtless work is progressing on developing a carrier design. However, this is very much a long term project and other requirements are far more pressing. Having said that, the perceived need to project naval power much further afield than hitherto leaves the surface fleet vulnerable in the area of air defence. Not until an aircraft carrier can be deployed will Chinese naval task forces operating far from the mainland be provided with a full air defence capability.

United Kingdom

As with many other nations, the core of UK policy now is counter-terrorism, particularly following the bombings of 7/7 in London. Countering international terrorism reflects on defence policy, and while the current UK policy is to maintain the direction set out in the Strategic Defence Review of 1998 and subsequent updates, there has to be a change in emphasis to meet these new threats. While previously plans have centred on operations around Europe, the Middle East and the Gulf and North African regions, frequently in co-operation with other European nations and the USA, there is now a recognition, borne out by events since 2002, that there may well be a requirement for the UK Royal Navy to operate more independently even further afield. This is now being given added impetus by the increasing frequency of violent piratical attacks on merchant vessels in vulnerable shipping lanes, some of which may well be connected with terrorist operations.

To provide adequate cover of any description, or just to be a 'policeman on the beat' demands that any task force operating far from friendly bases – and in today's climate there may be very few of these available – is provided with organic air cover. This requirement will now give added urgency to the completion of planning for the new carrier project and to commence its construction.

In this context it seems strange that the Government has deemed it wise to begin disposing of some of the Navy's escorts when they are only about half way through their life. It is true that they were designed for Cold War scenarios, but any vessel is capable of offering a deterrent image, and may well prevent an escalation of a crisis into one of hostile operations. The net result of the present decision is that the number of hulls available to the Navy to meet any possible future contingency is being severely reduced, particularly when vessels under maintenance or long term refit that are not immediately available for operational duties are taken into account. In fact it has been noted that of the planned force of 27 destroyers and frigates available to the Navy, only nine will be available for continuous overseas deployment at any one time. This is a totally inadequate force to meet any unforeseen situations in which the Government may wish to be involved.

Neither is this desperate situation likely to be resolved in the short term, for the first of the new 'Daring' class destroyers is not scheduled to be commissioned until 2007 at the earliest, with the second unit following some two years later in 2009.

A similar fate is befalling the submarine arm. The new 'Astute' class has, for a variety of reasons both technical and managerial, suffered serious delays and the first of class will not now commission until at least 2008, although construction commenced in 1999. In the meantime the seven 'Trafalgar' class boats will have to soldier on alone, the remaining 'Swiftsure' class already being well beyond their 25-year life expectancy and exhibiting an increasing number of deficiencies and faults. Neither is the 'Trafalgar' class free from problems and the early boats are approaching the limit of their life expectancy from the date of commissioning.

All in all the future for the Royal Navy would seem to be one of mixed fortunes.

The Turkish *Alanya* of the 'Aydin' class exhibits hull stealth features that are now common to many designs. (*Michael Nitz*)

That the Navy will one day have a fixed-wing aircraft carrier again seems assured, but will there be sufficient escorts, both surface and subsurface, to afford it adequate protection in a hostile area of operations where suicide terrorists would be willing to sacrifice themselves against such an inviting target?

Japan

The war in Iraq and the global need to counter the threat of terrorism has seen the beginnings of a major shift in the role of the Japanese armed forces from the purely self-defence role, which had been maintained since the end of the Second World War, to a much wider and expanded one. In the new world order Japan is engaging in much closer co-operation with other regional and global powers and operating over a much wider area as far as the navy is concerned. This has meant that the armed forces have had to undergo a re-organisation of the way in which they are structured and the type of equipment that they have hitherto deployed. Among the priorities that Japan now seeks to address is the potential for a ballistic missile attack against the country, most particularly from North Korea, but also possibly from China. The asymmetrical terrorist threat, as already mentioned, is one that urgently needs to be addressed.

These factors are now impinging heavily on the Navy and its future plans. Emphasis is being placed on the need to provide transport and support for the rapid deployment of security forces. As part of the restructuring to meet the new demands the Navy has laid down the first of a new generation of helicopter carriers (dubbed destroyers to allay any fears that the acquisition of carriers might have on the general population) that will eventually total four, the first of which will enter service around 2010. The vessels will not have a fixed wing capability and no ski-ramp for STOVL aircraft will be fitted.

For ballistic missile defence the 'Kongou' class are to be modernised and upgraded, with an improved design to follow in due course, the first of which was laid down in 2004.

In line with the need to provide an extended reach for the Navy, the first of the 'Improved Oyashio' class equipped with an AIP system has been laid down and will enter service in 2009.

France

French programmes are geared very closely to the needs of the ERRF (European Rapid Reaction Force) and the NRF (NATO Response Force). France has increased her defence equipment budget by 7.3 per cent, the major acquisition being a second carrier that will not be nuclear powered. As with the carrier acquisition programme in the UK, the drain on the defence budget of the second carrier will be enormous and there has been talk that France may join with the UK to build the two nations carriers. However, French requirements differ in many ways from British, and it may prove impossible for the two countries to find common

New threats lead to radical designs capable of meeting all possible contingencies. The US DD(X) design represents the latest thinking in a family of designs based on a common hull. (*Artwork courtesy Raytheon Co*)

ground on which to prepare a carrier design to meet their conflicting requirements. What would not be acceptable to either country would be to achieve a compromise design that would not meet the requirements of either navy.

In line with its avowed intent to support the ERRF France has commissioned the first of two new amphibious vessels, the *Mistral*. These new amphibious ships will replace the *Ouragan* and *Orage*.

In the area of escorts France and Italy are heavily involved in joint ventures, building the 'Horizon' class destroyers and a new class of multi-mission frigates. The latter will be built as two variants, one emphasizing ASW and the other land attack and surface warfare.

Germany

The first two Type 212A submarines under construction for Germany and Italy have been commissioned into the German Navy, and the third and fourth are to commission in 2006. The two boats for the Italian Navy are commissioning in 2005–06. With the commissioning of the third and last 'Sachsen' class unit Germany's frigate programme is now in the doldrums as there seems to be no progress with the follow on F125 frigate programme. Work is progressing on the 'Braunschweig' class (K130 corvettes), but there are no plans to build more than the five units already planned.

Italy

Troubled by her economic situation, and not considering it cost effective to modernise her fleet on her own, Italy has entered into a number of joint ventures with other European countries in an endeavour to maintain a modern and effective fleet. Much of the naval defence budget will be consumed by the new 'Cavour' carrier project. Other major programmes being managed as joint ventures are the Type 212A submarines, and the new 'Horizon' destroyer programme and the Multi-Mission frigate project to replace the 'Maestrale' class frigates.

Anthony J. Watts

About This Book

Jane's Warship Recognition Guide has been published to help readers identify any one of more than 2,200 ships featured, to provide information on the physical characteristics of the ships and the main weapons and to indicate helicopters and fixed wing aircraft that are embarked.

The most important feature of recognition is the visual impact of hulls, masts, radar aerials, funnels and major weapons systems. To help the reader to identify a particular ship, two different types of visual aid have been included:-

- Each entry has a photograph that has been chosen, where possible, for its clarity and the detail it shows.
- At the bottom of each entry is a silhouette that can be used in the traditional way to help with horizon or sun-backed views.

Composite diagrams of a theoretical warship and submarine are printed in the front of the book to help the less experienced reader identify parts of a ship's structure and to become familiar with the terminology used in the text.

Despite the sophistication of modern electronic sensors, visual ship recognition remains as important as ever and is still taught to armed forces in most countries. This book is intended to be a lead-in to the subject of recognition for the student and is not a comprehensive volume of ship types with full data on equipment and systems. Jane's Information Group publishes a series of authoritative titles in electronic or book formats covering ships and associated equipment in great detail. Examples are *Jane's Fighting Ships, Jane's Naval Weapons Systems, Jane's Underwater Warfare Systems*, and *Jane's Radar and Electronic Warfare Systems*. The journal, *Jane's Navy International* covers maritime developments with news and articles on designs, ships, weapons systems, and tactical and strategic issues.

Ship classes for *Jane's Warship Recognition Guide* have been selected for reasons ranging from those ships which may be the most numerous, the most heavily armed, the most tactically important, to those which are most likely to be seen away from their home country's territorial waters.

Navies' orders of battle constantly change with deletions from the strength of the fleet, sales to other countries, refits, and the arrival of new designs and constructions. This edition of *Jane's Warship Recognition Guide* includes details of 24 classes new to the book. A few classes have been deleted, because they are about to disappear; others remain, as whilst the country of origin may be paying them off, they stay in the service of other navies. The book has been structured to make its use as easy as possible.

There are nine sections which cover the major types of warships, namely:-

- Submarines
- Aircraft Carriers
- Cruisers
- Destroyers
- Frigates
- Corvettes
- Patrol Forces
- Amphibious Forces
- Mine Warfare Forces

There is no significance to a ship's strategic or tactical importance indicated by its position in the book. Each section is presented as far as possible in alphabetical order by the country where the ship is in operation. In this way, many more classes of warships and hulls are covered and the reader is able, for the first time, to compare the differences within classes and different navies.

General Notes
In the Name (Pennant Number) section of each entry, the names and pennant numbers of relevant ships are only included where applicable. Some countries do not use pennant numbers, or change them so frequently that the information would soon be of little value. In the case of submarines, pennant numbers are included where often they are not displayed on the boat's hull. There are some cases where the ships fall into the Patrol Forces category with one country and are designated as Corvettes by another, and vice versa. This also can apply in some cases to Frigates and Corvettes and Mine Warfare vessels. To avoid confusion, this has been pointed out in the text.

There are a few instances where a silhouette may not display exactly the same weapons fit as the photograph. This occurs when there are different versions of that class within a navy or a group of navies operating that class of ship.

The editor welcomes any news of corrections, changes or updates to the book as well as new illustrations. These should be forwarded either to the Publishers, or to the editor at his home address, or by e-mail. Any images forwarded by e-mail must be at least 300 dpi, to meet printing requirements.

Anthony J. Watts, Hunters Moon, Hogspudding Lane, Newdigate, Surrey, RH5 5DS, UK; e-mail: anthony.watts@virgin.net.

Composite Warship

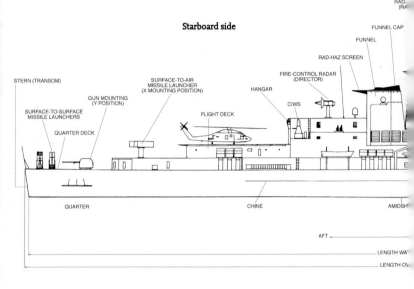

Starboard side

RAD.
(RA

FUNNEL CAP

FUNNEL

RAD-HAZ SCREEN

FIRE-CONTROL RADAR
(DIRECTOR)

STERN (TRANSOM)

SURFACE-TO-AIR
MISSILE LAUNCHER
(X MOUNTING POSITION)

HANGAR

GUN MOUNTING
(Y POSITION)

CIWS

SURFACE-TO-SURFACE
MISSILE LAUNCHERS

FLIGHT DECK

QUARTER DECK

QUARTER

CHINE

AMIDSH

AFT

LENGTH WA

LENGTH OV

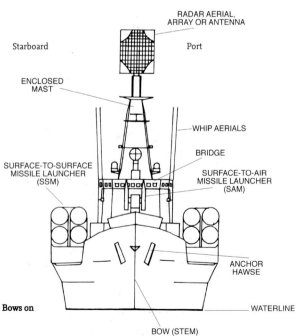

RADAR AERIAL,
ARRAY OR ANTENNA

Starboard

Port

ENCLOSED
MAST

WHIP AERIALS

BRIDGE

SURFACE-TO-SURFACE
MISSILE LAUNCHER
(SSM)

SURFACE-TO-AIR
MISSILE LAUNCHER
(SAM)

ANCHOR
HAWSE

Bows on

WATERLINE

BOW (STEM)

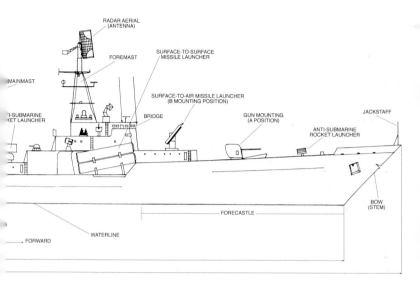

RADAR AERIAL
(ANTENNA)

FOREMAST

MAINMAST

SURFACE-TO-SURFACE
MISSILE LAUNCHER

SURFACE-TO-AIR MISSILE LAUNCHER
(B MOUNTING POSITION)

ANTI-SUBMARINE
ROCKET LAUNCHER

BRIDGE

GUN MOUNTING
(A POSITION)

JACKSTAFF

ANTI-SUBMARINE
ROCKET LAUNCHER

BOW
(STEM)

FORECASTLE

WATERLINE

FORWARD

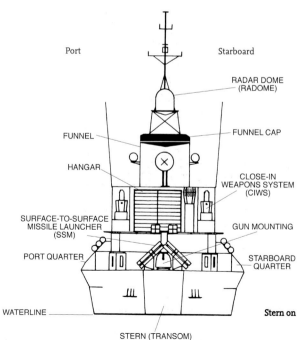

Port

Starboard

RADAR DOME
(RADOME)

FUNNEL

FUNNEL CAP

HANGAR

CLOSE-IN
WEAPONS SYSTEM
(CIWS)

SURFACE-TO-SURFACE
MISSILE LAUNCHER
(SSM)

GUN MOUNTING

PORT QUARTER

STARBOARD
QUARTER

WATERLINE

Stern on

STERN (TRANSOM)

23

Types of Warship Masts

AFT ────────→ FWD

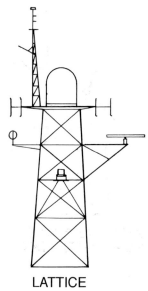

LATTICE

AFT ────────→ FWD

TRIPOD

AFT ────────→ FWD

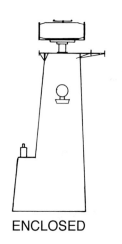

ENCLOSED

AFT ────────→ FWD

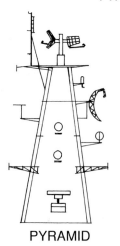

PYRAMID

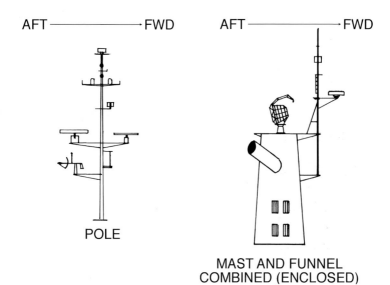

AFT ────────→ FWD

POLE

AFT ────────→ FWD

MAST AND FUNNEL
COMBINED (ENCLOSED)

Composite Submarine

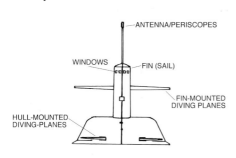

ANTENNA/PERISCOPES

WINDOWS

FIN (SAIL)

FIN-MOUNTED
DIVING PLANES

HULL-MOUNTED
DIVING-PLANES

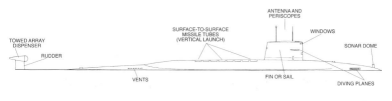

TOWED ARRAY
DISPENSER

RUDDER

VENTS

SURFACE-TO-SURFACE
MISSILE TUBES
(VERTICAL LAUNCH)

ANTENNA AND
PERISCOPES

WINDOWS

SONAR DOME

FIN OR SAIL

DIVING PLANES

Submarines

Type 209 ARGENTINA, BRAZIL, CHILE, COLUMBIA, ECUADOR, GREECE,

Chang Bogo (*Michael Nitz*)

- Blunt bow profile with bow mounted diving planes not visible
- Rounded-topped casing
- Low, long fin mounted on raised part of the casing (on some), with blunt profile forward and sloping profile aft
- Fin has vertical leading and after edges
- Rudder just visible right aft
- Type 1300/1400/1500 and South Korean Type 1200 have more streamlined curves to hull, without raised portion around fin

NOTE: These are a single hull design with two ballast tanks and forward and after trim tanks
NOTE 2: Portugal ordered two Type 209 in April 2004

SPECIFICATION:

COUNTRY OF ORIGIN: Germany
CLASS: Type 209 (Types 1100, 1200, 1300, 1400 and 1500) (Salta, Tupi, Thomson, Pijao, Glavkos, Shishumar, Cakra, Chang Bogo, Angamos, Casma, Atilay, Preveze, Sabalo) (SSK)
ACTIVE: 1 Argentina ('Salta' class, Type 1200), 4 Brazil ('Tupi' class, Type 1400), 2 Chile ('Thomson' class, Type 1300), 2 Colombia ('Pijao' class, Type 1200), 2 Ecuador ('Shyri' class, Type 1300), 8 Greece ('Glavkos' class, Types 1100 and 1200), 4 India ('Shishumar' class, Type 1500), 2 Indonesia ('Cakra' class, Type 1300), 9 South Korea ('Chang Bogo' class, Type 1200), 6 Peru ('Angamos' class, Type 1200), 6 Turkey ('Atilay' class, Type 1200), 5 Turkey ('Preveze' class, Type 1400), 2 Venezuela ('Sabalo' class, Type 1300)
BUILDING: 3 Turkey (Type 1400), 3 South Africa (Type 1400 Mod) (Sa)
NAME (PENNANT NUMBER):
ARGENTINA – Salta (S 31)
BRAZIL – Tupi (S 30), Tamoio (S 31), Timbira (S 33), Tapajó (ex-*Tapajós*) (S 33)

Types 1200/1300

INDIA, INDONESIA, KOREA (SOUTH), PERU, PORTUGAL, SOUTH AFRICA, TURKEY, VENEZUELA

CHILE – Thomson (20), Simpson (21)
COLOMBIA – Pijao (SO 28), Tayrona (SO 29)
ECUADOR – Shyri (S 101, ex-S 11), Huancavilca (S 102, ex-S 12)
GREECE – Glavkos (S 110), Nereus (S 111), Triton (S 112), Proteus (S 113, Type 1100), Poseidon (S 116), Amphitrite (S 117), Okeanos (S 118), Pontos (S 119, Type 1200)
INDIA – Shishumar (S 44), Shankush (S 45), Shalki (S 46), Shankul (S 47)
INDONESIA – Cakra (401), Nanggala (402)
SOUTH KOREA – Chang Bogo (061), Yi Chon (062), Choi Muson (063), Park (065), Lee Jongmu (066), Jung Woon (067), Lee Sunsin (068), Na Daeyong (069), Lee Eokgi (071)
PERU – Angamos (ex-Casma) (SS 31), Antofagasta (SS 32), Pisagua (SS 33), Chipana (SS 34), Islay (SS 35), Arica (SS 36)
SOUTH AFRICA – S 101, S 102, S 103
TURKEY – 'Atilay' class: Atilay (S 347), Saldiray (S 348), Batiray (S 349), Yildiray (S 350), Doganay (S 351), Dolunay (S 352); 'Preveze' class: Preveze (S 353), Sakarya (S 354), 18 Mart (S 355), Anafartalar

(S 356), Gür (S 357), Çanakkale (S 358), Burakreis (S 359), Birinci Inonu (S 360)
VENEZUELA – Sábalo (S 31, ex-S 21), Caribe (S 32, ex-S 22)

FEATURES:

DISPLACEMENT, SURFACED: 980 tons (Turkey 'Atilay' class); 1125 tons (Greece S 110-113), South Korea); 1180 tons (Colombia); 1185 tons (Peru); 1140 tons (Argentina); 1260 tons (Chile); 1285 tons (Ecuador, Indonesia, Venezuela); 1454 tons (Brazil, South Africa, Turkey 'Preveze' class); 1660 tons (India)
DISPLACEMENT, DIVED: 1185 tons (Turkey 'Atilay' class); 1235 tons (Greece S 110-113); 1248 tons (Argentina); 1285 tons (Colombia, Greece (S 116-119), South Korea); 1290 tons (Peru); 1390 tons (Chile, Ecuador, Indonesia); 1586 tons (Turkey 'Preveze' class); 1590 tons (Brazil); 1594 tons (South Africa); 1600 tons (Venezuela); 1850 tons (India)
LENGTH: 183.4 ft (55.9 m) (Argentina, Columbia, Greece); 183.7 ft (56 m) (South Korea, Peru); 195.2 ft (59.5 m) (Chile, Ecuador, Indonesia); 200.1 ft (61 m) (Venezuela); 200.8 ft (61.2 m) (Brazil, Turkey 'Atilay' class); 203.4 ft (62 m) (Turkey 'Preveze' class); 211.2 ft (64.4 m) (India)
BEAM: 20.5 ft (6.3 m) (Argentina, Columbia, Ecuador); 20.3 ft (6.2 m) (Chile, Greece, Brazil, Indonesia, South Korea, Peru, Turkey (both classes), Venezuela); 21.3 ft (6.5 m) (India)
DRAUGHT: 17.9 ft (5.5 m) (Argentina, Columbia, Ecuador, Turkey 'Atilay' class); 18 ft (5.5 m) (Brazil, Chile, South Korea, Turkey 'Preveze' class, Venezuela); 19.7 ft (6 m) (India)
SPEED: 11 kts surfaced; 21.5 kts dived
RANGE: 7500 miles at 8 kts snorting (South Korea, Turkey 'Atilay' class, Venezuela); 8000 miles at 8 kts snorting (India, Indonesia, Chile, Turkey 'Preveze' class); 400 miles at 4 kts dived

ARMAMENT:

MISSILES: McDonnell Douglas Sub-Harpoon (Greece, South Korea and Turkey 'Preveze' class

only); SSM also fitted to Indian boats S 48 and S 49
TORPEDOES: Eight 21 in (533 mm) bow tubes; AEG SST 4 (Argentina, Peru, Turkey 'Atilay' class, Venezuela); AEG SUT Mod 1 (Chile, Colombia, Ecuador, India); AEG SUT Mod 0 (Greece, Indonesia); SystemTechnik Nord (STN) SUT Mod 2 (South Korea); Marconi Mk 24 Tigerfish Mod 1/2 (Brazil, Turkey 'Preveze' class); STN Atlas DM 2A4 (Turkey S 357 on)
MINES: External 'strap-on' type for 24 (India); 28 in lieu of torpedoes (South Korea, Turkey 'Preveze' class)
DECOYS: C 303 acoustic decoys (India)

ELECTRONICS:

RADARS: Surface search – Thomson-CSF Calypso II/III (all except Turkey 'Atilay' class), S 63B (Turkey 'Atilay' class); Navigation – Thomson-CSF Calypso II, (Argentina), Terma Scanter (Brazil, Venezuela)
SONARS: Atlas Elektronik CSU 83-90 (DBQS-21) (Greece S 110-113); CSU 83/1 (Brazil, India, South Korea, Turkey 'Preveze' class); Atlas Elektronik CSU 3-4 (Argentina, Chile, Colombia, Ecuador, Greece (S 116-119), Peru, Turkey 'Atilay' class, Venezuela), hull-mounted; CSU 3-2 (Indonesia); Atlas Elektronik TAS-3 towed array (Turkey 'Preveze' class); Atlas Elektronik PRS-3-4, passive ranging (Colombia, Greece, Indonesia, Peru (in some)); Krupp Atlas PSU 83-55 (Colombia). Thomson Sintra DUUX 2C, (Argentina, Ecuador, Greece, Peru (in some), Venezuela); DUUX 5 (India); DUUG 1 D (Argentina); CSU-90 (South Africa)
EW: Argo (South Korea); Argo Phoenix II AR 700 (India); Thomson-CSF DR 2000U ESM (Argentina, Chile, Columbia, Ecuador, Indonesia, Venezuela); Thomson-CSF DR 4000 ESM (Brazil); Racal Porpoise (S 353-356) or Sealion (Turkey, S 357 on); Argo AR-700-S5 (Greece S 110-113); Thomson Arial DR 2000U (Greece S 116-119); Grintek Avionics ESM (South Africa)

Kilo ALGERIA, CHINA, INDIA, IRAN, POLAND, ROMANIA, RUSSIA

Russian 'Kilo' class submarine (*Michael Nitz*)

- Blunt, rounded bow
- Flat-topped casing, tapering towards after end
- Long, low fin with vertical leading and after edges and flat top
- Two windows either side at top, leading edge of fin
- Hull-mounted diving planes not visible
- Rudder just visible

NOTE: SA-N-8 SAM launcher may be fitted on top of the fin in Chinese hulls

SPECIFICATION:

COUNTRY OF ORIGIN: Russia
CLASS: Kilo/Kilo 4B (Vashavyanka) (Type 877E/877K/877M), (Sindhughosh) (SSK)
ACTIVE: 2 Algeria (Type 877E); 5 China (Type 877EKM/636); 10 India ('Sindhughosh' class, Type 877EM/8773); 3 Iran (Type 877EKM); 1 Poland (Type 877EM); 1 Romania (Type 877E); 17 Russia (Type 877K/877M/636)
BUILDING: 7 China (Type 636)
NAME (PENNANT NUMBER):
ALGERIA – Rais Hadj Mubarek (012), El Hadj Slimane (013)
CHINA – 364 (ex-B 171) (Type 877EKM), 365 (ex-177) (Type 877EKM), 366, 367 (remainder unknown)
INDIA – Sindhughosh (S 55), Sindhudhvaj (S 56), Sindhuraj (S 57), Sindhuvir (S 58) Sindhuratna (S 59), Sindhukesari (S 60), Sindhukirti (S 61), Sindhuvijay (S 62), Sindhurakshak (S 63), Sindhushastra (S 64)
IRAN – Tareq (901), Noor (902), Yunes (903)
POLAND – Orzel (291)
ROMANIA – Delfinul (521)
RUSSIA – Razboynik (B 260), — (B 227), — (B 405), Vologda (B 402), — (B 439), Tur (B 806), — (B 445), Jaroslavl (B 808), Magneto-Gorsk (B 800), Novosibirsk (B 401) (Type 636), Kaluga (B 471), Ust-Bolsheretsk (B 494), Alrosa (B 871), Lipetsk

(B 177), — (B 187) (Type 636), — (B 190) (Type 636), — (B 345)

FEATURES:

DISPLACEMENT: 2325 tons surfaced; 3076 tons dived
LENGTH: 238.2 ft (72.6 m); 242.1 ft (73.8 m) (China, Russia, Type 636); 243.8 ft (74.3 m) (Poland)
BEAM: 32.8 ft (9.9 m)
DRAUGHT: 21.7 ft (6.6 m)
SPEED: 10 kts surfaced; 17 kts dived
RANGE: 6000 miles at 7 kts, snorting; 400 miles at 3 kts dived

ARMAMENT:

MISSILES: SLCM – Novator Alfa Klub SS-N-27 (3M-54E1) (India and China); SAM – SA-N-8 Gremlin portable launcher (India); six to eight SA-N-5/8 (Russia); eight SA-N-5 (Strela 2M) portable launcher (Poland)
TORPEDOES: Six 21 in (533 mm) tubes; combination of TEST 71/96 and 53-65 (TEST-71ME Algeria only), (USET-80 Russia only)
MINES: 24 in lieu of torpedoes

ELECTRONICS:

RADARS: Surface search – Snoop Tray MRP-25 (Racal Decca Bridgemaster, Poland)
SONARS: MGK-400 Shark Teeth/Shark Fin, hull-mounted; Mouse Roar MG-519, hull-mounted
EW: Squid Head ESM (India, Iran); Brick Group MRP-25 ESM (Poland); Squid Head or Brick Pulp (Russia, China); Brick Pulp (Algeria); Brick Group (Romania)

Collins AUSTRALIA

'Collins' class

- Blunt bow with prominent pod
- Low, slim fin with forward edge sloping slightly aft
- Unusual, flat extension to the top after end of the fin
- Conventional diving planes low down on fin
- Rounded top to casing
- 'x'-form rudders visible above waterline, aft

SPECIFICATION:

COUNTRY OF ORIGIN: Sweden
CLASS: Collins (Kockums Type 471) (SSK)
ACTIVE: 6
NAME (PENNANT NUMBER):
Collins (73), Farncomb (74), Waller (75), Dechaineux (76), Sheean (77), Rankin (78)

FEATURES:

DISPLACEMENT: 3051 tons surfaced; 3353 tons dived
LENGTH: 255.2 ft (77.8 m)
BEAM: 25.6 ft (7.8 m)
DRAUGHT: 23. ft (7 m)
SPEED: 10 kts surfaced; 10 kts snorting; 20 kts dived
RANGE: 9000 miles at 10 kts snorting

ARMAMENT:

MISSILES: SSM – McDonnell Douglas Sub-Harpoon
TORPEDOES: Six 21 in (533 mm) forward tubes; Gould Mk 48 Mod 4
MINES: 44 in lieu of torpedoes
DECOYS: Two SSE torpedo decoys

ELECTRONICS:

RADARS: Navigation – Kelvin Hughes Type 1007
SONARS: Thomson-Sintra Scylla bow and flank arrays; GEC-Marconi Kariwara (73-74) or Thomson Marconi Narama or Allied Signal TB 23 passive towed array
EW: Condor CS-5600

Victoria

Victoria

- Blunt bow with prominent pod
- Tall rounded fin midships, with two bulges atop at aft end
- Rounded top to casing
- Casing slopes down more steeply at its after end
- Tall rudder with sloping forward edge and vertical after edge

SPECIFICATION:

COUNTRY OF ORIGIN: UK
CLASS: Victoria (ex-Upholder Type 2400) (SSK)
ACTIVE: 4
NAME (PENNANT NUMBER):
Victoria (ex-*Unseen*) (876, ex-S 41),
Windsor (ex-*Unicorn*) (877,
ex-S 43), Cornerbrook (ex-*Ursula*)
(878, ex-S 42), Chicoutimi
(ex-*Upholder*) (879, ex-S 40)

FEATURES:

DISPLACEMENT: 2168 tons
surfaced; 2455 tons dived
LENGTH: 230.6 ft (70.3 m)
BEAM: 25 ft (7.6 m)
DRAUGHT: 17.7 ft (5.5 m)
SPEED: 20 kts dived, 12 kts
surfaced
RANGE: 8000 miles at 8 kts
snorting

ARMAMENT:

TORPEDOES: Eight 21 in (533 mm)
bow tubes; Gould Mk 48 Mod 4
dual purpose
DECOYS: Two SSE launchers

ELECTRONICS:

RADARS: Navigation – Kelvin
Hughes Type 1007
SONARS: Thomson Sintra Type
2040 hull-mounted, passive;
BAE Type 2007 flank array,
passive; Thales Type 2046;
Thales Type 2019
EW: AR 900

Scorpene CHILE, INDIA, MALAYSIA

O'Higgins (DCN)

- Rounded, smooth-lined hull
- Rounded top to casing
- Slim fin forward of midships with vertical leading edge swept up from forward casing. Top of fin is slightly rounded in profile and slopes down at after end
- Diving planes sited near the top of the fin at its leading edge
- Silhouette of fin very similar to 'Le Triomphant' class
- Pronounced rudder at end of steeply sloped-down after casing

SPECIFICATION:

COUNTRY OF ORIGIN: France and Spain
CLASS: Scorpene
ACTIVE: 1 Chile
BUILDING: 1 Chile, 2 Malaysia
PLANNED: 6 India
NAME (PENNANT NUMBER):
CHILE – O'Higgins (22), Carrera (23)
MALAYSIA – — (—), — (—)

FEATURES:

DISPLACEMENT: 1668 tons surfaced, 1564 tons (Malaysia); 1711 tons dived
LENGTH: 217.9 ft (66.4 m)
BEAM: 20.3 ft (6.2 m)
DRAUGHT: 19 ft (5.8 m); 17.7 ft (5.4 m) (Malaysia)
SPEED: 20 kts dived, 12 kts surfaced
RANGE: 6500 miles at 8 kts surfaced; 550 miles at 4 kts dived; 360 miles at 4 kts dived (Malaysia)

ARMAMENT:

MISSILES: Aerospatiale SM39 Exocet (Malaysia)
TORPEDOES: Six 21 in (533 mm) bow tubes; Alenia Whitehead Black Shark

ELECTRONICS:

RADARS: Navigation – Sagem (Chile)
EW: Argos AR 900 ESM (Chile)

Han CHINA

'Han' class

- Fin sited well forward of midships with diving planes at its forward edge, just above mid-height
- Fin has vertical forward edge, top sloping down towards after end and sloping after edge, curved at the bottom
- Tall rudder with sloping forward edge and vertical after edge
- YJ 8-2 (C-801) SSM tubes fitted aft of the fin

SPECIFICATION:

COUNTRY OF ORIGIN: China
CLASS: Han (Type 091) (SSN)
ACTIVE: 4
NAME (PENNANT NUMBER): (402), (403), (404), (405)

FEATURES:

DISPLACEMENT: 4500 tons surfaced; 5550 tons dived
LENGTH: 321.5 ft (98 m); 347.8 ft (106 m) (403 onwards)
BEAM: 32.8 ft (10 m)
DRAUGHT: 24.2 ft (7.4 m)
SPEED: 25 kts dived; 12 kts surfaced

ARMAMENT:

MISSILES: SSM – YJ801Q (Eagle Strike) (C-801)
TORPEDOES: Six 21 in (533 mm) bow tubes; Yu-3 (SET-65E) and Yu-1 (Type 53-51) combination
MINES: 36 in lieu of torpedoes

ELECTRONICS:

RADARS: Surface search – Snoop Tray
SONARS: Trout Cheek, hull-mounted, active/passive search and attack; DUUX-5
EW: Type 921-A ESM

Song CHINA

'Song' class

- Forward hydroplanes mounted in lower part of fin beneath bridge, which is on a step lower than the part of the fin housing the masts
- The aft part of the fin sweeps down in a curve to join the casing
- Later boats show fin of different shape (ie there is no cutaway)
- Distinctive swelling of bow section presumably housing large spherical sonar array
- Aft casing slopes down below waterline before rudder

SPECIFICATION:

COUNTRY OF ORIGIN: China
CLASS: Song
ACTIVE: 9
BUILDING: 3
NAME (PENNANT NUMBER): (320),
(321), (322), (323), (324), (325), (314),
(—), (—), (—), (—), (—)

FEATURES:

DISPLACEMENT: 1700 tons
surfaced; 2250 tons dived
LENGTH: 246 ft (74.9 m)
BEAM: 24.6 ft (7.5 m)
DRAUGHT: 17.5 ft (5.3 m)
SPEED: 22 kts dived; 15 kts
surfaced

ARMAMENT:

MISSILES: YJ801Q (C-801)
TORPEDOES: Six 21 in (533 mm)
bow tubes; Yu-3 (SAET-60), Yu-1
(Type 53-51)
MINES: In lieu of torpedoes

ELECTRONICS:

SONARS: Passive/active MF bow-
mounted, passive LF flank array
EW: Type 921-A ESM

Yuan CHINA

'Yuan' class

- Tall, slim fin configuration similar to 'Song' class
- Large hydroplanes mounted at forward end of fin
- Low profile, blunt, rounded bow
- Flat-topped casing tapering towards stern
- Chin-mounted sonar and distinctive 'hump' on top of tear-drop-shaped hull
- In appearance very similar to Japanese 'Oyashio' class

SPECIFICATION:

COUNTRY OF ORIGIN: China
CLASS: Yuan
ACTIVE: 1
BUILDING: 1
NAME (PENNANT NUMBER):
— (—), — (—)

FEATURES:
LENGTH: 236.2 ft (72 m)
BEAM: 27.5 ft (8.4 m)

ARMAMENT:
MISSILES: Possibly Klub
TORPEDOES: Six 21 in (533 mm) bow tubes

Agosta/Agosta B FRANCE, PAKISTAN, SPAIN

Khalid

- Blunt, bull-nose bow with sonar pod atop forward end of casing
- Wide fin with rounded surfaces. Fin has vertical leading edge with straight, sloping after edge. Distinctive protrusion at top after end of fin
- Bow-mounted diving planes
- Flat-topped casing
- Rudder has steeply sloping forward edge

NOTE: French boat is test bed for the Project Barracuda SSN new equipment

SPECIFICATION:

COUNTRY OF ORIGIN: France
CLASS: Agosta/Agosta B (Hashmat, Galerna, Khalid) (SSK)
ACTIVE: 1 France, 2 Pakistan ('Hashmat' class), 2 Pakistan ('Khalid' class, 'Agosta B'), 4 Spain ('Galerna' class)
BUILDING: 1 Pakistan
NAME (PENNANT NUMBER):
FRANCE — Ouessant (S 623)
PAKISTAN — 'Agosta' class: Hashmat (ex-Astrant) (S 135), Hurmat (ex-Adventurous) (S 136); 'Agosta B': Khalid (S 137), Saad (S 138), Hamza (ex-Ghazi) (S 139)
SPAIN — Galerna (S 71), Siroco (S 72), Mistral (S 73), Tramontana (S 74)

FEATURES:

DISPLACEMENT, SURFACED: 1230 tons (France); 1490 tons (Pakistan); 1510 tons (Pakistan, 'Agosta B'); 1490 tons (Spain)
DISPLACEMENT, DIVED: 1760 tons (France); 1740 tons (Pakistan 'Agosta', and Spain); 1760 tons (Pakistan 'Agosta B')
LENGTH: 221.7 ft (67.7 m)
BEAM: 22.3 ft (6.8 m)
DRAUGHT: 17.7 ft (5.4 m)
SPEED: 12 kts surfaced; 20 kts dived
RANGE: 8500 miles at 9 kts snorting; 350 miles at 3.5 kts dived

ARMAMENT:

MISSILES: SSM — four Aerospatiale SM 39 Exocet launched from 533 mm tubes ('Agosta B'); McDonnell Douglas Sub-Harpoon (Pakistan 'Agosta')
TORPEDOES: Four 21 in (533 mm) bow tubes; ECAN F17P Mod 2; (additionally ECAN L5 Mod 3/4 in Spanish boats)
MINES: Stonefish (Pakistan); up to 19 (Spain)

ELECTRONICS:

RADARS: Search — Thomson-CSF DRUA 33C ('Agosta'); surface search — Kelvin Hughes 1007 ('Agosta B')
SONARS: Thomson-Sintra DSUV 22; DUUA 2D; DUUA 1D; DSUV 62A towed array (France); Thales TSM 2233 suite ('Agosta B'); Thomson-Sintra TSM 2233D; Thomson-Sintra DUUA 2B; Thomson-Sintra TSM 2933D (Pakistan); Thomson-Sintra DSUV 22; DUUA 2A/2B; DUUX 2A/5; SAES Solarsub towed passive array (Spain)
EW: Thorn-EMI/Inisel Manta E (Spain)

L'Inflexible FRANCE

L'Inflexible

- Large, flat-topped casing atop main pressure hull, housing the SLBM tubes
- Slim, rounded fin with diving planes forward and protrusion at after end
- Casing extends well aft of the fin and slopes down more steeply at its after end
- Square-topped rudder with slightly sloping forward edge, right aft

SPECIFICATION:

COUNTRY OF ORIGIN: France
CLASS: L'Inflexible (SNLE/SSBN)
ACTIVE: 1
NAME (PENNANT NUMBER):
L'Inflexible (S 615)*
*L'Inflexible will pay off when the last *Le Triomphant* class SSBN commissions

FEATURES:
DISPLACEMENT: 8080 tons surfaced; 8920 tons dived
LENGTH: 422.1 ft (128.7 m)
BEAM: 34.8 ft (10.6 m)
DRAUGHT: 32.8 ft (10 m)
SPEED: 20 kts surfaced; 25 kts dived
RANGE: 5000 miles at 4 kts on auxiliary propulsion only

ARMAMENT:
MISSILES: SLBM – 16 Aerospatiale M45/TN 75. SSM – Aerospatiale SM 39 Exocet, launched from 21 in (533 mm) torpedo tubes
TORPEDOES: Four 21 in (533 mm) tubes; ECAN L5 Mod 3 and ECAN F17 Mod 2

ELECTRONICS:
RADARS: Navigation – Thomson-CSF DRUA 33
SONARS: Thomson-Sintra DSUX 21B, passive bow and flank arrays; DUUX 5; DSUV 61B; towed array
EW: Thomson-CSF ARUR a5/DR 3000U ESM

Rubis FRANCE

Améthyste

- Rounded, smooth-lined hull
- Small, prominent pod atop casing forward of fin
- Rounded-topped casing
- Slim fin forward of midships with vertical leading edge and sloping after edge. Top of the fin is slightly rounded in profile and slopes down at the after end
- Diving planes sited near the top of the fin at its leading edge
- Rudder, right aft, has sloping forward edge

SPECIFICATION:

COUNTRY OF ORIGIN: France
CLASS: Rubis Améthyste (SSN)
ACTIVE: 6
NAME (PENNANT NUMBER): Rubis (S 601), Saphir (S 602), Casabianca (S 603), Émeraude (S 604), Améthyste (S 605), Perle (S 606)

FEATURES:

DISPLACEMENT: 2410 tons surfaced; 2670 tons dived
LENGTH: 241.5 ft (73.6 m)
BEAM: 24.9 ft (7.6 m)
DRAUGHT: 21 ft (6.4 m)
SPEED: 25 kts

ARMAMENT:

MISSILES: SSM – Aerospatiale SM 39 Exocet, launched from 21 in (533 mm) torpedo tubes
TORPEDOES: Four 21 in (533 mm) tubes; ECAN L5 Mod 3 and ECAN F17 Mod 2
MINES: Up to 32 FG 29 in lieu of torpedoes

ELECTRONICS:

RADARS: Navigation – Kelvin Hughes Type 1007
SONARS: Thomson-Sintra DMUX 20 multi-function; DSUV 62C; towed array; DSUV 22 listening suite
EW: Thomson-CSF ARUR 13/DR 3000U ESM

Le Triomphant   FRANCE

Le Téméraire

- Very thin, tall fin with large diving planes at forward end towards its top
- Rounded casing with flattened top with SLBM tubes aft of fin
- Casing slopes down steeply at aft end to square-topped rudder

SPECIFICATION:

COUNTRY OF ORIGIN: France
CLASS: Le Triomphant (SNLE-NG/SSBN)
ACTIVE: 3
BUILDING: 1
NAME (PENNANT NUMBER):
Le Triomphant (s 616),
Le Téméraire (s 617), Le Vigilant (s 618), Le Terrible (s 619)

FEATURES:

DISPLACEMENT: 12,640 tons surfaced; 14,335 tons dived
LENGTH: 453 ft (138 m)
BEAM: 41 ft (12.5 m)
DRAUGHT: 41 ft (12.5 m)
SPEED: 25 kts dived

ARMAMENT:

MISSILES: SLBM – 16 Aerospatiale M45/TN 75; SSM – Aerospatiale SM 39 Exocet
TORPEDOES: Four 21 in (533 mm) tubes; ECAN L5 Mod 3

ELECTRONICS:

RADARS: Search – Dassault
SONARS: Thomson-Sintra DMUX 80 multifunction passive bow and flank arrays; DSUV 61 towed array; DUUX 5 passive ranging intercept
EW: Thomson-CSF ARUR 13/DR 3000U ESM

Type 206A GERMANY

U 17 (old pennant number)

- Distinctive, bulbous bow narrowing down to slim casing
- Large, bulky, irregular shaped fin with vertical forward edge, rounded at top. Fin is stepped at its after end with sloping after edge down to casing
- Round top to casing of which very little is visible aft of the fin
- Bow-mounted diving planes not visible

NOTE: Unusual GRP mine containers are secured either side of the hull, forward of the fin

SPECIFICATION:

COUNTRY OF ORIGIN: Germany
CLASS: Type 206A (SSK)
ACTIVE: 11
NAME (PENNANT NUMBER): U 15 (S 194), U 16 (S 195), U 17 (S 196), U 18 (S 197), U 22 (S 171), U 23 (S 172), U 24 (S 173), U 25 (S 174), U 26 (S 175), U 29 (S 178), U 30 (S 179)

FEATURES:

DISPLACEMENT: 450 tons surfaced; 498 tons dived
LENGTH: 159.4 ft (48.6 m)
BEAM: 15.1 ft (4.6 m)
DRAUGHT: 14.8 ft (4.5 m)
SPEED: 10 kts surfaced; 17 kts dived
RANGE: 4500 miles at 5 kts surfaced

ARMAMENT:

TORPEDOES: Eight 21 in (533 mm) bow tubes; STN Atlas DM 2A3
MINES: GRP container secured outside hull each side containing 12 each, in addition to normal torpedo or mine armament

ELECTRONICS:

RADARS: Surface search – Thomson-CSF Calypso II
SONARS: Thomson-Sintra DUUX 2; Atlas Elektronik DBQS-21D
EW: Thomson-CSF DR 2000U ESM with Thorn EMI Sarie

Type 212A GERMANY, ITALY

U 31 (*Michael Nitz*)

- The partial double hull is of larger diameter forward of the fin, tapering to a smaller conical section aft of fin that houses the fuel cell plant
- Low profile, stream-lined, slim fin faired into side of casing and curving upwards
- Fin slopes back at aft end
- Forward hydroplanes mounted midway up fin
- Casing visible aft of fin
- 'x'-form rudder visible aft

SPECIFICATION:

COUNTRY OF ORIGIN: Germany
CLASS: Type 212A (U 31, Salvatore Todaro)
ACTIVE: 2 Germany, 1 Italy
BUILDING: 2 Germany, 1 Italy
NAME (PENNANT NUMBER):
GERMANY – U 31 (S 181), U 32 (S 182), U 33 (S 183), U 34 (S 184)
ITALY – Salvatore Todaro (S 526), Scire (S 527)

FEATURES:

DISPLACEMENT: 1450 tons surfaced; 1830 tons dived
LENGTH: 183.4 ft (55.9 m)
BEAM: 23 ft (7 m)
DRAUGHT: 19.7 ft (6 m)
SPEED: 12 kts surfaced; 20 kts dived
RANGE: 8000 miles at 8 kts surfaced

ARMAMENT:

TORPEDOES: Six 21 in (533 mm) bow tubes; STN DM 2A4 (Germany), Whitehead Black Shark (Italy)
MINES: In lieu of torpedoes
DECOYS: Tau (C 303) (Germany), Circe (Italy) torpedo countermeasures

ELECTRONICS:

RADARS: Navigation – Kelvin Hughes 1007
SONARS: STN Atlas DBQS-40, FAS-3

Type 214 GREECE, KOREA (SOUTH)

Papanikolis on first sea trials (*Michael Nitz*)

- Blunt, bull nose rounded bow
- Tall fin amidships faired into side of deck casing
- Rudder visible right aft with sloping forward edge
- Forward hydroplanes mounted on top of deck casing forward of fin (as in 'Dolphin' class)

SPECIFICATION:

COUNTRY OF ORIGIN: Germany
CLASS: Type 214 (Papanikolis, KSS-2)
ACTIVE: –
BUILDING: 4 Greece ('Papanikolis' class), 2 South Korea ('KSS-2' class)
NAME (PENNANT NUMBER):
GREECE – Papanikolis (S 120), Matrozos (S 121), Pipinos (S 122), Katsonis (S 123)
SOUTH KOREA – — (—), — (—)

FEATURES:

DISPLACEMENT: 1700 tons surfaced; 1800 tons dived, 1860 tons (Korea (South))
LENGTH: 213.3 ft (65 m)
BEAM: 20.7 ft (6.3 m)
DRAUGHT: 21.6 ft (6.6 m); 19.7 ft (6 m) (Korea (South))
SPEED: 11 kts surfaced; 20 kts dived, 12 kts (Korea (South))

ARMAMENT:

MISSILES: Sub Harpoon (Greece)
TORPEDOES: Six 21 in (533 mm) bow tubes; STN Atlas SUT, SST-4, DM 2A4 (Greece)
DECOYS: Circe torpedo countermeasures (Greece)

ELECTRONICS:

RADARS: Navigation – Thales Sphynx (Greece)
EW: Elbit TIMNEX II ESM (Greece)

Dolphin ISRAEL

'Dolphin' class (*Michael Nitz*)

- Blunt, rounded bow
- Diving planes flush with top of casing, aft of bow, with sonar dome between planes
- Flat top to casing
- Low profile, slim fin with sloping, tapering edges
- Short visible casing aft of fin

SPECIFICATION:

COUNTRY OF ORIGIN: Germany
CLASS: Dolphin (Type 800) (SSK)
ACTIVE: 3
NAME (PENNANT NUMBER):
Dolphin (—), Leviathan (—),
Tekuma (—)

FEATURES:

DISPLACEMENT: 1640 tons
surfaced; 1900 tons dived
LENGTH: 188 ft (57.3 m)
BEAM: 22.5 ft (6.8 m)
DRAUGHT: 20.3 ft (6.2 m)
SPEED: 11 kts snorting; 20 kts
dived
RANGE: 8000 miles at 8 kts
surfaced; 420 miles at 8 kts dived

ARMAMENT:

MISSILES: SSM/SLCM – Sub
Harpoon UGM-84C; SAM – Fitted
for Triton anti-helicopter system
TORPEDOES: Four 25.6 in
(650 mm) and six 21 in (533 mm)
bow tubes; STN Atlas DM24A4
Seehecht
MINES: In lieu of torpedoes

ELECTRONICS:

RADARS: Search/navigation – Elta
SONARS: Atlas Elektronik CSU 90;
Atlas Elektronik PRSW-3; FAS-3
flank array
EW: Elbit TIMNEX 4CH(V)2 ESM

Sauro ITALY

Sauro

- Blunt, rounded bow
- Three sets of diving planes, one at bow, one on fin and one aft
- Flat top to casing
- Low profile, slim fin with vertical forward edge and sloping after edge. Diving planes just under midway up fin
- Rudder visible right aft with vertical leading edge, Sauro (slopes in Improved Sauro) and sloping after edge

SPECIFICATION:

COUNTRY OF ORIGIN: Italy
CLASS: Sauro (Type 1081)/ Improved Sauro (SSK)
ACTIVE: 1 Sauro and 3 Improved Sauro
NAME (PENNANT NUMBER):
SAURO – Leonardo da Vinci (S 520)
IMPROVED SAURO – Salvatore Pelosi (S 522), Primo Longobardo (S 524), Gianfranco Gazzana Priaroggia (S 525)

FEATURES:

DISPLACEMENT: 1456 tons surfaced (Sauro), 1476 tons (Improved Sauro), 1653 tons (S 524-5); 1631 tons dived (Sauro), 1662 tons (Improved Sauro), 1862 tons (S 524-5)
LENGTH: 210 ft (63.9 m); 211.2 ft (64.4 m) (Improved Sauro); 217.8 ft (66.4 m) (S 524-5)
BEAM: 22.5 ft (6.8 m)
DRAUGHT: 18.9 ft (5.7 m); 18.4 ft (5.6 m) (Improved Sauro)
SPEED: 11 kts surfaced; 12 kts snorting; 19 kts dived
RANGE: 11,000 miles at 11 kts surfaced, 250 miles at 4 kts dived

ARMAMENT:

TORPEDOES: Six 21 in (533 mm) bow tubes; 12 Whitehead A184

ELECTRONICS:

RADARS: Search/navigation – SMA BPS-704
SONARS: Selenia Elsag IPD 70/S
EW: Elettronica BLD 727 ESM

Harushio JAPAN

Harushio (*Japanese Maritime Self-Defence Force*)

- Low profile bow
- Rounded top to casing
- Only short amount of casing visible forward of fin, which is sited well forward of midships
- Tall fin, tapered from forward to aft with vertical leading and after edge
- Diving planes on fin at leading edge, just below mid-height
- Curved, humpback profile to hull
- Rudder visible right aft sloping forward edge

NOTE: The slight growth in all dimensions and same basic shape suggests a natural progression from the 'Yuushio' class

SPECIFICATION:

COUNTRY OF ORIGIN: Japan
CLASS: Harushio (SSK)
ACTIVE: 7
NAME (PENNANT NUMBER):
Harushio (SS 583), Natsushio (SS 584), Hayashio (SS 585), Arashio (SS 586), Wakashio (SS 587), Fuyushio (SS 588), Asashio (TSS 3601, ex-SS 589)

FEATURES:

DISPLACEMENT: 2450 tons standard (2560 tons, TSS 3601); 2750 tons dived (2850 tons, TSS 3601)
LENGTH: 252.6 ft (77 m); 255.9 ft (78 m) (TSS 3601)
BEAM: 32.8 ft (10 m)
DRAUGHT: 25.3 ft (7.7 m)
SPEED: 12 kts surfaced; 20 kts dived

ARMAMENT:

MISSILES: SSM – McDonnell Douglas Sub-Harpoon, fired from torpedo tubes
TORPEDOES: Six 21 in (533 mm) tubes; Japanese Type 89 and Type 80

ELECTRONICS:

RADARS: Surface search – JRC ZPS 6
SONARS: Hughes/Oki ZQQ 5B; hull-mounted; ZQR 1 towed array similar to BQR 15
EW: NZLR-1 ESM

Oyashio JAPAN

Oyashio (*Japanese Maritime Self-Defence Force*)

- Low profile bow
- Rounded top to casing with prominent low sonar dome above bow
- Only short amount of casing visible forward of fin, which is sited well forward of midships
- Tall fin, tapered from forward to aft with vertical leading and sloping after edges
- Diving planes on fin at leading edge, around mid-height
- Rudder visible right aft with sloping forward edge

SPECIFICATION:

COUNTRY OF ORIGIN: Japan
CLASS: Oyashio (SSK)
ACTIVE: 8
BUILDING: 3
NAME (PENNANT NUMBER):
Oyashio (SS 590), Michishio
(SS 591), Uzushio (SS 592),
Makishio (SS 593), Isoshio (SS 594),
Narushio (SS 595), Kuroshio
(SS 596) Takashio (SS 597), Yaeshio
(SS 598), — (SS 599), — (SS 501)

FEATURES:

DISPLACEMENT: 2700 tons
standard; 3000 tons dived
LENGTH: 268 ft (81.7 m)
BEAM: 29.2 ft (8.9 m)
DRAUGHT: 25.9 ft (7.9 m)
SPEED: 12 kts surfaced;
20 kts dived

ARMAMENT:

MISSILES: SSM – McDonnell
Douglas Sub-Harpoon, fired
from torpedo tubes
TORPEDOES: Six 21 in (533 mm)
tubes; Japanese Type 89 and
Type 80

ELECTRONICS:

RADARS: Surface search –
JRC ZPS 6
SONARS: Hughes/Oki ZQQ 5B/6,
hull-mounted; ZQR 1 towed array
similar to BQR 15
EW: NZLR-1B ESM

Yuushio JAPAN

Sachishio (*Michael Nitz*)

- Low profile bow
- Rounded top to casing
- Only short amount of casing visible forward of fin, sited well forward of midships
- Very tall fin, tapered from forward to aft with vertical leading and after edges
- Diving planes on fin at leading edge, just below mid-height
- Curved, humpback profile to hull
- Rudder visible right aft with sloping forward edge

NOTE: The same basic shape as 'Harushio' class

SPECIFICATION:

COUNTRY OF ORIGIN: Japan
CLASS: Yuushio (SSK)
ACTIVE: 3
NAME (PENNANT NUMBER):
Hamashio (TSS 3604, ex-SS 578),
Yukishio (SS 581), Sachishio
(SS 582)

FEATURES:

DISPLACEMENT: 2250 tons
standard; 2450 tons dived
LENGTH: 249.3 ft (76 m)
BEAM: 32.5 ft (9.9 m)
DRAUGHT: 24.3 ft (7.4 m)
SPEED: 12 kts surfaced; 20 kts
dived

ARMAMENT:

MISSILES: SSM – McDonnell
Douglas Sub-Harpoon, fired
from torpedo tubes
TORPEDOES: Six 21 in (533 mm)
tubes; Japanese Type 89 and
Type 80

ELECTRONICS:

RADARS: Surface search –
JRC ZPS 6
SONARS: Hughes/Oki ZQQ 5B,
hull-mounted; ZQR 1 towed array
similar to BQR 15
EW: ZLR 5/6 ESM

Walrus NETHERLANDS

'Walrus' class

- Low bow with small pod at forward end of casing
- Flat top to casing
- Large slender fin, with leading edge sloping slightly aft and vertical after edge
- Diving planes at extreme forward edge of fin and just above mid-height
- 'x'-form rudders just visible right aft

NOTE: These are improved 'Zwaardvis' class, upon which the Taiwanese 'Hai Lung' class (active 2) is based

SPECIFICATION:

COUNTRY OF ORIGIN: Netherlands
CLASS: Walrus (SSK)
ACTIVE: 4
NAME (PENNANT NUMBER):
Walrus (S 802), Zeeleeuw (S 803),
Dolfijn (S 808), Bruinvis (S 810)

FEATURES:
DISPLACEMENT: 2465 tons
surfaced; 2800 tons dived
LENGTH: 223.1 ft (67.7 m)
BEAM: 27.6 ft (8.4 m)
DRAUGHT: 23 ft (7 m)
SPEED: 12 kts surfaced; 20 kts
dived
RANGE: 10,000 miles at 9 kts
snorting

ARMAMENT:
MISSILES: SSM – McDonnell
Douglas Sub-Harpoon
TORPEDOES: Four 21 in (533 mm)
tubes; Honeywell Mk 48 Mod 4

ELECTRONICS:
RADARS: Surface search –
Signaal/Racal ZW07
SONARS: Thomson-Sintra
TSM 2272 Eledone Octopus,
hull-mounted; GEC Avionics Type
2026, towed array; Thomson-
Sintra DUUX 5
EW: Argo 700

Ula NORWAY

Utsira

- Blunt, high bow
- Flat-topped casing slopes down from bow to water level right aft
- Diving planes sited at bow, not visible
- Fin sited just aft of midships
- Fin is unusually low in profile with vertical leading edge and sharp, sloping after edge with notch cut out at mid-point
- 'x'-form rudders just visible right aft

SPECIFICATION:

COUNTRY OF ORIGIN: Norway
CLASS: Ula (SSK)
ACTIVE: 6
NAME (PENNANT NUMBER): Ula (S 300), Uredd (S 305), Utvaer (S 303), Uthaug (S 304), Utstein (S 302), Utsira (S 301)

FEATURES:

DISPLACEMENT: 1040 tons surfaced; 1150 tons dived
LENGTH: 193.6 ft (59 m)
BEAM: 17.7 ft (5.4 m)
DRAUGHT: 15.1 ft (4.6 m)
SPEED: 11 kts surfaced; 23 kts dived
RANGE: 5000 miles at 8 kts

ARMAMENT:

TORPEDOES: Eight 21 in (533 mm) bow tubes; AEG DM 2A3

ELECTRONICS:

RADARS: Surface search – Kelvin Hughes 1007
SONARS: Atlas Elektronik CSU 83; Thomson-Sintra flank array
EW: Racal Sealion ESM

Daphné PAKISTAN, PORTUGAL, SPAIN

Barracuda

- Pointed bow, flat fronted in profile
- Flat, elongated sonar atop casing at bow
- Slim fin with vertical leading edge and sloping after edge
- Flat top to casing
- Bow-mounted diving planes and rudder not visible

SPECIFICATION:

COUNTRY OF ORIGIN: France
CLASS: Daphné (Hangor, Albacora, Delfin) (SSK)
ACTIVE: 4 Pakistan ('Hangor' class), 2 Portugal ('Albacora' class), 2 Spain ('Delfín' class)
NAME (PENNANT NUMBER):
PAKISTAN – Hangor (S 131), Shushuk (S 132), Mangro (S 133), Ghazi (ex-*Cachalote*) (S 134)
PORTUGAL – Barracuda (S 164), Delfim (S 166)
SPAIN – Tonina (S 62), Marsopa (S 63)

FEATURES:

DISPLACEMENT: 869 tons surfaced; 1043 tons dived
LENGTH: 189.6 ft (57.8 m)
BEAM: 22.3 ft (6.8 m)
DRAUGHT: 15.1 ft (4.6 m)
SPEED: 13.5 kts surfaced; 16 kts dived
RANGE: 4500 miles at 5 kts surfaced; 3000 miles at 7 kts snorting

ARMAMENT:

MISSILES: SSM – McDonnell Douglas Sub-Harpoon (Pakistan only)
TORPEDOES: Twelve 21.7 in (550 mm) (8 bow, 4 stem) tubes
MINES: Stonefish, (Pakistan only); twelve can be carried in lieu of torpedoes (Spain)

ELECTRONICS:

RADARS: Search – Thomson-CSF DRUA 31 (Pakistan); Kelvin Hughes Type 1007 (Portugal); DRUA 31 or 33A (Spain)
SONARS: TSM 2233D, DUUA 1 (Pakistan); DSUV 2, DUUA 2 (Portugal); DSUV 22, DUUA 2A (Spain)
EW: Thorn EMI Manta ESM (Spain); ARUD ESM (Pakistan); ARUR ESM (Portugal)

Akula I/II RUSSIA

Akula

- Blunt, bull-nosed bow
- Large diameter hull, flat-topped aft of fin
- Very distinctive, long low-profile fin, unusually long sloping edge aft with smoothly rounded hydrodynamic lines moulded into the casing
- Retractable diving planes not visible
- Large stern pod (towed array dispenser) on rudder

NOTE: Has the same broad hull as 'Sierra' class

NOTE 2: A number of non-acoustic sensors have begun to appear on the fin leading edge and on the forward casing of later 'Akulas'

SPECIFICATION:

COUNTRY OF ORIGIN: Russia
CLASS: Akula I/II (Bars) (Type 971/971U) (SSN)
ACTIVE: 7 Akula I; 2 Akula II
BUILDING: 1 Akula I, 7 Akula II
NAME (PENNANT NUMBER):
AKULA I – Magadan (ex-*Narwhal*) (K 331), Volk (K 461), Kuzbass (ex-*Morzh*) (K 419), Leopard (K 328), Tigr (K 154), Samara (ex-*Drakon*) (K 267), Nerpa (K 152); AKULA II – Vepr (K 157), Gepard (K 335), Cougar (K 337)

FEATURES:

DISPLACEMENT: 7500 tons surfaced; 9100 tons dived, 9500 tons (Akula II)
LENGTH: 360.1 ft (110 m) oa
BEAM: 45.9 ft (14 m)
DRAUGHT: 34.1 ft (10.4 m)
SPEED: 10 kts surfaced; 28 kts dived

ARMAMENT:

MISSILES: SLCM – Raduga SS-N-21 Sampson (RKV-500 Granat) fired from 533 mm tubes; SAM – SA-N-5/8 Strela portable launcher; A/S – Novator SS-N-15 Starfish fired from 533 mm tubes; SS-N-16 Stallion fired from 650 mm tubes, with 200 kT nuclear warhead or Veder Type 40 torpedoes
TORPEDOES: Four 21 in (533 mm) and four 25.6 in (650 mm) tubes (six extra 21 in in upper bow area of Akula II)

ELECTRONICS:

RADARS: Surface search – Snoop Pair or Snoop Half with back-to-back aerials on same mast as ESM
SONARS: Shark Gill (Skat MGK-503), hull-mounted; Mouse Roar MG-519, hull-mounted; Skat 3 towed array
EW: Rim Hat

Delta IV RUSSIA

Delta IV

- Blunt, rounded, low bow
- Low profile fin sited well forward
- Large diving planes on fin at leading edge, about mid-height
- Very large and distinctive raised flat-topped missile casing aft of the fin with its forward end moulded round after edge of fin. Missile casing runs straight for approximately half the distance to the stern where it smoothly tapers away
- Rudder, with sloping forward edge, just visible right aft

NOTE: Delta IV differs from III by being about 20 ft longer overall and has a pressure-tight fitting on the after end of the missile tube housing. Seven Delta III 'Kalmar' class are active

SPECIFICATION:

COUNTRY OF ORIGIN: Russia
CLASS: Delta IV (Delfin) (Type 667 BDRM) (SSBN)
ACTIVE: 6
NAME (PENNANT NUMBER):
Verchoture (K 51), Ekateringburg (K 84), Tula (K 114), Briansk (K 117), Karelia (K 18), Novomoskovsk (K 407)

FEATURES:
DISPLACEMENT: 10,800 tons surfaced; 13,500 tons dived
LENGTH: 544.6 ft (166 m) oa
BEAM: 39.4 ft (12 m)
DRAUGHT: 28.5 ft (8.7 m)
SPEED: 14 kts surfaced; 24 kts dived

ARMAMENT:
MISSILES: SLBM – 16 Makeyev SS-N-23 (RSM 54) Skiff with 4-10 MIRVed 100 kT warheads; A/S – Novator SS-N-15 Starfish with 200 kT warhead or Type 40 torpedo
TORPEDOES: Four 21 in (533 mm)

ELECTRONICS:
RADARS: Surface search – Snoop Tray MRP-25
SONARS: Shark Gill (Skat MGK-503), hull-mounted; Mouse Roar MG-519, hull-mounted; Shark Hide flank array; Pelamida towed array
EW: Brick Pulp/Group ESM

Oscar II RUSSIA

Oscar II

- Blunt, rounded low bow
- Exceptionally large diameter hull with rounded top
- Low, smooth profile fin forward of midships
- Fin is tapered at the leading and after edges
- Three windows at either side of top leading edge of fin
- Retractable diving planes, not visible
- Large rudder right aft

NOTE: Much shorter and much larger diameter than Delta IV

NOTE 2: SSM missile tubes are in banks of twelve either side and external to the 8.5 m diameter pressure hull

NOTE 3: All have a tube on the rudder fin as in Delta IV which may be used for dispensing a thin line-towed sonar array

SPECIFICATION:

COUNTRY OF ORIGIN: Russia
CLASS: Oscar II (Antyey) (Type 949A) (SSGN)
ACTIVE: 6
BUILDING: 1
NAME (PENNANT NUMBER): Smolensk (K 410), Cheliabinsk (K 442), Orel (ex-*Severodvinsk*) (K 266), Omsk (K 186), Tomsk (K 526), Voronezh (K 119), Belgorod (K 139)

FEATURES:

DISPLACEMENT: 13,900 tons surfaced; 18,300 tons dived
LENGTH: 505.2 ft (154 m)
BEAM: 59.7 ft (18.2 m)
DRAUGHT: 29.5 ft (9 m)
SPEED: 15 kts surfaced; 28 kts dived

ARMAMENT:

MISSILES: SSM – 24 Chelomey SS-N-19 Shipwreck (Granit); warhead 750 kg HE or 500 kT nuclear; A/S – Novator SS-N-15 Starfish fired from 21 in (533 mm) tubes; Novator SS-N-16 Stallion fired from 25.6 in (650 mm) tubes; payload Type 45 Veder torpedo or Vodopad 200 kT nuclear weapon
TORPEDOES: Four 21 in (533 mm) and two 25.6 in (650 mm) tubes; Type 53 and Type 65
MINES: 32 can be carried

ELECTRONICS:

RADARS: Surface search – Snoop Pair (Albatros) or Snoop Half
SONARS: Shark Gill (Skat MGK-503), hull-mounted; Shark Rib flank array; Mouse Roar MG-519, hull-mounted; Pelamida towed array
EW: Rim Hat ESM

Victor III   RUSSIA

Victor III

- Low, blunt bow
- Retractable, hull-mounted diving planes
- Large diameter, bulbous hull with a low profile
- Rounded top to casing
- Relatively small, rounded fin with slightly sloping leading edge and shallow sloping after edge
- Distinctive, large, streamlined pod, housing towed array dispenser, mounted on rudder

SPECIFICATION:

COUNTRY OF ORIGIN: Russia
CLASS: Victor III (Schuka)
(Type 671 RTM) (SSN)
ACTIVE: 5
NAME (PENNANT NUMBER):
Petrozavodsk (ex-*Snezhnogorsk*)
(B 388), Obninsk (B 138), Danil
Moskovoskiy (B 414), Tamboy
(B 448), Peram (B 292)

FEATURES:

DISPLACEMENT: 4850 tons
surfaced; 6300 tons dived
LENGTH: 351.1 ft (107 m)
BEAM: 34.8 ft (10.6 m)
DRAUGHT: 24.3 ft (7.4 m)
SPEED: 10 kts surfaced;
30 kts dived

ARMAMENT:

MISSILES: SLCM – SS-N-21
Sampson (Granat) fired from 21
in (533 mm) tubes; A/S – Novator
SS-N-15 Starfish fired from 21 in
(533 mm) tubes; SS-N-16 Stallion
fired from 25.6 in (650 mm)
tubes; payload Veder Type 40
torpedo or Vodopad
200 kT nuclear warhead
TORPEDOES: Four 21 in (533 mm)
and two 25.6 in (650 mm) tubes
MINES: Can carry 36 in lieu of
torpedoes

ELECTRONICS:

RADARS: Surface search – Snoop
Tray (MRP-25)
SONARS: Shark Gill (Skat
MGK-503), hull-mounted; Shark
Rib flank array; Mouse Roar
MG-519, hull-mounted; Skat 3
towed array; nuclear warhead
EW: Brick Spit and Brick Pulp
(Brick Group) ESM

Typhoon RUSSIA

Typhoon

- Easily identified, the largest submarine built
- Blunt, bull-nosed bows with huge cylindrical hull
- Flat-topped casing
- Streamlined fin, with windows at the top forward edge, sited well aft of midships
- The fin has a relatively low profile, with the lower part being larger and rounded where it moulds onto the main casing
- In profile the leading edge to the fin is vertical and the after edge has a slight slope
- Retractable diving planes are not visible
- The very large rudder at the after end gives this class an unmistakable profile
- Missile tubes are mounted forward of the fin

SPECIFICATION:

COUNTRY OF ORIGIN: Russia
CLASS: Typhoon (Akula)
(Type 941) (SSBN)
ACTIVE: 3
NAME (PENNANT NUMBER):
Arkhangelsk (TK 17), Severstal
(TK 20), Dmitriy Donskoy (TK 208)

FEATURES:

DISPLACEMENT: 18,500 tons
surfaced; 26,500 tons dived
LENGTH: 562.7 ft (171.5 m) oa
BEAM: 80.7 ft (24.6 m)
DRAUGHT: 42.7 ft (13 m)
SPEED: 12 kts surfaced;
25 kts dived

ARMAMENT:

MISSILES: SLBM – 20 Makeyev
SS-N-20 (RSM 52/3M20) Sturgeon
with 10 MIRVed warheads of
200 kT; SAM – SA-N-8 Gremlin
capability when surfaced; A/S –
Novator SS-N-15 Starfish fired
from 21 in (533 mm) tubes;
payload 200 kT Vodopad nuclear
warhead or Veder Type 40 torpedo
TORPEDOES: Six 21 in (533 mm)
MINES: Could be carried in lieu
of torpedoes

ELECTRONICS:

RADARS: Surface search – Snoop
Pair (Albatros)
SONARS: Shark Gill (Skat MGK-503),
hull-mounted; Shark Rib flank
array; Mouse Roar MG-519, hull-
mounted; Pelamida towed array
EW: Rim Hat (Nakat M) ESM

Sjöormen SINGAPORE

Conqueror

- Low, blunt bow
- Low profile hull with smooth, sloping forward and after ends
- Rounded top to casing
- Bulky fin with unusual curves to leading edge. Vertical after edge, slightly flared at bottom
- Fin-mounted diving planes sited at centre of fin and well below mid-height

NOTE: Albacore hull. Twin-decked

SPECIFICATION:

COUNTRY OF ORIGIN: Sweden
CLASS: Sjöormen (A 12) (SSK)
ACTIVE: 4
NAME (PENNANT NUMBER):
Challenger (ex-*Sjöbjörnen*),
Centurion (ex-*Sjöormen*),
Conqueror (ex-*Sjölejonet*),
Chieftain (ex-*Sjöhunden*)

FEATURES:

DISPLACEMENT: 1130 tons
surfaced; 1210 tons dived
LENGTH: 167.3 ft (51 m)
BEAM: 20 ft (6.1 m)
DRAUGHT: 19 ft (5.8 m)
SPEED: 12 kts surfaced;
20 kts dived

ARMAMENT:

TORPEDOES: Four 21 in (533 mm)
bow tubes; FFV Type 613; two
16 in (400 mm) tubes; FFV
Type 431

ELECTRONICS:

RADARS: Navigation – Terma
SONARS: Plessey Hydra,
hull-mounted

Götland SWEDEN

Uppland

- Blunt, bull-nosed rounded bow
- Flat top to casing
- Slim fin amidships with slightly sloped base, forward and aft
- Diving planes midway up centre of fin

SPECIFICATION:

COUNTRY OF ORIGIN: Sweden
CLASS: Götland (A 19) (SSK)
ACTIVE: 3
NAME (PENNANT NUMBER):
Götland (—), Uppland (—),
Halland (—)

FEATURES:

DISPLACEMENT: 1494 tons
surfaced; 1599 tons dived
LENGTH: 198.2 ft (60.4 m)
BEAM: 20.3 ft (6.2 m)
DRAUGHT: 18.4 ft (5.6 m)
SPEED: 10 kts surfaced,
20 kts dived

ARMAMENT:

TORPEDOES: Four 21 in (533 mm)
bow tubes; FFV Type 613/62; two
15.75 in (400 mm) bow tubes;
Swedish Ordnance Type 432/451
MINES: 12 Type 47 swim-out
mines in lieu of torpedoes

ELECTRONICS:

RADARS: Navigation – Terma
Scanter
SONARS: STN Atlas Elektronik
CSU 90-2, hull-mounted
EW: Racal Thorn Manta S ESM

Södermanland SWEDEN

Östergotland

- Rounded bow, small pod atop forward casing
- Smooth, symmetrical casing with rounded top
- Large, distinctive fin with sloping top at forward edge
- Fin is slightly flared out (in profile) for the lower one third of its height
- Fin-mounted diving planes, aft from forward edge below mid-height

NOTE: Single hulled, with an 'x'-form rudder/after hydroplane design

NOTE 2: Equipped with Stirling Mk III AIP

SPECIFICATION:

COUNTRY OF ORIGIN: Sweden
CLASS: Södermanland (A 17) (SSK)
ACTIVE: 2
NAME (PENNANT NUMBER):
Södermanland (—),
Östergötland (—)

FEATURES:
DISPLACEMENT: 1500 tons
surfaced; 1600 tons dived
LENGTH: 198.5 ft (60.5 m)
BEAM: 20 ft (6.1 m)
DRAUGHT: 18.4 ft (5.6 m)
SPEED: 10 kts surfaced;
20 kts dived

ARMAMENT:
TORPEDOES: Six 21 in (533 mm)
tubes; FFV Type 613; three 15.75 in
(400 mm) tubes; FFV Type 431/451
MINES: 12 Type 47 swim-out in
lieu of torpedoes

ELECTRONICS:
RADARS: Navigation – Terma
SONARS: Atlas Elektronik CSU 83,
hull-mounted
EW: Condor CS 3701

Astute UK

Artist's impression of 'Astute' class submarine (*BAe Systems*)

- Evolved version of 'Trafalgar' class with similar profile
- Long, low hull
- Flat-topped casing
- Retractable forward hull-mounted hydroplanes
- Fin sited just forward of midships, of same profile as Trafalgar, but slightly longer
- Fin slopes back on leading edge. After edge features less slope and tapers to a point

SPECIFICATION:

COUNTRY OF ORIGIN: UK
CLASS: Astute
ACTIVE: —
BUILDING: 3
PLANNED: 3
NAME (PENNANT NUMBER): Astute (S 20), Ambush (S 21), Artful (S 22), — (—), — (—), — (—)

FEATURES:

DISPLACEMENT: 6500 tons surfaced; 7800 tons dived
LENGTH: 318.2 ft (97 m)
BEAM: 37 ft (11.27 m)
DRAUGHT: 32.8 ft (10 m)
SPEED: 29 kts dived
RANGE: unlimited

ARMAMENT:

MISSILES: Tomahawk Block IV, Sub-Harpoon
TORPEDOES: Six 21 in (533 mm) tubes; BAE Systems Spearfish
MINES: In lieu of torpedoes

ELECTRONICS:

SONARS: Thomson Marconi 1076 sonar suite
EW: Racal UAP 4 ESM

Swiftsure UK

'Swiftsure' class

- Submarine has humpbacked appearance in profile
- The pressure hull maintains its diameter for most of the hull length
- Retractable, hull-mounted diving planes
- Prominent, slender sonar pod atop casing forward of fin
- Fin mounted just forward of midships. Fin has vertical leading and after edges and is tapered to point at after end
- Slopes steeply down at after end of hull compared with shallow slope at forward end
- Large, flat-topped rudder with sloping forward edge at after end of casing

SPECIFICATION:

COUNTRY OF ORIGIN: UK
CLASS: Swiftsure (SSN)
ACTIVE: 4
NAME (PENNANT NUMBER):
Sovereign (S 108), Superb (S 109),
Sceptre (S 104), Spartan (S 105)

FEATURES:

DISPLACEMENT: 4400 tons
standard; 4900 tons dived
LENGTH: 272 ft (82.9 m)
BEAM: 32.3 ft (9.8 m)
DRAUGHT: 28 ft (8.5 m)
SPEED: 30+ kts dived

ARMAMENT:

MISSILES: SLCM – Hughes Tomahawk Block III; SSM – McDonnell Douglas UGM-84B Sub-Harpoon
TORPEDOES: Five 21 in (533 mm) bow tubes; Marconi Spearfish
MINES: Can be carried in lieu of torpedoes

ELECTRONICS:

RADARS: Navigation – Kelvin Hughes Type 1007
SONARS: Marconi/Plessey Type 2074, hull-mounted, active/passive search and attack; Marconi 2072 flank array; Ferranti Type 2046, towed array; Thomson-Sintra Type 2019 Paris or Thorn EMI 2082 passive intercept and ranging; Marconi Type 2077 short-range classification, active
EW: Racal UAP ESM

61

Trafalgar UK

Talent

- Long, low hull with almost identical sloping profiles at the forward and after ends of the pressure hull
- Rounded top to casing
- Retractable, forward, hull-mounted diving planes
- Prominent, slender sonar pod atop casing just forward of fin
- Fin is mounted forward of midships. Fin has vertical leading and after edges and is tapered to point at after end
- Large, flat-topped rudder at after end of casing

NOTE: The pressure hull and outer surfaces are covered with conformal anechoic noise reduction coatings

NOTE 2: Strengthened fins for under ice operations

SPECIFICATION:

COUNTRY OF ORIGIN: UK
CLASS: Trafalgar (SSN)
ACTIVE: 7
NAME (PENNANT NUMBER):
Trafalgar (S 107), Turbulent (S 87),
Tireless (S 88), Torbay (S 90),
Trenchant (S 91), Talent (S 92),
Triumph (S 93)

FEATURES:

DISPLACEMENT: 4740 tons
surfaced; 5208 tons dived
LENGTH: 280.1 ft (85.4 m)
BEAM: 32.1 ft (9.8 m)
DRAUGHT: 31.2 ft (9.5 m)
SPEED: 32 kts dived

ARMAMENT:

MISSILES: SLCM – Hughes
Tomahawk Block IIIC; SSM –
McDonnell Douglas UGM-84B
Sub-Harpoon Block IC
TORPEDOES: Five 21 in (533 mm)
bow tubes; Marconi Spearfish

ELECTRONICS:

RADARS: Navigation – Kelvin
Hughes Type 1007
SONARS: Marconi 2072, hull-
mounted flank array; Plessey
Type 2020 or Marconi/Plessey
2074 or Thales 2076 passive/active
search and attack, hull-mounted;
Ferranti Type 2046 towed array;
Thomson-Sintra Type 2019 Paris
or Thorn EMI 2082 passive
intercept and ranging; Marconi
Type 2077 short range
classification, active
EW: Racal UAP ESM

Vanguard UK

Vengeance

- Casing slopes down forward of fin to waterline
- Slim, tapered fin well forward of midships
- Hull-mounted diving planes approximately midway between fin and bow
- Large, distinctive, flat-topped casing aft of fin, dropping down steeply at its after end. Casing houses SLBMS
- Large rudder with curved top

NOTE: Outer surface covered with conformal anechoic noise reduction coatings

SPECIFICATION:

COUNTRY OF ORIGIN: UK
CLASS: Vanguard (SSBN)
ACTIVE: 4
NAME (PENNANT NUMBER):
Vanguard (S 28), Victorious (S 29),
Vigilant (S 30), Vengeance (S 31)

FEATURES:
DISPLACEMENT: 15,900 tons dived
LENGTH: 491.8 ft (149.9 m)
BEAM: 42 ft (12.8 m)
DRAUGHT: 39.4 ft (12 m)
SPEED: 25 kts dived

ARMAMENT:
MISSILES: SLBM – Lockheed
Trident 2 (D5) with up to eight
MIRVed nuclear warheads of
100-120 kT
TORPEDOES: Four 21 in (533 mm)
tubes; Marconi Spearfish

ELECTRONICS:
RADARS: Navigation – Kelvin
Hughes Type 1007
SONARS: Marconi Type 2054, hull-mounted sonar suite; Marconi/
Ferranti Type 2046 towed array;
Type 2043 hull-mounted, active;
Type 2082 passive intercept and
ranging; Type 2081 environment
sensor system
EW: Racal UAP 3 ESM

Los Angeles USA

'Los Angeles' class

- Blunt bow, very low profile pressure hull
- Hull profile tapers gently and consistently down to water level from bow to stern
- Slender fin, with vertical leading and after edges, is sited well forward of midships
- Fin-mounted diving planes

NOTE: SSN 719 onwards fitted with Vertical Launch System with 12 launch tubes external to the pressure hull behind bow sonar

NOTE 2: Five are fitted with Dry Dock shelters on the aft casing for special forces operation (SSN 688, 690, 700, 701). Four being fitted to operate ASDS (SSN 772, 762, 766, 768)

SPECIFICATION:

COUNTRY OF ORIGIN: USA
CLASS: Los Angeles (SSN)
ACTIVE: 50
NAME (PENNANT NUMBER): Los Angeles (SSN 688), Philadelphia (SSN 690), Memphis (SSN 691), Bremerton (SSN 698), Jacksonville (SSN 699), Dallas (SSN 700), La Jolla (SSN 701), City of Corpus Christi (SSN 705), Albuquerque (SSN 706), Minneapolis-Saint Paul (SSN 708), Hyman G Rickover (SSN 709), Augusta (SSN 710), San Francisco (SSN 711), Houston (SSN 713), Norfolk (SSN 714), Buffalo (SSN 715), Salt Lake City (SSN 716), Olympia (SSN 717), Honolulu (SSN 718), Providence (SSN 719), Pittsburgh (SSN 720), Chicago (SSN 721), Key West (SSN 722), Oklahoma City (SSN 723), Louisville (SSN 724), Helena (SSN 725), Newport News (SSN 750), San Juan (SSN 751), Pasadena (SSN 752), Albany (SSN 753), Topeka (SSN 754), Miami (SSN 755), Scranton (SSN 756), Alexandria (SSN 757), Asheville (SSN 758), Jefferson City (SSN 759), Annapolis (SSN 760), Springfield (SSN 761), Columbus (SSN 762), Santa Fe (SSN 763), Boise (SSN 764), Montpelier (SSN 765), Charlotte (SSN 766), Hampton (SSN 767), Hartford (SSN 768), Toledo (SSN 769), Tucson (SSN 770), Columbia (SSN 771), Greeneville (SSN 772), Cheyenne (SSN 773)

FEATURES:

DISPLACEMENT: 6082 tons standard; 6927 tons dived
LENGTH: 362 ft (110.3 m)
BEAM: 33 ft (10.1 m)
DRAUGHT: 32.3 ft (9.9 m)
SPEED: 32 kts dived

ARMAMENT:

MISSILES: SLCM – GDC/Hughes Tomahawk (TLAM-N); SSM – GDC/Hughes Tomahawk (TASM); McDonnell Douglas Harpoon
TORPEDOES: Four 21 in (533 mm) tubes midships; Gould Mk 48 ADCAP
MINES: Can lay Mk 67 Mobile and Mk 60 Captor mines
DECOYS: Emerson Electric Mk 2, torpedo decoy

ELECTRONICS:

RADARS: Surface search/ navigation/fire control – Sperry BPS 15H/16
SONARS: IBM BQQ-5D/E passive/ active search and attack; BQG–5D (flank array, SSN 710 and SSN 773); TB 23/29 thin line array; TB 16 and TB 93 passive towed array; AMETEK BQS-15 active close range; MIDAS (mine and ice avoidance system) (SSN 751 on)
EW: BRD-7, WLR-1H (SSN 771-773); WLR-8(v)2/6 ESM, WLR-10 ESM

Ohio USA

Maryland

- Very long, low profile pressure hull
- Hull steeply sloped at the forward end with a long shallow slope down to the rudder aft
- Comparatively small, slim fin sited well forward with vertical leading and after edges. After end of fin is tapered
- Long, slender fin-mounted diving planes at mid-height

NOTE: *Florida, Georgia, Michigan* and *Ohio* converting to SSGNS carrying up to 143 Toma-hawk cruise missiles in place of Trident strategic missiles

SPECIFICATION:

COUNTRY OF ORIGIN: USA
CLASS: Ohio (SSBN)
ACTIVE: 18
NAME (PENNANT NUMBER): Ohio (SSBN 726), Michigan (SSBN 727), Florida (SSBN 728), Georgia (SSBN 729), Henry M Jackson (SSBN 730), Alabama (SSBN 731), Alaska (SSBN 732), Nevada (SSBN 733), Tennessee (SSBN 734), Pennsylvania (SSBN 735), West Virginia (SSBN 736), Kentucky (SSBN 737), Maryland (SSBN 738), Nebraska (SSBN 739), Rhode Island (SSBN 740), Maine (SSBN 741), Wyoming (SSBN 742), Louisiana (SSBN 743)

FEATURES:

DISPLACEMENT: 16,600 tons surfaced; 18,750 tons dived
LENGTH: 560 ft (170.7 m)
BEAM: 42 ft (12.8 m)
DRAUGHT: 36.4 ft (11.1 m)
SPEED: 24 kts dived

ARMAMENT:

MISSILES: SLBM – Lockheed Trident II (D5) up to 12 MIRVed nuclear warheads of 100-475 kt (734 onwards)
TORPEDOES: Four 21 in (533mm) Mk 68 bow tubes; Gould Mk 48 ADCAP
DECOYS: Eight launchers for Emerson Electric Mk 2; torpedo decoy

ELECTRONICS:

RADARS: Surface search/navigation/fire control – BPS-15A/H
SONARS: IBM BQQ-6 passive search; Raytheon BQS-13, spherical array for BQQ-6; Ametek BQS-15 active/passive for close contacts; Western Electric BQR-15 (with BQQ-9 signal processor) passive towed array; Raytheon BQR-19 active, for navigation; TB 23 towed array
EW: WLR-8(V)5, WLR-10 ESM

Seawolf USA

Seawolf

- Long, low profile pressure hull
- Characteristic integral rounded curve upwards from forward casing to low slim fin with notch above. After end of fin is tapered
- Casing flattened with a short, sharp slope down to the rudder aft

SPECIFICATION:

COUNTRY OF ORIGIN: USA
CLASS: Seawolf (SSN)
ACTIVE: 3
NAME (PENNANT NUMBER): Seawolf (SSN 21), Connecticut (SSN 22), Jimmy Carter (SSN 23)

FEATURES:

DISPLACEMENT: 8080 tons surfaced; 9142 tons dived, 12,139 tons (SSN 23)
LENGTH: 353 ft (107.6 m); 453.2 ft (138.1 m) (SSN 23)
BEAM: 42.3 ft (12.9 m)
DRAUGHT: 35.8 ft (10.9 m)
SPEED: 39 kts dived

ARMAMENT:

MISSILES: SLCM – Hughes Tomahawk (TLAM-N) land attack; SSM – GDC/Hughes Tomahawk (TASM) anti-ship
TORPEDOES: Four 26 in (660 mm); Gould Mk 48 ADCAP
MINES: 100 in lieu of torpedoes

ELECTRONICS:

RADARS: Navigation – BPS-16
SONARS: BSY-2 suite with bow spherical active/passive array and wide aperture passive flank arrays; TB 16 and TB 29 surveillance and tactical towed arrays

Virginia USA

uss Virginia (*Courtesy USN*)

- Acoustic cladding on hull
- Long, low profile pressure hull
- Integral rounded curve upwards from deck casing to low slim fin as in Seawolf
- Tapered after end to fin

SPECIFICATION:
COUNTRY OF ORIGIN: USA
CLASS: Virginia
ACTIVE: 1
BUILDING: 6
PLANNED: 3
NAME (PENNANT NUMBER):
Virginia (SSN 774), Texas (SSN 775),
Hawaii (SSN 776), North Carolina
(SSN 777), New Hampshire
(SSN 778), New Mexico (SSN 779),
— (SSN 780), — (SSN 781),
— (SSN 782), (SSN 783)

FEATURES:
DISPLACEMENT: 7800 tons dived
LENGTH: 377 ft (114.9 m)
BEAM: 34 ft (10.4 m)
DRAUGHT: 30.5 ft (9.3 m)
SPEED: 34 kts dived
RANGE: unlimited

ARMAMENT:
MISSILES: SLCM – Tomahawk;
12 VLS tubes for cruise missiles
TORPEDOES: Four 21 in (553 mm)
bow tubes; Mk 48 ADCAP
MINES: Can lay Mk 67 and Mk 60
Captor until new weapons
available
DECOYS: 14 external, one internal
(reloadable) launchers

ELECTRONICS:
RADARS: Navigation – BPS-16
SONARS: Bow spherical
active/passive array; wide
aperture passive flank array;
HF active keel and fin arrays;
TB 16 towed array; TB 29
towed array
EW: WLQ-4(V) ESM; BLQ-10 ESM

Aircraft
Carriers

São Paulo (Clemenceau) BRAZIL

São Paulo (H. M. Steele)

- Large thin island just forward of midships, starboard side (three bridges, flag, command and aviation)
- Black-capped, raked funnel atop centre of island
- Spherical landing approach control (NRBA 51) dome at after end of island
- Crane aft of island
- Single pole mainmast supporting air/surface search radar aerial forward and air search radar aerial aft
- Foldable mini ski-jump fitted to both deck catapults

SPECIFICATION:

COUNTRY OF ORIGIN: France
CLASS: Clemenceau (CV)
ACTIVE: 1
NAME (PENNANT NUMBER): São Paulo (ex-Foch) (A-12, ex-R 99)

FEATURES:

DISPLACEMENT: 27,307 tons standard; 33,673 tons full load
LENGTH: 869.4 ft (265 m) oa
BEAM: 104.1 ft (31.7 m) (hull); 168 ft (51.2 m) oa
DRAUGHT: 28.2 ft (8.6 m)
FLIGHT DECK LENGTH: 850 ft (259 m)
FLIGHT DECK WIDTH: 154 ft (47 m)
SPEED: 30 kts
RANGE: 7000 miles at 18 kts; 4800 miles at 24 kts

ARMAMENT:

MISSILES: SAM – two AESN Albatros Mk 2, Aspide (to be fitted)
DECOYS: Two CSEE Sagaie 10-barrel launchers

ELECTRONICS:

RADARS: Air search – Thomson-CSF DRBV 23B; air/surface search – two DRBI 10, Thomson-CSF DRBV 15; height finder – two DRBI 10; fire control – two AESN Orion RTN 30X; navigation – Racal Decca 1226; landing approach control – NRBA 51

AIR SUPPORT:

FIXED WING AIRCRAFT: 15-18 A-4 Skyhawk strike fighters
HELICOPTERS: Four to six Agusta-Sikorsky SH-3A/D Sea Kings; three Eurocopter UH-12/13 Esquilo (liaison/patrol); two Eurocopter UH-14 Cougar (SAR)

Charles de Gaulle FRANCE

Charles de Gaulle (*Michael Nitz*)

- Sweeping bow with near vertical stern
- Very distinctive, clean superstructure, angled surfaces for reduced radar signature
- Large angular island starboard side, well forward of midships
- Sturdy enclosed mainmast atop island, supporting tall pole mast and prominent fire control radar dome forward
- Large spherical air-search radar dome atop after end of bridge roof
- Angled flight deck terminating port side just forward of island
- Two VLS Eurosaam SAM launchers outboard of flight deck sited amid-ships, just forward of island, starboard side

SPECIFICATION:

COUNTRY OF ORIGIN: France
CLASS: Charles de Gaulle (CVN)
ACTIVE: 1
NAME (PENNANT NUMBER):
Charles de Gaulle (R 91)

FEATURES:

DISPLACEMENT: 36,600 tons
standard; 42,000 tons full load
LENGTH: 857.7 ft (261.5 m)
BEAM: 211.3 ft (64.4 m)
DRAUGHT: 30.9 ft (9.4 m)
FLIGHT DECK LENGTH: 857.7 ft
(261.5 m)
FLIGHT DECK WIDTH: 211.3 ft
(64.4 m)
SPEED: 27 kts

ARMAMENT:

MISSILES: SAM – four EUROSAAM
VLS octuple launchers,
Aerospatiale Aster 15 anti-missile
system, two Matra Sadral PDMS
sextuple launchers: Mistral
GUNS: Four Giat 20F2 20 mm
DECOYS: Four CSEE Sagaie
10-barrel launchers; Dassault LAD
offboard decoys; SLAT torpedo
decoys from 2006

ELECTRONICS:

RADARS: Air search – Thomson-
CSF DRBJ 11B, Thomson DRBV 26D
Jupiter; air/surface search –
Thomson-CSF DRBV 15C Sea Tiger
Mk 2; nagivation – two Racal
1229 (DRBN 34A); fire control –
Thomson-CSF Arabel 3D (SAM)
SONARS: To include SLAT torpedo
attack warning
EW: Two ARBB 33B jammers

AIR SUPPORT:

FIXED WING AIRCRAFT: 20 Super
Étendard strike fighters; two
E-2C Hawkeye Group 2 (AEW);
12 Rafale F1 air defence/strike
fighters
HELICOPTERS: Two Eurocopter
AS 565MB Panther, or two
Eurocopter AS 322 Cougar Mk II
or two Super Frelon and two
Dauphin (SAR)

Future Aircraft Carrier FRANCE

Future Aircraft Carrier (DCN)

- Two deck edge lifts fore and aft of island superstructure
- Compact island superstructure to starboard approximately one third from bow
- Large enclosed mast atop island supporting prominent spherical air-search radar dome
- Pole mainmast behind enclosed mast
- Two smaller spherical domes to port and starboard on island superstructure
- Angled flight deck
- Single catapult on main deck and second catapult on angled deck

SPECIFICATION:

COUNTRY OF ORIGIN: France
CLASS: –
ACTIVE: –
PLANNED: 1
NAME (PENNANT NUMBER):
— (—)

FEATURES:

DISPLACEMENT: 60,000 tons full load
LENGTH: 931.7 ft (284 m)
BEAM: 236.2 ft (72 m)
DRAUGHT: To be announced
FLIGHT DECK LENGTH: To be announced
FLIGHT DECK WIDTH: To be announced
SPEED: 27 kts
RANGE: To be announced

ARMAMENT:

MISSILES: SAM – Aster 15
GUNS: To be announced
DECOYS: To be announced

ELECTRONICS:

RADARS: To be announced

AIR SUPPORT:

FIXED WING AIRCRAFT: Up to 35 including Rafale M and E-2C Hawkeye
HELICOPTERS: Up to five NH 90

Jeanne d'Arc FRANCE

Jeanne d'Arc

- Long forecastle
- SSN launcher immediately forward of bridge
- Main superstructure one third of ship's length from bow
- Pole mainmast forward of funnel supporting air/surface search and air-search radar aerials
- Very tall black-capped funnel at after end of bridge structure
- Flight deck extending from bridge aft to break at short quarterdeck
- Two 3.9 in mountings on flight deck level, in line with forward edge of bridge, port and starboard

SPECIFICATION:

COUNTRY OF ORIGIN: France
CLASS: Jeanne d'Arc (CVH)
ACTIVE: 1
NAME (PENNANT NUMBER):
Jeanne d'Arc (ex-*La Résolue*) (R 97)

FEATURES:
DISPLACEMENT: 10,575 tons standard; 13,270 tons full load
LENGTH: 597.1 ft (182 m)
BEAM: 78.7 ft (24 m) (hull)
DRAUGHT: 24.6 ft (7.5 m)
FLIGHT DECK LENGTH: 203.4 ft (62 m)
FLIGHT DECK WIDTH: 68.9 ft (21 m)
SPEED: 26.5 kts
RANGE: 7500 miles at 15 kts

ARMAMENT:
MISSILES: SSM – Six Aerospatiale MM 38 Exocet, (2 triple launchers)
GUNS: Two DCN 3.9 in (100 mm)/ 55 Mod 1964 CADAM automatic; four 12.7 mm machine guns
DECOYS: Two CSEE/VSEL Syllex 8-barrel trainable chaff launchers (may not be fitted)

ELECTRONICS:
RADARS: Air search – Thomson-CSF DRBV 22D; air/surface search – DRBV 51; navigation – two Racal 1229 (DRBN 34A); fire control – two Thomson-CSF DRBC 32A
SONARS: Thomson Sintra DUBV 24C, hull-mounted, active search
EW: Thomson CSF ARBR 16/ARBX 10 intercept

AIR SUPPORT:
HELICOPTERS: Two Pumas and two Gazelles (Army); two Alouette III (Navy); war inventory includes eight Super Frelon or 10 mixed heavy/light

Vikrant INDIA

Vikrant (*Indian Navy*)

- Two angled decks providing extensive flight deck area
- Two deck edge lifts fore and aft of central island superstructure
- Ski ramp over bulbous bow
- Very large 3-D planar array antenna at forward end of island
- Solid mast sited between two enclosed funnel exhausts
- Solid mast supports small spherical dome partway up and radar antenna on top

SPECIFICATION:

COUNTRY OF ORIGIN: India
CLASS: Vikrant (Project 71)
ACTIVE: –
PLANNED: 1
NAME (PENNANT NUMBER): Vikrant (—)

FEATURES:

DISPLACEMENT: 38,000 tons full load
LENGTH: 826.8 ft (252.3 m)
BEAM: 186.3 ft (56.8 m)
DRAUGHT: 25.6 ft (7.8 m)
FLIGHT DECK LENGTH: –
FLIGHT DECK WIDTH: –
SPEED: 32 kts

ARMAMENT:

MISSILES: SAM – To be announced
GUNS: CIWS to be announced

ELECTRONICS:

RADARS: To be announced

AIR SUPPORT:

FIXED WING AIRCRAFT: 16 MiG 29
HELICOPTERS: 20 Helix and Sea King

Modified Kiev INDIA

Possible configuration of Admiral Gorshkov for Indian Navy

- Raked bow, square stem
- Angled flight deck only
- 14° ski jump
- Tall island just forward of midships, starboard side
- Distinctive cylindrical Tacan Cake Stand radar aerial housing centrally sited atop island
- Squat, low funnel

NOTE: Under refit, expected to enter service 2008

SPECIFICATION:

COUNTRY OF ORIGIN: Russia
CLASS: Modified Kiev (Krechyet)
(Project 1143.4) (CVG)
ACTIVE: 0 (In refit)
NAME (PENNANT NUMBER): —,
(ex-Admiral Gorshkov, ex-Baku)

FEATURES:

DISPLACEMENT: 45,400 tons full load
LENGTH: 928.5 ft (283 m) oa
BEAM: 167.3 ft (51 m) oa
DRAUGHT: 32.8 ft (10 m) (screws)
FLIGHT DECK LENGTH: 640 ft (195 m)
FLIGHT DECK WIDTH: 68 ft (20.7 m)
SPEED: 28 kts
RANGE: 13,800 miles at 18 kts

ARMAMENT:

MISSILES: SAM – six Altair
CADS-N-1 (Kortik/Kashtan) each with twin 30 mm Gatling combined with eight SA-N-11 Grisson and Hot Flash/Hot Spot fire control radar/optronic director
DECOYS: Two PK 2 twin chaff launchers; two towed torpedo decoys

ELECTRONICS:

RADARS: Air search – Plate Steer
Surface search – two Strut Pair
Aircraft control – Cake Stand
SONARS: Horse Jaw MG 355; hull-mounted, active search and attack
EW: Bharat intercept and jammers

AIR SUPPORT:

FIXED WING AIRCRAFT: Up to 24
MiG-29MTK 2002 Fulcrum air defence/strike fighters or Rafale
HELICOPTERS: Six Kamov
Ka-27/28/31 Helix (ASW) or
Westland Sea King 42A/42B

Viraat (Hermes) INDIA
Viraat

- Fitted with 12° ski jump ramp over bulbous bows
- Large midships island, starboard side
- Medium height, enclosed mast at forward end of island with air-search radar aerial atop
- Squat square profile funnel, mid-island
- Tall lattice mainmast at after end of island supporting air/surface search radar and communications aerials
- Crane derrick immediately aft of island, starboard side

NOTE: Completed refit at Mazagon Dock in 2001. Ship is planned to remain in service until around 2010

SPECIFICATION:

COUNTRY OF ORIGIN: UK
CLASS: Hermes
ACTIVE: 1
NAME (PENNANT NUMBER): Viraat (ex-HMS *Hermes*) (R 22)

FEATURES:
DISPLACEMENT: 23,900 tons standard; 28,700 tons full load
LENGTH: 685 ft (208.8 m) wl
BEAM: 90 ft (27.4 m)
DRAUGHT: 28.5 ft (8.7 m)
SPEED: 28 kts

ARMAMENT:
MISSILES: Two octuple Raphael Barak VLS/CIWS
GUNS: Four Oerlikon 20 mm; four 30 mm; two USSR 30 mm AK 230 Gatlings on aft sponsons
DECOYS: Two Knebworth Corvus chaff launchers

ELECTRONICS:
RADARS: Air search – Bharat RAWL-02 Mk II (PLN 517); air/surface search – Bharat RAWS (PFN 513); navigation – Bharat Rashmi; fire control – IAI/Elta EL/M-2221
SONARS: Graseby Type 184M; hull-mounted, active search and attack
EW: ESM Bharat Ajanta intercept

AIR SUPPORT:
FIXED WING AIRCRAFT: 12 Sea Harriers FRS Mk 51/60 air defence/strike fighters (capacity for 30)
HELICOPTERS: Seven Sea King Mk 42B/C (ASW/ASV) and Ka-27/31 Helix (ASW/AEW)

Giuseppe Garibaldi ITALY

Giuseppe Garibaldi

- 6.5° ski jump ramp
- Short mast forward of funnel supporting long-range air-search radar aerial
- Air-search radar aerial atop forward end of bridge with two low fire control radar domes immediately forward
- Integral, short funnel with four aerials
- Two tall pole masts, aft, supporting air/surface search radar aerial
- Angled SSM launchers, two port, two starboard, below after end of flight deck
- Three 40 mm/70 mountings, one port, one starboard below flight deck just aft of ski jump ramp, one centre-line aft quarterdeck
- Chaff launchers on sponsons aft and below flight deck

SPECIFICATION:

COUNTRY OF ORIGIN: Italy
CLASS: Garibaldi (CVS)
ACTIVE: 1
NAME (PENNANT NUMBER):
Giuseppe Garibaldi (C 551)

FEATURES:
DISPLACEMENT: 10,100 tons
standard; 13,850 tons full load
LENGTH: 591 ft (180 m)
BEAM: 110.2 ft (33.4 m)
DRAUGHT: 22 ft (6.7 m)
FLIGHT DECK LENGTH: 570.2 ft
(173.8 m)
FLIGHT DECK WIDTH: 99.7 ft
(30.4 m)
SPEED: 30 kts
RANGE: 7000 miles at 20 kts

ARMAMENT:
MISSILES: SAM – two Selenia Elsag
Albatros octuple launchers,
Aspide; upgrade to Aster 15
missiles planned
GUNS: Six Breda 40 mm/70
(3 twin) MB
TORPEDOES: Six 324 mm B-515
(2 triple) tubes; Honeywell Mk 46
anti-submarine (being replaced
by A 290)
DECOYS: AN/SLQ-25 Nixie
noisemaker torpedo decoy; two
Breda SCLAR 105 mm 20-barrel
trainable chaff launchers; SLAT
torpedo defence system planned

ELECTRONICS:
RADARS: Long range air-search –
Hughes SPS-52C, 3D; air-search –
Selenia SPS-768 (RAN 3L); air/
surface search – Selenia SPS-774
(RAN 10S); surface search/target
indication – SMA SPS-702 UPX; 718
beacon; navigation – SMA 753G(V);
fire control – three Selenia
SPG-75 (RTN 30X), three Selenia
SPG-74 (RTN 20X)
SONARS: WASS DMSS 2000; bow-
mounted, active search
EW: Elettronica Nettuno SLQ-732

AIR SUPPORT:
FIXED WING AIRCRAFT: 15 AV-8B
Harrier II Plus
HELICOPTERS: 17 Agusta-Sikorsky
SH-3D Sea King helicopters or EH
Industries EH 101 Merlin Mk 110
(ASW/anti-surface vessel) (12 in
hangar, six on deck); capacity is
either 15 Harriers or 17 Sea
Kings, but this leaves no space
for movement

Cavour ITALY

Artist's impression of Cavour (*Fincantieri*)

- Main deck continuous from stem to stern, with 12° ski jump
- Low island superstructure with funnels with twin exhausts at forward and aft ends
- Large deck crane forward of superstructure; smaller one aft
- Large enclosed mast above bridge, topped by bulbous EMPAR air search and missile guidance radome
- Slim enclosed mast at forward edge of aft funnel, topped by short pole mast

SPECIFICATION:

COUNTRY OF ORIGIN: Italy
CLASS: Cavour (CV)
BUILDING: 1*
*Expected to be commissioned – 2007
NAME (PENNANT NUMBER): Cavour (ex-*Andrea Doria*) (C 552)

FEATURES:

DISPLACEMENT: 27,100 tons full load
LENGTH: 772.9 ft (235.6 m) oa
BEAM: 128 ft (39 m)
DRAUGHT: 24.6 ft (7.5 m)
FLIGHT DECK LENGTH: 721.8 ft (220 m)
FLIGHT DECK WIDTH: 111.5 ft (34 m)
SPEED: 28 kts
RANGE: 7000 miles at 16 kts

ARMAMENT:

MISSILES: SAM – four Sylver VLS, Aster 15
GUNS: Two OTO Melara 3 in (76 mm) Super Rapid; two OTOBreda 25 mm
DECOYS: Two Breda SCLAR-H 20-barrel trainable chaff; two SLAT torpedo countermeasures TCM launchers

ELECTRONICS:

RADARS: Long range air-search – RAN-40; air-search and missile guidance – EMPAR; surface search – SPS-791; navigation – SPN-753G(V)
SONARS: SNA-2000 mine avoidance
EW: ESM/ECM radar and communications intercept and jammer

AIR SUPPORT:

FIXED WING AIRCRAFT: Eight AV-8B Harrier II or Joint Strike Fighter (JSF)
HELICOPTERS: 12 EH Industries EH 101 Merlin (also fitted for AB 212, NH 90 and SH-3D)

Admiral Kuznetsov RUSSIA

Admiral Kuznetsov

- Typical high, sweeping bow profile
- 14° ski jump ramp
- 7° angled flight deck
- SSM launchers forward end of flight deck in centre, with flush deck covers
- SAM VLS port and starboard, forward of angled deck
- High freeboard of 16.5 m
- Large island aft of midships, starboard side
- Distinctive cylindrical Tacan 'Cake Stand' radar aerial housing forward of funnel atop island/bridge
- Short, slightly raked funnel at after end of island structure
- Square stem with clear flight deck overhang

SPECIFICATION:

COUNTRY OF ORIGIN: Russia
CLASS: Admiral Kuznetsov (Orel) (Project 1143.5/6) (CV)
ACTIVE: 1
NAME (PENNANT NUMBER): Admiral Kuznetsov (ex-*Tbilisi*, ex-*Leonid Brezhnev*) (063)

FEATURES:

DISPLACEMENT: 45,900 tons standard; 58,500 tons full load
LENGTH: 918.6 ft (280 m) wl; 999 ft (304.5 m) oa
BEAM: 121.4 ft (37 m) wl; 229.7 ft (70 m) oa
DRAUGHT: 34.4 ft (10.5 m)
FLIGHT DECK LENGTH: 999 ft (304.5 m)
FLIGHT DECK WIDTH: 229.7 ft (70 m)
SPEED: 30 kts
RANGE: 3850 miles at 29 kts; 8500 miles at 18 kts

ARMAMENT:

MISSILES: SSM – 12 Chelomey SS-N-19 Shipwreck (3M-45) launchers (flush mounted); SAM – four Altair SA-N-9 Gauntlet (Klinok) sextuple vertical launchers; SAM/guns – eight Altair CADS-N-1 (Kortik/Kashtan), each with twin 30 mm Gatling combined with eight SA-N-11 Grisson and Hot Flash/Hot Spot fire control radar/optronic director

GUNS: Six 30 mm/65 AK 630; six barrels per mounting
A/S MORTARS: Two RBU 12000
DECOYS: Ten PK 10 and four PK 2 chaff launchers

ELECTRONICS:

RADARS: Air-search – Sky Watch, four planar phased arrays, 3D; air/surface search – Top Plate B; surface search – two Strut Pair; navigation – three Palm Frond; fire control – four Cross Sword (SAM), eight Hot Flash; aircraft control – Fly Trap B
SONARS: Bull Horn and Horse Jaw; hull-mounted, active search and attack
EW: Eight Foot Ball; four Wine Flask; four Flat Track; 10 Ball Shield

AIR SUPPORT:

FIXED WING AIRCRAFT: 18 Sukhoi Su-27K/Su-33 Flanker D air defence fighters; four Sukhoi Su-25UTG Frogfoot ground attack fighters
HELICOPTERS: 15 Kamov Ka-27PL Helix, (ASW); two Kamov Ka-31 RLD Helix (AEW)

Príncipe de Asturias SPAIN

Príncipe de Asturias

- 12° ski jump ramp
- Unusual, over-hanging aircraft lift at after end of flight deck
- Two 20 mm/120 12-barrel mountings at flare of bows, port and starboard
- Crane gantry forward of island, starboard side
- Island much further aft of midships than usual, starboard side
- Large lattice mainmast at forward end of island supporting square profile air-search radar aerial
- Raked funnel mid-island with four protruding individual exhausts at top
- Large aircraft control radar dome at after end of island structure
- Two 20 mm/120 mountings right aft, port and starboard on quarterdeck
- Two saluting guns on port quarter

SPECIFICATION:

COUNTRY OF ORIGIN: Spain
CLASS: Príncipe de Asturias (CVS)
ACTIVE: 1
NAME (PENNANT NUMBER):
Príncipe de Asturias (ex-*Almirante Carrero Blanco*) (R 11)

FEATURES:
DISPLACEMENT: 17,188 tons full load
LENGTH: 642.7 ft (195.9 m) oa
BEAM: 79.7 ft (24.3 m)
DRAUGHT: 30.8 ft (9.4 m)
FLIGHT DECK LENGTH: 575.1 ft (175.3 m)
FLIGHT DECK WIDTH: 95.1 ft (29 m)
SPEED: 25 kts
RANGE: 6500 miles at 20 kts

ARMAMENT:
GUNS: Four Bazán Mod 2A/2B Meroka 12-barrel 20 mm/120; two Rheinmetall 37 saluting guns
DECOYS: Loral Hycor SRBOC 6-barrel fixed Mk 36; SLQ-25 Nixie noisemaker towed torpedo decoy; US Prairie/Masker; hull noise/blade rate suppression

ELECTRONICS:
RADARS: Air-search – Hughes SPS-52 C/D, 3D; surface search – ISC Cardion SPS-55; aircraft control – ITT SPN-35A; fire control – one Selenia RAN 12L (target designation), four Sperry/Lockheed VPS 2 (for Meroka), one RTN 11L/X (missile warning)
EW: Elettronica Nettunel

AIR SUPPORT:
FIXED WING AIRCRAFT: Six to 12 BAe/McDonnell Douglas EAV-8B Harrier II/Harrier Plus
HELICOPTERS: Six to ten Sikorsky SH-3D/G Sea Kings (ASW/AEW); two to four Agusta AB 212EW

Chakri Naruebet THAILAND

Chakri Naruebet

- 12° ski jump ramp
- Squared, 'chunky' island aft of midships, starboard side
- Crane gantry forward end of island, starboard side
- One of two aircraft lifts at after end of flight deck
- Enclosed mainmast part of funnel structure
- Air-search radar, Hughes SPS-52C, atop bridge

NOTE: Similarities with Spanish carrier *Princípe de Asturias*

SPECIFICATION:

COUNTRY OF ORIGIN: Spain
CLASS: Chakri Naruebet (CVS)
ACTIVE: 1
NAME (PENNANT NUMBER): Chakri Naruebet (911)

FEATURES:

DISPLACEMENT: 11,485 tons full load
LENGTH: 599.1 ft (182.6 m) oa
BEAM: 73.8 ft (22.5 m) wl; 100.1 ft (30.5 m) oa
DRAUGHT: 20.3 ft (6.2 m)
FLIGHT DECK LENGTH: 572.8 ft (174.6 m)
FLIGHT DECK WIDTH: 90.2 ft (27.5 m)
SPEED: 26 kts; 16 kts diesels
RANGE: 10,000 miles at 12 kts

ARMAMENT:

MISSILES: SAM — one Mk 41 LCHR 8-cell VLS launcher, Sea Sparrow (to be fitted); three Matra Sadral sextuple launchers, Mistral
GUNS: Two 30 mm (to be fitted)
DECOYS: Four Tracor Mk 137 chaff launchers

ELECTRONICS:

RADARS: Air-search — Hughes SPS-52C; surface search — SPS-64 (to be fitted); fire control — (to be fitted); navigation — Kelvin Hughes; aircraft control — Kelvin Hughes

AIR SUPPORT:

FIXED WING AIRCRAFT: Six BAe/McDonnell Douglas AV-8S Matador (supplied to Spain and transferred in 1996)
HELICOPTERS: Six Sikorsky S-70B7 Seahawk (multi-mission); Chinook capable

Invincible UK

Invincible (*Michael Nitz*)

- 12° ski jump ramp fitted on offset, port side deck (*Invincible*); 13° (*Illustrious*, and *Ark Royal*)
- Very long and low island situated amidships, starboard side
- Twin funnels, one immediately aft of bridge, one aft of mainmast, forward funnel taller. Both funnels have twin, black painted exhausts atop
- Large fire control radar dome(s) aft extreme of island
- Central, enclosed mainmast supporting surface search radar aerial. *Illustrious* has SATCOM terminals midway mast and composite third mast at after end of island to support additional communications antennae
- *Ark Royal* to receive third advanced technology mast in 2005
- Goalkeeper CIWS mountings fitted at bows, port side aft and immediately forward of after funnel

SPECIFICATION:

COUNTRY OF ORIGIN: UK
CLASS: Invincible (CV)
ACTIVE: 3
NAME (PENNANT NUMBER):
Invincible (R 05), Illustrious
(R 06), Ark Royal (R 07)

FEATURES:

DISPLACEMENT: 20,600 tons
full load
LENGTH: 685.8 ft (209.1 m) oa
BEAM: 118 ft (36 m) oa
DRAUGHT: 26 ft (8 m)
FLIGHT DECK LENGTH: 550 ft
(167.8 m)
FLIGHT DECK WIDTH: 44.3 ft
(13.5 m)
SPEED: 28 kts
RANGE: 7000 miles at 19 kts

ARMAMENT:

GUNS: Three 30 mm 7-barrel
Gatling Goalkeeper (R 05/R 06);
three Vulcan Phalanx Mk.15
(R 07); two Oerlikon/BMARC
20 mm GAM-B01
DECOYS: Outfit DLH – eight Sea
Gnat 6-barrel 130/102 mm
dispensers; Prairie/Masker noise
suppression

ELECTRONICS:

RADARS: Air-search – Marconi/
Signaal Type 1022; air/surface
search – AMS Type 996;
navigation – two Kelvin Hughes
Type 1007
EW: Racal UAT

AIR SUPPORT:

FIXED WING AIRCRAFT: Eight
British Aerospace Sea Harrier
FA 2 air defence/strike fighters
and eight Harrier GR 7 ground
attack fighters
HELICOPTERS: EH 101 Merlin HM
Mk 1 (ASW); four Westland Sea
King ASAC Mk 7 AEW 2; Chinook
HC2 capable; mix of up to
24 aircraft

Queen Elizabeth UK

Artist's impression of Queen Elizabeth (*BAe Systems*)

- Swept back bow with ski ramp
- Two large island superstructures to starboard
- Funnel incorporated into forward superstructure
- After superstructure supports large enclosed mast housing 3-D phased array radar antenna and flight control position
- Forward superstructure features pole mast
- Forward superstructure supports large revolving radar antenna
- Aircraft parking spots sited on port side of flight deck overhang
- Deck edge lifts sited one between island structures and second aft of second superstructure

SPECIFICATION:

COUNTRY OF ORIGIN: UK
CLASS: Queen Elizabeth
ACTIVE: —
PLANNED: 2
NAME (PENNANT NUMBER):
Queen Elizabeth (—), Prince of Wales (—)

FEATURES:
DISPLACEMENT: 65,000 tons full load
LENGTH: 931.7 ft (284 m) oa
BEAM: 127.9 ft (39 m)
DRAUGHT: —
FLIGHT DECK LENGTH: —
FLIGHT DECK WIDTH: —
SPEED: 26+ kts
RANGE: To be announced

ARMAMENT:
MISSILES: To be announced
GUNS: To be announced
DECOYS: To be announced

ELECTRONICS:
RADARS: To be announced

AIR SUPPORT:
FIXED WING AIRCRAFT:
Approximately 36 JSF
HELICOPTERS: Merlin ASW

CVN 21 USA

Artist's impression of CVN 21

- Flight deck features extensions to increase deck parking area
- Four electromagnetic catapults – two on angled deck and two on main flight deck
- Improved island arrangement sited well aft
- Integrated island with composite mast supporting planar array radars
- Three deck edge aircraft lifts – two to starboard, one to port aft

SPECIFICATION:

COUNTRY OF ORIGIN: USA
CLASS: CVN 21
ACTIVE: –
BUILDING: 1
PLANNED: 1
NAME (PENNANT NUMBER):
— (CVN 78), — (CVN 79)

FEATURES:
DISPLACEMENT: 100,000 tons approx. standard
LENGTH: 836.6 ft (255 m)
BEAM: 265.1 ft (80.8 m)
DRAUGHT: –
FLIGHT DECK LENGTH: –
FLIGHT DECK WIDTH: –
SPEED: To be announced
RANGE: To be announced

ARMAMENT:
MISSILES: Evolved Sea Sparrow
GUNS: –
DECOYS: –

ELECTRONICS:
RADARS: Air-search – AN/SPY-3 MFR and S-VSR; navigation – to be announced; landing approach control – to be announced; fire control – to be announced

AIR SUPPORT:
FIXED WING AIRCRAFT: Joint Strike Fighter JSF
HELICOPTERS: –

Enterprise USA

Enterprise

- Angled flight deck
- Island aft of midships, starboard side
- Unusual box-shaped bridge supported on significantly narrower pedestal structure
- Square air-search radar atop bridge, forward
- SAM launchers mounted to port at after end of flight deck. Second launcher situated starboard side forward
- RAM launchers to port just forward of angled deck and aft on starboard edge of angled deck
- CIWS mountings situated right aft below flight deck overhang and on sponson on port side, forward of angled deck

SPECIFICATION:

COUNTRY OF ORIGIN: USA
CLASS: Enterprise (CVN)
ACTIVE: 1
NAME (PENNANT NUMBER):
Enterprise (CVN 65)

FEATURES:

DISPLACEMENT: 75,700 tons
standard; 89,600 tons full load
LENGTH: 1123 ft (342.3 m)
BEAM: 133 ft (40.5 m)
DRAUGHT: 39 ft (11.9 m)
FLIGHT DECK LENGTH: 1088 ft
(331.6 m)
FLIGHT DECK WIDTH: 252 ft
(76.8 m)
SPEED: 33 kts

ARMAMENT:

MISSILES: SAM – two Raytheon
GMLS Mk 29 octuple launchers,
NATO Sea Sparrow, two GMLS
Mk 49 RAM RIM-116
GUNS: Three GE/GD 20 mm
Vulcan Phalanx 6-barrel Mk 15
DECOYS: SSTDS; SLQ-36 Nixie
noisemaker torpedo decoy

ELECTRONICS:

RADARS: Air-search – ITT SPS-48E
3D, Raytheon SPS-49(v)5, Hughes
Mk 23 TAS; surface search –
Norden SPS-67; navigation –
Raytheon SPS-64(v)9, Furuno
900; fire control – four Mk 95
(for SAM)
EW: SLQ-32(v)4 ESM/ECM

AIR SUPPORT:

FIXED WING AIRCRAFT: 50 TACAIR
wing, depending on mission;
includes up to 12 McDonnell
Douglas F/A-18F Hornet, 36
McDonnell Douglas F/A-18A/C/E
Hornet (strike/interdiction), four
Grumman EA-6B Prowler (EW),
four Grumman E-2C Hawkeye
(AEW)
HELICOPTERS: Four Sikorsky
SH-60F Seahawk (ASW) and two
HH-60H Seahawk (strike/special
warfare support/SAR) and up to
nine SH-60B Seahawk

Kitty Hawk & John F Kennedy USA

Constellation (now decommissioned)

- Angled flight deck
- Complex thin pole mast on central island, fitted with air-search radar, WT and EW aerials, (topped by radome in CV67 alone)
- Funnel at rear of island structure, flush with top of bridge
- Tall lattice mast immediately aft of bridge supporting square profile air-search radar aerial
- Crane derrick starboard, aft of island, outboard of flight deck
- CIWS mountings mounted port and starboard at stern under flight deck overhang
- RAM sited one on port side forward of angled deck and one on opposite side to starboard
- Two deck-edge lifts fitted forward of island superstructure, a third aft of the island, and a fourth port side quarter

SPECIFICATION:

COUNTRY OF ORIGIN: USA
CLASS: Kitty Hawk and John F Kennedy (CV)
ACTIVE: 2
NAME (PENNANT NUMBER): Kitty Hawk (CV 63), John F Kennedy (CV 67)

FEATURES:

DISPLACEMENT: 83,960 tons full load; 81,430 tons (CV 67)
LENGTH: 1062.5 ft (323.6 m) (CV 63); 1052 ft (320.6 m) (CV 67)
BEAM: 130 ft (39.6 m)
DRAUGHT: 37.4 ft (11.4 m)
FLIGHT DECK LENGTH: 1046 ft (318.8 m)
FLIGHT DECK WIDTH: 252 ft (76.8 m)
SPEED: 32 kts
RANGE: 4000 miles at 30 kts, 12,000 at 20 kts

ARMAMENT:

MISSILES: SAM – two Raytheon GMLS Mk 29 octuple launchers; NATO Sea Sparrow; two GMLS Mk 49 RAM RIM-116
GUNS: Two GE/GD 20 mm Vulcan Phalanx 6-barrel Mk 15
DECOYS: SSTDS; SLQ-36 Nixie noisemaker torpedo decoy

ELECTRONICS:

RADARS: Air-search – ITT SPS-48E 3D, Raytheon SPS-49(V)5, Hughes Mk 23/7 TAS; surface search – Norden SPS-67; navigation – Furuno 900; fire control – four Mk 95 (SAM)
EW: SLW-32(V)4 ESM/ECM

AIR SUPPORT:

FIXED WING AIRCRAFT: 50 TACAIR air wing, depending on mission, including up to 12 McDonnell Douglas F/A-18F Hornet; 36 McDonnell Douglas F/A-18A/C/E Hornet (strike/interdiction); four Grumman EA-6B Prowler (EW); four Grumman E-2C Hawkeye
HELICOPTERS: Four Sikorsky SH-60F (ASW); two HH-60H Seahawk (strike/special forces/SAR) and up to nine SH-60B Seahawk

Nimitz USA

Nimitz

SPECIFICATION:

COUNTRY OF ORIGIN: USA
CLASS: Nimitz (CVN)
ACTIVE: 9
BUILDING: 1 – George W Bush (CVN 77)
NAME (PENNANT NUMBER): Nimitz (CVN 68), Dwight D Eisenhower (CVN 69), Carl Vinson (CVN 70), Theodore Roosevelt (CVN 71), Abraham Lincoln (CVN 72), George Washington (CVN 73), John C Stennis (CVN 74), Harry S Truman (ex-*United States*) (CVN 75), Ronald Reagan (CVN 76)

FEATURES:

DISPLACEMENT: 91,487 tons full load (CVN 68-70); 96,386 tons (CVN 71); 102,000 tons (CVN 72-77)
LENGTH: 1092 ft (332.9 m)
BEAM: 134 ft (40.8 m) wl
DRAUGHT: 37 ft (11.3 m) (CVN 68-70); 38.7 ft (11.8 m) (CVN 71); 39 ft (11.9 m) (CVN 72-76); 39.8 ft (12.1 m) (CVN 77)
FLIGHT DECK LENGTH: 1092 ft (332.9 m)
FLIGHT DECK ANGLED: 779.8 ft (237.7 m)
FLIGHT DECK WIDTH: 252 ft (76.8 m)
SPEED: 30+ kts

ARMAMENT:

MISSILES: SAM – two (CVN 68, 69, 76, 77) or three Raytheon GMLS Mk 29 octuple launchers, NATO Sea Sparrow, two GMLS Mk 49 RAM RIM-116 (CVN 68, 69, 76, 77)
GUNS: Three (CVN 71) or four GE/GD 20 mm Vulcan Phalanx 6-barrel Mk 15
DECOYS: SSTDS; SLQ-36 Nixie (Phase I) noisemaker torpedo decoy

ELECTRONICS:

RADARS: Air-search – ITT SPS-48E 3D, Raytheon SPS-49(V)5, Hughes Mk 23 TAS; surface search – Norden SPS-67(V)1; navigation – Raytheon SPS-64(V)9, Furuno 900; fire control – six Mk 95 (SAM)

AIR SUPPORT:
As in *Kitty Hawk*

- Large island well aft of midships. (Reshaped island in CVN 69)
- Square profile air-search radar aerial mounted atop forward end of island, above bridge
- Tall thin complex pole mainmast atop central bridge supporting array of radar, EW and WT aerials
- Enclosed isolated mast immediately aft of island supporting curved lattice bedstead air-search radar aerial (not on CVN-76)
- Two CIWS mountings fitted right aft, one port, one starboard below flight deck overhang
- Second two CIWS mountings, port and starboard, immediately forward of where flight deck narrows
- Octuple SAM missile launch boxes right aft, port and starboard on sponsons and on port side where flight deck narrows
- Large radome on narrow sponson, port side, forward of Mk 29 mountings

Cruisers

Almirante Grau PERU

Almirante Grau

- Two 6 in gun mountings forward of bridge in 'A' and 'B' mounting positions
- Cylindrical after funnel close to midships, sloped slightly aft with lattice mast built around it
- Forward funnel at after end of tall forward superstructure with mast above
- Dome-shaped Signaal WM25 fire control radar on pylon immediately forward of main mast
- Upper deck superstructure sited astern of after funnel with fire control director atop
- Two 6 in gun mountings on afterdeck in 'Y' and 'X' mounting positions
- No flight deck but long, low quarterdeck
- Spherical SATCOM dome aft of superstructure

NOTE: Sister ship *Aguirre* deleted in 1999

SPECIFICATION:

COUNTRY OF ORIGIN: Netherlands
CLASS: De Ruyter (CG)
ACTIVE: 1
NAME (PENNANT NUMBER):
Almirante Grau (ex-*De Ruyter*)
(CLM 81)

FEATURES:
DISPLACEMENT: 12,165 tons full load
LENGTH: 624.5 ft (190.3 m)
BEAM: 56.7 ft (17.3 m)
DRAUGHT: 22 ft (6.7 m)
SPEED: 32 kts
RANGE: 7000 miles at 12 kts

ARMAMENT:
MISSILES: SSM – eight OTO Melara
Otomat Mk 2 (TG 1)
GUNS: Eight Bofors 6 in (152 mm)
/53 (4 twin); four OTOBreda
40 mm/70 (2 twin); four Bofors
40 mm/70
DECOYS: Two Dagaie and one
Sagaie chaff launcher

ELECTRONICS:
RADARS: Air-search – Signaal
LW08; surface search/target
indication – Signaal DA08;
nagivation – Racal Decca 1226;
fire control – Signaal WM25
(6 in guns), Signaal STIR

Kara RUSSIA

Kerch (*Harmut Ehlers*)

- SAM (twin) SA-N-3 Goblet launcher on raised forecastle structure forward of bridge
- 'Head Light C' fire control director mounted on bridge roof, sited aft of funnel
- Forward tripod mast aft of bridge supporting air/surface search radar aerial
- Large pyramid mainmast sited amidships, supporting square profile Flat Screen air-search radar
- Two 3 in gun mountings, port and starboard, sited between forward and aftermasts
- Large, slightly tapered, square section funnel situated immediately aft of mainmast

SPECIFICATION:

COUNTRY OF ORIGIN: Russia
CLASS: Kara (Berkot-B) (Project
1134B/BF) (CG)
ACTIVE: 1
NAME (PENNANT NUMBER): Kerch
(713, ex-711)

FEATURES:

DISPLACEMENT: 7650 tons
standard; 9900 tons full load
LENGTH: 568 ft (173.2 m)
BEAM: 61 ft (18.6 m)
DRAUGHT: 22 ft (6.7 m)
SPEED: 32 kts
RANGE: 9000 miles at 15 kts;
3000 miles at 32 kts

ARMAMENT:

MISSILES: SAM – two SA-N-3
Goblet twin launchers, two
SA-N-4 Gecko twin launchers;
A/S – two Raduga SS-N-14 Silex
(Rastrub) quad launchers
GUNS: Four 3 in (76 mm)/60
(2 twin); four 30 mm/65; six
barrels per mounting
TORPEDOES: Ten 21 in (533 mm)
(2 quintuple) tubes
A/S MORTARS: Two RBU 6000
12-tubed, trainable; two RBU
1000 6-tubed
DECOYS: Two PK 2 chaff
launchers; one BAT-1 torpedo
decoy

ELECTRONICS:

RADARS: Air-search – Flat Screen;
air/surface search – Head Net C,
3D; navigation – two Don Kay,
Don 2 or Palm Frond; fire
control – two Head Light B/C (for
SA-N-3 and SS-N-14), two Pop
Group (SA-N-4), two Owl Screech
(76 mm guns), two Bass Tilt
(30 mm guns)
SONARS: Bull Nose, (Titan
2-MG 332) hull-mounted, active
search and attack; Mare Tail
(Vega-M 325); VDS
EW: Eight Side Globe; two Bell
Slam; two Bell Clout; four
Rum Tub

AIR SUPPORT:

HELICOPTERS: One Kamov Ka-27
Helix (ASW)

Kirov RUSSIA

Pyotr Velikiy (old pennant number)

- Very large tall mast and funnel combined sited amidships, supporting Top Pair air-search radar aerials
- Raised raked bows, sloping forecastle, break in deck aft of superstructure
- Secondary masts and upper deck structures aft of mainmast supporting (from forward to aft) Top Plate air/surface search and Top Dome fire control radar aerials
- 130 mm/70 gun mounting fitted immediately forward of flight deck
- CADS-N-1 SAM/gun mounting and Hot Flash/Hot Spot fire control radar/optronic director on raised platforms each side of SS-N-19 launch silos; four more on after superstructure

SPECIFICATION:

COUNTRY OF ORIGIN: Russia
CLASS: Kirov (Orlan) (Project 1144.1/1144.2) (CGN)
ACTIVE: 1
NAME (PENNANT NUMBER):
Pyotr Velikiy (ex-Yuri Andropov) (099, ex-183)

FEATURES:

DISPLACEMENT: 19,000 tons standard; 24,300 full load
LENGTH: 826.8 ft (252 m)
BEAM: 93.5 ft (28.5 m)
DRAUGHT: 29.5 ft (9.1 m)
SPEED: 30 kts
RANGE: 14,000 miles at 30 kts

ARMAMENT:

MISSILES: SSM – 20 Chelomey SS-N-19 Shipwreck (Granit); SAM – 12 SA-N-20 Grumble (Fort) vertical launchers; two SA-N-4 Gecko twin launchers; two SA-N-9 Gauntlet (Klinok) octuple vertical launchers; SAM/guns – six CADS-N-1 (Kortik/Kashtan) with twin 30 mm Gatling combined with eight SA-N-11 Grisson missiles; A/S – Novator SS-N-15 (Starfish) fired from fixed torpedo tubes behind shutters in superstructure
GUNS: Two 130 mm/70 (twin) AK 130
TORPEDOES: 10 21 in (533 mm) (2 quin) tubes
A/S MORTARS: One RBU 12000; 10 tubes per launcher; two RBU 1000 6-tubed
DECOYS: Two twin PK2 150 mm chaff launchers; towed torpedo decoy

ELECTRONICS:

RADARS: Air-search – Top Pair (Top Sail plus Big Net) 3D; air/surface search – Top Plate 3D; navigation – three Palm Frond; fire control – Cross Sword (SA-N-9), one Top Dome for SA-N-6, Tomb Stone (SA-N-20), two Pop Group (SA-N-4), Kite Screech (130 mm guns), six Hot Flash (CADS-N-1)
AIRCRAFT CONTROL: Flyscreen B
SONARS: Horse Jaw; hull-mounted, active search and attack; Horse Tail; VDS active search

AIR SUPPORT:

HELICOPTERS: Three Kamov Ka-27PL Helix (ASW)

Slava RUSSIA

Marshal Ustinov

- High raked bow, sloping forecastle
- 130 mm/70 gun mounting at after end of forecastle
- Distinctive angled ssm launchers adjacent to the bridge structure, four pairs port and four pairs starboard
- Large pyramid mainmast at after end of bridge structure with lattice gantry protruding horizontally astern at the top. Mainmast supports the air/surface search Top Steer or Top Plate radar aerial
- Smaller aftermast supporting the Top Pair air-search radar aerials
- Short, squat twin funnels, side by side, immediately astern of aftermast
- Notable gap abaft the twin funnels (sa-n-6 area) is traversed by a large crane which stows between the funnels
- Prominent Top Dome fire control director aft situated just forward of small flight deck

SPECIFICATION:

COUNTRY OF ORIGIN: Russia
CLASS: Slava (Atlant) (Project 1164)
(CG)
ACTIVE: 3
NAME (PENNANT NUMBER):
Moskva (ex-Slava) (121), Marshal
Ustinov (055), Varyag (ex-Chervona
Ukraina) (011)

FEATURES:
DISPLACEMENT: 9380 tons
standard; 11,490 full load
LENGTH: 611.5 ft (186.4 m)
BEAM: 68.2 ft (20.8 m)
DRAUGHT: 27.6 ft (8.4 m)
SPEED: 32 kts
RANGE: 7500 miles at 15 kts;
2200 miles at 30 kts

ARMAMENT:
MISSILES: SSM – 16 Chelomey
SS-N-12 (8 twin) Sandbox (Bazalt)
launchers; SAM – eight SA-N-6
Grumble (Fort) vertical launchers,
two SA-N-4 Gecko twin launchers
GUNS: Two 130 mm/70 (twin)
AK 130; six 30 mm/65 AK 650; six
barrels per mounting
TORPEDOES: 10 21 in (533 mm)
(2 quin)
A/S MORTARS: Two RBU 6000
12-tubed, trainable
DECOYS: Two PK 2 chaff launchers

ELECTRONICS:
RADARS: Air-search – Top Pair
(Top Sail plus Big Net), 3D; air/
surface search – Top Steer or Top
Plate (Varyag), 3D; navigation –
three Palm Frond; fire control –
Front Door (SS-N-12), Top Dome
(SA-N-6 SAM), two Pop Group
(SA-N-4 SAM), three Bass Tilt
(30 mm guns), Kite Screech
(130 mm gun)
SONARS: Bull Horn and Steer
Hide (Platina); hull-mounted,
active search and attack
EW: Eight Side Globe, four
Rum Tub

AIR SUPPORT:
HELICOPTERS: One Kamov
Ka-27PL Helix (ASW)

Ticonderoga USA

Mobile Bay

- High raked bow with unusual raised solid sides surrounding forecastle
- 5 in gun mounting on forecastle at break in maindeck profile
- Two SAM or A/S Mk 26 Mod 5 launchers (CG 49-51), or two Mk 41 Mod 0 vertical launchers (CG 52 onwards), one between forward turret and bridge structure and one at the after break to quarterdeck. This is the clearest way to differentiate between the two versions of the class
- Large, boxlike forward superstructure just forward of midships. Bridge at forward end, small lattice mast on bridge roof supporting dome for SPQ-9A fire control radar
- Twin funnels, both with three exhausts. Forward funnel has two larger diameter exhausts forward of a smaller one, after funnel has smaller diameter exhaust of three at the forward end
- Tall lattice mainmast supporting radar aerials situated between funnels, exactly amidships.
- Both versions of class have 5 in mounting on quarterdeck

SPECIFICATION:

COUNTRY OF ORIGIN: USA
CLASS: Ticonderoga (Aegis) (CG)
ACTIVE: 25
NAME (PENNANT NUMBER):
Vincennes (CG 49), Valley Forge
(CG 50), Thomas S Gates (CG 51),
Bunker Hill (CG 52), Mobile Bay
(CG 53), Antietam (CG 54), Leyte
Gulf (CG 55), San Jacinto (CG 56),
Lake Champlain (CG 57),
Philippine Sea (CG 58), Princeton
(CG 59), Normandy (CG 60),
Monterey (CG 61), Chancellors-
ville (CG 62), Cowpens (CG 63),
Gettysburg (CG 64), Chosin
(CG 65), Hue City (CG 66), Shiloh
(CG 67), Anzio (CG 68), Vicksburg
(CG 69), Lake Erie (CG 70), Cape
St George (CG 71), Vella Gulf
(CG 72), Port Royal (CG 73)

FEATURES:

DISPLACEMENT: 9407 tons full
load (CG 49-51); 9957 tons
(remainder)
LENGTH: 567 ft (172.8 m)
BEAM: 55 ft (16.8 m)
DRAUGHT: 31 (9.5) (sonar)
SPEED: 30+ kts
RANGE: 6000 miles at 20 kts

ARMAMENT:

MISSILES: SLCM – GDC Tomahawk
(CG 52 onwards), eight
McDonnell Douglas Harpoon
(2 quad); SAM – GDC Standard
SM-2MR; A/S – Honeywell ASROC,
(CG 49-51) and Loral ASROC VLA
(CG 52 onwards) (SAM and A/S
missiles are fired from two twin
Mk 26 Mod 5 launchers (CG 49-
51) and two Mk 41 Mod 0 vertical
launchers (CG 52 onwards);
Tomahawk is carried in CG 52
onwards with eight missiles in
each VLS launcher
GUNS: Two FMC 5 in (127 mm)/54
Mk 45 Mod 0 (CG 49-50); Mod 1
(CG 51 onwards); two GE/GD
20 mm/76 Vulcan Phalanx 6-
barrel Mk 15 Mod 2; two
McDonnell Douglas 25 mm; four
12.7 mm machine guns
TORPEDOES: Six 324 mm Mk 32
(2 triple) Mod 14 tubes with
Honeywell Mk 46 Mod 5
DECOYS: Up to eight Loral Hycor
SRBOC 6-barrel fixed Mk 36,
firing IR flares and chaff; SLQ-25
Nixie; towed torpedo decoy

ELECTRONICS:

RADARS: Air-search/fire control –
RCA SPY-1A phased arrays, 3D and
Raytheon SPY-1B phased arrays,
3D (CG 59 on); air-search –
Raytheon SPS-49(V)7 or 8; surface
search – ISC Cardion SPS-55;
navigation – Raytheon SPS-64(V)9;
fire control – Lockheed SPQ-9A/B;
four Raytheon/RCA SPG-62
SONARS: General Electric/Hughes
SQS-53B (CG 49-51), bow-
mounted, active search and
attack; Gould SQR-19 (CG 54-55),
passive towed array; Gould/
Raytheon SQQ-89(V)3 (CG 52
onwards); combines hull-
mounted SQS-53B (CG 52-67) or
SQS-53C (CG 68-73) and passive
towed array SQR-19
EW: Raytheon SLQ-32V(3)/SLY-2

AIR SUPPORT:

HELICOPTERS: Two Sikorsky
SH-60B Seahawk LAMPS III; two
Kaman SH-2F LAMPS I (CG 47-48)

Destroyers

Meko 360 ARGENTINA, NIGERIA

Sarandi

- Short forecastle, 5 in gun mounting in 'A' position
- 40 mm/70 gun mountings immediately forward of bridge in 'B' position
- Short, stubby pyramid mast at after end of bridge structure with WM25 fire control radome atop
- Exocet SSM launchers, port and starboard, immediately forward of funnels
- Two side-by-side funnels angled outboard in 'V' formation with pole 'T' mast at forward edge
- DA08A Air/surface search and STIR fire control radars on raised superstructure aft of funnels
- Short flight deck right aft with open quarterdeck below
- Nigerian hull has solid deckhouse supporting lattice pylon aft of funnels with prominent Albatros octuple launcher further aft

SPECIFICATION:

COUNTRY OF ORIGIN: Germany
CLASS: Almirante Brown
(Meko 360) (DDG/FFG)
ACTIVE: 4 Argentina, 1 Nigeria
NAME (PENNANT NUMBER):
ARGENTINA – Almirante Brown
(D 10), La Argentina (D 11),
Heroina (D 12), Sarandi (D 13)
NIGERIA – Aradu (ex-Republic)
(F 89)

FEATURES:

DISPLACEMENT: 2900 tons
standard; 3360 tons full load
LENGTH: 413.1 ft (125.9 m);
412 ft (125.6 m) (Aradu)
BEAM: 46 ft (14 m), 49.2 ft (15 m)
(Aradu)
DRAUGHT: 19 ft (5.8 m) (screws)
SPEED: 30.5 kts
RANGE: 4500 miles at 18 kts

ARMAMENT:

MISSILES: SSM – eight
Aerospatiale MM 40 Exocet
(2 quad) launchers (Argentine
units), eight OTO Melara/Matra
Otomat Mk 1 (Aradu); SAM –
Selenia/Elsag Albatros octuple
launcher, Aspide
GUNS: One OTO Melara 5 in
(127 mm)/54 automatic, eight
Breda/Bofors 40 mm/70 (4 twin)
TORPEDOES: Six 324 mm ILAS 3
(2 triple) tubes; Whitehead A 244
(Argentine hulls); six 324 mm
Plessey STWS-1B (2 triple) tubes;
Whitehead A244S (Aradu)
DEPTH CHARGES: One rack (Aradu)
DECOYS: CSEE Dagaie double
mounting; Graseby G1738 towed
torpedo decoy system (Argentine
hulls only); two Breda 105 mm
SCLAR chaff launchers

ELECTRONICS:

RADARS: Air/surface search –
Signaal DA08A (Plessey AWS 5,
Aradu); surface search – Signaal
ZW06 (Argentina only);
navigation – Decca 1226; fire
control – Signaal STIR, Signaal
WM 25 (Aradu only)
SONARS: Atlas Elektronik 80
(DSQS-21BZ); hull-mounted,
active search and attack

AIR SUPPORT:

HELICOPTERS: Aerospatiale AS 555
Fennec, (ASW/ASV) (Argentina);
one Lynx Mk 89 (Aradu)

Iroquois CANADA

Athabaskan

- SAM VLS at after end of forecastle
- 3 in gun mounting in 'B' position
- Signaal SPQ-502 air-search radar aerial atop short pylon aft end of bridge structure
- Tall lattice mainmast forward of funnel
- Unusual, large, square funnel amidships
- Distinctive break in superstructure abreast lattice mast
- Large SATCOM domes alongside funnel
- CIWS mounting immediately aft of funnel, atop after superstructure
- Helicopter flight deck raised above quarter-deck level with torpedo tubes visible below

SPECIFICATION:

COUNTRY OF ORIGIN: Canada
CLASS: Iroquois (DDG)
ACTIVE: 3
NAME (PENNANT NUMBER):
Iroquois (280), Athabaskan (282), Algonquin (283)

FEATURES:

DISPLACEMENT: 5300 tons full load
LENGTH: 426 ft (129.8 m) oa
BEAM: 50 ft (15.2 m)
DRAUGHT: 15.5 ft (4.7 m)
SPEED: 27 kts
RANGE: 4500 miles at 15 kts

ARMAMENT:

MISSILES: SAM – one Martin Marietta Mk 41 VLS, Standard SM-2MR Block III
GUNS: One OTO Melara 3 in (76 mm)/62 Super Rapid; one GE/GD 20 mm/76 6-barrel Vulcan Phalanx Mk 15
TORPEDOES: Six 324 mm Mk 32 (2 triple) tubes; Honeywell Mk 46, Mod 5
DECOYS: Four Plessey Shield Mk 2 6-tubed trainable launchers; chaff or IR flares, Nulka; SLQ-25 Nixie torpedo decoy

ELECTRONICS:

RADARS: Air-search – Signaal SPQ-502 (LW08); surface search – Signaal SPQ-501 (DA08); navigation – two Raytheon Pathfinder, Koden MD 373 (Iroquois only, on hangar roof); fire control – two Signaal SPG-501 (STIR 1.8)
SONARS: Two GD SQS-510; combined VDS and hull-mounted, active search and attack
EW: MEL SLQ-501 Canews

AIR SUPPORT:

HELICOPTERS: Two Sikorsky CH-124A Sea King (ASW)

Prat CHILE

Cochrane (*Maritime Photographic*)

- High freeboard
- 4.5 in gun mounting in 'A' position immediately forward of ssm launchers in 'B' mounting position
- Slim pyramid mast aft of bridge
- Squat funnels with pyramid mainmast centrally situated between them. Double bedstead air-search radar aerial atop
- Enlarged hangar and flight deck continued right aft, making hulls effectively flush-decked.

SPECIFICATION:

COUNTRY OF ORIGIN: UK
CLASS: Prat (ex-*County*)
ACTIVE: 2
NAME (PENNANT NUMBER):
Prat (ex-*Norfolk*) (11), Cochrane (ex-*Antrim*) (12)

FEATURES:

DISPLACEMENT: 6200 tons full load
LENGTH: 520.5 ft (158.7 m)
BEAM: 54 ft (16.5 m)
DRAUGHT: 20.5 ft (6.3 m)
SPEED: 30 kts
RANGE: 3500 miles at 28 kts

ARMAMENT:

MISSILES: SSM – four Aerospatiale MM 38 Exocet; SAM – two octuple IAI/Rafael Barak 1
GUNS: Two Vickers 4.5 in (115 mm) Mk 6 semi-automatic twin mounting; two or four Oerlikon 20 mm Mk 9
TORPEDOES: Six 324 mm Mk 32 (2 triple) tubes; Honeywell Mk 46 Mod 2
DECOYS: SLQ-25 Nixie towed noisemaker

ELECTRONICS:

RADARS: Air-search – Marconi Type 966; Elta LM 2228s (for Barak); surface search – Marconi Type 992 Q or R; navigation – Decca Type 978/1006; fire control – Plessey Type 903 (guns), two Elta EL/M-2221GM (Barak)
SONARS: Kelvin Hughes Type 162 M, hull-mounted; Graseby Type 184 M hull mounted; active search and attack
EW: Elisra 9003 ESM; Type 667 ECM

AIR SUPPORT:

HELICOPTERS: Two (one in *Prat*) Nurtanio NAS 332C Cougar (ASW/ASV)

Luda I/II CHINA

Luda I

- Lattice mainmast with sloping forward edge just forward of forward funnel. Smaller lattice tapered aftermast about midships
- Twin, black-capped funnels angled astern
- Two large HY-2 SSM missile launchers. One set immediately aft of forward funnel, the second immediately aft of after funnel
- Isolated after superstructure supports Rice Lamp fire control director at forward end and 37 mm/63 mounting
- 5.1 in gun mounting in 'Y' position
- Large deck house helicopter hangar with raised flight deck aft

SPECIFICATION:

COUNTRY OF ORIGIN: China
CLASS: Luda I/II (Type 051/051D/051Z) (DDG)
ACTIVE: 12
NAME (PENNANT NUMBER): Jinan (105) (Type 051), Xian (106) (Type 051), Yinchuan (107) (Type 051), Xining (108), Nanjing (131) (Type 051), Hefei (132) (Type 051Z), Chongqing (133), Zunyi (134), Changsha (161) (Type 051), Nanning (162) (Type 051), Nanchang (163), Guilin (164)

FEATURES:

DISPLACEMENT: 3250 tons standard; 3670 tons full load
LENGTH: 433.1 ft (132 m)
BEAM: 42 ft (12.8 m)
DRAUGHT: 15.1 ft (4.6 m)
SPEED: 32 kts
RANGE: 2970 miles at 18 kts

ARMAMENT:

MISSILES: SSM – six HY-2 (C-201) (CSS-C-3A Seersucker) (2 triple) launchers
GUNS: Four (Type 051) or two (Type 051D) USSR 5.1 in (130 mm)/58 (2 twin) (Type I); eight China 57 mm/70 (4 twin) or eight China 37 mm/63 (4 twin); eight USSR 25 mm/60 (4 twin)
TORPEDOES: Six 324 mm Whitehead B515 (2 triple tubes) (fitted in some Type 051); Yu-2 (Mk 46 Mod 1)
A/S MORTARS: Two FQF 2500 12-tubed launchers similar in design to the RBU 1200
DEPTH CHARGES: Two or four BMB projectors; two or four racks (Type 051)
MINES: 38 can be carried
DECOYS: Chaff launchers (fitted to some)

ELECTRONICS:

RADARS: Air-search – Type 515 Bean Sticks, Type 381 Rice Screen, 3D (on mainmast in some); surface search – Type 354 Eye Shield, Square Tie (not in all); navigation – Fin Curve or Racal Decca 1290; fire control – Wasp Head (Wok Won) or Type 343 Sun Visor B (Series 2), two Type 347G
SONARS: Pegas 2M and Tamir 2; hull-mounted, active search and attack

AIR SUPPORT:

HELICOPTERS: Two Harbin Z-9C Haitun (Dauphin 2)

Luda III CHINA

Zhuhai

- High bow with sweeping forecastle aft to bridge. One maindeck level through to stern
- Large distinctive 5.1 in gun mounting in 'A' position with 37 mm/63 turret in 'B' position
- Lattice mainmast with sloping forward edge just forward of forward funnel. Smaller lattice tapered aftermast about midships
- Twin, black-capped funnels angled astern
- Two large YJ-1 Eagle Strike SSM box missile launchers. One set immediately aft of forward funnel, the second immediately aft of after funnel
- Isolated after superstructure supports Type 347G fire control director at forward end and turreted 37 mm/63 mounting
- 5.1 in gun mounting in 'Y' position

NOTE: Secondary gun armament in turrets

SPECIFICATION:

COUNTRY OF ORIGIN: China
CLASS: Luda 051DT (DDG)
ACTIVE: 4
NAME (PENNANT NUMBER):
Kaifeng (109), Dalian (110), Zhanjiang (165), Zhuhai (166) (168 when out of area)

FEATURES:

DISPLACEMENT: 3250 tons standard; 3730 tons full load
LENGTH: 433.1 ft (132 m)
BEAM: 42 ft (12.8 m)
DRAUGHT: 15.3 ft (4.7 m)
SPEED: 32 kts
RANGE: 2970 miles at 18 kts

ARMAMENT:

MISSILES: SSM – 16 YJ-1 Eagle Strike (C-801) (CSS-N-4 Sardine) (4 quad launchers); SAM – one HQ-7 (Crotale) octuple launcher
GUNS: Two USSR 5.1 in (130 mm)/58; four 3.9 in (2 twin); six China 37 mm/63 Type 76A (3 twin); six China 57 mm/63 (3 twin)
TORPEDOES: Six 324 mm Whitehead B515 (2 triple tubes) Yu-2 (Mk 46 Mod 1)
A/S MORTARS: Two FQF 2500 12-tubed fixed launchers, similar in design to the RBU 1200
DECOYS: Two 15-tubed fixed Chaff/IR flare launchers

ELECTRONICS:

RADARS: Air-search – Type 517 Knife Rest; surface search – Type 363 Sea Tiger, Type 354 Eye Shield; navigation – Racal Decca 1290; fire control – Type 343 Sun Visor B, Type 344 (MR34), Type 345 (MR35), Type 347G
SONARS: DUBV 23 (165 and 166), hull-mounted, active search/attack
EW: Type 825 ESM, Type 981 ECM

Luhai CHINA

Shenzhen

- Raised bow with one maindeck level through to stern
- 3.9 in gun twin turret in 'A' position
- HQ-7 (Crotale) SAM launcher in 'B' position
- Tall superstructure, forward and helicopter hangar aft of midships with two funnels separated by aft pylon mast and two C-802 SSM missile box launchers
- Short forward mast atop bridge super-structure with low vertical lattice pylon behind Type 360 air/surface search radar aerial. Two low pylons with fire control radars forward of mast
- Four Twin 37 mm turret mountings atop hangar
- Triple torpedo tubes just aft of forward funnel on main deck

SPECIFICATION:

COUNTRY OF ORIGIN: China
CLASS: Luhai (DDG)
ACTIVE: 1
PLANNED: 1
NAME (PENNANT NUMBER):
Shenzhen (167)

FEATURES:

DISPLACEMENT: 6000 tons full load
LENGTH: 505 ft (154 m)
BEAM: 52.5 ft (16 m)
DRAUGHT: 19.7 ft (6 m)
SPEED: 29 kts
RANGE: 4500 miles at 14 kts

ARMAMENT:

MISSILES: SSM – C-802 (CSS-N-8 Saccade), two octuple box launchers; SAM – one HQ-7 (Crotale) octuple launcher
GUNS: Two 3.9 in (100 mm)/56 (twin); eight 37 mm/63 Type 76A (4 twin)
TORPEDOES: Six 324 mm B5 15 (2 triple) tubes with Yu-2/5/6
DECOYS: Two Type 946 15-tube 100 mm and two Type 947 10-tube 130 mm chaff launchers

ELECTRONICS:

RADARS: Air-search – Type 517 Knife Rest, Type 381C Rice Shield; air/surface search – Type 360 Seagull; navigation – Racal Decca 1290; fire control – Type 344 (MR34) (SSM/100 mm guns), two Type 347G Rice Lamp (37 mm), Type 345 (MR35) (HQ-7)
SONARS: DUBV-23; hull-mounted, active search and attack
EW: Type 826 ESM, Type 984 and Type 985 ECM

AIR SUPPORT:

HELICOPTERS: Two Harbin Zhi-9C Haitun (Dauphin 2) (ASW/ASV) or Kamov Ka-28 Helix

Luhu CHINA

Qingdao

- Acute angled high bow. Single maindeck level from stem to stern
- Sloping forecastle with 3.9 in gun mounting in 'A' position
- Crotale SAM octuple launcher ('B' mounting position)
- Two 37 mm/63 gun turret mountings immediately forward of bridge
- Short, tapered, lattice mainmast at after end of main superstructure
- Single funnel amidships with black, wedge-shaped, RAD-HAZ screen at after end
- Two SSM missile launchers. One set between enclosed aftermast and funnel, second aft of aftermast
- Square after superstructure supports large curved Type 518 air-search radar aerial at forward end and 37 mm/63 gun mounting at after end
- Helicopter flight deck aft with open quarterdeck below

NOTE: Forecastle gun and SAM mounting may cause confusion with 'Luhai' class but 'Luhu' has single funnel and prominent, raised 37 mm gun turrets immediately forward of bridge as quick distinguishing features

SPECIFICATION:

COUNTRY OF ORIGIN: China
CLASS: Luhu (Type 052) (DDG)
ACTIVE: 2
NAME (PENNANT NUMBER):
Harbin (112), Quingdao (113)

FEATURES:
DISPLACEMENT: 4600 tons full load
LENGTH: 472.4 ft (144 m)
BEAM: 52.5 ft (16 m)
DRAUGHT: 16.7 ft (5.1 m)
SPEED: 31 kts
RANGE: 5000 miles at 15 kts

ARMAMENT:
MISSILES: SSM – 16 YJ-82 (C-802) (CSS-N-8 Saccade); SAM – one HQ-7 (Crotale) octuple launcher
GUNS: Two 3.9 in (100 mm)/56 (twin); eight 37 mm/63 Type 76 (4 twin)
TORPEDOES: Six 324 mm Whitehead B5 15 (2 triple) tubes; Yu-2 (Mk 46 Mod 1)
A/S MORTARS: Two FQF 2500 12-tubed fixed launchers
DECOYS: Two Type 946 15-barrel chaff launchers

ELECTRONICS:
RADARS: Air-search – Type 518; air/ surface search – Type 363S Sea Tiger, Type 360 Seagull; surface search – China Type 362 (ESR 1); navigation – Racal Decca 1290; fire control – Type 344 (MR34) (for SSM and 100 mm gun), two Type 347G Rice Lamp (37 mm gun); Type 345 (MR35) (Crotale)
SONARS: DUBV-23; hull-mounted, active search and attack; DUBV-43 VDS, active attack
EW: Rapido and Type 826 ESM; Ramses and Type 984 ECM

AIR SUPPORT:
HELICOPTERS: Two Harbin Zhi-9C Haitun (Dauphin 2) (ASW/ASV)

Luyang I/II CHINA

Luyang

- Luyang I based on Luhai design incorporating more advanced stealth features
- Luyang I aft superstructure houses hangar to port and aft, missile magazine to starboard
- Luyang I solid mast to rear of forward superstructure supporting Top Plate air-search radar
- Solid mast with spherical dome housing Type 364 radar sited immediately forward of aft superstructure
- C 803 missile launchers mounted forward of after mast
- Luyang II uses same basic hull as Luyang I
- Luyang II has taller, slab sided forward superstructure mounting four phase array antennas
- Luyang II helicopter hangar as in Type I
- CIWS mounted on raised platforms forward and aft on top of hangar to port
- Type 517 radar mounted on squat solid mast aft of funnel
- Quadruple C 803 missile launchers in Luyang II sited in fixed positions facing port and starboard immediately in front of hangar aft

SPECIFICATION:

COUNTRY OF ORIGIN: China
CLASS: Luyang I, Luyang II
ACTIVE: 2 (Luyang I), 2 (Luyang II)
NAME (PENNANT NUMBER):
Guangzhou (168), Wuhan (169)
(Luyang I), Lanzhou (170), Haikou
(171) (Luyang II)

FEATURES:
DISPLACEMENT: 7000 tons
full load
LENGTH: 508.5 ft (155 m)
BEAM: 55.8 ft (17 m)
DRAUGHT: 19.7 ft (6 m)
SPEED: 29 kts
RANGE: 4500 miles at 15 kts

ARMAMENT:
MISSILES: SSM – 16 C-802 (SS-N-2
Saccade) (4 quad), eight C-803
(2 quad) (Luyang II); SAM – SA-N-12
Grizzly (Luyang II), HHQ-9 8 vertical
revolving sextuple launchers
(six forward, two aft) (Luyang II)
GUNS: One 3.9 in (100 mm)/56;
two 30 mm Type 730
A/S MORTARS: Four multiple
rocket launchers
DECOYS: Four 18-tube 100 mm
launchers

ELECTRONICS:
RADARS: Air-search – Top Plate,
Type 517 Knife Rest (Luyang II);
air/surface search – Type 364
Seagull; air-search/fire control –
Type 346 phased array (Luyang II
only); fire control – four Front
Dome (not in Luyang II), Type
344, Type 347G Rice Lamp
EW: SRW 210A ESM, Type 984, Type
985 ECM (Luyang I)

AIR SUPPORT:
HELICOPTERS: 1 (two in Luyang II)
Harbin Zhi-9A Haitun or Kamov
KA-28 Helix

Type 051C   CHINA

Type 051c fitting out

- Slab-sided superstructure fore and aft with sloping sides to reduce radar signature
- Solid mast on top of forward superstructure
- Solid main mast probably mounting Top Plate radar sited in front of funnel which is sited in front of after superstructure
- Aft superstructure incorporates hangar
- c 803 missiles probably to be mounted facing port and starboard between forward superstructure and mainmast
- 3.9 in gun in 'A' mounting position
- Profile exhibits strong similarities to that of 'Luhai'

SPECIFICATION:

COUNTRY OF ORIGIN: China
CLASS: Type 051c
ACTIVE: 0
BUILDING: 2
NAME (PENNANT NUMBER):
— (115), — (—)

FEATURES:

DISPLACEMENT: 7000 tons full load
LENGTH: 508.5 ft (155 m)
BEAM: 55.8 ft (17 m)
DRAUGHT: 19.7 ft (6 m)
SPEED: To be announced
RANGE: To be announced

ARMAMENT:

MISSILES: SSM — eight (final details to be verified) c-803 (2 quad); SAM — six (two forward, four aft) SA-N-6 Grumble revolving vertical launchers
GUNS: One 3.9 in (100 mm)/56; two Type 730 30 mm
TORPEDOES: To be announced
A/S MORTARS: To be announced
DECOYS: To be announced

ELECTRONICS:

RADARS: Air-search — Top Plate 3D; air/surface search — Type 364 Seagull; navigation — to be announced; fire control — to be announced
SONARS: Bow mounted
EW: To be announced

AIR SUPPORT:

HELICOPTERS: One Harbin Zhi-9A Haitun or Kamov KA-28 Helix

Cassard FRANCE

Jean Bart

- Continuous maindeck from stem to stern
- Long forecastle with 3.9 in gun mounting in 'A' position
- High forward superstructure with tall lattice mainmast
- Large curved DRBV 26C air/surface search radar aerial immediately forward of mainmast
- High superstructure amidships with very distinctive DRBJ 11B air-search radar dome
- Two SPG-51C fire control directors on after end of central superstructure
- Mk 13 Mod 5 SAM launcher isolated, aft of central superstructure
- Matra Sadral PDMS SAM sextuple launchers outboard at after end of hangar
- Hangar and small flight deck right aft

SPECIFICATION:

COUNTRY OF ORIGIN: France
CLASS: Cassard (Type F 70 (A/A)) (DDG)
ACTIVE: 2
NAME (PENNANT NUMBER): Cassard (D 614), Jean Bart (D 615)

FEATURES:

DISPLACEMENT: 4230 tons standard; 5000 tons full load
LENGTH: 455.9 ft (139 m)
BEAM: 45.9 ft (14 m)
DRAUGHT: 21.3 ft (6.5 m) (sonar)
SPEED: 29 kts
RANGE: 8000 miles at 17 kts

ARMAMENT:

MISSILES: SSM – eight Aerospatiale MM 40 Exocet; SAM – GDC Pomona Standard SM-1MR, Mk 13 Mod 5 launcher, two Matra Sadral PDMS sextuple launchers, Mistral
GUNS: One DCN 3.9 in (100 mm)/55 Mod 68 CADAM automatic; two Oerlikon 20 mm; four 12.7 mm machine guns
TORPEDOES: Two fixed launchers model KD 59E; ECAN L5 Mod 4
DECOYS: Two CSEE Dagaie and two AMBL Sagaie 10-barrel Chaff/IR launchers; SLQ-25 Nixie; towed torpedo decoy

ELECTRONICS:

RADARS: Air-search – Thomson-CSF DRBJ 11B, 3D; air/surface search – DRBV 26C; navigation – two Racal DRBN 34A; fire control – Thomson-CSF DRBC 33A (guns), two Raytheon SPG-51C (missiles)
SONARS: Thomson-Sintra DUBA 25A (D 614) or DUBA 25C (D 615); hull-mounted, active search and attack
EW: ARBR 17B ESM, ARBB 33 ECM, DIBV 1A Vampir IR detector

AIR SUPPORT:

HELICOPTERS: One Aerospatiale AS 565MA Panther (SSM targeting)

Georges Leygues FRANCE

Jean de Vienne

- Long forecastle with 3.9 in gun mounting in 'A' position close to superstructure
- Tall lattice mainmast at after end of bridge with vertical after edge and sloping forward edge. Tall pole mast with ESM array further forward on lattice mainmast in D 645
- Tall funnel amidships with vertical forward edge and sloping after edge, funnel cap angled down at after end
- Two Exocet SSM launchers atop forward end of after superstructure immediately aft of funnel
- Crotale SAM launcher atop after superstructure
- Flight deck aft of hangar
- VDS towing equipment on quarterdeck

NOTE: Bridge raised one deck in the last three of the class. INMARSAT aerial can be fitted forward of the funnel or between the Syracuse SATCOM domes

SPECIFICATION:

COUNTRY OF ORIGIN: France
CLASS: Georges Leygues
(Type F 70 (ASW)) (DDG)
ACTIVE: 7
NAME (PENNANT NUMBER):
Georges Leygues (D 640), Du-
pleix (D 641), Montcalm (D 642),
Jean de Vienne (D 643), Primau-
guet (D 644), La Motte-Picquet
(D 645), Latouche-Tréville (D 646)

FEATURES:

DISPLACEMENT: 4300 tons full load
(D 640-643); 4750 tons (D 644-646)
LENGTH: 455.9 ft (139 m)
BEAM: 45.9 ft (14 m)
DRAUGHT: 18.7 ft (5.7 m)
SPEED: 30 kts; 21 kts (diesels)
RANGE: 8500 miles at 18 kts

ARMAMENT:

MISSILES: SSM – four MM 40 Exocet
(MM 38 in D 640); SAM – Crotale
Naval EDIR octuple launcher, two
Matra Sadral/Mistral sextuple
launchers being fitted to D 640-
643 (two Matra Simbad twin laun-
chers may be mounted in place
of 20 mm guns in D 644-646)
GUNS: One 3.9 in (100 mm)/55
Mod 68 CADAM automatic; two
Breda/Mauser 30 mm guns
(D 640-643); two Oerlikon 20 mm;
four M2HB 12.7 mm machine guns
TORPEDOES: Two fixed launchers;
Eurotorp Mu 90
DECOYS: Two CSEE Dagaie Mk 1
or two 10-barrel double trainable
chaff/IR flare launcher

ELECTRONICS:

RADARS: Air-search – DRBV 26A
(D 640-643); air/surface search –
DRBV 15A (DD 640, 641, 645), DRBV
15B (DD 642-644, 646); navigation
– two Decca 1226; fire control –
Vega with DRBC 32E (D 640-643),
DRBC 33A (D 644-646) (Crotale),
Castor II (SAM)
SONARS: DUBV 23D (DUBV 24C in
D 644-646), bow-mounted active
search and attack; DUBV 43B (43C
in D 643-646) VDS, paired with
DUBV 23D/24; DSBV 61B (in D 644
on) passive linear towed array
EW: ARBR 17 ESM, ARBB 32B or
ARBB 36A (DD 641-646) ECM, DIBV
2A Vampir IR detector (DD 641-643)

AIR SUPPORT:

HELICOPTERS: Two Westland Lynx
Mk 4 (FN) (ASW) except D 640

Horizon FRANCE, ITALY

Horizon Class

- Sylver VSL SAM in forecastle in 'A' position
- Two 76 mm gun turrets in 'B' position
- Tall pyramid mast above bridge superstructure with Alenia EMPAR surveillance/fire control radar atop
- Low, squat funnel with integral narrow pyramid mast, topped by pole mast
- SSM box launchers between forward and after superstructure
- Short pyramid mast on forward edge of after superstructure with air surface radar atop
- 76 mm gun turret (Italian hulls) Sadral SAM launchers (French) atop helicopter hangar
- Short helicopter landing deck on quarterdeck

SPECIFICATION:

COUNTRY OF ORIGIN: France, Italy
CLASS: Forbin, Andrea Doria
BUILDING: 2 France, 2 Italy
PLANNED: 2 France, 2 Italy
NAME (PENNANT NUMBER):
FRANCE – Forbin (D 620),
Chevalier Paul (D 621)
ITALY – Andrea Doria (ex-*Carlo Bergamini* (—), Caio Duilio (—)

FEATURES:

DISPLACEMENT: 6700 tons full load
LENGTH: 502 ft (153 m) oa (France); 494.1 ft (150.6 m) oa (Italy)
BEAM: 66.6 ft (20.3 m) (France); 57.4 ft (17.5 m) (Italy)
DRAUGHT: 15.7 ft (4.8 m) (France); 16.7 ft (5.1 m) (Italy)
SPEED: 29 kts; 18 kts (diesels)
RANGE: 7000 miles at 18 kts

ARMAMENT:

MISSILES: SSM – eight Aerospatiale MM 40 Block III Exocet (France), eight (2 quad) Teseo Mk 2 (Italy); SAM – DCN Sylver A50 VLS, with Aster 15 and 30 weapons (two Sadral sextuple launchers, France only)
GUNS: Two OTOBreda 76 mm/62 Super Rapid (three in Italian hulls); two GIAT (France); two Breda Oerlikon 20 mm/80 (Italy)
TORPEDOES: Two launchers, Eurotorp Mu 90
DECOYS: Two OTOBreda SCLAR H chaff launchers (Italy); four Matra Defense chaff/IR (France); SLAT torpedo decoy

ELECTRONICS:

RADARS: Air/surface search – Thomson-CSF/Marconi DRBV 27 (S 1850M) (Astral); surveillance/fire control – Alenia EMPAR; surface search – two SPN 753 (France), Alenia RASS (Italy); fire control – two Alenia Marconi NA 25XP (Italy), Alenia Marconi NA 25 (France)
SONARS: Thomson-Marconi 4110CL; hull-mounted, active search/attack
EW: SIGEN suite integrating decoys, ESM, ECM

AIR SUPPORT:

HELICOPTERS: One Marine Nationale NH 90 (France); one EH Industries EH 101 Merlin (ASW)

Suffren FRANCE

Duquesne

- Two 3.9 in gun mountings in 'A' and 'B' positions
- Very large and distinctive air-search radome at after end of bridge structure, flanked by small SATCOM domes
- Solid, rounded mast and funnel combined amidships with main engine exhausts at top
- Exocet SSM box launcher on slightly raised after superstructure immediately forward of short lattice aftermast
- Masurca SAM twin launcher at forward end of quarter deck
- VDS towing equipment at after end of quarter deck

SPECIFICATION:

COUNTRY OF ORIGIN: France
CLASS: Suffren (DDG)
ACTIVE: 1
NAME (PENNANT NUMBER):
Duquesne (D 603)

FEATURES:
DISPLACEMENT: 5335 tons
standard; 6780 tons full load
LENGTH: 517.1 ft (157.6 m)
BEAM: 50.9 ft (15.5 m)
DRAUGHT: 23.8 ft (7.25 m)
SPEED: 34 kts
RANGE: 5100 miles at 18 kts,
2400 miles at 29 kts

ARMAMENT:
MISSILES: SSM – four Aerospatiale
MM 38 Exocet; SAM – ECAN Ruelle
Masurca twin launcher
GUNS: Two DCN/Cruesot-Loire
3.9 in (100 mm)/55 Mod 1964
CADAM automatic; four or six
Oerlikon 20 mm; two 12.7 mm
machine guns
TORPEDOES: Four launchers (two
each side); 10 ECAN L5
DECOYS: Two CSEE Sagaie
10-barrel trainable chaff/IR flare
launchers; two Dagaie launchers

ELECTRONICS:
RADARS: Air-search (radome) –
DRBI 23; air/surface search – DRBV
15A; navigation – Racal Decca
1229 (DRBN 34A); fire control –
two Thomson-CSF DRBR 51
(Masurca), Thomson-CSF
DRBC 33A (guns)
SONARS: Thomson-Sintra
DUBV 23; hull-mounted, active
search/attack; DUBV 43 VDS
EW: ARBR 17 ESM, ARBB 33 ECM

Tourville FRANCE

De Grasse

- Two 3.9 in gun mountings in 'A' and 'B' positions
- Short lattice mast atop after end of forward superstructure
- Exocet SSM launchers immediately aft of forward superstructure
- Large solid combined mainmast and funnel amidships
- Distinctive DRBV 26 air-search radar aerial supported on projecting gantry forward end of mainmast
- Two domed SATCOM aerials, port and starboard, immediately aft of mainmast
- Crotale SAM launcher atop raised after superstructure
- VDS towing gear on quarterdeck down from after end of flight deck

SPECIFICATION:

COUNTRY OF ORIGIN: France
CLASS: Tourville (Type F 67) (DDG)
ACTIVE: 2
NAME (PENNANT NUMBER):
Tourville (D 610); de Grasse
(D 612)

FEATURES:
DISPLACEMENT: 4650 tons
standard; 6100 tons full load
LENGTH: 501.6 ft (152.8 m)
BEAM: 51.8 ft (15.8 m)
DRAUGHT: 21.6 ft (6.6 m)
SPEED: 32 kts
RANGE: 5000 miles at 18 kts

ARMAMENT:
MISSILES: SSM – six Aerospatiale
MM 38 Exocet; SAM – Thomson-
CSF Crotale Naval EDIR octuple
launcher
GUNS: Two DCN/Creusot-Loire
3.9 in (100 mm)/55 Mod 68
CADAM automatic; two Giat
20 mm; four 12.7 mm
machine guns
TORPEDOES: Two launchers,
ten ECAN L5
DECOYS: Two CSEE/VSEL Syllex
8-barrel trainable chaff launchers

ELECTRONICS:
RADARS: Air-search – DRBV 26A;
air/surface search – Thomson-
CSF DRBV 51D; navigation – two
Racal Decca Type 1226; fire
control – Thomson-CSF DRBC
321D (Crotale)
SONARS: Thomson-Sintra DUBV
23, bow-mounted, active
search/attack; DSBX 1A (ATBF)
active VDS; DSBV 62C; passive
linear towed array

AIR SUPPORT:
HELICOPTERS: Two Westland Lynx
Mk 4 (FN) (ASW); armed with
Mk 46 or Eurotorp MU 90

Delhi INDIA

Mumbai

SPECIFICATION:

COUNTRY OF ORIGIN: India
CLASS: Delhi (DDG) (Project 15)
ACTIVE: 3
NAME (PENNANT NUMBER):
Delhi (D 61), Mysore (D 60),
Mumbai (D 62)

FEATURES:
DISPLACEMENT: 6700 tons
full load
LENGTH: 534.8 ft (163 m)
BEAM: 55.8 ft (17 m)
DRAUGHT: 21.3 ft (6.5 m)
SPEED: 32 kts
RANGE: 4500 miles at 18 kts

ARMAMENT:
MISSILES: SSM – 16 Zvezda
SS-N-25 (4 quad) (KH 35E Uran);
SAM – two SA-N-7 Gadfly (Kashmir
Uragan), two octuple Barak VLS
GUNS: One USSR 3.9 in (100 mm)/
59 AK 100; four USSR 30 mm/65
AK 630, 6 barrels per mounting
TORPEDOES: Five PTA 21 in
(533 mm) (quin) tubes
A/S MORTARS: Two RBU 6000,
12-tubed trainable
DEPTH CHARGES: Two rails
DECOYS: Two PK 2 chaff
launchers; towed torpedo decoy

ELECTRONICS:
RADARS: Air-search – Bharat/
Signaal RALW (LW08); air/surface
search – Half Plate; navigation –
three Nyada MR-212/201; fire
control – six Front Dome (SAM),
Kite Screech (100 mm gun),
two Bass Tilt (30 mm guns),
(D60 and 62) Plank Shave
(Granit Harpun B) (SSM)
SONARS: Bharat HUMVAD, hull
mounted (D 62) active search;
Bharat HUMSA hull mounted
(D 62); Thales ATAS active towed
array (D 62); India/Garden Reach
Model 15-750 VDS
EW: Bharat Ajanta Mk 2 ESM,
Elettronica TQN-2 ECM

AIR SUPPORT:
HELICOPTERS: Two Westland Sea
King Mk 42B (ASV) or two
Hindustan Aeronautics ALH,
(ASW/ASV)

- High bow with sweeping forecastle aft to bridge. One maindeck level through to stern
- Squat 3.9 in gun mounting in 'A' position
- SA-N-7 SAM launcher in 'B' position with two RBU 6000 A/S launchers aft
- Four angled, tubular quad launcher tubes for SS-N-25 SSM, (two port, two starboard) alongside and forward of bridge superstructure
- Prominent square Half Plate air/surface search radar aerial at top of short mainmast atop bridge superstructure
- Second low pyramid mast between two squared funnels, with Bharat/Signaal RALW (LW08) air-search aerial atop
- Long, low helicopter hangar aft of second funnel

Audace ITALY

Ardito

- Continuous maindeck from stem to stern
- 5 in gun mounting in 'A' position with Albatros SAM launcher in 'B' position
- Unusually high forward superstructure
- Forward mast and funnel, combined at after end of forward superstructure, supports air-search radar aerial. Twin exhausts in 'V' protruding aft
- Aftermast and funnel combined has sloping forward edge supporting large, angled square-shaped long-range air-search radar aerial
- Ship's boat alongside after funnel and mast
- Teseo SSM launchers sited between funnels, above 76 mm gun mountings
- Two prominent fire control radars on pylons aft of after funnel/mast
- Standard SAM launcher atop forward end of hangar which rises at an angle aft
- Flight deck right aft with open quarterdeck below

SPECIFICATION:

COUNTRY OF ORIGIN: Italy
CLASS: Audace (DDG)
ACTIVE: 2
NAME (PENNANT NUMBER):
Ardito (D 550), Audace (D 551)

FEATURES:

DISPLACEMENT: 3600 tons standard; 4400 tons full load
LENGTH: 448 ft (136.6 m)
BEAM: 46.6 ft (14.2 m)
DRAUGHT: 15.1 ft (4.6 m)
SPEED: 34 kts
RANGE: 3000 miles at 20 kts

ARMAMENT:

MISSILES: SSM – eight OTO Melara/Matra Teseo Mk 2 (TG 2) (4 twin); SAM – GDC Pomona Standard SM-1MR, Mk 13 Mod 4 launcher, Selenia Albatros octuple launcher for Aspide
GUNS: One OTO Melara 5 in (127 mm)/54; three OTO Melara 3 in (76 mm)/62 Compact (Ardito) and one (Ardito) or four (Audace) Super Rapid
TORPEDOES: Six 324 mm US Mk 32 (2 triple) tubes; Honeywell Mk 46
DECOYS: Two Breda 105 mm SCLAR 20-barrel chaff launchers; SLQ-25 Nixie towed torpedo decoy

ELECTRONICS:

RADARS: Long range air-search – Hughes SPS-52C, 3D; air-search – Selenia SPS-768 (RAN 3L); air/surface search – Selenia SPS-774 (RAN 10S); surface search – SMA SPQ-2D; navigation – SMA SPN-748; fire control – three Selenia SPG-76 (RTN 30X), two Raytheon SPG-51 (standard SAM)
SONARS: CWE 610; hull-mounted, active search and attack
EW: Elettronica SLQ-732 Nettuno ESM/ECM

AIR SUPPORT:

HELICOPTERS: Two Agusta-Bell AB 212 (ASW) or one EH Industries EH 101 Merlin

De la Penne ITALY

Francesco Mimbelli

- High bow, continuous maindeck from stem to stern
- 5 in gun mounting in 'A' position with Albatros SAM octuple box launcher in 'B' mounting position
- Slim pyramid foremast atop forward superstructure
- Slightly shorter, enclosed aftermast supporting square long range air-search radar aerial on platform protruding aft. Pole mast atop aftermast with air/surface search radar atop
- Three square section funnels, one at after end of forward superstructure and twin 'v' funnels just abaft aftermast. Both sets slightly tapered towards top
- Teseo SSM launchers amidships between forward funnel and after mast
- Prominent fire control arrays on pylons aft of after mast
- Standard SAM launcher and 3 in gun mounting atop after superstructure
- Flight deck right aft with open quarterdeck below

Asagiri JAPAN

Yuugiri

- Continuous maindeck line from stem to stern with rising bows
- 3 in gun mounting in 'A' position
- ASROC A/S missile octuple box launcher immediately forward of bridge
- Two black-capped funnels, after one partially obscured by superstructure
- Lattice mainmast at aft of bridge supporting several radar aerials. Lattice aftermast just abaft after funnel
- Two CIWS mountings immediately forward of mainmast, atop bridge
- Fire control radome sited aft of aftermast on tall superstructure
- Helicopter deck aft, raised above maindeck, with Sea Sparrow SAM box launcher right aft at maindeck level

NOTE: The mainmast now offset to port, (more so in last four of class) as is the forward funnel but the after funnel has been offset to starboard, all to reduce IR signature and damage to electronic systems on the mainmast

SPECIFICATION:

COUNTRY OF ORIGIN: Japan
CLASS: Asagiri (DDG/DD)
ACTIVE: 8
NAME (PENNANT NUMBER):
Asagiri (DD 151), Yamagiri
(DD 152), Yuugiri (DD 153), Amagiri
(DD 154), Hamagiri (DD 155),
Setogiri (DD 156), Sawagiri
(DD 157), Umigiri (DD 158)

FEATURES:
DISPLACEMENT: 4200 tons full load
LENGTH: 449.4 ft (137 m)
BEAM: 48 ft (14.6 m)
DRAUGHT: 14.6 ft (4.5 m)
SPEED: 30 kts

ARMAMENT:
MISSILES: SSM – eight McDonnell
Douglas Harpoon (2 quad)
launchers; SAM – Raytheon Sea
Sparrow Mk 29 (Type 3/3A)
octuple box launcher; A/S –
Honeywell ASROC Mk 112 octuple
launcher; payload – Mk 46 Mod 5
Neartip torpedoes
GUNS: One OTOBreda 3 in
(76 mm)/62 Compact; two GE/GD
20 mm Phalanx Mk 15 CIWS
TORPEDOES: Six 324 mm Type 68
(2 triple) HOS 301 tubes;
Honeywell Mk 46 Mod 5 Neartip
DECOYS: Two Loral Hycor SRBOC
6-barrel Mk 36 chaff launchers;
one SLQ-51 Nixie or Type 4 towed
anti-torpedo decoy

ELECTRONICS:
RADARS: Air-search – Melco
OPS-14C (DD 151-154), Melco
OPS-24 (DD 155-158), 3D; surface
search – JRC OPS-28C (DD 151, 152,
155-158), JRC OPS-28C-1Y (DD 153-
154); fire control – Type 2-22
(guns), Type 2-12E (DD 151-154),
Type 2-12G (for SAM) (DD 155-158)
SONARS: Mitsubishi OQS-4A (II);
hull-mounted, active search/
attack; OQR-1 towed array
EW: Nec NOLR 6C or NOLR 8
(DD 152) ESM, Fujitsu OLT-3 ECM

AIR SUPPORT:
HELICOPTERS: One Sikorsky/
Mitsubishi SH-60J Sea Hawk (ASW)

Haruna JAPAN

Hiei

- Continuous maindeck line from bow to stern
- Forecastle identical to 'Shirane' class
- Similar large, slab-sided central superstructure to 'Shirane' class. Main difference is single mast/funnel combined, offset slightly to port
- Lattice mast and curved Melco OPS-11C air-search radar aerial atop funnel
- Prominent fire control radome aft of main-mast and funnel
- Aft of funnel almost identical to 'Shirane' class
- Appearance of weapons fit on forecastle is very similar in appearance to 'Shirane' class

SPECIFICATION:

COUNTRY OF ORIGIN: Japan
CLASS: Haruna (DD/DDH)
ACTIVE: 2
NAME (PENNANT NUMBER): Haruna (DDH 141), Hiei (DDH 142)

FEATURES:

DISPLACEMENT: 4950 tons standard, 5050 tons (DD 142); 6900 tons full load
LENGTH: 502 ft (153 m)
BEAM: 57.4 ft (17.5 m)
DRAUGHT: 17.1 ft (5.2 m)
SPEED: 31 kts

ARMAMENT:

MISSILES: SAM – Raytheon Sea Sparrow Mk 29 (Type 3A) octuple box launcher; A/S – Honeywell ASROC Mk 112 octuple launcher; payload – Mk 46 Mod 5 Neartip torpedoes
GUNS: Two FMC 5 in (127 mm)/54 Mk 42 automatic; two GE/GD 20 mm Phalanx Mk 15 CIWS
TORPEDOES: Six 324 mm HOS 301 (2 triple) tubes; Honeywell Mk 46 Mod 5 Neartip
DECOYS: Four Loral Hycor SRBOC 6-barrel Mk 36 chaff launchers

ELECTRONICS:

RADARS: Air-search – Melco OPS-11C; surface search – JRC OPS-28C/28C-Y; navigation – Koden OPN-11; fire control – one Type 1A (guns), one Type 2-12 (SAM)
SONARS: Sangamo/Mitsubishi OQS-3; bow-mounted, active search/attack
EW: Melco NOLQ-1 ESM/ECM, Fujitsu OLR9 ESM

AIR SUPPORT:

HELICOPTERS: Three Sikorsky/Mitsubishi SH-60J Seahawk (ASW)

Hatakaze JAPAN

Shimakaze

- Break in upper deck profile just aft from bow, continuous maindeck from stem to stern
- Three weapons fitted on long forecastle, from forward to aft, Standard SAM launcher, raised 5 in gun mounting, ASROC A/S missile launcher
- Central superstructure with lattice mainmast atop after end supporting square profile SPS-52C air-search radar aerial
- Thin break in superstructure just aft of mainmast
- Black-capped, slightly tapered single funnel just aft of midships
- Short lattice aftermast supporting curved, OPS-11C air-search radar
- 5 in gun mounting forward end flight deck in 'Y position'
- Long flight deck with open quarterdeck below

SPECIFICATION:

COUNTRY OF ORIGIN: Japan
CLASS: Hatakaze (DDG)
ACTIVE: 2
NAME (PENNANT NUMBER):
Hatakaze (DDG 171), Shimakaze
(DDG 172)

FEATURES:
DISPLACEMENT: 6400 tons
full load
LENGTH: 492 ft (150 m)
BEAM: 53.8 ft (16.4 m)
DRAUGHT: 15.7 ft (4.8 m)
SPEED: 30 kts

ARMAMENT:
MISSILES: SSM – eight McDonnell
Douglas Harpoon; SAM – GDC
Pomona Standard SM-1MR, Mk 13
Mod 4 launcher; A/S – Honeywell
ASROC Mk 112 octuple box
launcher; payload – Mk 46 Mod
5 Neartip torpedoes
GUNS: Two FMC 5 in (127 mm)/54
Mk 42 automatic; two GE/GD
20 mm Phalanx Mk 15 CIWS
TORPEDOES: Six 324 mm Type 68
or HOS 301 (2 triple) tubes;
Honeywell Mk 46 Mod 5 Neartip
DECOYS: Two Loral Hycor SRBOC
6-barrel Mk 36 chaff launchers

ELECTRONICS:
RADARS: Air-search – Hughes
SPS-52C, 3D, Melco OPS-11C;
surface search – JRC OPS-28B;
fire control – two Raytheon
SPG-51C, Melco 2-21, Type 2-12
SONARS: Nec OQS-4 Mod 1;
bow-mounted, active
search/attack
EW: Melco NOLQ-1 ESM/ECM;
Fujitsu OLR9B ESM

AIR SUPPORT:
HELICOPTERS: Platform for one
Sikorsky/Mitsubishi SH-60J
Seahawk (ASW)

Hatsuyuki JAPAN

Asayuki (*Michael Nitz*)

- Continuous maindeck with break down to quarterdeck
- 3 in gun mounting in 'A' position
- ASROC A/S missile box launcher immediately forward of bridge
- Large black-capped funnel, slightly tapered, amidships
- Lattice mainmast at after end of bridge structure supporting several radar aerials, most prominent, OPS-14B air-search on forward gantry. CIWS mountings at base of mainmast
- Fire control radome mounted atop hangar, offset to starboard
- Flight deck aft raised above maindeck level
- Sea Sparrow SAM launcher just forward of quarterdeck

NOTE: Last of class, *Shimayuki* converted to training ship (TV 35 13) March, 1999. Lecture room added to helicopter hangar

SPECIFICATION:

COUNTRY OF ORIGIN: Japan
CLASS: Hatsuyuki (DDG/DD)
ACTIVE: 11
NAME (PENNANT NUMBER):
Hatsuyuki (DD 122), Shirayuki
(DD 123), Mineyuki (DD 124),
Sawayuki (DD 125), Hamayuki
(DD 126), Isoyuki (DD 127),
Haruyuki (DD 128), Yamayuki
(DD 129), Matsuyuki (DD 130),
Setoyuki (DD 131), Asayuki
(DD 132)

FEATURES:
DISPLACEMENT: 3700 tons full
load; 3800 tons (DD 129 onwards)
LENGTH: 426.4 ft (130 m)
BEAM: 44.6 ft (13.6 m)
DRAUGHT: 13.8ft (4.02 m); 14.4 ft
(4.4 m) (DD 129 onwards)
SPEED: 30 kts

ARMAMENT:
MISSILES: SSM – McDonnell
Douglas Harpoon (2 quad)
launchers; SAM – Raytheon Sea
Sparrow Type 3A launcher;
A/S – Honeywell ASROC Mk 112
octuple box launcher; payload –
Mk 46 Mod 5 Neartip torpedoes
GUNS: One OTOBreda 3 in
(76 mm)/62 Compact; two GE/GD
20 mm Phalanx Mk 15 CIWS
TORPEDOES: Six 324 mm Type 68
or HOS 301 (2 triple) tubes;
Honeywell Mk 46 Mod 5 Neartip
DECOYS: Two Loral Hycor SRBOC
6-barrel Mk 36 chaff launchers

ELECTRONICS:
RADARS: Air-search – Melco
OPS-14B; surface search – JRC
OPS-18; fire control – Type 2-12 A
(SAM), two Type 2-21/21A (guns)
SONARS: Nec OQS-4A (II) (SQS-23
type); bow-mounted active
search/attack; OQR-1 TACTASS
(in some) passive
EW: Nec NOLR6C ESM; Fujitsu
OLT3 ECM

AIR SUPPORT:
HELICOPTERS: One Sikorsky/
Mitsubishi SH-60J Seahawk (ASW)

Kongou JAPAN

Kirishima

- Continuous maindeck line from stem to stern
- Sole visible armament on long foredeck 5 in gun mounting in 'A' position
- CIWS mounting immediately forward of bridge and at after end of after superstructure
- High forward superstructure topped by lattice mast sloping aft
- SPY 1D panels on forward face of bridge superstructure
- Two unusually large angular funnels, close together amidships. Funnels tapered and with several black exhausts protruding at top
- Harpoon SSM launchers between funnels
- Standard SAM VLS cells at after end of foredeck and forward end of flight deck; not obvious from side aspect of ship
- Long flight deck aft

NOTE: This is an enlarged and improved version of the US 'Arleigh Burke' class with a lightweight version of the Aegis system

SPECIFICATION:

COUNTRY OF ORIGIN: Japan
CLASS: Kongou (DDG)
ACTIVE: 4
NAME (PENNANT NUMBER):
Kongou (DDG 173), Kirishima
(DDG 174), Myoukou (DDG 175),
Choukai (DDG 176)

FEATURES:

DISPLACEMENT: 7250 tons
standard; 9485 tons full load
LENGTH: 528.2 ft (161 m)
BEAM: 68.9 ft (21 m)
DRAUGHT: 20.3 ft (6.2 m); 32.7 ft
(10 m) sonar
SPEED: 30 kts
RANGE: 4500 miles at 20 kts

ARMAMENT:

MISSILES: SSM – eight McDonnell
Douglas Harpoon (2 quad)
launchers; SAM – GDC Pomona
Standard SM-2MR, FMC Mk 41 VLS
(29 cells) forward, Martin
Marietta Mk 41 VLS (61 cells) aft;
A/S – Vertical launch ASROC;
payload – Mk 46 torpedoes
GUNS: One OTO Melara 5 in
(127 mm)/54 Compatto; two
GE/GD 20 mm/76 Mk 15
Vulcan Phalanx
TORPEDOES: Six 324 mm (2 triple)
HOS 302 tubes; Honeywell Mk 46
Mod 5 Neartip
DECOYS: Four Loral Hycor SRBOC
6-barrel Mk 36 chaff launchers;
Type H towed torpedo decoy

ELECTRONICS:

RADARS: Air-search – RCA SPY-1D,
3D; surface search – JRC OPS-28D;
navigation – JRC OPS-20; fire
control – three SPG-62, one
Mk 2/21
SONARS: Nec OQS-102 (SQS-53B/C)
bow-mounted, active
search/attack; Oki OQR-2 Tactass
towed array, passive
EW: Melco NOLQ-2 ESM/ECM

AIR SUPPORT:

HELICOPTERS: Platform and
refuelling facilities for
Sikorsky/Mitsubishi SH-60J
Seahawk

Murasame JAPAN

Harusame

- Curved, sweeping bow
- 3 in gun mounting sited at mid-forecastle
- VL ASROC abaft forward gun mounting
- CIWS mounting on raised platform immediately forward of bridge
- Slab-like forward superstructure has winged bridge; large lattice mainmast at after end
- Two large, twin, square profile funnels, one at after end of forward superstructure and one at forward end of after superstructure
- Break in superstructure between funnels. Harpoon launchers immediately forward of this break
- Large flight deck at after end of superstructure
- CIWS mounting on helicopter hangar

NOTE: ASROC missiles are not carried

SPECIFICATION:

COUNTRY OF ORIGIN: Japan
CLASS: Murasame (DDG/DD)
ACTIVE: 9
NAME (PENNANT NUMBER):
Murasame (DD 101), Harusame
(DD 102), Yuudachi (DD 103),
Kirisame (DD 104), Inazuma
(DD 105), Samidare (DD 106),
Ikazuchi (DD 107), Akebono
(DD 108), Ariake (DD 109)

FEATURES:
DISPLACEMENT: 4550 tons
standard; 5100 tons full load
LENGTH: 495.4 ft (151 m)
BEAM: 57.1 ft (17.4 m)
DRAUGHT: 17.1 ft (5.2 m)
SPEED: 30 kts

ARMAMENT:
MISSILES: SSM – eight SSM-1B
Harpoon; SAM – Raytheon Mk 48
VLS Sea Sparrow; A/S – Mk 41 VL
ASROC
GUNS: One OTOBreda 3 in
(76 mm)/62 Compact; two GE/GD
20 mm Vulcan Phalanx Mk 15
TORPEDOES: Six 324 mm HOS 302
(2 triple) tubes Mk 46 Mod 5
DECOYS: Four Mk 36 SRBOC chaff
launchers; Type 4 towed torpedo
decoy

ELECTRONICS:
RADARS: Air-search – Melco
OPS-24B, 3D; surface search – JRC
OPS-28D; navigation – OPS-20;
fire control – two Type 2-31
SONARS: Mitsubishi OQS-5;
hull-mounted, active search/
attack OQR-1 towed array, passive
search
EW: Nec NOLQ-3 ESM/ECM

AIR SUPPORT:
HELICOPTERS: One Sikorsky/
Mitsubishi SH-60J Seahawk (ASW)

Takanami (Improved Murasame) JAPAN

Takanami

- Curved, sweeping bow, square, near vertical stern
- Larger, 5 in gun mounting sited at mid-forecastle (compared with low rounded turret of 3 in in 'Murasame' class)
- SAM VLS abaft forward gun mounting on low superstructure, with CIWS mounting above, on platform immediately forward of bridge
- Slab-like forward superstructure has winged bridge; large lattice mainmast at after end, very similar to 'Murasame' class
- Two large, twin, square profile funnels, one at after end of forward superstructure and one at forward end of after superstructure, as 'Murasame' class
- Wider break in superstructure between funnels. Harpoon launchers immediately forward of after funnel
- Large flight deck at after end of superstructure
- CIWS mounting on helicopter hangar

SPECIFICATION:

COUNTRY OF ORIGIN: Japan
CLASS: Improved Murasame
(DDG/DD)
ACTIVE: 4
PLANNED: 1
NAME (PENNANT NUMBER):
Takanami (DD 110), Oonami
(DD 111), Makinami (DD 112),
Sazanami (DD 113), Suzanami
(DD 114)

FEATURES:
DISPLACEMENT: 4600 tons
standard; 5300 tons full load
LENGTH: 495.4 ft (151 m)
BEAM: 57.1 ft (17.4 m)
DRAUGHT: 17.4 ft (5.3 m)
SPEED: 30 kts

ARMAMENT:
MISSILES: SSM – eight SSM-1B
Harpoon (2 quad); SAM –
Raytheon Mk 41 32-cell VLS Sea
Sparrow; A/S – Mk 41 VL ASROC
GUNS: One OTOBreda 5 in
(127 mm)/54; two GE/GD 20 mm
Vulcan Phalanx Mk 15
TORPEDOES: Six 324 mm HOS 302
(2 triple) tubes Mk 46 Mod 5
Neartip
DECOYS: Four Mk 36 SRBOC chaff
launchers, SLQ-25 Nixie towed
torpedo decoy

ELECTRONICS:
RADARS: Air-search – Melco
OPS-24B, 3D; surface search –
JRC OPS-28D; navigation –
OPS-20; fire control – two
FCS 2-3/B
SONARS: OQS-5 bow-mounted,
active search/attack; OQR-1
towed array, passive search
EW: Nec NOLQ-2/3 ESM/ECM

AIR SUPPORT:
HELICOPTERS: One
Sikorsky/Mitsubishi SH-60J
Seahawk (ASW)

Shirane JAPAN

Shirane (*Michael Nitz*)

- High bow, sweeping continuous maindeck line from stem to stern
- Two 5 in gun mountings in 'A' and 'B' positions with ASROC A/S missile octuple box launcher between after mounting and bridge ('B' position) on raised platform
- High, slab-sided centrally sited superstructure, similar to 'Haruna' class
- Two funnels and masts combined with distinctive black, wedge-shaped exhaust diffusers/RAD-HAZ screens atop. The after funnel is set to starboard and the forward one to port
- Lattice mast mounted atop forward funnel and WM 25 fire control radar dome atop after one
- Long flight deck with open quarterdeck below
- Sea Sparrow SAM octuple box launcher atop hangar

NOTE: Almost identical to and easily confused with 'Haruna' class from bow to bridge. Number and type of funnels distinguish

SPECIFICATION:

COUNTRY OF ORIGIN: Japan
CLASS: Shirane (DD/DDH)
ACTIVE: 2
NAME (PENNANT NUMBER): Shirane (DDH 143), Kurama (DDH 144)

FEATURES:
DISPLACEMENT: 5200 tons standard; 7500 tons full load
LENGTH: 521.5 ft (159 m)
BEAM: 57.5 ft (17.5 m)
DRAUGHT: 17.5 ft (5.3 m)
SPEED: 31 kts

ARMAMENT:
MISSILES: SAM – Raytheon Sea Sparrow Mk 25 octuple launcher; A/S – Honeywell ASROC Mk 112 octuple box launcher; payload – Mk 46 Mod 5 Neartip torpedoes
GUNS: Two FMC 5 in (127 mm)/54 Mk 42 automatic; two GE/GD 20 mm Phalanx Mk 15 CIWS
TORPEDOES: Six 324 mm HOS 301 (2 triple) tubes; Honeywell Mk 46 Mod 5 Neartip
DECOYS: Four Mk 36 SBROC chaff launchers; Prairie Masker blade rate suppression system

ELECTRONICS:
RADARS: Air-search – Nec OPS-12, 3D; surface search – JRC OPS-28; navigation – JRC OFS-2D; fire control – Signaal WM 25 (DDH 143), two Type 72-1A FCS, Type 2-12
SONARS: EDO/Nec SQS-35(J); VDS active/passive search; EDO/Nec OQS-101, bow-mounted; EDO/Nec SQR-18A; towed array, passive
EW: Melco NOLQ-1 ESM/ECM; Fujitsu OLR-9B ESM

AIR SUPPORT:
HELICOPTERS: Three Sikorsky/ Mitsubishi SH-60J Sea Hawk (ASW)

Tachikaze JAPAN

Tachikaze

- High bow, continuous sweeping maindeck line from stem to stern
- 5 in gun mounting in 'A' position
- ASROC A/S missile octuple box launcher immediately forward of bridge
- Forward mast and funnel combined at after end of main superstructure topped by lattice mast with air-search radar on forward gantry
- Wide break in superstructure between funnels
- Aftermast and tall funnel combined has SPS-52B/C square profile radar aerial mounted atop
- Two sets of triple torpedo tubes mounted between funnels
- After 5 in gun mounting in 'X' position (removed from Tachikaze to allow increased Flag accommodation)
- Standard SAM launcher on long afterdeck

SPECIFICATION:

COUNTRY OF ORIGIN: Japan
CLASS: Tachikaze (DDG)
ACTIVE: 3
NAME (PENNANT NUMBER):
Tachikaze (DDG 168), Asakaze
(DDG 169), Sawakaze (DDG 170)

FEATURES:
DISPLACEMENT: 3850 tons
standard, 3950 tons (DD 170);
5500 tons full load
LENGTH: 469 ft (143 m)
BEAM: 47 ft (14.3 m)
DRAUGHT: 15.1 ft (4.6 m)
SPEED: 32 kts

ARMAMENT:
MISSILES: SSM – eight McDonnell
Douglas Harpoon (DDG 170 only);
SAM – GDC Pomona Standard
SM-1MR, Mk 13 Mod 1 or 4
launcher; A/S – Honeywell ASROC
Mk 112 octuple launcher;
payload – Mk 46 Mod 5 Neartip
torpedoes
GUNS: One (DDG 168) or two FMC
5 in (127 mm)/54 Mk 42
automatic; two GE/GD 20 mm
Phalanx CIWS Mk 15
TORPEDOES: Six 324 mm Type 68
or HOS 301 (2 triple) tubes;
Honeywell Mk 46 Mod 5 Neartip
DECOYS: Four Loral Hycor
SRBOC 6-barrel Mk 36 chaff
launchers; SLQ-25 Nixie towed
torpedo decoy

ELECTRONICS:
RADARS: Air-search – Melco
OPS-11C, Hughes SPS-52B or C
(DDG 170), 3D; surface search –
JRC OPS-16D (DDG 168) JRC OPS-28
(DD 170), JRC OPS-18-3 (DDG 169);
fire control – two Raytheon
SPG 51, Type 2 FCS
SONARS: Nec OQS-3A (Type 66);
bow-mounted, active
search/attack
EW: Nec NOLR-6 (DDG 168);
Nec NOLQ-1 (rest) ESM; Fujitsu
OLT-3 ECM

Yamagumo JAPAN

Yuugumo

- High bow, continuous sweeping maindeck line from stem to stern
- 3 in gun mountings in 'A' and 'Y' positions
- Bofors 375 mm 4-barrel A/s mortar on raised platform immediately forward of bridge superstructure
- Lattice mainmast supporting Melco OPS-11B/11C and OPS-18-3 air-search radar and surface search radar on gantries
- Two rounded, tapering funnels with second, short lattice mast forward of squat, aft funnel
- ASROC A/s missile octuple box launcher between funnels

SPECIFICATION:

COUNTRY OF ORIGIN: Japan
CLASS: Yamagumo (DD/DDK)
ACTIVE: 1
NAME (PENNANT NUMBER):
Yuugumo (DDK 121)

FEATURES:

DISPLACEMENT: 2150 tons
standard; 2900 tons full load
LENGTH: 377.2 ft (114.9 m)
BEAM: 38.7 ft (11.8 m)
DRAUGHT: 13.1 ft (4 m)
SPEED: 27 kts
RANGE: 7000 miles at 20 kts

ARMAMENT:

MISSILES: A/s – Honeywell ASROC
Mk 112 octuple launcher with
payload, Mk 46 Mod 5 Neartip
GUNS: Four USN 3 in (76mm)/50
Mk 33 (2 twin)
TORPEDOES: Six 324 mm Type 68
(2 triple) tubes with Honeywell
Mk 46 Mod 5 Neartip
A/s MORTARS: One Bofors
375 mm Type 71 4-barrel trainable
rocket launcher

ELECTRONICS:

RADARS: Air-search – Melco
OPS-11B/11C; surface search –
RC OPS-118-3; fire control – two
GE Mk 35
SONARS: Nec OQS-3A, hull-
mounted, active search/attack;
EDO SQS-35(J)
EW: Nec NOLR-6 ESM

KDX-2 KOREA (SOUTH)

Chungmugong Yi Sun-Shin (*Michael Nitz*)

- High bow, break in forecastle abreast 5 in gun and, from there to stern, continuous sweeping maindeck
- 5 in gun mounting in 'A' position
- VLS SAM system in raised platform immediately aft of forward gun
- Slab sided bridge superstructure supporting pyramid mast with surface search radar
- Wide, clear break between bridge superstructure and funnel
- Low squat tapering funnel aft of midships
- Two pylons supporting air-search and fire control radars atop aft superstructure
- Helicopter landing deck aft
- Harpoon launchers in break between funnel and aft superstructure

NOTE: See entry on 'Kwanggaeto the Great' class on page 126 which has hull and superstructure similarities

See entry on 'Kwanggaeto the Great' class on page 126

SPECIFICATION:

COUNTRY OF ORIGIN: Korea (South)
CLASS: KDX-2 (DDG)
ACTIVE: 2
PLANNED: 1
NAME (PENNANT NUMBER):
Chungmugong Yi Sun-Shin
(DDG 975), Moonmu Daewang
(DDG 976), Daejoyoung (DDG 977)

FEATURES:

DISPLACEMENT: 4800 tons full load
LENGTH: 506.6 ft (154.4 m)
BEAM: 55.5 ft (16.9 m)
DRAUGHT: 14.1 ft (4.3 m)
SPEED: 29 kts
RANGE: 4000 miles at 18 kts

ARMAMENT:

MISSILES: SSM – Harpoon (Block 1C) (2 quad); SAM – Standard SM-2MR (Block IIIA), Lockheed Martin Mk 41 32-cell VLS Launcher, Raytheon RAM Mk 31 Mk 1 with Mk 116 Block 1 missiles, ASROC VLS
GUNS: One 5 in (127 mm)/62 Mk 45 Mod 4; one Goalkeeper 30 mm, 7-barrels
DECOYS: Four chaff launchers

ELECTRONICS:

RADARS: Air-search – Raytheon SPS-49(V)5; surface search – Signaal MW08; fire control – two Signaal STIR 240
SONARS: DSQS-23, hull-mounted, active search/attack; Daewoo Telecom towed array

AIR SUPPORT:

HELICOPTERS: One Westland Super Lynx Mk 99

Kwanggaeto the Great (KDX-1) KOREA (SOUTH)

Euljimundok (*Sattler/Steele*)

- High bow, continuous sweeping maindeck line from stem to stern
- 5 in gun mounting in 'A' position
- VLS SAM system in raised platform immediately aft of forward gun
- CIWS mounting atop bridge
- Slab-sided bridge superstructure supporting lattice mast with surface search radar atop, and navigation radar on forward gantry
- Clear break between bridge superstructure and funnel – narrower than KDX-2 class
- Low squat tapering funnel aft of midships
- Separate squat lattice mast supporting air-search radar, and pylon with fire control radars atop aft superstructure
- Helicopter deck above open quarterdeck

NOTE: Hull and superstructure has similarities with KDX-2 class

SPECIFICATION:

COUNTRY OF ORIGIN: Korea (South)
CLASS: Kwanggaeto the Great (KDX-1) (DDG)
ACTIVE: 3
NAME (PENNANT NUMBER): Kwanaggaeto the Great (DDG 971), Euljimundok (DDG 972), Yangmanchun (DDG 973)

FEATURES:

DISPLACEMENT: 3855 tons full load
LENGTH: 444.2 ft (135.4 m)
BEAM: 46.6 ft (14.2 m)
DRAUGHT: 13.8 ft (4.2 m)
SPEED: 30 kts
RANGE: 4000 miles at 18 kts

ARMAMENT:

MISSILES: SSM – Harpoon (Block 1C) (2 quad); SAM – Sea Sparrow Mk 48 Mod 2 VLS launcher
GUNS: One OTOBreda 5 in (127 mm)/54; two Goalkeeper 30 mm
TORPEDOES: Six 324 mm (two triple Mk 32) Mk 46 Mod 5
DECOYS: Four CSEE Dagaie Mk 2 chaff launchers; SLQ-25 Nixie towed torpedo decoy

ELECTRONICS:

RADARS: Air-search – Raytheon SPS-49(V)5; surface search – Signaal MW08; navigation – Daewoo DTR 92 (SPS-55M); fire control – two Signaal STIR 180
SONARS: DSQS-21BZ hull-mounted, active search/attack, towed array
EW: Argo AR 700/APECS ESM/ECM

AIR SUPPORT:

HELICOPTERS: One Westland Super Lynx Mk 99

Gearing (FRAM-1) KOREA (SOUTH), MEXICO, PAKISTAN, TAIWAN
Netzahualcoyotl

- Blunt bow, low freeboard
- Continuous maindeck from stem to stern
- 5 in twin gun mounting in 'A' position. (OTO Melara 3 in (76 mm) in Taiwan conversions)
- Twin funnels sloping aft with distinctive black tapered tops
- Large lattice mainmast astride forward funnel, smaller tapering mast aft of after funnel

NOTE: The general recognition features above apply to all of the class. There are too many variants to be covered in this publication. Further details can be obtained from *Jane's Fighting Ships* yearbook
NOTE 2: Remaining Pakistan unit now with Maritime Safety Agency, with hull painted white with a distinctive diagonal blue and red band, together with the letters 'MSA'

contd.

Gearing contd.

SPECIFICATION:

COUNTRY OF ORIGIN: USA
CLASS: Gearing (Fram I)
(Wu Chin III conversion) (DD)
ACTIVE: 3 (South Korea);
1 (Mexico); 1 (Pakistan, Maritime
Safety Agency), 7 (Taiwan,
Wu Chin III)
NAME (PENNANT NUMBER):
SOUTH KOREA – Taejon (ex-*New*)
(DD 919, ex-DD 818), Kwang Ju
(ex-*Richard E Kraus*) (DD 921,
ex-DD 849); Kang Won
(ex-*William R Rush*) (DD 922,
ex-DD 714)
MEXICO – Netzahualcoyotl
(ex-*Steinaker*) (E 11, ex-E O4,
ex-DD 863)
PAKISTAN (MARITIME SAFETY
AGENCY) – Nazim (ex-*Tughril*,
ex-*Henderson*), (D 156, ex-D 167,
ex-DD 785)
TAIWAN – Wu Chin III – Chien
Yang (ex-*James E Kyes*) (912,
ex-DD 787), Liao Yang (ex-*Hanson*)
(921, ex-DD 832), Shao Yang
(ex-*Hollister*) (929, ex-DD 788),
Te Yang (ex-*Sarsfield*) (925,
ex-DD 837), Chen Yang
(ex-*Johnston*) (928, ex-DD 821),
Shen Yang (ex-*Power*) (923,
ex-DD 839), Yun Yang
(ex-*Hamner*) (927, ex-DD 718)

FEATURES:

DISPLACEMENT: 3540 tons full
load (Korea (South), Taiwan);
3500 tons (Pakistan); 3690 tons
(Mexico)
LENGTH: 390.5 ft (119 m); 390.2 ft
(118.7 m) (Mexico)
BEAM: 41.2 ft (12.6 m); 41.9 ft
(12.7 m) (Mexico)
DRAUGHT: 19 ft (5.8 m); 15 ft
(4.6 m) (Mexico)
SPEED: 30 kts (Korea (South));
15 kts (Mexico); 32 kts (Pakistan);
32.5 kts (Taiwan)
RANGE: 5800 miles at 15 kts;
6080 miles at 15 kts (Taiwan)

ARMAMENT:

MISSILES: SSM – McDonnell
Douglas Harpoon (Korea (South),
2 quad), four Hsiung Feng (quad)
(Taiwan); SAM – General
Dynamics Standard SM1-MR
(2 triple, 2 twin) (Taiwan);
A/S – Honeywell ASROC Mk 112
octuple launcher; payload –
Mk 46 torpedoes (Taiwan)
NOTE: No missiles fitted to
Mexican ships and have been
removed from Pakistani hull
GUNS: Four US 5 in (127 mm)/38
(2 twin) Mk 38 (Korea (South),
Mexico); one US 5 in (127 mm)/38
Mk 38 (Pakistan); one OTO Melara
3 in (76 mm)/62 (Taiwan); one
GE/GD 20 mm Vulcan Phalanx
Block 1, 6-barrel Mk 15 (Korea
(South), Taiwan); two Bofors
40 mm/70 (Taiwan); USN/Bofors
40 mm/56 (twin) (Korea (South);
one 57 mm/70 Mk 2 (Mexico);
four 25 mm (Pakistan); four or six
12.7 mm machine guns (Taiwan)
TORPEDOES: Six 324 mm US
Mk 32 (2 triple) tubes; Honeywell
Mk 46 (not Mexico)
DEPTH CHARGES: One Mk IX rack
(Korea (South) only)
DECOYS: Two Plessey Shield
6-barrel fixed chaff launchers
(Pakistan); four Kung Fen, six
16-tubed chaff launchers;
Mk T-6 Fanfare torpedo
decoy (Taiwan)

ELECTRONICS:

RADARS: Air-search – SPS-40
(Korea (South), Mexico), Signaal
DAo8 (Taiwan with DAo5 aerial),
not fitted to Pakistani ship;
surface search – Raytheon
SPS-10/SPS-58, Kelvin Hughes
17/9 (Mexico); navigation –
Marconi LN66 (Mexico), KH 1007
(Pakistan); fire control – Western
Electric Mk 12/12 (Mexico),
Western Electric Mk 25 (Korea
(South), Pakistan), Signaal STIR
(Standard and 76mm) (Taiwan),
Westinghouse W-160 (Bofors
guns) (Taiwan)
SONARS: Sangamo SQS-23,
hull-mounted (Korea (South);
Raytheon SQS-23H, hull-mounted
(Taiwan); no sonar Mexico or
Pakistan
EW: Chang Feng III (Hughes
SLQ-17/SLQ-31) ESM/ECM (Taiwan),
WLR-1 ESM (Korea (South) and
Mexico)

AIR SUPPORT:

HELICOPTERS: Aerospatiale
SA 316B Alouette III (marine
support) or Westland Super
Lynx Mk 99/100 (ASW/ASV)
(Korea (South), except for
DD 925); MBB BO 105CB (Mexico);
McDonnell Douglas MD 500
(ASW) (Taiwan); no air support
in Pakistani ship

De Zeven Provincien NETHERLANDS

De Zeven Provincien *(Michael Nitz)*

- Continuous sweeping maindeck line from stem to stern with open quarterdeck below
- 5 in gun mounting in 'A' position
- Rounded, smooth slab-sided bridge structure
- Squat, stumpy pyramid mast atop bridge with air/surface search and fire control radars
- SATCOMS on wings off mainmast
- Very low 'v' shaped twin funnels
- Slab-sided helicopter hangar aft with landing deck above open quarterdeck
- CIWS atop bridge, forward of mainmast, and on aft hangar, just above doors
- Air-search radar atop pylon above hangar

SPECIFICATION:

COUNTRY OF ORIGIN: Netherlands
CLASS: De Zeven Provincien (DDG)
ACTIVE: 4
NAME (PENNANT NUMBER):
De Zeven Provincien (F 802),
De Ruyter (F 804), Tromp (F 803),
Evertsen (F 805)

FEATURES:
DISPLACEMENT: 6048 tons full load
LENGTH: 473.1 ft (144.2 m) oa
BEAM: 61.7 ft (18.8 m)
DRAUGHT: 17.1 ft (5.2 m)
SPEED: 28 kts
RANGE: 5000 miles at 18 kts

ARMAMENT:
MISSILES: SSM – eight Harpoon in VL tubes behind mainmast; SAM – Mk 41 VLS Standard SM2-MR Block IIIA, Evolved Sea Sparrow
GUNS: One OTOBreda 5 in (127 mm)/54; two Thales Goalkeeper 30 mm; two 12.7 mm
TORPEDOES: Four 323 mm (2 twin) tubes; Mk 32 Mod 9 fixed launchers with Mk 46 Mod 5 torpedoes
DECOYS: Four SRBOC Mk 36 chaff launchers; SLQ-25 Nixie towed torpedo decoy

ELECTRONICS:
RADARS: Air-search – Thales SMART L; air/surface search – Thales APAR; surface search – Thales Scout
SONARS: STN Atlas DSQS-24C bow-mounted, active search/attack
EW: Racal Sabre ESM/ECM

AIR SUPPORT:
HELICOPTERS: One NFH 90/ Lynx (ASW)

Ferré (Daring) PERU

Ferré

- Main deck break aft of bridge superstructure
- 4.5 in guns at 'A', 'B' and 'Y' positions
- Slim pyramid mast behind bridge with air/surface search radar, with pole mast atop
- Single slim funnel well aft of midships
- Exocet SSM launchers aft of funnel
- Raised helicopter landing platform at stern

SPECIFICATION:

COUNTRY OF ORIGIN: UK
CLASS: Daring (DDG)
ACTIVE: 1
NAME (PENNANT NUMBER):
Ferré (ex-*Decoy*), (DM 74)

FEATURES:
DISPLACEMENT: 2800 tons
standard; 3600 tons full load
LENGTH: 390 ft (118.9 m)
BEAM: 43 ft (13.1 m)
DRAUGHT: 18 ft (5.5 m)
SPEED: 32 kts
RANGE: 3000 miles at 20 kts

ARMAMENT:
MISSILES: SSM – eight
Aerospatiale MM 38 Exocet
GUNS: Six (3 twin) Vickers 4.5 in
(114 mm)/45 Mk 5; four Breda
40 mm/70 (2 twin)

ELECTRONICS:
RADARS: Air/surface search –
Plessey AWS 1; surface search –
Racal Decca TM 1226; fire control
– Selenia RTN 10X

AIR SUPPORT:
HELICOPTERS: Platform only

Kashin RUSSIA, INDIA

Smetlivy

Russian units:
- High bow sloping down to stern
- 3 in gun in 'A' position and SA-N-1 Goa SAM in 'B' position
- Owl Screech fire control dish immediately forward of bridge
- Two isolated, massive lattice masts, with 'Head Net C' air/surface radar aerial atop forward mast
- Two slab-sided squat funnels, aft well back from midships
- Gun mounting in 'Y' position, SA-N-1 SAM in 'X' position
- Low helicopter landing platform on quarterdeck
- Angled Styx tubular launchers, facing astern, port and starboard, alongside aft funnel

NOTE: Indian units, as Russian except: Helicopter hangar replaces 'Y' position gun mounting; SS-N-2D Mod 2 Styx tubular launchers forward of bridge; aft Owl Screech fire control director omitted

contd.

Kashin contd.

SPECIFICATION:

COUNTRY OF ORIGIN: Russia
CLASS: Kashin (Type 61), Kashin II
(Rajput, Type 61ME) (DDG)
ACTIVE: 1 Russia (Kashin Project
61; 5 India (Kashin II/Rajput class)
NAME (PENNANT NUMBER):
RUSSIA — Smetlivy (810)
INDIA — Rajput (ex-*Nadiozny*)
(D 51), Rana (ex-*Gubitielny*)
(D 52) Ranjit (ex-*Lovky*) (D 53), Ranvir
(ex-*Twiordy*) (D 54), Ranvijay
(ex-*Tolkovy*) (D 55)

FEATURES:

DISPLACEMENT: 4010 tons
standard; 4750 tons full load
(Kashin), 4974 tons (Kashin II)
LENGTH: 472.4 ft (144 m);
480.5 ft (146.5 m) (Indian)
BEAM: 51.8 ft (15.8 m)
DRAUGHT: 15.4 ft (4.7 m)
SPEED: 32 kts, 35 kts (Indian)
RANGE: 4000 miles at 18 kts;
4500 miles at 18 kts (Indian)

ARMAMENT:

MISSILES: SSM — eight Zvezda
SS-N-25 (Kh 35 Uran) (2 quad)
(Russia), four SS-N-2D Mod 2
Styx (Indian); SAM — two SA-N-1
Goa twin launchers
GUNS: Two 3 in (76 mm)/60
(1 twin), AK 762; four 30 mm/65
AK 630 6-barrel (eight with
4 twin AK 230 in Indian ships,
Raijput, *Rana* and *Ranjit*, and
four 30 mm/65 ADG 630 in
Ranvir and *Ranvijay*)
TORPEDOES: Five 21 in (533 mm)
(quin tubes)
A/S MORTARS: Two RBU 6000
12-tubed trainable
DECOYS: Four PK 16 chaff
launchers; two towed torpedo
decoys (Russia)

ELECTRONICS:

RADARS: Air/surface search —
'Head Net C' Big Net, ('Big Net A'
in Indian ships as well for air-
search); navigation — two Don
2/Don Kay/Palm Frond (Russia),
two Don Kay (India); fire control
— two Peel Group (SA-N-1), Owl
Screech (guns), two Bass Tilt
(30 mm guns, in Indian D 54-55)
(Drum Tilt in Indian D 51-53)
SONAR: Bull Nose (MGK 336) or
Wolf Paw, hull-mounted, active
search/attack; Mare Tail VDS or
Vega in *Smetlivy* and Indian
hulls; Vycheda MG 311 (India)
EW: Two Bell Shroud; two Watch
Dog ESM/ECM; two Bell
Squat/Bell Shroud (*Ranvir*,
Ranvijay) ESM; two Bell Clout/
Bell Slam/Bell Tap (*Rajput*,
Rana, *Ranjit*) ESM; two Top Hat
(India) ECM

AIR SUPPORT:

HELICOPTERS: Platform only
(Russia); one Kamov Ka-27/28
Helix (ASW) (India)

Sovremenny RUSSIA, CHINA
Nastoychivy

- High bow. Sweeping maindeck aft to break at bridge where tubular quad SSM launchers are fitted, port and starboard
- 130 mm/70 gun mounts in 'A' and 'Y' positions
- SA-N-7 Gadfly SAM launcher in 'B' mounting position
- Prominent Band Stand weapons control dome atop bridge
- High forward super-structure with large enclosed mainmast at its after end. Large distinctive Top Plate air-search radar aerial atop
- Single, large, square funnel aft of midships
- Lattice aftermast immediately aft of funnel with telescopic helicopter hangar below
- Small raised flight deck forward of aft SA-N-7 SAM launcher

SPECIFICATION:

COUNTRY OF ORIGIN: Russia
CLASS: Sovremenny (Sarych) (Type 956/956A/956EM) (DDG)
ACTIVE: 6 Russia; 2 China
BUILDING: 2 China
PLANNED: 2 China
NAME (PENNANT NUMBER):
RUSSIA – Burny (778), Bespokoiny (620), Nastoychivy (ex-Moskowski Komsomolets) (610), Bystry (715), Bezboyaznenny (754), Marshal Ushakov (ex-Besstrashny) (434)
CHINA – Hangzhou (ex-Vazhny, ex-Yekaterinburg) (136, ex-698), Fuzhou (ex-Alexander Nevsky) (137)

FEATURES:

DISPLACEMENT: 6500 tons standard; 7940 tons full load
LENGTH: 511.8 ft (156 m)
BEAM: 56.8 ft (17.3 m)
DRAUGHT: 21.3 ft (6.5 m)
SPEED: 32 kts
RANGE: 6500 miles at 20 kts

ARMAMENT:

MISSILES: SSM – eight Raduga SS-N-22 Sunburn (3M-80 Zubr) (2 quad) launchers (from Bespokoiny onwards, the launchers are longer and fire a modified missile 3M-82 Moskit); SAM – two SA-N-7 Gadfly 3S 90 (Uragan) (from Bespokoiny onwards, the same launcher is used for the SA-N-17 Grizzly/SA-N-12 Yezh)
GUNS: Four 130 mm/70 AK 130 (2 twin); four 30 mm/65 6-barrel AK 630

TORPEDOES: Four 21 in (533 mm) (2 twin) tubes
A/S MORTARS: Two RBU 1000 6-barrelled
MINES: Rails for up to 22 (40 in China)
DECOYS: Eight PK 10 and two PK 2 chaff launchers

ELECTRONICS:

RADARS: Air-search – Top Plate 3D; surface search – three Palm Frond; fire control – six Front Dome (SA-N-7/17), Kite Screech (130 mm guns), two Bass Tilt (30 mm guns)
SONARS: Bull Horn (MGK-335 Platina) and Whale Tongue; hull-mounted active search/attack
EW: Four Foot Ball (or two Bell Shroud and two Bell Squat in some Russian) ESM/ECM; six Half Cup laser warner

AIR SUPPORT:

HELICOPTERS: One Kamov Ka-27PL Helix (ASW); one Harbin Zhi-9A Haitun (Dauphin 2) or Kamov KA-28 Helix (ASW/ASV) (Chinese)

Udaloy RUSSIA

Admiral Levchenko (*Michael Nitz*)

- High bow with sweeping maindeck aft to break at after funnel
- 3.9 in gun mountings in 'A' and 'B' positions
- SA-N-9 SAM VLS set into the ship's structure on the forecastle and forward of hangars
- Two SS-N-14 Silex A/s quad launchers, tucked beneath bridge, port and starboard
- Two square section, twin funnels side by side with tapered RAD-HAZ screens at after end
- Two lattice masts forward and aft of funnels. After mainmast is larger with Top Plate air-search radar aerial atop
- Small pyramid mast on bridge supports Kite Screech radar

SPECIFICATION:

COUNTRY OF ORIGIN: Russia
CLASS: Udaloy (Fregat) (Type 1155) (DDG)
ACTIVE: 9
NAME (PENNANT NUMBER): Vitse Admiral Kulakov (400), Marshal Vasilevsky (687), Admiral Tributs (564), Marshal Shaposhnikov (543), Severomorsk (ex-*Simferopol*, ex-*Marshal Budienny*) (619), Admiral Levchenko (ex-*Kharbarovsk*) (605), Admiral Vinogradov (572), Admiral Kharlamov (678), Admiral Panteleyev (648)

FEATURES:

DISPLACEMENT: 6700 tons standard; 8500 tons full load
LENGTH: 536.4 ft (163.5 m)
BEAM: 63.3 ft (19.3 m)
DRAUGHT: 24.6 ft (7.5 m)
SPEED: 29 kts
RANGE: 7700 miles at 18 kts

ARMAMENT:

MISSILES: SAM – eight SA-N-9 Gauntlet (Klinok) vertical launchers; a/s – two Raduga SS-N-14 Silex (Rastrub) quad launchers; payload – nuclear or Type 40 or E53-72 torpedo
GUNS: Two 3.9 in (100 mm)/59; four 30 mm/65 AK 630 6-barrelled
TORPEDOES: Eight 21 in (533 mm) (2 quad) tubes
A/S MORTARS: Two RBU 6000 12-tubed, trainable
MINES: Rails for 26 mines
DECOYS: Two PK 2 and eight PK 10 chaff launchers; US Prairie Masker type noise reduction

ELECTRONICS:

RADARS: Air-search – Strut Pair, Top Plate 3D; surface search – three Palm Frond; fire control – two Eye Bowl, (SS-N-14), two Cross Sword (SA-N-9), Kite Screech (100 mm guns), two Bass Tilt (30 mm guns)
SONARS: Horse Jaw (Polinom), hull-mounted, active search/attack; Mouse Tail VDS, active search
EW: Two Foot Ball (605 onwards); two Wine Glass; six Half Cup laser warner (605 onwards)
ESM/ECM: two Bell Squat ECM

AIR SUPPORT:

HELICOPTERS: Two Kamov Ka-27 Helix A (ASW) housed in two side-by-side hangars with inclined elevating ramps to flight deck

Udaloy II RUSSIA

Admiral Chabanenko

As 'Udaloy I' class, except:
- 130 mm gun only in 'A' position
- PK 2 chaff launchers in 'B' position
- Full length of SS-N-22 Sunburn SSM tubular quad launchers exposed, port and starboard, below bridge
- Torpedo tubes protected by hinged flap in hull above chine aft of second funnel
- Crane deck forward of deck break, which is further aft than 'Udaloy I'

SPECIFICATION:

COUNTRY OF ORIGIN: Russia
CLASS: Udaloy II (Fregat) (Project 1155.1) (DDG)
ACTIVE: 1
NAME (PENNANT NUMBER): Admiral Chabanenko (650, ex-437)

FEATURES:

DISPLACEMENT: 7700 tons standard; 8900 tons full load
LENGTH: 536.4 ft (163.5 m)
BEAM: 63.3 ft (19.3 m)
DRAUGHT: 24.6 ft (7.5 m)
SPEED: 28 kts
RANGE: 4000 miles at 18 kts

ARMAMENT:

MISSILES: SSM – eight Raduga SS-N-22 Sunburn (3M-82 Moskit) (2 quad launchers); SAM – eight SA-N-9 Gauntlet (Klinok) VLS; SAM/guns – two CADS-N-1 (Kashtan) each with 30 mm 6-barrel gun, combined with SA-N-11 (Grisson) SAMs and Hot Flash/Hot Spot fire control radar/optronic director; A/S – Novator SS-N-15 Starfish, Type 40 torpedo
GUNS: Two 130 mm/70 (twin) AK 130
TORPEDOES: Eight 21 in (533 mm) (2 quad tubes)
A/S MORTARS: Two RBU 6000, 12-tubed trainable
DECOYS: Eight PK 10 and two PK 2 chaff launchers

ELECTRONICS:

RADARS: Air-search – Strut Pair II, Top Plate 3D; surface search – three Palm Frond; fire control – two Cross Swords (SA-N-9), Kite Screech (100 mm gun)
SONARS: Horse Jaw (Polinom) hull-mounted, active search/attack; Horse Tail VDS, active search
EW: Two Wine Glass ESM; two Bell Shroud; two Bell Squat; four Half Cup laser warner; two Shot Dome

AIR SUPPORT:

HELICOPTERS: Two Kamov KA-27 Helix A (ASW)

135

Kidd TAIWAN

Callaghan, when in US service

- Armament and electronics may differ in Taiwanese service
- In US service almost identical profile to 'Spruance' class
- Distinguished from Spruance by two twin Standard missile launchers – one in front of bridge and second aft in place of Sea Sparrow SAM box launcher just aft of flight deck
- Large radar array on top of after lattice mast

SPECIFICATION:

COUNTRY OF ORIGIN: USA
CLASS: Kidd
ACTIVE: 4
NAME (PENNANT NUMBER):
Chi Teh (ex-Scott) 1801
(ex-DD 995), Ming Teh (ex-Kidd)
1802 (ex-DD 993), Tong Teh
(ex-Chandler) 1803 (ex-DD 996),
Wu Teh (ex-Callaghan) 1805
(ex-DD 994)

FEATURES:

DISPLACEMENT: 9574 full load
LENGTH: 563.3 ft (171.7 m)
BEAM: 55 ft (16.8 m)
DRAUGHT: 20 ft (6.2 m)
SPEED: 33 kts
RANGE: 6000 miles at 20 kts

ARMAMENT:

MISSILES: Eight McDonnell
Douglas Harpoon (2 quad);
52 GDC Standard SM-2 Block IIIA;
two twin Mk 26 launchers;
16 Honeywell ASROC
GUNS: Two FMC 5 in (127 mm)/54;
two GE/GD 20 mm Vulcan
Phalanx 6-barrelled Mk 15;
four 12.7 mm machine guns
TORPEDOES: Six 324 mm Mk 32
(2 triple); Honeywell Mk 46 Mod 5
DECOYS: Four Loral Hycor SRBOC
6-barrelled fixed Mk 36; SLQ-25
Nixie torpedo decoy

ELECTRONICS:

RADARS: Air/surface search –
Cardion SPS-55; air-search – ITT
SPS-48E; navigation – Raytheon
SPS-64; fire control – two
Raytheon SPG-51D, one Lockheed
SPG-60, one Lockheed SPQ-9A
SONARS: GE/Hughes SQS-53A
bow-mounted; Gould SQR-19
(TACTAS) passive towed array
(may be fitted)

AIR SUPPORT:

HELICOPTERS: Two medium size

Type 42 (Batch 3) UK

Manchester (*Patrick Allen*)

- Extremely long forecastle, some 50 ft more than UK Type 42 Batches 1 & 2. Otherwise, very similar
- Stretched Batch 3s are fitted with a strength-ening beam on each side which increases width by 2 feet
- Break in superstructure forward of funnel

NOTE: See also Type 42 Batch 1 & 2 on page 138 in Argentine and UK service

SPECIFICATION:

COUNTRY OF ORIGIN: UK
CLASS: Type 42 (Batch 3) (DDG)
ACTIVE: 4
NAME (PENNANT NUMBER):
Manchester (D 95), Gloucester
(D 96), Edinburgh (D 97),
York (D 98)

FEATURES:
DISPLACEMENT: 5200 tons
full load
LENGTH: 462.8 ft (141.1 m) oa
BEAM: 49.9 ft (15.2 m)
DRAUGHT: 19 ft (5.8 m) (screws)
SPEED: 30+ kts
RANGE: 4000 miles at 18 kts

ARMAMENT:
MISSILES: SAM – British Aerospace
Sea Dart twin launcher
GUNS: Vickers 4.5 in (114 mm)/55
Mk 8; two Oerlikon/BMARC
20 mm GAM-B01; two GE/GD
20 mm Vulcan Phalanx Mk 15
DECOYS: Four Sea Gnat
130/102 mm 6-barrel launchers;
SLQ-25A (Type 2070) towed
torpedo decoys; Irvin DLF 3
offboard decoys

ELECTRONICS:
RADARS: Air-search – Marconi/
Signaal Type 1022; air/surface
search – AMS Type 996;
navigation – Kelvin Hughes Type
1007 and Racal Decca Type 1008;
fire control – two Marconi Type
909 Mod 1
SONARS: Ferranti/Thomson
Type 2050 or Plessey Type 2016,
hull-mounted
EW: Racal UAT ESM

AIR SUPPORT:
HELICOPTERS: One Westland
Lynx HAS Mk 3/8 (ASV/ASW)

Type 42 (Batch 1 & 2) UK, ARGENTINA
Exeter

- Continuous maindeck line from stem to stern, high freeboard
- 4.5 in gun mounting halfway between bows and bridge
- Sea Dart SAM twin launcher immediately forward of bridge
- High forward superstructure with large Type 909 fire control radar dome atop
- Large single, black-capped funnel with sloping after end, just aft of midships
- Large lattice Type 1022 air-search radar aerial at after end of forward superstructure
- Tall, black-topped pole foremast forward of funnel
- Tall, enclosed, black-topped mainmast aft of funnel, supporting surface search radar aerial
- Hangar superstructure at forward end of flight deck with large Type 909 fire control radar dome at forward end
- Open quarterdeck below after end of flight deck

Argentine ships:
- Most obvious differences are Type 965P air-search bedstead radar aerial atop forward superstructure, large black exhausts on side of funnel
- Aft fire control radome missing

NOTE: See Type 42 Batch 3 in UK service on page 137

SPECIFICATION:

COUNTRY OF ORIGIN: UK
CLASS: UK – Type 42 (Batch 1 & 2)
ARGENTINA – Hercules (DDG)
ACTIVE: 4 UK, 1 Argentina
NAME (PENNANT NUMBER):
UK – Batch 2: Exeter (D 89),
Southampton (D 90),
Nottingham (D 91), Liverpool
(D 92)
ARGENTINA – Hercules (D 1, ex-28)

FEATURES:

DISPLACEMENT: 4100 tons full
load; 4800 tons (Batch 2); 4100
tons (Argentina)
LENGTH: 412 ft (125 m) oa
BEAM: 47 ft (14.3 m)
DRAUGHT: 19 ft (5.8 m) (screws)
SPEED: 29 kts
RANGE: 4000 miles at 18 kts

ARMAMENT:

MISSILES: SAM – British Aerospace
Sea Dart twin launcher
GUNS: Vickers 4.5 in (114 mm)/55
Mk 8; two Oerlikon/BMARC
20 mm GAM-B01 (two Oerlikon
20 mm Mk 7 in Argentine ships);
two GE/GD 20 mm Vulcan
Phalanx Mk 15 (British ships only)
DECOYS: Four Marconi Sea Gnat
130/102 mm 6-barrel launchers
(Corvus, Argentina); Irvin DLF 3
offboard decoys; SLQ-25A (Type
2070) towed torpedo decoy;
Graseby GI 738 towed torpedo
decoy in Argentine ships

ELECTRONICS:

RADARS: Air-search – Marconi/
Signaal Type 1022 (Marconi Type
965P, Argentina); Air/surface
search – AMS Type 996; surface
search – Marconi Type 992Q
(Argentina); navigation – Kelvin
Hughes Type 1007 and Racal
Decca Type 1008 (Kelvin Hughes
Type 1006, Argentina); fire
control – two Marconi Type 909
SONARS: Ferranti Type 2050 or
Plessey Type 2016, hull-mounted;
Graseby Type 184M hull-
mounted, active search/attack
(Argentina); Kelvin Hughes
Type 162M
EW: Racal UAT 1 ESM (Racal RDL
257 ESM, Racal RCM 2 Argentina)

AIR SUPPORT:

HELICOPTERS: One Westland Lynx
HMA 3/8 (ASV/ASW); two Sea King
(ASW/ASV) (Argentina)

Daring UK

Daring (Computer graphic)

- Extremely long forecastle with 4.5 in gun in 'A' position, with, further aft, raised area housing Sylver VLS SAM
- Space in 'B' position for Harpoon SSM launchers
- Slab-sided superstructure forward of funnel, with very prominent and tall enclosed pyramidal mast with Sampson surveillance and fire control radome atop with satcom domes on sponsons to port and starboard
- Small tapering funnel
- Slender enclosed tapering mast, topped by thin pole mast aft of funnel
- Prominent air/surface search radar on aft superstructure

NOTE: Some details speculative
NOTE 2: Later units may be fitted with 155 mm gun

SPECIFICATION:

COUNTRY OF ORIGIN: UK
CLASS: Daring (DDG)
BUILDING: 6
PLANNED: 2
NAME (PENNANT NUMBER):
Daring (D 32), Dauntless (D 33),
Diamond (D 34), Defender (D 35),
Dragon (D 36), Duncan (D 37)

FEATURES:
DISPLACEMENT: 7350 tons full load
LENGTH: 500.1 ft (152.4 m) oa
BEAM: 69.6 ft (21.2 m)
DRAUGHT: 17.4 ft (5.3 m) (screws)
SPEED: 29 kts
RANGE: 7000 miles at 18 kts

ARMAMENT:
MISSILES: SSM – Space for
Harpoon (2 quad); SAM –
DCN Sylver A 50 48-cell PAAMS
VLS, Aster 15 and Aster 30
GUNS: Vickers 4.5 in (114 mm)/55
Mk 8 Mod 1; two 20 mm Vulcan
Phalanx CIWS; two 30 mm
DECOYS: Four DLH chaff/IR
launchers; SSTD torpedo defence

ELECTRONICS:
RADARS: Air/surface search –
Signaal/Marconi S1850M;
surveillance/fire control – BAE
Systems Sampson
SONARS: Ultra MFS-7000
EW: Thales Type UAT (Mod) RESM

AIR SUPPORT:
HELICOPTERS: One Westland Lynx
HMA 8 (first batch) or EH Industries
EH 101 Merlin HM 1 (ASV/ASW)

Spruance USA
Cushing

SPECIFICATION:

COUNTRY OF ORIGIN: USA
CLASS: Spruance (DD/DDG)
ACTIVE: 3
NAME (PENNANT NUMBER):
Spruance (DD 963), Cushing
(DD 985), O'Bannon (DD 987)

FEATURES:
DISPLACEMENT: 8040 tons full load
LENGTH: 563.2 ft (171.7 m)
BEAM: 55.1 ft (16.8 m)
DRAUGHT: 19 ft (5.8 m)
SPEED: 33 kts
RANGE: 6000 miles at 20 kts

ARMAMENT:
MISSILES: SLCM/SSM – GDC
Tomahawk, eight McDonnell
Douglas Harpoon (2 quad);
SAM – Raytheon GMLS Mk 29
octuple launcher, Sea Sparrow,
GDC RAM quadruple launcher;
A/S – Loral ASROC VLS can be
carried; payload – Mk 46 Mod 5
Neartip torpedoes
GUNS: Two FMC 5 in (127 mm)/54
Mk 45 Mod 0/1; two GE/GD
20 mm/76 6-barrel Mk 15
Vulcan Phalanx; four 12.7 mm
machine guns
TORPEDOES: Six 324 mm Mk 32
(2 triple) tubes; Honeywell Mk 46
DECOYS: Four Loral Hycor SRBOC
6-barrel fixed Mk 36; SLQ-39 chaff
buoy; SLQ-25 Nixie torpedo
decoy; Prairie Masker hull/blade
rate noise suppression system

ELECTRONICS:
RADARS: Air-search – Lockheed
SPS-40B/C/D, Hughes Mk 23 TAS;
surface search – ISC Cardion
SPS-55; navigation – Raytheon
SPS-64(v)9; fire control –
Lockheed SPG-60, Lockheed
SPQ-9A, Raytheon Mk 95
SONARS: SQQ-89(v)6 including
GE/Hughes SQS-53B/C, bow-
mounted; Gould SQR-19 (TACTAS);
passive towed array
EW: Raytheon SLQ-32(v)2 ESM/ECM

AIR SUPPORT:
HELICOPTERS: Two Sikorsky
SH-60B LAMPS III or Kaman
SH-2G Seasprite

- High bow, high freeboard, sweeping maindeck aft to break at flight deck
- 5 in gun mounting on forecastle forward of A/S missile launcher and SSM or VLS tubes (on some)
- Unusually high and long main superstructure giving a slab-sided impression
- Large, square section twin funnels just proud of superstructure, each with several exhausts protruding at the top. After funnel offset to starboard
- Complex lattice foremast supporting various aerials immediately atop bridge roof
- Large central, lattice mainmast between funnels supporting air-search radar aerial
- Raised flight deck immediately aft of superstructure
- Sea Sparrow SAM box launcher just aft of flight deck with 5 in gun mounting in 'Y' position. GDC RAM SAM launcher, starboard side, right aft
- 5 in mounting on quarterdeck

Arleigh Burke USA

Oscar Austin

- High bow with sweeping maindeck aft to break down to flight deck
- Only obvious armament on forecastle is 5 in gun mounting midway between bow and bridge
- Missile vls tubes situated between forward gun mounting and bridge and just forward of flight deck
- High main superstructure with aft-sloping pole mainmast atop
- Large twin funnels of unusual square section with black exhausts protruding at top. Funnels sited either side of midships
- ciws mountings on raised platform immediately forward of bridge and forward of Harpoon ssm launcher
- Flight deck right aft

NOTE: Helicopter hangars incorporated in Flight iiA version with extended transom to increase size of flight deck

NOTE 2: Japan operates an improved 'Arleigh Burke' class named 'Kongou' class (see Japanese entry on page 119)

ARMAMENT:

MISSILES: SLCM – 56 GDC/Hughes Tomahawk; SSM – eight McDonnell Douglas Harpoon (2 quad); SAM – GDC Standard SM-2MR Block 4 (SM-2ER in DDG 72 onwards and in Flight IIA); A/S – Loral Asroc VLA; payload – Mk 46 Mod 5 Neartip torpedoes, two Lockheed Martin Mk 41 Vertical Launch Systems (VLS) for Tomahawk, Standard and ASROC

GUNS: One FMC/UDLP 5 in (127 mm)/54 Mk 45 Mod 1 (Mod 2 in DDG 79-80); 5 in (127 mm)/62 in DDG 81 onwards); two GE/GD 20 mm Vulcan Phalanx 6-barrel Mk 15 in Flights I and II; two Hughes 20 mm Vulcan Phalanx Mk 15 in Flight IIA

TORPEDOES: Six 324 mm Mk 32 Mod 14 (2 triple) tubes; Alliant Mk 46 Mod 5

DECOYS: Two Loral Hycor SRBOC 6-barrel fixed Mk 36, Mod 12; SLQ-25 Nixie torpedo decoy; NATO Sea Gnat SLQ-95 AEB, SLQ-39 chaff buoy

SPECIFICATION:

COUNTRY OF ORIGIN: USA
CLASS: Arleigh Burke (Flights I,II, IIA) – (Aegis) (DDG)
ACTIVE: 28 (Flights I and II), 19 (Flight IIA)
BUILDING: 15 (Flight IIA)
NAME (PENNANT NUMBER):
FLIGHTS I and II – Arleigh Burke (DDG 51), Barry (ex-John Barry) (DDG 52), John Paul Jones (DDG 53), Curtis Wilbur (DDG 54), Stout (DDG 55), John S McCain (DDG 56), Mitscher (DDG 57), Laboon (DDG 58), Russell (DDG 59), Paul Hamilton (DDG 60), Ramage (DDG 61), Fitzgerald (DDG 62), Carney (DDG 63), Benfold (DDG 65), Gonzalez (DDG 66), Cole (DDG 67), The Sullivans (DDG 68), Milius (DDG 69), Hopper (DDG 70), Ross (DDG 71), Mahan (DDG 72), Decatur (DDG 73) McFaul (DDG 74), Donald Cook (DDG 75), Higgins (DDG 76), O'Kane (DDG 77), Porter (DDG 78)
FLIGHT IIA – Oscar Austin (DDG 79), Roosevelt (DDG 80),

Winston S Churchill (DDG 81), Lassen (DDG 82), Howard (DDG 83), Bulkeley (DDG 84), McCampbell (DDG 85), Shoup (DDG 86), Mason (DDG 87), Preble (DDG 88), Mustin (DDG 89), Chaffee (DDG 90), Pinckney (DDG 91), Momsen (DDG 92), Chung-hoon (DDG 93), Nitze (DDG 94), James E Williams (DDG 95), Bainbridge (DDG 96), Halsey (DDG 97), Forrest Sherman (DDG 98), Farragut (DDG 99), Kidd (DDG 100), Gridley (DDG 101), Sampson (DDG 102), Truxtun (DDG 103), Sterett (DDG 104), Dewey (DDG 105), — (DDG 106-112)

FEATURES:

DISPLACEMENT: 8315 tons full load (DDG 51-71); 8400 tons (DDG 72-78); 9200 tons (Flight IIA)
LENGTH: 504.5 ft (153.8 m) oa; 509.5 (155.3) oa (Flight IIA)
BEAM: 66.9 ft (20.4 m)
DRAUGHT: 20.7 ft (6.3 m), 32.7 ft (9.9 m) (sonar)
SPEED: 32 kts
RANGE: 4400 miles at 20 kts

ELECTRONICS:

RADARS: Air-search/fire control – RCA SPY-1D, 3D; surface search – Norden DRS SPS-67(v)3; navigation – Raytheon SPS-64(v)9; fire control – three Raytheon/RCA SPG-62
SONARS: Gould/Raytheon/GE SQQ-89(v)6; combines SQS-53C, bow-mounted active search/attack with SQR-19B passive towed array (SQQ-89(v)10 in Flight IIA)
EW: Raytheon SLQ-32(v)2; SLQ-32(v)3 (SLY-2 from DDG 72 onwards and being retrofitted)§

AIR SUPPORT:

HELICOPTERS: Platform facilities to refuel/re-arm Sikorsky SH-60B/F (LAMPS III) in Flight I/II and hangar for two SH-60B-F in Flight IIA

Frigates

Koni ALGERIA, BULGARIA, LIBYA, SERBIA & MONTENEGRO

Rais Kellich

- High bow, sweeping maindeck line through to stern
- 3 in gun twin mounting in 'A' position
- RBU 6000 A/S mortar in 'B' mounting position
- Stepped main superstructure with enclosed mast at after end supporting Strut Curve air/surface or air-search radar aerials
- Single, squat funnel just aft of midships
- Short enclosed pyramid mast just forward of funnel supporting Drum Tilt fire control radar aerial
- SA-N-4 Gecko SAM launcher in 'X' position
- 3 in gun twin mounting in 'Y' position
- Pop Group fire control director just forward of SAM launcher at aft end of superstructure

SPECIFICATION:

COUNTRY OF ORIGIN: Russia
CLASS: Koni I/II/III (Type 1159) (FF)
ACTIVE: 1 Bulgaria, 2 Libya (FFG)
NAME (PENNANT NUMBER):
BULGARIA – Smeli (ex-*Delfin*) (11)
LIBYA – Al Hani (F 212),
Al Qirdabiyah (F 213)
CLASS: Mourad Rais (Koni II)
(Type 1159.2) (FF)
ACTIVE: 3 Algeria
NAME (PENNANT NUMBER):
Mourad Rais (901), Rais Kellich
(902), Rais Korfou (903)
CLASS: Beograd (Koni) (FFG)
ACTIVE: 1 Serbia & Montenegro
NAME (PENNANT NUMBER):
Beograd (ex-*Split*) (31)

FEATURES:

DISPLACEMENT: 1900 tons full
load; 1590 tons (Serbia &
Montenegro)
LENGTH: 316.3 ft (96.4 m); 316.7 ft
(96.5 m) (Serbia & Montenegro)
BEAM: 41.3 ft (12.6 m); 41 ft
(12.5 m) (Serbia & Montenegro)
DRAUGHT: 11.5 ft (3.5 m); 13.5 ft
(4.1 m) (Serbia & Montenegro)
SPEED: 27 kts
RANGE: 1800 miles at 14 kts

ARMAMENT:

MISSILES: SSM – four SS-N-2C Styx
(Libya (2 twin) and Serbia, not
Algeria or Bulgaria); SAM –
SA-N-4 Gecko
twin launcher
GUNS: Four 3 in (76 mm)/60
(2 twin); four 30 mm/65 (2 twin)
TORPEDOES: Four 533 mm (2 twin
tubes, Algeria 903 only); four
406 mm USET-95 (Libya only)
A/S MORTARS: Two RBU 6000,
12-barrel, trainable (one
RBU 6000, Libya only)
DEPTH CHARGES: Two racks
(not Serbia)
MINES: Rails; capacity 22
(20, Libya)
DECOYS: Two PK 16 chaff
launchers (Algeria, Bulgaria and
Libya)

ELECTRONICS:

RADARS: Air/surface search –
Strut Curve (Algeria 901 and 902,
Pozitiv-ME1.2 in 903); surface
search – Plank Shave (Libya only);
navigation/surface search – Don
2; fire control – Hawk Screech
(Algeria 901, 902) (Owl Screech,
Serbia), Drum Tilt, Pop Group
SONARS: Herkules (MG 322) or
Bull Nose (Serbia 33 and 34);
hull-mounted
EW: Two Watch Dog ESM

NOTE: The above features apply to Algerian and
Bulgarian ships, which could easily be confused.
Obvious differences in Libyan ships are: forward
end of superstructure removed to fit
SS-N-2C SSM launcher and lattice mast fitted
forward of Pop Group fire control director.
Camouflage paint applied to Libyan ships in 1991.
Algerian and Libyan ships have extended deck
housing aft of funnel
NOTE 2: Serbian units have SS-N-2C Styx in four
launchers, two port and two starboard, aft of the
funnel, facing astern

D'Estienne d'Orves ARGENTINA, FRANCE, TURKEY

Commandant Blaison

- Low profile forecastle with 3.9 in gun mounting in 'A' position
- Substantial forward superstructure
- Single funnel just aft of midships with vertical forward and sloping after end
- Mast and funnel combined with lattice mainmast atop
- Break in deck level aft of funnel, with low deckhouse continuing in Argentine ships
- Exocet ssm launchers, port and starboard, just aft of funnel
- Ship's boat stowed in davits aft of ssm launchers
- 375 mm A/S mortar launcher atop after superstructure. 40 mm/70 turret vice A/S mortar launcher on after superstructure in Argentine ships and Syracuse satcom dome in some French ships
- Torpedo tubes in 'Y' position in 'Drummond' class

SPECIFICATION:

COUNTRY OF ORIGIN: France
CLASS: D'Estienne d'Orves (Type
A69)/Drummond/Burak (FFG)
ACTIVE: 3 Argentina (Drummond),
9 France, 6 Turkey
NAME (PENNANT NUMBER):
ARGENTINA – Drummond
(ex-*Good Hope*, ex-*Lieutenant de
Vaisseau le Hénaff*) (31, ex-F 789),
Guerrico (ex-*Transvaal*, ex-
Commandant l'Herminier) (32, ex-F
791), Granville (33)
FRANCE – Lieutenant de Vaisseau
le Hénaff (F 789), Lieutenant de
Vaisseau Lavallée (F 790),
Commandant L'Herminier (F 791),
Premier Maître l'Her (F 792),
Commandant Blaison (F 793),
Enseigne de Vaisseau Jacoubet
(F 794), Commandant Ducuing
(F 795), Commandant Birot (F 796),
Commandant Bouan (F 797)
TURKEY – Bozcaada (ex-*Comman-
dant de Pimodan*) (F 500, ex-F 787),

Bodrum (ex-*Drogou*) (F 501,
ex-F 783), Bandirma (ex-*Quartier
Maître Anquetil*) (F 502, ex-F 786),
Beykoz (ex-*d'Estienne d'Orves*)
(F 503, ex-F 781), Bartin (ex-*Amyot
d'Inville*) (F 504, ex-F 782), Bafra
(ex-*Second Maître le Bihan*)
(F 505, ex-F 788)

NOTE: The French government
has offered to lease a ship of this
class to the Philippines Navy

FEATURES:

DISPLACEMENT: 1170 tons full
load (Argentina); 1250 tons
(France and Turkey, 1330 tons on
later ships); 1290 tons on 792-
793; 1330 tons on 794-797 ships
LENGTH: 262.5 ft (80 m)
(Argentina); 264.1 ft (80.5 m)
(France and Turkey)
BEAM: 33.8 ft (10.3 m)
DRAUGHT: 18 ft (5.5 m) (sonar)
SPEED: 23 kts
RANGE: 4500 miles at 15 kts

ARMAMENT:

MISSILES: SSM – four Aerospatiale
MM 40 (two MM 38 in 789-791
and Turkey) Exocet (four MM 38,
twin launchers, Argentina);
SAM – Matra Simbad twin
launcher for Mistral fitted aft of
A/S mortar or Syracuse SATCOM
(France and Turkey)
GUNS: One DCN/Cruesot-Loire
3.9 in (100 mm)/55 Mod 68
CADAM automatic (Creusot-Loire
3.9 in (100 mm)/55 Mod 1953
'Drummond' class); two Giat
20 mm (two Oerlikon 20 mm),
two Breda 40 mm/70 (twin)
(Argentina) and two 12.7 mm
machine guns (four 12.7 mm
machine guns, France
and Turkey)
TORPEDOES: Four fixed tubes;
ECAN L5 (France and Turkey);
six 324 mm Mk 32 (2 triple
tubes); Whitehead A 244
(Argentina only)
A/S MORTARS: One Creusot-Loire
375 mm Mk 54 6-tubed launcher
(France and Turkey only, removed
from F 792 and 797)
DECOYS: Two CSEE Dagaie
10-barrel trainable chaff/IR
launchers; Nixie SLQ-25 torpedo
decoy (France and Turkey);
CSEE Dagaie double mounting,
chaff, decoys; Corvus sextuple
chaff launchers (Argentina only)

ELECTRONICS:

RADARS: Air/surface search –
Thomson-CSF DRBV 51A;
navigation – Racal Decca 1290
(DRBN 34) (1226, Argentina and
Turkey); fire control –
Thomson-CSF DRBC 32E
SONARS: Thomson-Sintra DUBA
25; hull-mounted, active search/
attack (Diodon in Argentina)
EW: ARBR 16 ESM (DR 2000/Dahlia
500 ESM); Thomson-CSF
Allligator ECM (Argentina)

Espora ARGENTINA

Parker

- Blunt bow. Maindeck level raised for the length of the superstructure
- 3 in gun mounting in 'A' position
- 40 mm/70 gun twin mountings in 'B' and 'Y' positions
- Exocet SSM ribbed launchers forward of 40 mm/70 gun mounting on quarterdeck
- Low integral funnel at after end of upper superstructure. Black exhaust protrudes from centre of main funnel
- Tripod style mainmast atop after end of bridge structure supporting fire control radome
- Raised flight deck
- *Parker* and later ships fitted with a telescopic hangar

NOTE: Scaled down Meko 360s

SPECIFICATION:

COUNTRY OF ORIGIN: Germany
CLASS: Espora (Meko 140) (FFG)
ACTIVE: 6
NAME (PENNANT NUMBER):
Espora (41), Rosales (42), Spiro
(43), Parker (44), Robinson (45),
Gomez Roca (46)

FEATURES:
DISPLACEMENT: 1836 tons
full load
LENGTH: 299.1 ft (91.2 m)
BEAM: 36.4 ft (11.1 m)
DRAUGHT: 11.2 ft (3.4 m)
SPEED: 27 kts
RANGE: 4000 miles at 18 kts

ARMAMENT:
MISSILES: SSM – four Aerospatiale
MM 38 Exocet
GUNS: One OTO Melara 3 in
(76 mm)/62 Compact; four Breda
40 mm/70 (2 twin); two 12.7 mm
machine guns
TORPEDOES: Six 324 mm ILAS 3
(2 triple) tubes; Whitehead
A 244/S
DECOYS: CSEE Dagaie double
mounting

ELECTRONICS:
RADARS: Air/surface search –
Signaal DA05; navigation –
Decca TM 1226; fire control –
Signaal WM28
SONARS: Atlas Elektronik ASO-4;
hull-mounted, active
search/attack
EW: Racal RQN-2B ESM;
Racal TQN-2X ECM

AIR SUPPORT:
HELICOPTERS: One Aerospatiale
SA 319B Alouette III or
Aerospatiale AS 555 Fennec
(ASW) in 44-46

Meko 200 AUSTRALIA, GREECE, NEW ZEALAND, PORTUGAL, TURKEY

Anzac (*Michael Nitz*)

- High bow with break down to after end of forecastle
- 5 in gun mounting in 'A' position (3.9 in gun mounting in Portuguese ships)
- CIWS mounting in 'B' mounting position in Greek and Australian ships.
  25 mm Sea Zenith CIWS in Turkish ships in same position. Space left for VLS
  Sea Sparrow SA in Portuguese hulls
- High, flat sided superstructure extending from bridge aft to flight deck
- Lattice mainmast at after end of bridge structure
- Harpoon SSM launchers immediately aft of mainmast in Greek, Turkish and
  Portuguese ships. They are absent in Australian and NZ units
- Twin, outward sloping, side-by-side funnels aft of midships
- Ship's boats hoisted unusually high on midship davits
- CIWS mounting at after end of hangar roof in Greek, NZ and Portuguese ships.
  Sea Zenith/Sea Guard CIWS in Turkish ships
- Sea Sparrow SAM box launcher on superstructure aft of funnels in Turkish
  hulls F240-245
- Turkish 'Yavuz' class has prominent WM25 fire control radome forward of
  mainmast
- Flight deck right aft with open quarterdeck below

contd.

Meko 200 contd.

SPECIFICATION:

COUNTRY OF ORIGIN: Germany
CLASS: Anzac, Hydra (Meko
200HN) Vasco da Gama, Yavuz,
Barbaros (modified Meko 200)
(FF/FFG)
ACTIVE: 6 Australia (Anzac),
4 Greece (Hydra), 2 New Zealand
(Anzac), 3 Portugal (Vasco da
Gama), 4 Turkey 'Barbaros'
class), 4 Turkey ('Yavuz' class)
BUILDING: 2 (Australia)
NAME (PENNANT NUMBER):
AUSTRALIA – Anzac (150), Arunta
(ex-Arrernte) (151), Warramunga
(ex-Warumungu) (152), Stuart (153),
Parramatta (154), Ballarat (155),
Toowoomba (155), Perth (157)
GREECE – Hydra (F 452),
Spetsai (F 453), Psara (F 454),
Salamis (F 455)
NEW ZEALAND – Te Kaha (F 77),
Te Mana (F 111)
PORTUGAL – Vasco da Gama
(F 330), Alvares Cabral (F 331),
Corte Real (F 332)
TURKEY ('Barbaros' class) –
Barbaros (F 244), Orucreis
(F 245), Salihreis (F 246),
Kemalreis (F 247)
TURKEY ('Yavuz' class) – Yavuz
(F 240), Turgutreis (ex-Turgut)
(F 241), Fatih (F 242),
Yildirim (F 243)

FEATURES:

DISPLACEMENT: 3600 tons full
load (Australia/NZ); 3350 tons
(Greece); 3300 tons (Portugal);
3380 tons (Turkey, 'Barbaros'
class); 2919 tons (Turkey, 'Yavuz'
class)
LENGTH: 380.3 ft (115.9 m)
(Portugal); 383.9 ft (117 m)
(Greece); 387.1 ft (118 m)
(Australia/NZ/Turkey, 'Barbaros'
classes); 378.9 ft (115.5 m)
(Turkey, 'Yavuz' class)
BEAM: 48.6 ft (14.8 m) (Greece,
Turkey, Australia/NZ); 48.7 ft
(14.8 m) (Portugal); 46.6 ft
(14.2 m) (Turkey, 'Yavuz' class)
DRAUGHT: 19.7 ft (6 m) (Greece);
13.5 ft (4.1 m) (Turkey, 'Yavuz'
class); 14.1 ft (4.3 m) (Turkey);
14.3 ft (4.4 m) (Australia/NZ);
20 ft (6.1 m) (Portugal)
SPEED: 27 kts (Australia/NZ,
Turkey, 'Yavuz' class); 31 kts
(Greece); 32 kts (Portugal/Turkey,
'Barbaros' classes)
RANGE: 4100 miles at 16 kts
(Greece); 4100 miles at 18 kts
(Turkey); 6000 miles at 18 kts
(Australia/NZ); 4900 miles at
18 kts (Portugal)

ARMAMENT:

MISSILES: SSM – eight McDonnell
Douglas Harpoon Block 1C
(2 quad launchers) (Greece,
Portugal, Turkey; none in NZ
units); SAM – Raytheon NATO Sea
Sparrow Mk 48 vertical launcher
(Greece), Mk 29 Mod 1 octuple
launcher (Portugal), (Aspide;
Turkish hulls, apart from
F 246-247), Sea Sparrow RIM-7NP
Mk 41 Mod 5 octuple VLS
(Australia F 150-151/NZ), (Turkey
F 246 and F 247, with Aspide
missiles)
GUNS: One United Defense Mk
45 Mods 2/2A/4 5 in (127 mm)/54
(Australia/NZ, Greece, Turkey;
Mod 1 in Turkish 'Yavuz' class);
Creusot-Loire 3.9 in (100 mm)/55
Mod 68 CADAM (Portugal); two
GD/GE Vulcan Phalanx 20 mm
Mk 15 Mod 12 (Greece, one only
in Portuguese and NZ ships);
three Oerlikon-Contraves 25 mm
Sea Zenith CIWS 4-barrels
(Turkey); two 12.7 mm machine
guns (Australia)

TORPEDOES: Six 324 mm Mk 32
Mod 5 (2 triple) tubes; Honeywell
Mk 46 Mod 5 Neartip
DECOYS: SRBOC 6-barrelled Mk 36
Mod 1/2 (Nulka quad expendable
decoy launchers, Australia/NZ
only); SLQ-25 Nixie torpedo
decoy; two Loral Hycor 6-tubed
fixed Mk 36 (Portugal, Turkey)

ELECTRONICS:

RADARS: Air-search – Raytheon
SPS-49(V)8 (Australia/NZ), Signaal
MW08 3D (Greece, Portugal),
Siemens/Plessey AWS 9 (Turkey,
'Barbaros' class), Signaal DA08
(Turkey 'Yavuz' class); air/surface
search – Ericsson Sea Giraffe
(Australia), CelsiusTech 9LV 453
TIR (Australia/NZ), Signaal/
Magnavox, DA08 (Greece,
Portugal), Siemens/Plessey AWS 6
Dolphin (Turkey); navigation –
Atlas Electronik 9600 ARPA
(Australia/NZ), Racal Decca 2690
BT (Greece, Turkey, 'Barbaros'
class), Kelvin Hughes Type 1007
(Portugal), Racal Decca TM 1226
(Turkey, 'Yavuz' class); fire control
– CelsiusTech 9LV 453
(Australia/NZ), two Signaal STIR
(Greece, Portugal, Turkey),
Seaguard (for 25 mm) (Turkey),
Signaal WM25 (Turkey, 'Yavuz'
class)
SONARS: Thomson-Sintra
Spherion B Mod 5 (Australia/NZ);
Raytheon SQS-56/DE 1160, hull-
mounted and VDS (Greece,
Turkey); CDC SQS-510(V)
(Portugal); Petrel (Australia/NZ)
EW: Racal Sceptre A ESM being
replaced by Thales Centaur
(Australia); APECS II (Portugal);
Argo AR 700 ESM, Argo APECS II
ECM (Greece); Racal Cutlass/
Scorpion ESM/ECM (Turkey);
Signaal Rapids/Ramses ESM/ECM
(Turkey, 'Yavuz' class); DASA
Maigret, Racal Sceptre A ESM (NZ)

AIR SUPPORT:

HELICOPTERS: One Sikorsky
S-70B6 Seahawk (Greece); two
Westland Super Sea Lynx Mk 95
(Portugal); Agusta AB 212 or
S-70B Seahawk (ASW) (Turkey),
one S-70B-2 Seahawk or one
Kaman SH-2G Seasprite
(Australia/NZ)

Oliver Hazard Perry
Sabha

AUSTRALIA, BAHRAIN, EGYPT, POLAND, SPAIN, TAIWAN, TURKEY, USA

- High bow with raised, solid sides to forward end of forecastle
- SAM/SSM launcher only in 'A' position
- Hsiung Feng SSM angled launchers between masts in Taiwanese ships
- Slab-sided, box-like superstructure running from forecastle to flight deck
- Distinctive WM 28 fire control radar dome atop the bridge (RCA Mk 92 in Spanish ships; Unisys Mk 92 in Taiwanese units) with the lattice foremast immediately aft supporting large curved SPS-49 air-search radar aerial
- Large lattice mainmast just forward of midships
- 3 in gun mounting forward of funnel
- Low single funnel just showing towards after end of superstructure
- After end of superstructure flush with ship's side
- Vulcan Phalanx CIWS mounting atop after end of hangar roof, (Meroka CIWS in Spanish ships)
- Bofors 40 mm/70 gun mountings on sponsons outboard of superstructure just forward of funnel (Taiwanese ships only)
- SATCOM terminals removed from Bahrain unit

contd.

Oliver Hazard Perry contd.

SPECIFICATION:

COUNTRY OF ORIGIN: USA

CLASS: Oliver Hazard Perry/
Adelaide/Santa María/Cheng
Kung/Gaziantep (FFGs)

ACTIVE: 5 Australia, 1 Bahrain,
4 Egypt, 2 Poland, 6 Spain ('Santa
María' class), 8 Taiwan ('Cheng
Kung' class), 8 Turkey, 30 USA

NAME (PENNANT NUMBER):
AUSTRALIA – Adelaide (01), Sydney
(03), Darwin (04), Melbourne (05),
Newcastle (06)

BAHRAIN – Sabha (ex-*Jack
Williams*) (90, ex-FFG 24)

EGYPT – Mubarak (ex-*Copeland*)
(F 911, ex-FFG 25), Taba (ex-
Gallery) (F 916, ex-FFG 26), Sharm
el Sheikh (ex-*Fahrion*) (F 901,
ex-FFG 22), Toushka (ex-*Lewis
B Puller*) (F 906, ex-FFG 23)

POLAND – General Kazimierz
Pulaski (ex-*Clark*) (272, ex-FFG 11),
General T Kosciuszko (ex-*Sides*)
(272, ex-FFG 14)

SPAIN – Santa María (F 81),
Victoria (F 82), Numancia (F 83),
Reina Sofía (ex-*América*) (F 84),
Navarra (F 85), Canarias (F 86)

TAIWAN – Cheng Kung (1101),
Cheng Ho (1103), Chi Kuang
(1105), Yueh Fei (1106), Tzu-I
(1107), Pan Chao (1108), Chang
Chien (1109), Tien Tan (1110)

TURKEY – Gaziantep (ex-*Clifton
Sprague*) (F 490, ex-FFG 16),
Giresun (ex-*Antrim*) (F 491,
ex-FFG 20), Gemlik (ex-*Flatley*)
(F 492, ex-FFG 21), Gelibolu
(ex-*Reid*) (F 493, ex-FFG 30),
Gökçeada (ex-*Mahlon S Tisdale*)
(F 494, ex-FFG 27), Gediz (ex-*John
A Moore*) (F 495, ex-FFG 19),
Gokova (ex-*Samuel Eliot Morrison*)
(F 496, ex-FFG 13), Göksu
(ex-*Estocin*) (F 497, ex-FFG 15)

USA – McInerney (FFG 8), Boone
(FFG 28), Stephen W Groves
(FFG 29), John L Hall (FFG 32),
Jarrett (FFG 33), Underwood
(FFG 36), Crommelin (FFG 37),
Curts (FFG 38), Doyle (FFG 39),
Halyburton (FFG 40), McClusky
(FFG 41), Klakring (FFG 42), Thach
(FFG 43), de Wert (FFG 45), Rentz
(FFG 46), Nicholas (FFG 47),
Vandegrift (FFG 48), Robert G
Bradley (FFG 49), Taylor (FFG 50),
Gary (FFG 51), Carr (FFG 52),
Hawes (FFG 53), Ford (FFG 54),
Elrod (FFG 55), Simpson (FFG 56),
Reuben James (FFG 57), Samuel B
Roberts (FFG 58), Kauffman
(FFG 59), Rodney M Davis
(FFG 60), Ingraham (FFG 61)

FEATURES:

DISPLACEMENT: 4100 tons full
load; 4105 tons (Taiwan); 3638
tons (Bahrain, Egypt, Poland,
Turkey); 3969 tons (Spain)

LENGTH: 453 ft (138.1 m); 445 ft
(135.6 m) (Bahrain, Egypt, Poland,
Turkey, US FFG 33); 451.2 ft
(137.7 m) (Spain); 453 ft (138.1 m)
(Taiwan)

BEAM: 45 ft (13.7 m); 46.9 ft
(14.3 m) (Spain)

DRAUGHT: 14.8 ft (4.5 m)

SPEED: 29 kts

RANGE: 4500 miles at 20 kts

ARMAMENT:

MISSILES: SSM – McDonnell
Douglas Harpoon; SAM – GDC
Pomona Standard SM-1MR, Mk 13
Mod 4 launcher for both SAM
and SSM systems (not in US)
(Hsiung Feng II (2 quad) SSM in
Taiwanese ships)

GUNS: One OTO Melara 3 in
(76 mm)/62 Mk 75 Compact; one
GE/GD 20 mm/76 Mk 15 Vulcan
Phalanx; up to four 12.7 mm
machine guns (not Taiwan); one
Bazán 20 mm/120 12-barrel
Meroka Mod 2A or 2B CIWS
(Spain); two additional Bofors
40 mm/70 and three 20 mm
Type 75 on hangar roof, when
fitted (Taiwan only); two
McDonnell Douglas 25 mm
Mk 38 can be fitted amidships
in US ships

TORPEDOES: Six 324 mm Mk 32
(2 triple) tubes; Honeywell
Mk 46 Mod 5

DECOYS: Two Loral Hycor SRBOC
6-barrel Mk 34/36; SLQ-25 Nixie
towed torpedo decoy (Prairie
Masker hull noise/blade rate
suppression in Spanish ships);
four Kung Fen 6 chaff launchers
(Taiwan only)

ELECTRONICS:

RADARS: Air-search – Raytheon
SPS-49(V)4 or 5; surface
search/navigation – ISC Cardion
SPS-55 (Raytheon SPS-55 in
Spanish ships); navigation –
Furuno (Raytheon 1650/9, Spain);
fire control – Lockheed STIR
(modified SPG-60), Sperry Mk 92
(Signaal WM 28), (RCA Mk 92
Mod 4/6, Signaal STING, Selenia
RAN 30L/X (RAN 12L), Spain),
(USN UD 417 STIR, Unisys Mk 92
Mod 6, Taiwan)

SONARS: Raytheon SQS-53B, hull-
mounted, active search/attack;
Gould SQR-18A passive towed
array; Raytheon SQS-56 hull-
mounted (Australia, Bahrain,
Egypt, Turkey); Raytheon SQS-56
(DE 1160) hull-mounted and
Gould SQR-19(V)2 tactical towed
array (Spain); Raytheon SQS-56/DE
1160P and SQR-18A(V)2 passive
towed array or BAE/Thomson-
Sintra ATAS towed array (Taiwan
from 1105 on); Raytheon
SQQ-89(V)2, hull-mounted,
active search/attack (US)

EW: SLQ-32(V)2 (Bahrain, Egypt,
Poland, US); Elbit EA-2118 ECM
(Australia); Elettronica Nettunel
or Mk 3000 Neptun (F 84-86)
ESM/ECM (Spain); Chang Feng IV
ESM/ECM (Taiwan)

AIR SUPPORT:

HELICOPTERS: Two Sikorsky
S-70B-2 Seahawks, or one
Seahawk and one Aerospatiale
AS 350B Squirrel (Australia); two
(normally only one embarked)
Sikorsky SH-60B Seahawk
(LAMPS III) (Spain); two Sikorsky
S-70C(M) Thunderhawks (only
one embarked) (Taiwan); two
Kaman SH-2G Seasprite (LAMPS 1)
(Egypt, Poland, US) or two
Sikorsky SH-60B Seahawk
(ASW/ASV/OTHT) (US); one
Eurocopter BO 105 (Bahrain),
one S-70B Seahawk (Turkey)

Leopard BANGLADESH

Ali Haider (*Michael Nitz*)

- Raised forecastle with break down to 4.5 in gun mounting
- Prominent Type 275 fire control director atop after end of bridge roof
- Two masts, lattice foremast immediately aft of fire control director, enclosed mainmast supporting distinctive single bedstead Type 965 air-search radar aerial
- Engine exhausts from short funnel inside lattice mainmast and at top aft end of aftermast
- 4.5 in gun mounting in 'Y' position
- Break in maindeck, sloping down to very short quarterdeck

SPECIFICATION:

COUNTRY OF ORIGIN: UK
CLASS: Leopard (Type 41) (FF)
ACTIVE: 2
NAME (PENNANT NUMBER):
Abu Bakr (ex-*Lynx*) (F 15), Ali Haider (ex-*Jaguar*) (F 17)

FEATURES:

DISPLACEMENT: 2520 tons full load
LENGTH: 339.8 ft (103.6 m)
BEAM: 40 ft (12.2 m)
DRAUGHT: 15.5 ft (4.7 m) (screws)
SPEED: 24 kts
RANGE: 7500 miles at 16 kts

ARMAMENT:

GUNS: Four Vickers 4.5 in (115 mm)/45 (2 twin) Mk 6; one Bofors 40 mm/60 Mk 9
DECOYS: Corvus chaff launchers

ELECTRONICS:

RADARS: Air-search – Marconi Type 965 with single AKE 1 array; air/surface search – Plessey Type 993; navigation – Decca Type 978, Kelvin Hughes Type 1007; fire control – Type 275

Salisbury BANGLADESH

Umar Farooq

- Raised forecastle with break down to 4.5 in gun mounting in 'A' position
- Low superstructure with Type 275 fire control director at aft end of bridge
- Two large, black-topped mast and funnel combined structures, aftermast supporting double bedstead Type 965 air-search radar aerial
- Engine exhausts at top after end of masts
- Short lattice mast supporting Type 278M height finder radar aerial between forward mast and fire control director
- Prominent Type 982 radar aerial on short pylon aft (non-operational)
- 40 mm/60 gun mounting in 'Y' position
- Break down to short quarterdeck

SPECIFICATION:

COUNTRY OF ORIGIN: UK
CLASS: Salisbury (Type 61) (FF)
ACTIVE: 1
NAME (PENNANT NUMBER): Umar Farooq (ex-*Llandaff*) (F 16)

FEATURES:
DISPLACEMENT: 2408 tons full load
LENGTH: 339.8 ft (103.6 m)
BEAM: 40 ft (12.2 m)
DRAUGHT: 15.5 ft (4.7 m)
SPEED: 24 kts
RANGE: 7500 miles at 16 kts

ARMAMENT:
GUNS: Two Vickers 4.5 in (115 mm)/45 (twin) Mk 6; two Bofors 40 mm/60 Mk 9
A/S MORTARS: One triple-barrelled Squid Mk 4
DECOYS: Corvus chaff launchers

ELECTRONICS:
RADARS: Air-search – Marconi Type 965 with double AKE 2 array; air/surface search – Plessey Type 993; heightfinder – Type 278M; navigation – Decca Type 978; fire control – Type 275
SONARS: Type 174, hull-mounted, active search/attack; Graseby Type 170B, hull-mounted, active attack

Wielingen BELGIUM, BULGARIA
Westdiep (*Michael Nitz*)

SPECIFICATION:

COUNTRY OF ORIGIN: Belgium
CLASS: Wielingen (E-71)
ACTIVE: 2 Belgium, 1 Bulgaria
NAME (PENNANT NUMBER):
BELGIUM – Wielingen (F 910),
Westdiep (F 911)
BULGARIA – — (ex-*Wandelaar*),
— (ex-F 912)

FEATURES:
DISPLACEMENT: 2430 tons full load
LENGTH: 349 ft (106.4 m)
BEAM: 40.3 ft (12.3 m)
DRAUGHT: 18.4 ft (5.6 m)
SPEED: 26 kts
RANGE: 6000 miles at 15 kts

ARMAMENT:
MISSILES: SSM – four Aerospatiale
MM 38 Exocet (2 twin) launchers;
SAM – Raytheon Sea Sparrow Mk
29 octuple launcher
GUNS: One Creusot-Loire 3.9 in
(100 mm)/55 Mod 68
TORPEDOES: Two 21 in (533 mm)
launchers; ECAN L5 Mod 4
A/S MORTARS: Creusot-Loire
375 mm 6-barrel, trainable
DECOYS: Two Tracor MBA SRBOC
6-barrel Mk 36; Nixie SLQ-25
towed anti-torpedo decoy

ELECTRONICS:
RADARS: Air/surface search –
Signaal DA05; surface search/fire
control – Signaal WM25;
navigation – Signaal Scout
SONARS: Computing Devices
Canada SQS-510, hull-mounted
active search/attack
EW: Argos AS 900 ESM

- High freeboard with continuous maindeck from bow aft to break for very short quarterdeck
- 3.9 in gun mounting in 'A' position
- Creusot-Loire 375 mm A/S mortar launcher in 'B' mounting position
- Enclosed mainmast atop superstructure supporting Signaal WM 25 search/fire control radar dome
- Large distinctive funnel amidships with large central exhaust and smaller exhausts protruding at top
- Short enclosed aftermast supporting DA05 air/surface search radar aerial
- Two Exocet SSM launchers in 'x' mounting position
- Sea Sparrow SAM box launcher forward of quarterdeck

Broadsword (Type 22, Batch 1) BRAZIL, CHILE, ROMANIA

Dodsworth (now decommissioned) (*Royal Navy Colours*)

- Blunt bow with short forecastle
- Exocet SSM box launcher in 'A' mounting position (in Brazilian hulls)
- Seawolf SAM six-barrel launcher in 'B' mounting position
- Raised central maindeck section giving high freeboard
- High enclosed mainmast at after end of forward superstructure
- Large funnel, aft of midships, with sloping top and black exhausts just protruding at top
- SATCOM dome atop superstructure just forward of funnel
- Large enclosed black-topped aftermast aft of funnel. This mast is only slightly shorter than the mainmast
- After superstructure has Type 910/11 fire control radar aerial atop raised forward section and Seawolf SAM 6-barrel launcher atop hangar
- Flight deck aft with open quarterdeck below

SPECIFICATION:

COUNTRY OF ORIGIN: UK
CLASS: Broadsword (Type 22)
(Batch 1) (FFG)
ACTIVE: 3 Brazil, 1 Chile,
2 Romania
NAME (PENNANT NUMBER):
BRAZIL – Greenhalgh
(ex-*Broadsword*) (F 48, ex-F 88),
Bosisio (ex-*Brazen*) (F 48, ex-F 91),
Rademaker (ex-*Battleaxe*)
(F 49, ex-F 89)
CHILE – Almirante Williams
(ex-*Sheffield*) (19 ex-F 96)
ROMANIA – Regina Maria
(ex-*London*) (222, ex-F 95),
Regele Ferdinand (ex-*Coventry*)
(221, ex-F 98)

FEATURES:
DISPLACEMENT: 4731 tons full load
LENGTH: 430 ft (131.2 m) oa
BEAM: 48.5 ft (14.8 m)
DRAUGHT: 19.9 ft (6 m) (screws)
SPEED: 30 kts
RANGE: 4500 miles at 18 kts

ARMAMENT:
MISSILES: SSM – four MM 40 Block
II Exocet; SAM – two British
Aerospace 6-barrel Seawolf
GWS 25 Mod 4
GUNS: Two Bofors 40 mm/70
(F 46 only); two Oerlikon/BMARC
20 mm GAM-B01
TORPEDOES: Six 324 mm Plessey
STWS Mk 2 (2 triple) tubes;
Marconi Stingray
DECOYS: Four Loral Hycor SRBOC
Mk 36; Graseby Type 182 towed
torpedo decoy

ELECTRONICS:
RADARS: Air/surface search –
Marconi Type 967/968; navigation
– Kelvin Hughes Type 1006;
fire control – two Marconi
Type 911
SONARS: Ferranti/Thomson-Sintra
Type 2050, hull-mounted
EW: MEL UAA-2 ESM; Type 670
ECM

AIR SUPPORT:
HELICOPTERS: Two Westland
Super Lynx AH-11A

Niteroi BRAZIL

Defensora

General Purpose design:

- Short forecastle with 4.5 in gun mounting in 'A' position and Bofors 375 mm A/S mortar launcher in 'B' mounting position
- High forward superstructure flush with ship's side
- Foremast at after end of forward superstructure
- Pyramid mainmast immediately forward of funnel supporting air/surface search radar aerial
- Squat, wide, black-capped funnel sited just aft of midships. Funnel has sloping top from forward to aft
- Flight deck on maindeck level with break down to long quarterdeck
- Albatros octuple launcher for Aspide SAM on the quarterdeck
- Ships boats, in davits, port and starboard, adjacent to funnel

NOTE: Modified 'Niteroi' class Brasil serves as training ship with pennant number U 27. Only two Bofors 40 mm/70 are carried, together with four saluting guns

NOTE 2: Similar in appearance to six 'Tariq' class frigates in Pakistan navy

SPECIFICATION:

COUNTRY OF ORIGIN: UK
CLASS: Niteroi
ACTIVE: 6
NAME (PENNANT NUMBER):
Niteroi (F 40), Defensora (F 41),
Constituição (F 42*), Liberal
(F 43*), Independência (F 44),
União (F 45)
* General Purpose design;
remainder are anti-submarine
configuration

FEATURES:

DISPLACEMENT: 3707 tons
full load
LENGTH: 424 ft (129.2 m)
BEAM: 44.2 ft (13.5 m)
DRAUGHT: 18.2 ft (5.5 m) (sonar)
SPEED: 30 kts
RANGE: 5300 miles at 17 kts

ARMAMENT:

MISSILES: SSM – Aerospatiale
MM 40 Exocet (2 twin) launchers;
SAM – Albatros octuple launcher
for Aspide
GUNS: One Vickers 4.5 in
(115 mm)/55 Mk 8 (GP version);
two Bofors Sea Trinity SAK
40 mm/70 Mk 3
TORPEDOES: Six 324 mm Plessey
STWS-1 (2 triple) tubes;
Honeywell Mk 46 Mod 5 Neartip
A/S MORTARS: One Bofors 375
mm rocket launcher (twin-tube)
DECOYS: Two Plessey Shield chaff
launchers; four IPQM/Elebra
MDLS octuple launcher

ELECTRONICS:

RADARS: Air/surface search –
AESN RAN 20 S (3L); surface
search – Terma Scanter MIP;
navigation – Furuno FR-1942
Mk 2; fire control – two AESN
RTN 30X
SONARS: EDO 997F hull-mounted
active search/attack; EDO 700E
VDS (F 40 and 41)
EW: Racal Cutlass B-1B ESM;
Racal Cygnus or IPQM/Elebra
ET/SLQ-2X ECM

AIR SUPPORT:

HELICOPTERS: One Westland
Super Lynx AH-11 (ASW)

Pará BRAZIL

Paraná (now decommissioned) (*Mario R. V. Carneiro*)

- Very long forecastle with continuous maindeck line from stem to stern
- 5 in gun mounting on forecastle, approximately mid-point between bow and bridge
- ASROC A/S missile box launcher between forward mounting and bridge
- Single black-capped funnel amidships
- Mast and funnel combined with pole mast atop after end. Large air-search radar aerial at forward end of funnel
- 5 in gun mounting atop after superstructure forward of hangar
- Flight deck right aft

SPECIFICATION:

COUNTRY OF ORIGIN: USA
CLASS: Pará (ex-US *Garcia*) (FF)
ACTIVE: 1
NAME (PENNANT NUMBER): Pará
(ex-*Albert David*) (D 27, ex-FF 1050)

FEATURES:

DISPLACEMENT: 3560 tons full load
LENGTH: 414.5 ft (126.3 m)
BEAM: 44.2 ft (13.5 m)
DRAUGHT: 14.5 ft (4.4 m) (keel)
SPEED: 27.5 kts
RANGE: 4000 miles at 20 kts

ARMAMENT:

MISSILES: A/S – Honeywell ASROC
Mk 116 Mod 3 octuple launcher
GUNS: Two USN 5 in (127 mm)/38
Mk 30
TORPEDOES: Six 324 mm Mk 32
(2 triple) tubes; 14 Honeywell
Mk 46 Mod 5 Neartip
DECOYS: Two Loral Hycor Mk 33
RBOC 4-tubed launchers; Mk T-6
Fanfare; torpedo decoy system;
Prairie/Masker; hull/blade rate
noise suppression

ELECTRONICS:

RADARS: Air-search – Lockheed
SPS-40B; surface search –
Raytheon SPS-10C; navigation –
Marconi LN 66; fire control –
General Electric Mk 35
SONARS: EDO/General Electric
SQS-26B, bow-mounted
EW: WLR-1, WLR-6 ESM; ULQ-6 ECM

AIR SUPPORT:

HELICOPTERS: Westland Super
Lynx AH-11

Halifax CANADA

Regina (*Michael Nitz*)

- Squat 57 mm/70 gun mounting mid-forecastle
- Short and squat lattice mast supporting large SPS-49(v)5 air-search radar aerial mid-forward superstructure
- Tall lattice mainmast after end of forward superstructure
- Unusually large, square section funnel amidships, offset to port with grilled intakes top, forward
- Break in superstructure aft of funnel with Harpoon launchers
- High after super-structure with CIWS mounting at after end
- Flight deck aft of hangar with small break down to short, shallow quarterdeck

SPECIFICATION:

COUNTRY OF ORIGIN: Canada
CLASS: Halifax (FFH/FFG)
ACTIVE: 12
NAME (PENNANT NUMBER):
Halifax (330), Vancouver (331),
Ville de Québec (332), Toronto
(333), Regina (334), Calgary (335),
Montreal (336), Fredericton (337),
Winnipeg (338), Charlottetown
(339), St John's (340), Ottawa (341)

FEATURES:
DISPLACEMENT: 4770 tons
full load
LENGTH: 441.9 ft (134.7 m) oa
BEAM: 53.8 ft (16.4 m)
DRAUGHT: 16.4 ft (5 m)
SPEED: 29 kts
RANGE: 9500 miles at 13 kts

ARMAMENT:
MISSILES: SSM – eight McDonnell
Douglas Harpoon Block 1C
(2 quad) launchers; SAM – two
Raytheon Sea Sparrow RIM-7P
Mk 48 octuple vertical launchers
GUNS: One Bofors 57 mm/70
Mk 2; one GE/GD 20 mm Vulcan
Phalanx Mk 15 Mod 1; eight
12.7 mm machine guns
TORPEDOES: Four 324 mm Mk 32
Mod 9 (2 twin) tubes; Honeywell
Mk 46 Mod 5 Neartip
DECOYS: Four Plessey Shield
Mk 2 decoy launchers; Nixie
SLQ-25 towed acoustic decoy

ELECTRONICS:
RADARS: Air-search – Raytheon
SPS-49(v)5; air/surface search –
Ericsson Sea Giraffe HC150;
navigation – Sperry Mk 340,
being replaced by Kelvin Hughes
1007; fire control – two Signaal
SPG-503 STIR 1.8
SONARS: Westinghouse SQS-510,
hull-mounted; GD CDC SQR-501
CANTASS towed array
EW: MEL/Lockheed Canews
SLQ-501, SRD 502, AN/ULR-501
(sea search) ESM; MEL/Lockheed
Ramses SLQ-503 ECM

AIR SUPPORT:
HELICOPTERS: One Sikorsky
CH-124A ASW or one CH-124B
Heltas Sea King

Jacob van Heemskerck CHILE

Witte de With

- Continuous maindeck from stem to stern
- No weapons on forecastle
- Sea Sparrow SAM octuple launcher in 'B' mounting position
- Forward superstructure has large pyramid enclosed mast at after end supporting Signaal smart 3D air/surface search radar aerial
- Pole mast immediately aft of mainmast
- Harpoon angled quad SSM launchers immediately aft of mainmast
- Prominent spherical SATCOM domes at port and startboard on raised platforms aft of mainmast
- Large funnel with sloping top just aft of midships
- After superstructure with raised forward section supporting large LW08 air-search radar aerial at forward end and STIR 240 fire control radar aft
- Standard SM-1MR SAM launcher aft of raised superstructure
- Goalkeeper CIWS mounting on quarterdeck

NOTE: *Jacob van Heemskerck* transferred to Chile 12/05 and *Witte de With* is due to be transferred 6/06

SPECIFICATION:

COUNTRY OF ORIGIN: Netherlands
CLASS: Jacob van Heemskerck (FFG)
ACTIVE: 2
NAME (PENNANT NUMBER):
Latorre (ex-*Jacob van Heemskerck*)
(ex-F 812), — (ex-*Witte de With*)
(ex-F 813)

FEATURES:

DISPLACEMENT: 3750 tons full load
LENGTH: 428 ft (130.5 m)
BEAM: 47.9 ft (14.6 m)
DRAUGHT: 14.1 ft (4.3 m)
SPEED: 30 kts
RANGE: 4700 miles at 16 kts

ARMAMENT:

MISSILES: SSM – eight McDonnell
Douglas Harpoon (2 quad)
launchers; SAM – 40 GDC Pomona
Standard SM-1MR, Mk 13 Mod 1
launcher, Raytheon Sea Sparrow
Mk 29 octuple launcher
GUNS: One Signaal SGE-30 Goal-
keeper CIWS with General Electric
30 mm; two Oerlikon 20 mm
TORPEDOES: Four 324 mm US
Mk 32 (2 twin) tubes; Honeywell
Mk 46 Mod 5
DECOYS: Two Loral Hycor SRBOC
6-barrel Mk 36 (quad) launchers

ELECTRONICS:

RADARS: Air-search – Signaal
LW08; air/surface search –
Signaal SMART, 3D; surface search
– Signaal Scout; fire control –
two Signaal STIR 240, Signaal
STIR 180
SONARS: Westinghouse SQS-509
hull-mounted, active
search/attack
EW: Ramses ESM/ECM

Karel Doorman CHILE, NETHERLANDS

Van Nes (*Michael Nitz*)

- Continuous maindeck from stem to stern
- 3 in gun mounting in 'A' position
- High forward super-structure topped by tall enclosed mainmast at after end supporting smart air/surface search radar aerial
- Squat, square shaped funnel with sloping after end, just aft of midships
- After superstructure has distinctive pedestal mounted LWO8 air-search radar aerial at forward end. Small, white SATCOM dome immediately forward
- Large hangar with Goalkeeper CIWS mounting atop at after end
- Long flight deck with open quarterdeck below

SPECIFICATION:

COUNTRY OF ORIGIN: Netherlands
CLASS: Karel Doorman (FFG)
ACTIVE: 1 Chile, 7 Netherlands
NAME (PENNANT NUMBER):
CHILE – Almirante Blanco
Encalada (ex-*Abraham van der Hulst*) (ex-F 832)
NETHERLANDS – Karel Doorman
(F 827), Willem van der Zaan
(F 829), Tjerk Hiddes (F 830), Van
Amstel (F 831), Van Nes (F 833), Van
Galen (F 834), Van Speijk (F 828)

FEATURES:

DISPLACEMENT: 3320 tons full load
LENGTH: 401.2 ft (122.3 m) oa
BEAM: 47.2 ft (14.4 m)
DRAUGHT: 14.1 ft (4.3 m)
SPEED: 30 kts
RANGE: 5000 miles at 18 kts

ARMAMENT:

MISSILES: SSM – McDonnell
Douglas Harpoon Block 1C
(2 quad) launchers; SAM –
Raytheon Sea Sparrow Mk 48
vertical launchers
GUNS: One OTO Melara 3 in
(76 mm)/62 Compact Mk 100;
one Signaal SGE-30 Goalkeeper
with General Electric 30 mm;
two Oerlikon 20 mm
TORPEDOES: Four 324 mm US
Mk 32 (2 twin) tubes (mounted
inside the after superstructure);
Honeywell Mk 46 Mod 5
DECOYS: Two Loral Hycor SRBOC
6-barrel Mk 36 (quad) fixed
launchers; SLQ-25 Nixie towed
torpedo decoy

ELECTRONICS:

RADARS: Air/surface search –
Signaal SMART, 3D; air-search –
Signaal LWO8; surface search –
Signaal Scout; navigation – Racal
Decca 1226; fire control – two
Signaal STIR
SONARS: Signaal PHS-36, hull-
mounted active search/attack;
Thomson-Sintra Anaconda DSBV
61, towed array
EW: Argo Apecs II ESM/ECM

AIR SUPPORT:

HELICOPTERS: One Westland
SH-14D Lynx (NAS 332SC Cougar
in Chile)

Leander CHILE, ECUADOR, INDIA, NEW ZEALAND, PAKISTAN

Almirante Lynch

- High forecastle, break at after end of bridge with continuous maindeck to stern
- 4.5 in gun twin mounting in 'A' position (MM 38 Exocet SSM launchers on forecastle in Ecuadorian ships)
- Substantial midships superstructure with tall enclosed mainmast aft of bridge
- Twin Matra Simbad SAM launchers atop bridge and at aft of superstructure in Ecuadorian units
- Single funnel just aft of bridge (extensions fitted to funnel uptakes on Canterbury)
- After superstructure has large enclosed aftermast atop (Chilean ships have MM 40 Exocet launchers adjacent to after superstructure (F 06, 07) and alongside funnel (F 08)
- Larger hangars for Chetak or Sea King helicopters in Indian ships *Taragiri* and *Vindhyagiri*
- Limbo A/S mortar on quarterdeck of Pakistani units

NOTE: India acquired Broad-beamed Leander frigate *Andromeda* in 1995 from UK and converted her into the training ship *Krishna* (F 46, ex-F 57). Armament reduced to two Bofors 40 mm/60

NOTE 2: The six 'Ahmad Yani' ('Van Speijk') class FFGs of the Indonesia Navy are based on Leander design and were acquired 1986-90 from the Netherlands

SPECIFICATION:

COUNTRY OF ORIGIN: UK
CLASS: Leander/Leander broad-
beamed/Nilgiri (FF/FFG)
ACTIVE: 3 Chile (broad-beamed
Leander/FFG), 2 Ecuador
(Leander/FFG), 5 India (Nilgiri/FF),
1 New Zealand (broad-beamed
Leander/FF), 1 Pakistan broad-
beamed Leander/FF)
NAME (PENNANT NUMBER):
CHILE – Almirante Condell (o6),
Almirante Lynch (07), Ministro
Zenteno (ex-Achilles) (o8, ex-F 12)
ECUADOR – Presidente Eloy Alfaro
(ex-Penelope) (FM 01, ex-F 127),
Moran Valverde (ex-Danae)
(FM 02, ex-F 42)
INDIA – Himgiri (F 34), Udaygiri
(F 35), Dunagiri (F 36), Taragiri
(F 41), Vindhyagiri (F 42)
NEW ZEALAND – Canterbury (F 421)
PAKISTAN – Zulfiquar (ex-Apollo)
(F 262)

FEATURES:

DISPLACEMENT: 3200 tons full load
(Ecuador); 2945 tons (broad-
beamed); 2962 tons (Chile, India
Pakistan); 3093 tons (India F 41-42)
LENGTH: 372 ft (113.4 m) oa
BEAM: 41 ft (12.5 m); 43 ft (13.1 m)
(broad-beamed, Chile); 36.1 ft
(11 m) (India); 44.3 ft (13.5 m)
(India F 41-42)
DRAUGHT: 18 ft (5.6 m) (screws)
SPEED: 28 kts; 27 kts (Chile)
RANGE: 5500 miles at 15 kts (NZ);
4000 miles at 15 kts (Ecuador,
Pakistan); 4500 miles at 12 kts
(Chile, India)

ARMAMENT:

MISSILES: SSM – four MM 38/40
Exocet (Chile), MM 38 Exocet
(Ecuador); SAM – Short Bros
Seacat GWS 22 quad launchers in
Chilean units, three twin Matra
Simbad launchers for Mistral,
Ecuadorian units only (no
missiles fitted in Indian, NZ
and Pakistan ships)
GUNS: Vickers 4.5 in (114 mm)/45
Mk 6 (twin) semi-automatic (not
Ecuador); two Bofors 40 mm/60
Mk 9 (Ecuador); one GE/GD
20 mm Vulcan Phalanx CIWS
Mk 15, Mod 11 (Chile); four
30 mm/65 (2 twin) AK 630 (India);
six 25 mm/60 (3 twin) (Pakistan);
two Oerlikon/BMARC 20 mm
GAM-BO1 (Ecuador); four
Oerlikon 20 mm Mk 9 (2 twin)
(Chile); two Oerlikon 20 mm/70
(India); four or six 12.7 mm
machine guns (NZ)
A/S MORTARS: UK MOD Mortar
Mk 10, 3-barrel (Pakistan); one
Limbo Mk 10 triple-tubed
launcher (India, except Taragiri
and Vindhyagiri which have
Bofors 375 mm twin-tubed
launcher); no mortars in
other units
TORPEDOES: Six 324 mm Mk 32
(2 triple) Honeywell Mk 46, Mod
2 (Chile and NZ only); six 324 mm
ILAS-3 (2 triple) tubes, Whitehead
A 244 (Ecuador and India, Taragiri
and Vindhyagiri only)

DECOYS: Two Loral Hycor SRBOC
Mk 36 6-barrel launchers (NZ,
four in Ecuador); Graseby Type
182 towed torpedo decoy
(Ecuador, NZ and Pakistan);
Graseby Type 738 towed torpedo
decoy (India); two Vickers Corvus
8-barrel chaff launchers (Chile,
Ecuador, Pakistan); Wallop
Barricade double layer chaff
launchers (Chile)

ELECTRONICS:

RADARS: Air-search – Marconi
Type 965/966 (Chile, Ecuador,
Pakistan), Signaal LWo8 (NZ),
Signaal LWo4 (India); surface
search – Marconi Type 992 Q or
Plessey Type 994 (F o8) (Chile),
Plessey Type 994 (Ecuador,
Pakistan, NZ), Signaal DAo5
(India); navigation – one Kelvin
Hughes Type 1006 (Chile,
Ecuador, NZ, Pakistan), Kelvin
Hughes Type 1007 (Pakistan),
Decca 1226, Signaal ZW o6
(India); fire control – RCA TR 76
(NZ), Plessey Type 903/904, (Chile,
Pakistan), Signaal M45 (India),
Selenia (Ecuador)
SONARS: Graseby Type 184M/P,
hull-mounted, active search/
attack; Graseby Type 170 B, hull-
mounted, active; Kelvin Hughes
Type 162M hull-mounted,
sideways-looking (Chile, Pakistan);
Graseby Type 184P/Kelvin Hughes
Type 162M (Ecuador, Pakistan);
Westinghouse SQS-505/Graseby
750 (India); Westinghouse VDS in
first two Indian ships; Thomson
Diodon (India, F41-42); Graseby
Type 750 (NZ)
EW: Elta (Chile); Elisra NS-9010
ESM, Type 667/668 ECM (Ecuador);
UA-8/9/13 ESM, Type 668 ECM
(Pakistan); Argo Phoenix
ESM/ECM (NZ); Bharat Ajanta ESM;
Racal Cutlass ESM (India)

AIR SUPPORT:

HELICOPTERS: One Bell 206B
JetRanger (ASW) or Nurtanio NAS
332C Cougar (ASV/ASW) (Chile);
Bell 206B (Ecuador); one HAL
SA 319B Chetak (Alouette III) (ASW)
in Indian ships; one Sea King
Mk 42A (ASW) in Taragiri and
Vindhyagiri; one Kaman SH-2G
Seasprite (NZ); one Aerospatiale
SA 319B Alouette III (ASW)
(Pakistan)

165

Jianghu I/II   CHINA, BANGLADESH, EGYPT

Zhaoqing (*Jianghu I*)

- Long slim hull with a high bow, low in water
- 3.9 in gun single or twin mounting in 'A' position (Creusot-Loire 3.9 in gun in 'Jianghu II'; Egyptian ships have 57 mm/70 twin mounting)
- Squat rounded funnel aft of midships
- Box-like HY-2 SSM launchers forward and aft of funnel (only one in 'Jianghu II', forward of funnel)
- Tall lattice mainmast aft of forward superstructure
- Two 37 mm/63 gun mountings forward of bridge, two outboard of mainmast (in some) and two atop after superstructure in 'x' position (in some) (*Dongguan* has 37 mm/63 turrets in 'B' and 'x' positions. In 'Jianghu II', 'x' position mounting omitted in lieu of helicopter hangar; 37 mm/63 gun mountings just aft of funnel)
- 3.9 in twin gun mounting in 'Y' position (omitted in 'Jianghu II', in lieu of flight deck). Egyptian ships have 57 mm/70 twin gun mountings in 'Y' position

NOTE: There are several variants of the 'Jianghu I' class, but the basic outline is similar

NOTE 2: 'Jianghu II' are similar to 'Jianghu I' class except that aft of the funnel, is a through deck with hangar forward of flight deck

SPECIFICATION:

COUNTRY OF ORIGIN: China
CLASS: Jianghu I/II (Type 053)
(FFG)
ACTIVE: 1 Bangladesh (Osman
Jianghu I/Type 053 H1), 27 China
(Jianghu I), 1 China (Jianghu II),
2 Egypt (Jianghu I)
NAME (PENNANT NUMBER):
BANGLADESH – Osman
(ex-*Xiangtan*) (F 18, ex-556)
CHINA – (JIANGHU I): Chang De
(509), Shaoxing (510), Nantong
(511), Wuxi (512), Huayin (513),
Zhenjiang (514), Xiamen (515),
Jiujiang (516), Nanping (517), Jian
(518), Changzhi (519), Ningpo
(533), Jinhua (534), Dandong (543),
Linfen (545), Maoming (551), Yibin
(552), Shaoguan (553), Anshun
(554), Zhaotong (555), Jishou (557),
Zigong (558), Kangding (559),
Dongguan (560), Shantou (561),
Jiangmen (562), Zhaoqing (563);
(JIANGHU II): Siping (544)
EGYPT – Najim al Zaffer (951),
El Nasser (956)

FEATURES:

DISPLACEMENT: 1702 tons full
load; 1865 tons ('Jianghu II')
LENGTH: 338.5 ft (103.2 m)
BEAM: 35.4 ft (10.8 m)
DRAUGHT: 10.2 ft (3.1 m)
SPEED: 26 kts
RANGE: 4000 miles at 15 kts

ARMAMENT:

MISSILES: SSM – four HY-2 (C-201)
(2 twin) launchers (CSSC-3
Seersucker) (1 twin in 'Jianghu II')
GUNS: Two or four China 3.9 in
(100 mm)/56 (2 twin); one
Creusot-Loire 3.9 in (100 mm)/55
('Jianghu II'); four China 57 mm/
70 (2 twin) in Egyptian ships;
12 China 37 mm/63 (6 twin)
(eight (4 twin) in some
Chinese units)
TORPEDOES: Six 324 mm ILAS
(2 triple) tubes ('Jianghu II'); Yu-2
(Mk 46 Mod 1) (none in 'Jianghu I',
Bangladesh or Egypt)
A/S MORTARS: Two RBU 1200
5-tubed fixed launchers (four
in some)

DEPTH CHARGES: Two BMB-2
projectors; two racks (none in
'Jianghu II')
MINES: Up to 60 can be carried
(none in 'Jianghu II')
DECOYS: Two SRBOC 6-barrel
Mk 33 chaff launchers or two
China 26-barrel launchers;
two Loral Hycor SRBOC Mk 36
6-barrel chaff launchers
(Bangladesh ship) ('Jianghu I/II')

ELECTRONICS:

RADARS: Air-search – Type 517
Knife Rest (not in 'Jianghu II');
air/surface search – MX 902
Eye Shield (Type 354), Type 765
(Egypt), Rice Screen/Shield in
Chinese units, *Zigong* onwards;
surface search/fire control –
Square Tie (352); navigation –
Don 2 or Fin Curve or Racal
Decca (Decca RM 1290A, Egypt);
fire control – Type 347G Rice
Lamp (in some), Type 343 (Wok
Won) (Wasp Head) in some,
Fog Lamp (Egypt)
SONARS: Echo Type 5; hull-
mounted, active search/attack
EW: Jug Pair or Watch Dog ESM
(Elettronica Beta or Litton Triton
ESM/ECM, Egypt)

AIR SUPPORT:

HELICOPTERS: Harbin Z-9C
Haitun (Dauphin 2) (ASV, in
'Jianghu I')

Jianghu III CHINA

Huangshi (*Ships of The World*)

- High bow, with 3.9 in gun twin mounting in 'A' position
- Maindeck higher in the midships section
- Forward superstructure with enclosed mainmast at after end, enclosed lower section lattice top
- Large, low funnel aft of midships with ship's boats in davits outboard
- Two 37 mm/63 gun mountings forward of bridge and two at after end of maindeck level, port and starboard, outboard of short mast with Rice Lamp fire control radar atop
- Distinctive 'x' shape communications aerial aft of funnel on short lattice mast
- YJ-1 SSM launchers in pairs, trained outboard, port and starboard, forward and aft of funnel
- 3.9 in gun twin mounting in 'Y' position

NOTE: See modified 'Jianghu III', 'Chao Phraya' class of Thailand on page 224

NOTE 2: CIWS PL 8H (combined gun/SAM) may be mounted instead of some of the 37 mm guns

SPECIFICATION:

COUNTRY OF ORIGIN: China
CLASS: Jianghu III (Type 053 HT) (FFG)
ACTIVE: 1
NAME (PENNANT NUMBER): Huangshi (535)

FEATURES:
DISPLACEMENT: 1924 tons full load
LENGTH: 338.5 ft (103.2 m)
BEAM: 35.4 ft (10.8 m)
DRAUGHT: 10.2 ft (3.1 m)
SPEED: 28 kts
RANGE: 4000 miles at 15 kts

ARMAMENT:
MISSILES: SSM – eight YJ-1 (Eagle Strike) (C-801) (CSS-N-4 Sardine), Jianghu IV fitted for improved C-802 (CSS-N-8 Saccade)
GUNS: Four China 3.9 in (100 mm)/56 (2 twin); eight China 37 mm/63 (4 twin)
A/S MORTARS: Two RBU 1200 5-tubed launchers
DEPTH CHARGES: Two BMB-2 projectors; two racks
MINES: Can carry up to 60
DECOYS: Two China 26-barrel chaff launchers

ELECTRONICS:
RADARS: Air-search – Type 517 Knife Rest; air/surface search – MX 902 Eye Shield (Type 354); surface search/fire control – Square Tie (Type 352); navigation – Fin Curve; fire control – Rice Lamp (Type 347G), Type 343G (Wok Won) (Wasp Head)
SONARS: Echo Type 5; hull-mounted active search/attack
EW: Elettronica Newton ESM; Elettronica 929 (Type 981) ECM

Jiangkai CHINA

Maanshan

- High pronounced bow with distinctive tumblehome
- 3.9 in gun in 'A' position
- HQ-7 SAM on raised platform abaft 3.9 in gun
- Main deck higher in midships section
- Forward superstructure with large enclosed mainmast at aft end
- SSM launchers between forward superstructure and funnel, facing out to port and starboard
- Enclosed aftermast built into forward part of funnel and supporting large spherical radome
- Fire control radar mounted on top of hangar aft
- Flight deck on quarterdeck aft

SPECIFICATION:

COUNTRY OF ORIGIN: China
CLASS: Jiangkai (Type 054)
ACTIVE: 2
BUILDING: 1
NAME (PENNANT NUMBER):
Maanshan (525), Wenzhou (526),
— (—)

FEATURES:
DISPLACEMENT: 3900 tons full load
LENGTH: 433.2 ft (132 m)
BEAM: 49.2 ft (15 m)
DRAUGHT: 16.4 ft (5 m)
SPEED: 27 kts
RANGE: 3800 miles at 18 kts

ARMAMENT:
MISSILES: SSM – eight C-802
(Saccade); SAM – one HQ-7
(Crotale)
GUNS: One 3.9 in (100 mm)/56;
four 300 mm/65 AK 630
TORPEDOES: Six 324 mm B515;
Yu-2/6/7
DECOYS: To be announced

ELECTRONICS:
RADARS: Air/surface search – Type
363S Sea Tiger; surface search
Type 364 Seagull; fire control –
Type 344 (MR 34), Type 345 (MR
35), Type 347G Rice Lamp
SONARS: To be announced
EW: To be announced

Jiangwei I/II CHINA

Huainan

* Long forecastle, one third length of ship (shorter forecastle in 'Jiangwei II')
* Weapons on forecastle of 'Jiangwei I' from forward to aft, RBU 1000 A/S mortar launcher, 3.9 in gun twin mounting and HQ-61 SAM tubular launchers in two banks
* 'Jiangwei II' has rounded turret for 3.9 gun twin mounting; HQ-7 SAM box launcher in raised 'B' position
* Stepped superstructure with 37 mm/63 gun mountings, port and starboard, outboard at forward end of bridge
* Large fire control radome atop bridge (Type 347G director in 'Jiangwei II')
* Mainmast, enclosed bottom lattice topped by Knife Rest air/surface search radar, at after end of forward superstructure (more hidden in 'Jiangwei II')
* Single, squat funnel just aft of midships
* Ship's boats in davits, port and starboard, adjacent to funnel
* YJ-1 SSM angled triple launchers forward (trained to starboard) and aft (trained to port) of funnel
* Large hangar with flight deck right aft and open quarterdeck below (37 mm/63 Type 76A mounting atop hangar in 'Jiangwei II', outboard of hangar on sponsons, 'Jiangwei I')

SPECIFICATION:

COUNTRY OF ORIGIN: China
CLASS: Jiangwei I/II (Type 053/053 H2G) (FFG)
ACTIVE: 4 (Jiangwei I), 8 (Jiangwei II)
BUILDING: 2 (Jiangwei II)
NAME (PENNANT NUMBER):
JIANGWEI I – Anqing (539), Huainan (540) (548 out of area), Huaibei (541), Tongling (542)
JIANGWEI II – Jiaxin (521, ex-597), Lianyungang (522), Sanming (523), Putian (524), Yichang (564), Yulin (565), Yuxi (566), — (527), — (528)

FEATURES:

DISPLACEMENT: 2250 tons full load
LENGTH: 366.5 ft (111.7 m)
BEAM: 39.7 ft (12.1 m)
DRAUGHT: 15.7 ft (4.8 m)
SPEED: 25 kts
RANGE: 4000 miles at 18 kts

ARMAMENT:

MISSILES: SSM – six YJ-1 (Eagle Strike) (C-801) or C-802 (2 triple) launchers; SAM – one HQ-61 sextuple launcher ('Jiangwei I'), HQ-7 Crotale octuple launcher ('Jiangwei II')
GUNS: Two China 3.9 in (100 mm)/56 (twin); eight China 37 mm/63 Type 76A (4 twin)
A/S MORTARS: Two Type 87 6-tubed launchers ('Jiangwei I'; two RBU 1200 5-tubed fixed launchers ('Jiangwei II')
DECOYS: Two SRBOC Mk 33 6-barrel chaff launchers ('Jiangwei I'); two China Type 945 26-barrel launchers

ELECTRONICS:

RADARS: Air-search – Type 517 Knife Rest ('Jiangwei I and II'); air/surface search – Type 360 Seagull S ('Jiangwei II'); fire control – Type 343 (Wok Won) (Wasp Head) ('Jiangwei I'), Type 347G Rice Lamp, Fog Lamp; navigation – Racal Decca 1290 and China Type 360
SONARS: Echo Type 5; hull-mounted, active search/attack
EW: RWD-8 ESM, NJ 81-3 ECM ('Jiangwei I'); SR-210 ESM, 981-3, RWD-8 ECM ('Jiangwei II')

AIR SUPPORT:

HELICOPTERS: One Harbin Z-9C

Type FS 1500 COLOMBIA, MALAYSIA
Almirante Padilla

SPECIFICATION:

COUNTRY OF ORIGIN: Germany
CLASS: Almirante Padilla (Type
FS 1500) (FL), Kasturi (FSG)
ACTIVE: 4 Columbia, 2 Malaysia*
* Rated as corvettes
NAME (PENNANT NUMBER):
COLUMBIA – Almirante Padilla
(FL 51), Caldas (FL 52), Antioquia
(FL 53), Independiente (FL 54)
MALAYSIA – Kasturi (25), Lekir (26)

FEATURES:
DISPLACEMENT: 2100 tons full load
(Colombia); 1850 tons (Malaysia)
LENGTH: 325.1 ft (99.1 m); 319.1 ft
(97.3 m) (Malaysia)
BEAM: 37.1 ft (11.3 m)
DRAUGHT: 12.1 ft (3.7 m); 11.5 ft
(3.5 m) (Malaysia)
SPEED: 27 kts; 28 kts (Malaysia)
RANGE: 7000 miles at 14 kts;
5000 miles at 14 kts (Malaysia)

ARMAMENT:
MISSILES: SSM – eight MM 40
Exocet (Colombia); SAM – two
Simbad (Mistral) (twin launchers)
(Colombia)
GUNS: One OTO Melara 3 in (76
mm)/ 62 Compact; one Creusot-
Loire 3.9 in (100 mm)/55 Mk 2
Compact (Malaysia); two Breda
40 mm/70 (twin) (Colombia); one
Bofors 57 mm/70 and four Emerson
Electric 30 mm (2 twin) (Malaysia)
TORPEDOES: Six 324 mm Mk 32
(2 triple) tubes (none Malaysia)
A/S MORTARS: One 375 mm twin
trainable launcher (Malaysia only)
DECOYS: One CSEE Dagaie
double mounting (two Malaysia)

ELECTRONICS:
RADARS: Air/surface search – Sea
Tiger, DA08 (Malaysia); navigation
– Kelvin Hughes 1007 (Malaysia),
Furuno (Colombia); fire control –
Castor II B, WM22 (Malaysia)
SONARS: ASO-4-2, hull-mounted;
DSQS-21C, hull-mounted (Malaysia)
EW: Argo AC672 ESM; Scimitar
ECM; Rapids ESM; Scimitar ECM
(Malaysia)

AIR SUPPORT:
HELICOPTERS: One MBB BO 105CB,
(ASW); platform for one medium
(Malaysia)

- Low forecastle with break up to high midships maindeck and down to short quarterdeck
- 3 in gun mounting (Colombian ships), 3.9 in gun mounting (Malaysian ships), in 'A' position
- Bofors twin 375 mm A/s mortar in 'B' position in Malaysian ships with prominent angled screen
- Tall flat fronted bridge structure with large enclosed mainmast at after end. Pole mast atop after end of mainmast. WM 22 radome atop mainmast in Malaysian ships
- Large, tapered funnel with wedge shaped smoke deflector atop
- Exocet SSM launchers between funnel and forward superstructure
- Flight deck aft of after superstructure at main deck level
- 40 mm/70 gun mounting in 'Y' position (Colombian ships). 57 mm/70 mounting in Malaysian ships
- DA 08 air/surface search radar aerial on raised platform atop after superstructure in Malaysian ships

Niels Juel DENMARK

Olfert Fischer

- Unusual profile and easily identified frigate
- Low forecastle with 3 in gun mounting in 'A' position
- High midships maindeck section, slab-sided
- Unusually robust enclosed mainmast amidships, supporting 9GR 600 surface search radar aerial, on forward gantry, and DASA TRS-3D air-search radar atop
- Large, black-capped funnel with sloping top sited well aft of midships
- Harpoon SSM angled launchers, port and starboard, aft of funnel
- Two fire control directors mounted on sturdy pedestals aft of bridge and forward of quarterdeck
- Sea Sparrow SAM octuple or VLS modular launcher on quarterdeck

SPECIFICATION:

COUNTRY OF ORIGIN: Denmark
CLASS: Niels Juel (FFG)
ACTIVE: 3
NAME (PENNANT NUMBER): Niels Juel (F 354), Olfert Fischer (F 355), Peter Tordenskiold (F 356)

FEATURES:

DISPLACEMENT: 1320 tons full load
LENGTH: 275.5 ft (84 m)
BEAM: 33.8 ft (10.3 m)
DRAUGHT: 10.2 ft (3.1 m)
SPEED: 28 kts
RANGE: 2500 miles at 18 kts

ARMAMENT:

MISSILES: SSM – eight McDonnell Douglas Harpoon (2 quad) launchers; SAM – 12 (sextuple) Raytheon NATO Sea Sparrow MK 48 or Mk 56 VLS modular launchers, four Stinger mountings (2 twin)
GUNS: One OTO Melara 3 in (76 mm)/62 Compact; four Oerlikon 20 mm (one each side of the funnel, two abaft the mast) can be fitted, to be replaced by two 12.7 mm machine guns
DEPTH CHARGES: One rack
DECOYS: Two DL-12T Sea Gnat 12-barrel chaff launchers

ELECTRONICS:

RADARS: Air-search – TRS-3D; surface search – 9GR 600; navigation – Terma Scanter Mil 009; fire control – two Mk 95 (SAM), 9LV 200 Mk 1 Rakel 203C (guns, SSM)
SONARS: Plessey PMS 26; hull-mounted, active search/attack

Thetis DENMARK

Hvidbjørnen

- Short forecastle with 3 in gun mounting in 'A' position
- High, slab-sided midships section
- Large enclosed mainmast at after end of forward superstructure with distinctive AWS 6 air/surface search radome atop
- Large, very squat, black-capped funnel amidships
- Ship's boats in davits outboard of funnel, port and starboard
- Long flight deck with domed SATCOM aerial on pedestal atop hangar roof

SPECIFICATION:

COUNTRY OF ORIGIN: Denmark
CLASS: Thetis (FF)
ACTIVE: 4
NAME (PENNANT NUMBER): Thetis (F 357), Triton (F 358), Vaedderen (F 359), Hvidbjørnen (F 360)

FEATURES:

DISPLACEMENT: 3500 tons full load
LENGTH: 369.1 ft (112.5 m) oa
BEAM: 47.2 ft (14.4 m)
DRAUGHT: 19.7 ft (6 m)
SPEED: 20 kts
RANGE: 8500 miles at 15.5 kts

ARMAMENT:

MISSILES: SAM – four Stinger (2 twin)
GUNS: One OTO Melara 3 in (76 mm)/62 Super Rapid
DEPTH CHARGES: Two rails (door in stern)
DECOYS: Two DL-12T Sea Gnat 12-barrel chaff/IR flares

ELECTRONICS:

RADARS: Air/surface search – Plessey AWS 6; surface search – Furuno 2135; navigation – Furuno 2115; fire control – CelsuisTech 9LV Mk 3
SONARS: Thomson-Sintra TSM 2640 Salmon; hull-mounted and VDS
EW: Racal Sabre ESM

AIR SUPPORT:

HELICOPTERS: One Westland Lynx Mk 91 (surface search)

NOTE: Thetis has a modified stern for seismological equipment

173

Descubierta   EGYPT, MOROCCO, SPAIN

Descubierta

SPECIFICATION:

COUNTRY OF ORIGIN: Spain
CLASS: Descubierta/Modified
Descubierta (FFG)
ACTIVE: 2 Egypt, 1 Morocco
(modified Descubierta), 6 Spain
NAME (PENNANT NUMBER):
EGYPT – Abu Qir (ex-*Serviola*)
(F 941), El Suez (ex-*Centinela*)
(F 946)
MOROCCO – Lieutenant Colonel
Errahamani (501)
SPAIN – Descubierta (P 75,
ex-F 31), Diana (M 11, ex-F 32),
Infanta Elena (F 33), Infanta
Cristina (P 77, ex-F 34), Cazadora
(P 78, ex-F 35), Vencedora (P 79,
ex-F 36)

- Short forecastle with 3 in gun mounting in 'A' position
- Distinctive Bofors 375 mm A/S mortar mounting forward of bridge in 'B' mounting position
- Short forward superstructure with pyramid mainmast at after end. WM 22/41 or WM 25/41 fire control radome atop; surface search ZW 06 radar on forward gantry
- Harpoon SSM angled launchers between mainmast and funnels (Spain and Egypt); MM 38 Exocet in Moroccan ship
- Unusual, black-capped 'V' formation funnels amidships with a large aerial atop each one
- Short aftermast aft of funnels supporting DA 05 air/surface search radar aerial
- Two 40 mm/70 gun mountings, on two levels, aft of aftermast (Breda/Bofors turrets, Morocco)
- Aspide SAM Albatros octuple box launcher on afterdeck in 'Y' position

FEATURES:

DISPLACEMENT: 1666 tons full
load (Spain); 1479 tons (Egypt,
Morocco)
LENGTH: 291.3 ft (88.8 m)
BEAM: 34 ft (10.4 m)
DRAUGHT: 12.5 ft (3.8 m)
SPEED: 25 kts
RANGE: 4000 miles at 18 kts

ARMAMENT:

MISSILES: SSM – eight Harpoon
(2 quad) launchers (normally two
pairs are embarked) (MM 38
Exocet, Morocco); SAM – Albatros
octuple launcher, Aspide
GUNS: One OTO Melara 3 in (76 mm)
/62 Compact; one or two Bofors
40 mm/70; two Oerlikon 20 mm
(Spain, P 75, P 77–P 79 and M 11)
TORPEDOES: Six 324 mm US
Mk 32 (2 triple) tubes; Mk 46
Mod 5 Neartip (Spain) (Mod 1,
Morocco); Stingray (Egypt)
A/S MORTARS: One 375 mm twin-
barrel, trainable launcher
DECOYS: Two SRBOC 6-barrel Mk 36;
two Dagaie launchers (Morocco)

ELECTRONICS:

RADARS: Air/surface search –
DAO5/2; surface search – ZW06;
navigation – two Furuno (Spain);
fire control – WM 22/41 or
WM 25/41 system
SONARS: DE 1160B (F 33, Egypt
and Moocco), hull-mounted
Raytheon 1167 VDS (Egypt)
EW: Mk 1000 or Mk 1600 ESM,
Ceselsa Canopus or Mk 1900
ECM (Spain); Beta
ESM/ECM (Egypt); ELT 715
(Morocco) ESM/ECM

Knox EGYPT, GREECE, MEXICO, SPAIN, TAIWAN, THAILAND, TURKEY

Phuttha Loetla Naphalai

- Long forecastle with 5 in gun mounting well forward of ASROC A/S box missile launcher
- Very unusual and prominent large cylindrical mast and funnel combined amidships; air-search radar aerial at forward end and short lattice mast atop after end supporting large surface search radar aerial
- 'Baleares' class has prominent square air-search radar atop mast
- 'Baleares' class also has Harpoon launchers atop aft low superstructure, immediately aft of short lattice mast omitted from other 'Knox' class units
- CIWS in 'Y' position on 'Knox' class ships. Standard SAM launch in 'X' position at aft end of superstructure in 'Baleares' class
- Flight deck aft, except 'Baleares' class

NOTE: 'Baleares' class built in Spain after very close co-operation between Spain and the USA. 'Knox' class units transferred from the US Navy

NOTE 2: In Mexican hulls, SAM launcher only in Ignacio Allende in 'Y' position

contd.

Knox contd.

COUNTRY OF ORIGIN: USA/Spain

CLASS: Knox/Epirus/Baleares (F 70)/'Tepe' class (FF/FFG)

ACTIVE: 2 Egypt, 1 Greece ('Epirus' class), 4 Mexico (FF), 3 Spain ('Baleares' class), 8 Taiwan, 2 Thailand, 4 Turkey ('Tepe' class)

NAME (PENNANT NUMBER):

EGYPT – Damyat (ex-*Jesse L Brown*) (961, ex-FF 1089), Rasheed (ex-*Moinester*) (966, ex-FF 1097)

GREECE – Epirus (ex-*Connole*) (F 456, ex-FF 1056)

MEXICO – Ignacio Allende (ex-*Stein*) (E 50, ex-FF 1065), Mariano Abasolo (ex-*Marvin Shields*) (E 51, ex-FF 1066), Guadaloupe Victoria (ex-*Pharris*) (E 52, ex-FF 1094), Francisco Javier Mina (ex-*Whipple*) (F214, ex-FF 1062)

SPAIN – Andalucía (F 72), Asturias (F 74), Extremadura (F 75)

TAIWAN – Chin Yang (ex-*Robert E Peary*) (932, ex-FF 1073), Fong Yang (ex-*Brewton*) (933, ex-FF 1086), Feng Yang (ex-*Kirk*) (934, ex-FF 1087), Lan Yang (ex-*Joseph Hewes*) (935, ex-FF 1078), Hae Yang (ex-*Cook*) (936, ex-FF 1083), Hwai Yang (ex-*Barbey*) (937 ex-FF 1088), Ning Yang (ex-*Downes*) (938, ex-FF 1070), Yi Yang (ex-*Aylwin*) (939, ex-FF 1081)

THAILAND – Phuttha Yotfa Chulalok (ex-*Truett*) (461, ex-FF 1095), Phuttha Loetla Naphalai (ex-*Ouellet*) (462, ex-FF 1077)

TURKEY – Muavenet (ex-*Capodanno*) (F 250, ex-FF 1093), Zafer (ex-*Thomas C Hart*) (F 253, ex-FF 1092), Karadeniz (ex-*Donald B Beary*) (F 255, ex-FF 1085), Ege (ex-*Ainsworth*) (F 256, ex-FF 1090)

DISPLACEMENT: 4177 tons full load ('Baleares' class); 4260 tons ('Knox' class)

LENGTH: 438 ft (133.6 m) ('Baleares' class); 439.6 ft (134 m) ('Knox' class)

BEAM: 46.9 ft (14.3 m) ('Baleares' class); 46.8 ft (14.3 m) ('Knox' class)

DRAUGHT: 15.4 ft (4.7 m) ('Baleares' class); 15 ft (4.6 m) ('Knox' class)

SPEED: 28 kts ('Baleares' class); 27 kts ('Knox' class)

RANGE: 4000 miles at 22 kts; 4500 miles at 20 kts ('Baleares' class)

MISSILES: SSM – eight McDonnell Douglas Harpoon (four normally carried), (not carried in Mexican hulls); SAM – 16 GDC Pomona Standard SM-1MR, Mk 22 Mod 0 launcher ('Baleares' class, but see note); A/S – Honeywell ASROC Mk 112 octuple launcher; payload – Mk 46 torpedoes ('Baleares' class), ASROC Mk 16 octuple launcher (with two cells modified to fire Harpoon) ('Knox' class), Greek ships have four Stinger or Redeye SAM posts fitted

GUNS: One FMC 5 in (127 mm)/54 Mk 42 Mod 9 (all ships); two Bazán 20 mm/120 12-barrel Meroka ('Baleares' class); one GE/GD 20 mm/76 Vulcan Phalanx Mk 15 ('Knox' class, not Mexican); two Rheinmetall 20 mm; four 12.7 mm machine guns, (Greek ships); two 12.7 mm machine guns ('Baleares' class); four Type 75 20 mm (Taiwan)

TORPEDOES: Four 324 mm US Mk 32 (2 twin) tubes; Honeywell Mk 46 Mod 5 (all ships)

MINES: Rail for eight mines can be fitted in Greek ships

DECOYS: Four Loral Hycor SRBOC 6-barrelled Mk 36, (all ships); T Mk-6 Fanfare/SLQ-25 Nixie torpedo decoy; Prairie Masker hull and blade rate noise suppression ('Knox' class)

RADARS: Air-search – Hughes SPS-52B, 3D ('Baleares' class), Lockheed SPS-40B/D ('Knox' class); surface search – Raytheon SPS-10 ('Baleares' class), SPS-10 or Norden SPS-67 ('Knox' class); navigation – Raytheon Marine Pathfinder ('Baleares' class), Marconi LN66 ('Knox' class); fire control – Western Electric SPG-53B, Raytheon SPG-51C, Selenia RAN 12L, two Sperry VPS 2 ('Baleares' class), SPG-53A/D/F ('Knox' class)

SONARS: Raytheon SQS-56 (DE 1160), hull-mounted; EDO SQS-35V VDS ('Baleares' class); EDO/GE SQS-26CX ('Knox' class); EDO SQR-18(V) TACTASS (Thailand); EDO SQS-35 (Greece)

EW: SLQ-32(V)2 ESM/ECM ('Knox' class); Ceselsa Deneb or Mk 1600 ESM, Ceselsa Canopus or Mk 1900 ECM ('Baleares' class)

HELICOPTERS: One Kaman SH-2G Seasprite (Egypt); one Agusta AB 212 (ASW) (Greece); one MBB BO 105CB (Patrol) (Mexico); one Hughes MD 500 (short-range ASW) (Taiwan); one Bell 212 (Thailand); one Agusta AB 212 (ASW) (Turkey)

Modified Hvidbjørnen ESTONIA

Admiral Pitka (*Harald Caestens*)

- Short forecastle with maindeck line dipping to superstructure
- 3 in gun mounting on forecastle approximately mid-point between bow and bridge
- Single black-capped tapering funnel amidships
- Mast atop bridge superstructure topped by prominent bulbous radome
- Short pylon mast on after superstructure
- Flight deck right aft above open quarterdeck

NOTE: Transferred by gift from Denmark in July 2000. Strengthened for ice operations

SPECIFICATION:

COUNTRY OF ORIGIN: Denmark
CLASS: Modified Hvidbjørnen (FF)
ACTIVE: 1
NAME (PENNANT NUMBER):
Admiral Pitka (ex-*Beskytteren*)
(A 230)

FEATURES:
DISPLACEMENT: 1970 tons
full load
LENGTH: 245 ft (74.7 m)
BEAM: 40 ft (12.2 m)
DRAUGHT: 17.4 ft (5.3 m) (keel)
SPEED: 18 kts
RANGE: 6000 miles at 13 kts

ARMAMENT:
GUNS: One USN 3 in (76 mm)/50
Mk 22

ELECTRONICS:
RADARS: Litton Marine;
nagivation – two Litton Decca
EW: Racal Cutlass ESM

AIR SUPPORT:
HELICOPTERS: Platform for one
Westland Lynx type

Floréal FRANCE, MOROCCO

Germinal

- Low forecastle with 3.9 in gun mounting raised above in 'B' position. (Probably 76 mm in Moroccan hulls)
- High central superstructure with complex enclosed mainmast at after end of bridge
- Unusual, twin, rectangular side-by-side funnels with exhausts protruding at top
- Exocet SSM angled launchers sited between funnel and mainmast
- Syracuse II SATCOM atop slab-sided platform adjacent funnels (missing in Moroccan hulls)
- 20 mm gun mounting on hangar roof
- Long flight deck with break down to small quarterdeck
- Ship's boat in starboard side davits adjacent to SSM launcher

SPECIFICATION:

COUNTRY OF ORIGIN: France
CLASS: Floréal (FFG)
ACTIVE: 6 France, 2 Morocco
NAME (PENNANT NUMBER):
FRANCE – Floréal (F 730), Prairial (F 731), Nivôse (F 732), Ventôse (F 733), Vendémaire (F 734), Germinal (F 735)
MOROCCO – Mohammed V (611), Hassan II (612)

FEATURES:

DISPLACEMENT: 2950 tons full load
LENGTH: 306.8 ft (93.5 m)
BEAM: 45.9 ft (14.4 m)
DRAUGHT: 14.1 ft (4.3 m)
SPEED: 20 kts
RANGE: 10,000 miles at 15 kts

ARMAMENT:

MISSILES: SSM – two Aerospatiale MM 38 Exocet; SAM – one or two Matra Simbad twin launchers can replace 20 mm guns or Dagaie launcher
GUNS: One DCN 3.9 in (100 mm)/55 Mod 68 CADAM (one OTOBreda 76 mm/62 in Moroccan hulls); two Giat 20 F2 20 mm
DECOYS: One or two CSEE Dagaie Mk II; 10-barrel trainable chaff/IR launchers

ELECTRONICS:

RADARS: Air/surface search – Thomson-CSF Mars DRBV 21A, Thales WM 28 (Morocco); navigation – two Racal Decca 1229 (DRBN 34A), two Decca Bridgemaster (Morocco)
EW: Thomson-CSF ARBR 17 ESM

AIR SUPPORT:

HELICOPTERS: One Aerospatiale AS 565MA Panther or platform for one AS 332F Super Puma

Multi Mission Frigate FRANCE, ITALY

Model of Multi Mission Frigate

- All external equipment and upper deck fittings concealed or placed in low positions
- Main gun in 'A' position
- High flush central superstructure with short cylindrical mainmast on top of bridge

NOTE: All superstructure inclined to reduce radar echo

SPECIFICATION:

COUNTRY OF ORIGIN: France, Italy
CLASS: Multi Mission Frigate
ACTIVE: 0
BUILDING: 8 France, 4 Italy
PLANNED: 9 France, 3 Italy
NAME (PENNANT NUMBER): FRANCE – None allocated
ITALY – None allocated

FEATURES:

DISPLACEMENT: 5700 tons full load (approx); 5750 tons (Italy)
LENGTH: 459.3 ft (140 m); 456 ft (139 m) Italy
BEAM: 62.3 ft (19 m)
DRAUGHT: 16.4 ft (5 m)
SPEED: 27 kts
RANGE: 6000 miles at 18 kts; 6000 miles at 15 kts (Italy)

ARMAMENT:

MISSILES: SSM – eight Exocet MM 40, four (eight in GP variant) Teseo Mk 2 (Italy); SLCM – 16-cell Sylver A70 VLS for Scalp Naval (Italy to be decided); SAM – 16-cell Sylver A43 for Aster 15
GUNS: One OTO Melara 127 mm/64; one (two in Italian air defence) OTO Melara 76 mm; two 20 mm
TORPEDOES: Two Eurotorp TLS launchers (four (2 twin) in Italy); Eurotorp MU 90 Impact
A/S MORTARS: Four MILAS (ASW variant of Italy, none in rest or in France)

DECOYS: Two EADS NGDS 12-barrelled chaff launcher (France); two Breda SCLAR-H (Italy); SLAT anti-torpedo defence system

ELECTRONICS:

RADARS: Air/surface search – Thales Herakles 3D, Alenia EMPAR (Italy); surface search – to be decided, SPS 791 (Italy); navigation – two (to be decided); fire control – Alenia Marconi NA 25XP
SONARS: Thales 4110CL hull-mounted active; Thales Captas active/passive (only in ASW variant in Italy)
EW: To be decided

AIR SUPPORT:

HELICOPTERS: One NH 90 (for ASW variant of France); two NH 90 or one NH 90 plus one Merlin EH 101 in Italy

La Fayette   FRANCE, SAUDI ARABIA, TAIWAN

Surcouf

- 3.9 in gun mounting in 'A' position. OTO Melara 76 mm/62 in Taiwanese ships
- High, flush central superstructure with pyramid mainmast amidships. Short mainmast in Taiwanese ships
- Unusual forward-sloping mast and funnel combined, supporting ESM aerial (SATCOM on forward gantry in French ships)
- Saudi ships have additional two pylon masts on superstructure. First, atop forward superstructure, is squat, and supports air-search radar. Second, tall, cylindrical, aft of midships, with Thomson-CSF Arabel 3D surveillance/fire control radome atop
- Taiwanese hulls have shorter mast funnel, supporting distinctive air/surface radar. Second, squat mast aft with pole mast atop, with surface search and fire control radars on very chunky gantries facing aft
- Crotale Naval CN 2 SAM launcher at after end of main superstructure in French ships. CIWS in Taiwanese hulls
- Long flight deck right aft

NOTE: All superstructure inclines at 10° to the vertical to reduce radar echo area

180

NOTE 2: External equipment such as capstans and bollards are either hidden or installed as low as possible

NOTE 3: Unusual smooth uncluttered profile for a warship

NOTE 4: La Fayette will have short cylindrical mast, topped by a bulbous fire control radome after mid-life modernisation

SPECIFICATION:

COUNTRY OF ORIGIN: France
CLASS: La Fayette/Type F-3000S/ Arrivad (modified La Fayette)/ Kang Ding (Kwang Hua Project II) (FFG)
ACTIVE: 5 France, 6 Taiwan (Kang Ding), 3 Saudi Arabia (Type F-3000S)
ORDERED: 6 Singapore
NAME (PENNANT NUMBER):
FRANCE – La Fayette (F 710), Surcouf (F 711), Courbet (F 712), Aconite (ex-Jauréguiberry) (F 713), Guépratte (F 714)
SAUDI ARABIA – Al Ryadh (812), Makkah (814), Al Dammam (816)
TAIWAN – Kang Ding (1202), Si Ning (1203), Kun Ming (1205), Di Hua (1206), Wu Chang (1207), Chen Te (1208)

FEATURES:

DISPLACEMENT: 3750 tons full load (France); 3800 tons (Taiwan); 4650 tons (Saudi Arabia)
LENGTH: 407.5 ft (124.2 m) oa (France, Taiwan); 438.43 ft (133.6 m) (Saudi Arabia)
BEAM: 50.5 ft (15.4 m) (France, Taiwan); 56.4 ft (17.2 m) (Saudi Arabia)
DRAUGHT: 19 ft (5.8 m) (France); 18 ft (5.5 m) (Taiwan); 13.5 ft (4.1 m) (Saudi Arabia)
SPEED: 25 kts
RANGE: 9000 miles at 12 kts

ARMAMENT:

MISSILES: SSM – eight Aerospatiale MM 40 Block II Exocet (France and Saudi Arabia), Hsiung Feng II (2 quad) (Taiwan); SAM – Thomson-CSF Crotale Naval CN 2 octuple launcher (France), Eurosam SAAM octuple VLS for Aster 15 (Saudi Arabia), Sea Chaparral quad launcher (Taiwan)
GUNS: One DCN 3.9 in (100 mm)/55 Mod 68 CADAM (France); one OTO Melara 3 in (76 mm)/62 Super Rapid (Saudi Arabia); one OTO Melara 76 mm/62 Mk 75 (Taiwan); two Giat 20F2 20 mm; two 12.7 mm machine guns (France, Saudi Arabia); one Hughes 20 mm/76 Vulcan Phalanx Mk 15 Mod 2; two Bofors 40 mm/70; two CS 20 mm Type 75 (Taiwan)

TORPEDOES: Four 21 in (533 mm) tubes, ECAN F17P (Saudi Arabia); six 324 mm Mk 32 (2 triple) tubes, Alliant Mk 36 Mod 5 (Taiwan)
DECOYS: Two CSEE Dagaie Mk 2 10-barrel launchers (all ships); SLAT anti-wake homing torpedoes system (France, Saudi Arabia)

ELECTRONICS:

RADARS: Air/surface search – Thomson-CSF Sea Tiger (DRBV 15C) (France), DRBV 26D Jupiter II (Saudi Arabia and Taiwan); surface search – Thomson-CSF Triton G (Taiwan); surveillance/fire control – Thomson-CSF Arabel 3D (Saudi Arabia); navigation – two Racal Decca 1226 (DRBN 34A), two Racal Decca 20V90 (Taiwan); fire control – Thomson-CSF Castor 2J
SONARS: Thomson Marconi CAPTAS 20 (Saudi Arabia); BAE/Thomson-Sintra ATAS(V)2 active towed array; Thomson-Sintra Spherion B, bow-mounted active search (Taiwan)
EW: Thomson-CSF ARBR 21 (DR 3000-S), ARBG 2 Maigret ESM; Dassault ARBB 33 ECM (can be fitted) (France); Thomson-CSF DR-3000S2 ESM; two Thales Salamandre ECM (Saudi Arabia); Thomson-CSF DR-3000S, ESM/ECM, Chang-Feng IV ESM/ECM (Taiwan)

AIR SUPPORT:

HELICOPTERS: One Aerospatiale AS565 MA Panther or platform for one Super Frelon (France); one Aerospatiale SA 365 Dauphin 2 (Saudi Arabia); one Sikorsky S-70C(M)1 (ASW) (Taiwan)

Brandenburg GERMANY

Brandenburg (*Michael Nitz*)

SPECIFICATION:

COUNTRY OF ORIGIN: Germany
CLASS: Brandenburg (Type 123)
(FFG)
ACTIVE: 4
NAME (PENNANT NUMBER):
Brandenburg (F 215),
Schleswig-Holstein (F 216),
Bayern (F 217), Mecklenburg-
Vorpommern (F 218)

FEATURES:

DISPLACEMENT: 4900 tons
full load
LENGTH: 455.7 ft (138.9 m) oa
BEAM: 54.8 ft (16.7 m)
DRAUGHT: 22.3 ft (6.8 m)
SPEED: 29 kts
RANGE: 4000 miles at 18 kts

ARMAMENT:

MISSILES: SSM – four Aerospatiale
MM 38 Exocet (2 twin); SAM –
Martin Marietta VLS Mk 41 Mod 3
for NATO Sea Sparrow, two
RAM 21 cell Mk 49 launchers
GUNS: One OTO Melara 76
mm/62 Mk 75; two Rheinmetall
20 mm Rh 202 (to be replaced
by Mauser 27 mm)
TORPEDOES: Four 324 mm
Mk 32 Mod 9 (2 twin) tubes;
Honeywell 46 Mod 2
DECOYS: Two Breda SCLAR

ELECTRONICS:

RADARS: Air-search – Signaal
LW08; air/surface search –
Signaal SMART, 3D; navigation –
two Raytheon Raypath;
fire control – two Signaal
STIR 180 trackers
SONARS: Atlas Elektronik
DSQS-23BZ; hull-mounted,
active search/attack
EW: TST FL 1800S ESM/ECM

AIR SUPPORT:

HELICOPTERS: Two Westland Sea
Lynx Mk 88 or 88A (ASW/ASV)

- High freeboard, continuous maindeck from bow to break down to flight deck
- 76 mm/62 gun mounting in 'A' position
- RAM SAM box launcher in 'B' position
- High central superstructure with bridge well aft from bows
- NATO Sea Sparrow SAM (VLS) tubes immediately forward of bridge
- Large, sturdy, enclosed mainmast forward of midships
- Large twin angled funnels between forward and after superstructures
- After superstructure with aftermast atop, supporting large Signaal LW08 air-search radar aerial
- Exocet SSM twin launchers between funnel and mainmast
- RAM SAM box launcher atop hangar
- Flight deck right aft with open quarterdeck below

NOTE: Germany's new 'Sachsen' class based on Type 123 hull

Kortenaer GERMANY, GREECE, UNITED ARAB EMIRATES (UAE)

Aegeon

- Similar hull and basic profile to the 'Jacob Van Heemskerck' class
- Easily identifiable differences are: 3 in gun mounting in 'A' position, WM 25 fire control radar dome atop mainmast, Pomona Standard SAM launcher not fitted, low hangar, flight deck with open quarterdeck below
- Sea Sparrow SAM box launcher in 'B' position
- Harpoon SSM launchers, angled port and starboard, in break in superstructure
- LW08 air-search radar atop short open pylon, forward edge of hangar, aft of funnel
- Greek ships have 3 in gun mounting atop hangar
- 'Bremen' class has tall lattice mast immediately forward of funnel and main deck not continuous. Taller hangar aft

contd.

Kortenaer contd.

SPECIFICATION:

COUNTRY OF ORIGIN: Netherlands

CLASS: Kortenaer/Bremen (modified Kortenaer Type 122)/ Elli (FFG)

ACTIVE: 8 Germany (Bremen/ modified Kortenaer/Type 122), 10 Greece (Elli), 2 UAE (Kortenaer)

NAME (PENNANT NUMBER):
GERMANY – Bremen (F 207), Niedersachsen (F 208), Rheinland-Pfalz (F 209), Emden (F 210), Köln (F 211), Karlsruhe (F 212), Augsburg (F 213), Lübeck (F 214)
GREECE – Elli (ex-*Pieter Florisz*) (F 450), Limnos (ex-*Witte de With*) (F 451, ex-F 813), Aegeon (ex-*Banckert*) (F 460, ex-F 810), Adrias (ex-*Callenburgh*) (F 459, ex-F 808), Navarinon (ex-*Van Kinsbergen*) (F 461, ex-F 809), Kountouriotis (ex-*Kortenaer*) (F 462, ex-F 807), Bouboulina (ex-*Pieter Floris, ex-Willem van der Zaan*) (F 463, ex-F 826), Kanaris (ex-*Jan van Brakel*) (F 464, ex-F 825), Themistocles (ex-*Philips Van Almonde*), (F 465, ex-F 823), Nikiforos Fokas (ex-*Bloys van Treslong*) (F 466, ex-F 824)
UNITED ARAB EMIRATES – Abu Dhabi (ex-*Abraham Crijnssen*) (F 01, ex-F 816), Al Emirat (ex-*Piet Heyn*) (F 02, ex-F 811)

FEATURES:

DISPLACEMENT: 3630 tons full load; 3680 tons (Germany)

LENGTH: 428 ft (130.5 m); 426.4 ft (130 m) (Germany)

BEAM: 47.9 ft (14.6 m); 47.6 ft (14.5 m) (Germany)

DRAUGHT: 20.3 ft (6.2 m) (screws); 21.3 ft (6.5 m) (Germany)

SPEED: 30 kts

RANGE: 4700 miles at 16 kts

ARMAMENT:

MISSILES: SSM – McDonnell Douglas Harpoon (2 quad) launchers; SAM – Raytheon Sea Sparrow Mk 29 octuple launcher, two GDC RAM (Germany only)

GUNS: One OTO Melara 3 in (76 mm)/62 Mk 75 Compact (F 459-462) (two in F 450-451); Signaal SGE-30 Goalkeeper with General Electric 30 mm (UAE); one or two GE/GD Vulcan Phalanx 20 mm Mk 15 (none in F 463-466) (Greece); two Oerlikon 20 mm (UAE only); two Rheinmetall 20 mm Rh 202, to be replaced by Mauser 27 mm (Germany only)

TORPEDOES: Four 324 mm US Mk 32 (2 twin) tubes; Honeywell Mk 46 Mod 5 Neartip (Mod 2 in German ships, to be replaced by Mu 90; Mod 5 in Greek ships)

DECOYS: Two Loral Hycor SRBOC 6-barrel Mk 36 chaff launchers (four in Germany); SLQ-25 Nixie towed torpedo decoy; Prairie Bubble noise reduction (Germany)

ELECTRONICS:

RADARS: Air-search – Signaal LW08 (Greece, UAE); air/surface search – DASA TRS-3D/32 (Germany only); surface search – Signaal ZW06 (Greece), Signaal Scout (UAE); navigation – SMA 3 RM 20 (Germany only); fire control – Signaal STIR, Signaal WM25 (Germany only)

SONARS: SQS-505, hull-mounted, (Greece, UAE); Atlas Elektronik DSQS-21BZ (BO) (Germany)

EW: Ramses ESM/ECM; Elettronica Sphinx; MEL Scimitar ESM; Elettronica ELT 715 ESM (Greece); TST FL 1800 ESM/ECM (Germany only)

AIR SUPPORT:

HELICOPTERS: Two Westland Sea Lynx Mk 88 or 88A (ASW/ASV) (Germany); two Agusta AB 212 (ASW) (Greece); two Eurocopter AS 545 Panther (ASW) (UAE)

Sachsen GERMANY

Sachsen (*Michael Nitz*)

SPECIFICATION:

COUNTRY OF ORIGIN: Germany
CLASS: Sachsen (Type 124) (FFG)
ACTIVE: 2
BUILDING: 1
NAME (PENNANT NUMBER):
Sachsen (F 219), Hamburg
(F 220), Hessen (F 221)

FEATURES:

DISPLACEMENT: 5600 tons full load
LENGTH: 469.2 ft (143 m) oa
BEAM: 57.1 ft (17.4 m)
DRAUGHT: 14.4 ft (4.4 m)
SPEED: 29 kts
RANGE: 4000 miles at 18 kts

ARMAMENT:

MISSILES: SSM – eight Harpoon
(2 quad); SAM – VLS Mk 41 for
Standard SM-2; two RAM 21-cell
Mk 49 launchers
GUNS: One OTOBreda 76 mm/62
IRDF; two Mauser 27 mm
TORPEDOES: Six 324 mm Mk 32
Mod 9 (2 triple) tubes; Eurotorp
Mu 90 Impact
DECOYS: Six SRBOC 130 mm chaff
launchers

ELECTRONICS:

RADARS: Air-search – Signaal
SMART L; air/surface search –
Signaal APAR, phased array;
navigation – two sets
SONARS: Atlas DSQS-21B; bow-
mounted, active search/attack;
active towed array
EW: DASA FL 1800S ESM/ECM

AIR SUPPORT:

HELICOPTERS: Two NFH 90 or
Westland Sea Lynx Mk 88A
(ASW/ASV)

- High freeboard, continuous maindeck from bow to break down to short flight deck
- 76 mm/62 gun mounting in 'A' position
- RAM SAM box launcher in 'B' position
- High central superstructure with bridge well aft from bows
- Mk 41 (VLS) SAM tubes immediately forward of bridge
- Massive, sturdy, enclosed mainmast forward of midships with circular APAR phased arrays at apex; above thin, short pole mast
- Thin pyramid enclosed mast forward of funnels
- Large twin angled funnels aft of midships, atop superstructure
- After superstructure with aftermast atop, supporting large rectangular smart air-search radar aerial
- Harpoon twin launchers between funnel and mainmast
- RAM SAM box launcher atop hangar
- Flight deck right aft

NOTE: Based on German Type 123 Brandenburg hull with improved stealth features

Godavari/Improved Godavari INDIA

Gomati

- Unusually long forecastle
- Three major weapons systems forward of the bridge; from the bow aft, 57 mm/70 gun twin mounting, Styx SSM launchers (F 20-22) (SS-N-25, F 31 onwards), SA-N-4 or Trishful SAM launchers
- Bows are flared to accommodate the large SSM launchers sited either side of the Muff Cob or Seaguard fire control director
- Midships superstructure with pyramid mainmast at after end
- Small, tapered funnel just aft of midships (resembles 'Leander' class)
- Slab-sided after superstructure (hangars) with small enclosed aftermast at forward end and LW08 air-search radar aerial atop
- Flight deck with break down to short quarterdeck

NOTE: First three further modification of original 'Leander' class design. The second three modified 'Godavari' class are larger and with different profile. Some refer to the latter class as 'Brahmaputra'

SPECIFICATION:

COUNTRY OF ORIGIN: India
CLASS: Godavari/modified Godavari (Project 16A) (FFG)
ACTIVE: 5
BUILDING: 1
NAME (PENNANT NUMBER): Godavari (F 20), Gomati (F 21), Ganga (F 22), Brahmaputra (F 31), Beas (F 37), Betwa (F 32)

FEATURES:

DISPLACEMENT: 4209 tons full load; 4450 tons (modified Godavari)
LENGTH: 414.9 ft (126.5 m)
BEAM: 47.6 ft (14.5 m)
DRAUGHT: 14.8 ft (4.5 m)
SPEED: 27 kts
RANGE: 4500 miles at 12 kts

ARMAMENT:

MISSILES: SSM – four SS-N-2D Styx (F 20-22), SS-N-25 (4 quad), 16 SS-N-25 Sapless (Kh 35 Uran) quad (F 31-32, 37); SAM – SA-N-4 Gecko twin launcher (F 20-21), Barak launcher to be fitted in F 31-33, one octuple IAI/Rafael Barak VLS (F 22, mod. Godavari)
GUNS: Two 57 mm/70 (twin) (replaced by OTO Melara 76 mm/62 gun in mod. Godavari); eight 30 mm/65 (4 twin) AK 230 (replaced by four 30 mm/65 AK 630 in mod. Godavari)
TORPEDOES: Six 324 mm ILAS 3 (2 triple) tubes; Whitehead A244S
DECOYS: Two Super Barricade chaff launchers; Graseby G738 towed torpedo decoy

ELECTRONICS:

RADARS: Air-search – Signaal LW 08 (LW 08/Bharat RAWL PLN 517, mod. Godavari); air/surface search – 'Head Net C,' 3D (Bharat RAWS 03 PFN 513, mod. Godavari); navigation/helo control – two Signaal ZW 06 or Don Kay; fire control – two Drum Tilt (30 mm), Muff Cob (57 mm), Pop Group (SA-N-4) (F 20-22), Contraves Seaguard (30 mm and SSM), Bharat Aparna (SAM) (F 31-32, 37)
SONARS: Bharat APSOH; Thomson-Sintra DSBV 62 (Ganga) passive towed array; VDS; Type 162M
EW: Selenia INS-3 ESM/ECM

AIR SUPPORT:

HELICOPTERS: Two Sea King or one Sea King and one HAL SA 319B Chetak (Alouette III) (ASW)

Shivalik INDIA

Shivalik

- Enlarged modified version of 'Talwar'
- Unusually long forecastle
- Four weapons systems forward of the bridge; from the bow aft, OTO Melara 76 mm/62 gun mounting; SA-N-7 Gadfly SAM launcher; SS-N-27 Klub SSM in raised VLS silo; RBU 6000 A/S Mortar on raised platform immediately forward of bridge
- Midships superstructure with pyramid mainmast at after end and enclosed pyramid pylon immediately above bridge
- Funnel aft of midships with pylon immediately aft supporting Front Dome fire control radar
- Aft section resembles 'Delhi' class
- Slab-sided after superstructure (hangars) with air-search radar and Shikari fire control mounted on top
- Long flight deck aft

SPECIFICATION:

COUNTRY OF ORIGIN: India
CLASS: Shivalik (Project 17)
ACTIVE: 1
BUILDING: 2
NAME (PENNANT NUMBER):
Shivalik (—), Satpura (—),
Sahyadi (—)

FEATURES:

DISPLACEMENT: 4900 tons full load
LENGTH: 469.3 ft (143 m)
BEAM: 55.5 ft (16.9 m)
DRAUGHT: 17.4 ft (5.3 m)
SPEED: 32 kts
RANGE: 4500 miles at 18 kts

ARMAMENT:

MISSILES: SSM – eight SS-N-27 Alfa Klub; SAM – SA-N-7 Gadfly; SAM/guns – two CADS-N-1 Kashtan combined with eight SA-N-11 Grisson
GUNS: One 3 in (76 mm)/62 Super Rapid
TORPEDOES: Six 324 mm ILAS-3 (2 triple)
A/S MORTARS: Two RBU 6000 12-barrelled launcher
DECOYS: Two PK 2 chaff launchers

ELECTRONICS:

RADARS: Air-search – Bharat RAWL-02; air/surface search – Top Plate 3D; navigation – one BEL Rashmi; fire control – two BEL Shikari, one Bharat Aparna, four Front Dome
SONARS: Bharat MF HUMSA, hull-mounted, active
EW: Bharat Ajanta ESM; ASOR 11356 ECM

Talwar INDIA

Talwar

- Unusually long forecastle
- Four weapons systems forward of the bridge; from the bow aft, 100 mm/59 gun mounting; SA-N-7 Gadfly SAM launcher; SS-N-27 Klub SSM in raised VLS silo; RBU 6000 A/S mortar on raised platform immediately forward of bridge
- Midships superstructure with pyramid mainmast at after end and enclosed pyramid pylon immediately above bridge
- Sloping tapered lattice mast at aft end of bridge superstructure
- Low funnel well aft of midships with pylon immediately forward supporting Front Dome fire control radar
- Slab-sided after superstructure (hangars) with dome at aft end, and GADS-N-1 SAM/guns system adjacent, port and starboard
- Flight deck with break down to very short quarterdeck

NOTE: First three are a dramatic modification of the original 'Krivak III' class design. Later ships will incorporate stealth features

SPECIFICATION:

COUNTRY OF ORIGIN: India
CLASS: Talwar (Type 1135.6/Project 17) (FFG)
ACTIVE: 3
PLANNED: 3
NAME (PENNANT NUMBER): Talwar (F40), Trishul (F43), Tabar (F44)

FEATURES:

DISPLACEMENT: 4035 tons full load
LENGTH: 409.6 ft (124.8 m)
BEAM: 49.9 ft (15.2 m)
DRAUGHT: 15.1 ft (4.6 m)
SPEED: 32 kts
RANGE: 4850 miles at 14 kts

ARMAMENT:

MISSILES: SSM – eight SS-N-27 Novator Alfa Klub (3M-5-54E1) in VLS silo; SAM – SA-N-7 Gadfly (Kashmir/Uragan); SAM/guns – two CADS-N-1 (Kashtan) with twin 30 mm Gatling combined with SA-N-11 'Grisson' and Hot Flash/Hot Spot radar/optronic director
GUNS: One 3.9 in (100 mm)/59 A 190
TORPEDOES: Four PTA-53 533 mm (2 twin) tubes
A/S MORTARS: One RBU 6000 12-barrel launcher
DECOYS: Two PK 2 chaff launchers

ELECTRONICS:

RADARS: Air/surface search – 'Top Plate', 3D; surface search – Cross Dome; fire control – four Front Dome (SA-N-7) Plank Shave (SSM), Ratrep 5P-10E Puma (100 mm); navigation – Kelvin Hughes Nucleus 6000, two Palm Frond
SONARS: HUMSA
EW: Bharat Ajanta ESM, ASOR 11356 ESM

AIR SUPPORT:

HELICOPTERS: One Kamov Ka-28/Ka-31 Helix (ASW) or HAL Advanced Light Helicopter (ASV/ASW)

Van Speijk INDONESIA

Ahmad Yani

- Similar to British 'Leander' class
- Long, raised forecastle with Oto Melara 3 in (76 mm)/62 Compact gun mounting in 'A' position
- Midships superstructure with pyramid mainmast atop, just aft of bridge
- Single, 'capped' funnel just aft of midships
- Short aftermast supporting large LW03 air-search radar aerial
- Mistral SAM Simbad launchers on hangar roof (replacing Seacat quad launchers)
- Torpedo tubes, port and starboard, on maindeck at forward end of long flight deck

SPECIFICATION:

COUNTRY OF ORIGIN: Netherlands
CLASS: Van Speijk/Ahmad Yani (FFG)
ACTIVE: 6
NAME (PENNANT NUMBER):
Ahmad Yani (ex-*Tjerk Hiddes*) (351), Slamet Riyadi (ex-*Van Speijk*) (352), Yos Sudarso (ex-*Van Galen*) (353), Oswald Siahaan (ex-*Van Nes*) (354), Abdul Halim Perdanakusuma (ex-*Evertsen*) (355), Karel Satsuitubun (ex-*Isaac Sweers*) (356)

FEATURES:

DISPLACEMENT: 2835 tons full load
LENGTH: 372 ft (113.4 m)
BEAM: 41 ft (12.5 m)
DRAUGHT: 13.8 ft (4.2 m)
SPEED: 28.5 kts
RANGE: 4500 miles at 12 kts

ARMAMENT:

MISSILES: SSM – eight McDonnell Douglas Harpoon; SAM – two Short Bros Seacat quad launchers (being replaced by two Matra Simbad twin launchers for Mistral)
GUNS: One OTO Melara 3 in (76 mm)/62 Compact; four 12.7 mm machine guns
TORPEDOES: Six 324 mm Mk 32 (2 triple) tubes; Honeywell Mk 46
DECOYS: Two Knebworth Corvus 8-tubed trainable launchers

ELECTRONICS:

RADARS: Air-search – Signaal LW03; air/surface search – Signaal DA05; navigation – Racal Decca 1229; fire control – Signaal M 45 (76 mm and SSM), two Signaal M 44 (for Seacat SAM, being removed)
SONARS: Signaal CWE 610, hull-mounted, VDS
EW: UA 8/9, UA 13 ESM

AIR SUPPORT:

HELICOPTERS: One Westland Wasp HAS Mk 1 (ASW) or NBO 105C

Fatahillah INDONESIA

Fatahillah

- 4.7 in gun mounting in 'A' position with Bofors 375 mm A/S mortar launcher in 'B' mounting position
- Low, slab-sided superstructure centred forward of midships
- Very substantial pyramid mainmast with pole mast atop its after end
- WM28 fire control radome atop short pyramid mainmast above bridge
- Large, square-shaped, low profile funnel well aft of midships
- Exocet SSM launchers between funnel and after superstructure
- Large DA05 air/surface search radar aerial on pedestal atop small after superstructure
- 40 mm/70 gun mounting aft of maindeck at break down to small quarterdeck

NOTE: *Nala* has no after mounting and the maindeck is extended to provide a hangar and short flight deck

SPECIFICATION:

COUNTRY OF ORIGIN: Netherlands
CLASS: Fatahillah (FFG)
ACTIVE: 3
NAME (PENNANT NUMBER):
Fatahillah (361), Malahayati (362),
Nala (363)

FEATURES:

DISPLACEMENT: 1450 tons full load
LENGTH: 276 ft (84 m)
BEAM: 36.4 ft (11.1 m)
DRAUGHT: 10.7 ft (3.3 m)
SPEED: 30 kts
RANGE: 4250 miles at 16 kts

ARMAMENT:

MISSILES: SSM – four Aerospatiale
MM 38 Exocet
GUNS: One Bofors 4.7 in
(120 mm)/46; one or two Bofors
40 mm/70 (two in *Nala*); two
Rheinmetall 20 mm
TORPEDOES: Six 324 Mk 32 or
ILAS 3 (2 triple) tubes (none in
Nala); 12 Mk 46 (or A244S)
torpedoes
A/S MORTARS: One Bofors 375
mm twin-barrelled
DECOYS: Two Knebworth Corvus
8-tubed trainable launchers; one
T-Mk 6 torpedo decoy

ELECTRONICS:

RADARS: Air/surface search –
Signaal DA05; surface search –
Racal Decca AC 1229; fire control
– Signaal WM28
SONARS: Signaal PHS-32; hull-
mounted active search/attack
EW: MEL Susie 1 (UAA-1) ESM

AIR SUPPORT:

HELICOPTERS: One Westland
Wasp HAS (Mk 1) (ASW) (*Nala* only)

Ki Hajar Dewentara INDONESIA

Ki Hajar Dewantara

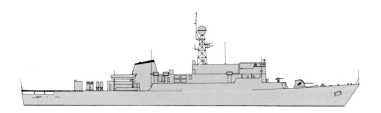

- 4.7 in gun mounting in 'A' position with 20 mm cannon in 'B' mounting position on raised platform
- Long, slab-sided superstructure centred forward of midships
- Very substantial lattice mainmast with fire control radome at top at aft end of bridge superstructure with pole mast atop its after end
- Large, rounded and tapered funnel well aft of midships
- Ships boats on davits just aft of funnel
- Exocet SSM launchers aft of funnel and after superstructure
- Flight deck above open quarterdeck

SPECIFICATION:

COUNTRY OF ORIGIN: Yugoslavia
CLASS: Ki Hajar Dewantara (FFG)
ACTIVE: 1
NAME (PENNANT NUMBER): Ki Hajar Dewantara (364)

FEATURES:
DISPLACEMENT: 2050 tons full load
LENGTH: 317.3 ft (96.7 m)
BEAM: 36.7 ft (11.2 m)
DRAUGHT: 15.7 ft (4.8 m)
SPEED: 26 kts
RANGE: 4000 miles at 18 kts

ARMAMENT:
MISSILES: SSM – four Aerospatiale MM 38 Exocet
GUNS: One Bofors 57 mm/70; two Rheinmetall 20 mm
TORPEDOES: Two 21 in (533 mm) tubes; AEG SUT dual purpose torpedoes
DEPTH CHARGES: One projector
DECOYS: Two 128 mm twin-tubed flare launchers

ELECTRONICS:
RADARS: Surface search – Racal Decca AC 1229; fire control – Signaal WM28
SONARS: Signaal PHS-32; hull-mounted active search/attack
EW: MEL Susie ESM

AIR SUPPORT:
HELICOPTERS: Platform for Nurtanio NBO 105C (support)

Claud Jones INDONESIA, TURKEY

Martadinata

- 3 in gun mounting on raised platform forward of bridge
- Tall, slab-sided superstructure centred forward of midships. Bridge has circular structure above
- Tall thin cylindrical mainmast with triangular support aft. Short pole mast atop its after end
- Large, rounded and tapered funnel aft of midships (Turkish ship)
- Two shorter funnels in Indonesian units, one above each other
- Ships boats on davits just aft of funnel
- Deck break aft of superstructure to long quarterdeck. Turkish unit has 3 in gun on quarterdeck and Indonesian ships can have a 37 mm (or 76 mm gun) twin mounting here
- Tall pole mast aft of funnel (Indonesian units only)

SPECIFICATION:

COUNTRY OF ORIGIN: USA
CLASS: Claud Jones/Samadikun/
Berk (modified Claud Jones)
(FFG/FF)
ACTIVE: 2 Indonesia ('Samadikun'
class), 1 Turkey ('Berk' class)
NAME (PENNANT NUMBER):
INDONESIA – Samadikun (ex-*John
R Perry*) (341, ex-DE 1034),
Martadinata (ex-*Charles Berry*)
(342, ex-DE 1035)
TURKEY – Peyk (D 359)

FEATURES:
DISPLACEMENT: 1968 tons full
load (Indonesia); 1950 tons
(Turkey)
LENGTH: 310 ft (95 m) (Indonesia);
311.7 ft (95.3 m) (Turkey)
BEAM: 38.7 ft (11.8 m)
DRAUGHT: 18 ft (5.5 m)
SPEED: 22 kts
RANGE: 3000 miles at 18 kts

ARMAMENT:
GUNS: One or two USN 3 in
(76 mm)/50 Mk 34 (Indonesia);
four USN 3 in (76 mm)/50 (2 twin)
(Turkey); two USSR 37 mm/63
(twin) (Indonesia only)
TORPEDOES: Six 364 mm Mk 32
(2 triple tubes); Honeywell Mk 46
A/S MORTARS: Two Mk 11
Hedgehog rocket launchers
(Turkey only)
DEPTH CHARGES: One rack
(Turkey); two throwers
(Indonesia)

ELECTRONICS:
RADARS: Air-search –
Westinghouse SPS-6E (Indonesia),
Lockheed SPS-40 (Turkey);
surface search – Raytheon
SPS-5D, Raytheon SPS-10 (Turkey);
navigation – Racal Decca 1226;
fire control – Lockheed SPG-52
(Indonesia), two Western Electric
Mk 34 (Turkey)
SONARS: EDO (*Samadikun*) SQS-45V
(*Martadinata*); hull-mounted
active search/attack; Sangamo
SQS-29/31, hull-mounted active
search and attack (Turkey)
EW: WLR-1C (except *Samadikun*)
ESM

AIR SUPPORT:
HELICOPTERS: Platform for AB 212
(ASW) (Turkey)

Parchim INDONESIA, RUSSIA

Untung Suropati (M. *Declerck*)

- High bow, short forecastle
- Low main superstructure with high central superstructure atop
- 30 mm/65 AK 630 CIWS mounting at forward end of main superstructure
- RBU 6000 A/s mortar mounting forward of bridge
- Lattice mainmast atop central superstructure. 'Y'- shaped (in profile) lattice mast aft
- Cross Dome search radome atop mainmast
- SA-N-5 quad launcher at after end of forward superstructure (Russia)
- Large, enclosed aftermast supporting Bass Tilt fire control radar
- 3 in gun mounting in 'Y' position

SPECIFICATION:

COUNTRY OF ORIGIN: East Germany
CLASS: Parchim I (Type 1331) (Kapitan Patimura) (FS)*
* Officially rated as corvettes
ACTIVE: 16 (Indonesia)
NAME (PENNANT NUMBER): Kapitan Patimura (ex-*Prenzlau*) (371, ex-231), Untung Suropati (ex-*Ribnitz*) (372, ex-233), Nuku (ex-*Waren*) (373, ex-224), Lambung Mangkurat (ex-*Angermünde*) (374, ex-214), Cut Nyak Dien (ex-*Lübz*) (375, ex-P 6169, ex-221), Sultan Thaha Syaifuddin (ex-*Bad Doberan*) (376, ex-222), Sutanto (ex-*Wismar*) (377, ex-P 6170, ex-241), Sutedi Senoputra (ex-*Parchim*) (378, ex-242), Wiratno (ex-*Perleberg*) (379, ex-243), Memet Sastrawiria (ex-*Bützow*) (380, ex-244), Tjiptadi (ex-*Bergen*) (381, ex-213), Hasan Basri (ex-*Güstrow*) (382, ex-223), Iman Bonjol (ex-*Teterow*) (383, ex-P 6168, ex-234), Pati Unus (ex-*Ludwiglust*) (384, ex-232), Teuku Umar (ex-*Grevesmühlen*) (385, ex-212), Silas Papare (ex-*Gadebusch*) (386, ex-P 6167, ex-211)
CLASS: Parchim II (Type 1331) (FFL)
ACTIVE: 10 (Russia)
NAME (PENNANT NUMBER): MPK 67 (242), MPK 99 (308), MPK 105 (245), MPK 192 (304), MPK 205 (311), MPK 213 (222), MPK 216 (258), MPK 224 (218), MPK 227 (243), MPK 229 (232)

FEATURES:

DISPLACEMENT: 960 tons full load; 769 tons ('Parchim I')
LENGTH: 246.7 ft (75.2 m)
BEAM: 32.2 ft (9.8 m)
DRAUGHT: 14.4 ft (4.4 m); 11.5 ft (3.5 m) ('Parchim I')
SPEED: 26 kts; 24 kts ('Parchim I')
RANGE: 2500 miles at 12 kts

ARMAMENT:

MISSILES: SAM – two SA-N-5 Grail quad launchers
GUNS: One 3 in (76 mm)/66 AK 176; one 30 mm/65 AK 630 6-barrels ('Parchim II'); one USSR 57 mm/ 80 (twin) automatic; two 30 mm (twin) ('Parchim I')
TORPEDOES: Four 21 in (533 mm) (2 twin) tubes; four 400 mm tubes ('Parchim I')
A/s MORTARS: Two RBU 6000
DEPTH CHARGES: Two racks
DECOYS: Two PK 16 chaff launchers

ELECTRONICS:

RADARS: Air/surface search – Cross Dome (Strut Curve, Indonesia); navigation – TSR 333 or Nayala or Kivach III; fire control – Bass Tilt (Muff Cob, Indonesia)
SONARS: Bull Horn (MGT 332T) hull-mounted; Lamb Tail; helicopter type VDS
EW: Two Watchdog ESM

193

Alvand IRAN

Alvand (Guy Toremons)

- Similar hull and superstructure profile to Pakistani British 'Type 21' frigates
- Long forecastle with 4.5 in gun mounting in 'A' position
- Short pyramid mainmast just forward of midships
- Low profile, sloping funnel, well aft with distinctive gas turbine air intakes forward of funnel, port and starboard
- AWS 1 air/surface radar aerial immediately forward of funnel
- Sited on afterdeck, from forward to aft, YJ-2 or Sea Killer II SSM launcher, Limbo A/S mortar and 35 mm/90 twin gun turret mounting

SPECIFICATION:

COUNTRY OF ORIGIN: UK
CLASS: Alvand (Vosper Mark 5) (FFG)
ACTIVE: 3
NAME (PENNANT NUMBER): Alvand (ex-Saam) (71), Alborz (ex-Zaal) (72), Sabalan (ex-Rostam) (73)

FEATURES:
DISPLACEMENT: 1350 tons full load
LENGTH: 310 ft (94.5 m)
BEAM: 36.4 ft (11.1 m)
DRAUGHT: 14.1 ft (4.3 m)
SPEED: 29 kts
RANGE: 3650 miles at 18 kts

ARMAMENT:
MISSILES: SSM – four China YJ-2 (C-802, CSS-N-8 Saccade) (2 twin)
GUNS: One Vickers 4.5 in (114 mm)/55 Mk 8; two Oerlikon 35 mm/90 (twin); three Oerlikon GAM-BO1 20 mm; two 12.7 mm machine guns
A/S MORTARS: One 3-tubed Limbo Mk 10
DECOYS: Two UK Mk 5 rocket flare launchers

ELECTRONICS:
RADARS: Air/surface search – Plessey AWS 1, Rice Screen (Sabalan); surface search – Racal Decca 1226; navigation – Decca 629; fire control – two Contraves Sea Hunter
SONARS: Graseby 174, hull-mounted, active search; Graseby 170, hull-mounted, active attack
EW: Decca RDL 2AC ESM

Lupo ITALY, PERU, VENEZUELA

Perseo (now decommissioned)

- High bow, sweeping forecastle with 5 in gun mounting in 'A' position
- High forward superstructure. Distinctive surface search/target indication radome atop bridge roof in Peruvian FM 55-56 only
- Enclosed mast, with pole mast at after end, atop bridge superstructure
- Shorter pyramid aftermast immediately forward of funnel with RAN 10S air-search radar atop (all ships). Lattice mast in Peruvian ships
- After superstructure (hangar) with SAM box launcher on roof (Sea Sparrow in Peruvian FM 55-56; Aspide in Peruvian and Venezuelan ships)
- Forward-trained, angled SSM launchers on maindeck level, port and starboard, immediately aft and forward of funnel (Teseo in Italian and Venezuelan ships; Otomat in Peruvian ships)
- Two 40 mm/70 gun mountings on maindeck level, port and starboard, abaft aft SSM launchers. Peruvian and Venezuelan ships have raised mountings
- Flight deck right aft with open quarterdeck below. Peruvian and Venezuelan ships have extended flight deck, Venezuelan with break down to short quarterdeck

contd.

Lupo contd.

SPECIFICATION:

COUNTRY OF ORIGIN: Italy
CLASS: Lupo, Artigliere, Carvajal,
modified Lupo (FFG)
ACTIVE: 4 Italy (Artigliere)*, 6 Peru
(Carvajal),
6 Venezuela (modified Lupo)
* Originally built for Iraq
NAME (PENNANT NUMBER):
ITALY – Artigliere (ex-*Hittin*)
(F 582, ex-F 14), Aviere
(ex-*Thi Qar*) (F 583 ex-F 15),
Bersagliere (*Al Yarmouk*) (F 584
ex-F 17), Granatiere
(ex-*Al Qadisiya*) (F 585 ex-F 16)
PERU – Carvajal (FM 51),
Villavicencio (FM 52), Montero
(FM 53), Mariategui (FM 54),
Aguirre (ex-*Orsa*) (FM 55,
ex-F 567), Palacios (ex-*Lupo*)
(FM 56, ex-F 564)
VENEZUELA – Mariscal Sucre
(F 21), Almirante Brión (F 22),
General Urdaneta (F 23), General
Soublette (F 24), General Salom
(F 25), Almirante Garcia
(ex-*José Felix Fibas*) (F 26)

FEATURES:

DISPLACEMENT: 2525 tons
full load (Italy); 2500 tons (Peru);
2520 tons (Venezuela)
LENGTH: 371.3 ft (113.2 m)
BEAM: 37.1 ft (11.3 m)
DRAUGHT: 12.1 ft (3.7 m)
SPEED: 35 kts
RANGE: 3450 miles at 20.5 kts;
5000 miles at 15 kts (diesels)

ARMAMENT:

MISSILES: SSM – eight OTO Melara
Teseo Mk 2 (TG 2) (Italy,
Venezuela), eight OTO Melara/
Matra Otomat Mk 2 (TG 1) (Peru);
SAM – Raytheon NATO Sea
Sparrow Mk 29 octuple launcher
(FM 55-56 Peru), Albatros/Aspide
octuple launcher ('Artigliere'
class, Peru, Venezuela)
GUNS: One OTO Melara 5 in
(127 mm)/54; four Breda
40 mm/70 (2 twin) Compact;
two Oerlikon 20 mm can be
fitted in Italian ships
TORPEDOES: Six 324 mm ILAS or
Mk 32 (2 triple) tubes; Whitehead
A244S, (Peru, Venezuela)
DECOYS: Two Breda 105 mm
SCLAR 20-tubed (all ships)

ELECTRONICS:

RADARS: Air-search – Selenia
SPS-774 (RAN 10S); surface search
– SMA SPQ-2 F (FM 55-56 Peru),
SPQ-712 (RAN 12L/X) (Italy), Selenia
RAN 11LX (Peru, Venezuela),
Signaal LW08 (Peru); navigation –
SMA SPN-748 (FM 55-56 Peru),
SMA SPN-703 (Italy), SMA 3RM 20R
(Peru, Venezuela); fire control –
Selenia SPG-70 (RTN 10X), two
Selenia SPG-74 (RTN 20X) (all
ships but also two Orion RTN
10XP in Venezuelan ships)
SONARS: Raytheon DE 1160B,
hull-mounted (FM 55-56 Peru);
EDO SQS-29 Mod 610E in
Peruvian and Venezuelan ships
(Northrop Grumman 21 HS-7 in
Venezuelan F 21-22); none fitted
in 'Artigliere' class
EW: Selenia SLQ-747 (INS-3M)
ESM/ECM (Italy); Elettronica
Lambda ESM (Peru), Elisra
NS 9003/9005 ESM (Venezuela)

AIR SUPPORT:

HELICOPTERS: One Agusta AB 212
(ASW); one Augsta ASH-3D Sea
King (deck only on FM 51 and 54)

Maestrale ITALY

Aliseo

- Bridge well aft from bows
- 5 in gun mounting in 'A' position
- Albatros/Aspide SAM launcher in 'B' mounting position
- High forward superstructure with pointed pyramid mainmast atop
- Single, rectangular funnel with wedge shaped, black smoke diffuser at top
- Teseo SSM launchers, two port, two starboard, angled outboard sited immediately aft of funnel
- Small, white, domed SATCOM aerial atop hangar roof
- Flight deck right aft with open quarterdeck below

SPECIFICATION:

COUNTRY OF ORIGIN: Italy
CLASS: Maestrale (FFG)
ACTIVE: 8
NAME (PENNANT NUMBER): Maestrale (F 570), Grecale (F 571), Libeccio (F 572), Scirocco (F 573), Aliseo (F 574), Euro (F 575), Espero (F 576), Zeffiro (F 577)

FEATURES:

DISPLACEMENT: 3200 tons full load
LENGTH: 405 ft (122.7 m)
BEAM: 42.5 ft (12.9 m)
DRAUGHT: 15.1 ft (4.6 m)
SPEED: 32 kts
RANGE: 6000 miles at 16 kts

ARMAMENT:

MISSILES: SSM – four OTO Melara Teseo Mk 2 (TG 2); SAM – Selenia Albatros octuple launcher, Aspide
GUNS: One OTO Melara 5 in (127 mm)/54 automatic; four Breda 40 mm/70 (2 twin) Compact; two Oerlikon 20 mm (two Breda Oerlikon 20 mm fitted for Gulf deployments in 1990-91)
TORPEDOES: Six 324 mm US Mk 32 (2 triple) tubes; Honeywell Mk 46; two 21 in (533 mm) B516 tubes in transom; Whitehead A184
DECOYS: Two Breda 105 mm SCLAR 20-tubed rocket launchers; SLQ-25 towed torpedo decoy; Prairie Masker; noise suppression system

ELECTRONICS:

RADARS: Air/surface search – Selenia SPS-774 (RAN 10S); surface search – SMA SPS-702; navigation – SMA SPN-703; fire control – Selenia SPG-75 (RTN 30X), two Selenia SPG-74 (RTN 20X)
SONARS: Raytheon DE 1164; hull-mounted; VDS
EW: Elettronica SLR-4 ESM, two SLQ-D ECM

AIR SUPPORT:

HELICOPTERS: Two Agusta AB 212 (ASW)

Abukuma JAPAN

Ooyodo (*Hachiro Nakai*)

- Long, sweeping, uncluttered forecastle with 3 in gun mounting midway between bow and vertical bridge front
- High forward superstructure with large lattice mainmast at after end, top half offset
- Distinctive curved, OPS-14C lattice air-search radar aerial on platform at forward end of mast
- Two rectangular shaped black-capped funnels, forward one slightly taller
- ASROC A/S missile box launcher sited between funnels
- Gas turbine air intakes aft of after funnel, port and starboard
- Short lattice aftermast atop after superstructure
- Harpoon SSM angled launchers on raised structure immediately aft of aftermast
- CIWS mounting on afterdeck

NOTE: Non-vertical and rounded surfaces are employed for stealth reasons

SPECIFICATION:

COUNTRY OF ORIGIN: Japan
CLASS: Abukuma (FFG/DE)
ACTIVE: 6
NAME (PENNANT NUMBER):
Abukuma (DE 229), Jintsu
(DE 230), Ooyodo (DE 231),
Sendai (DE 232), Chikuma
(DE 233), Tone (DE 234)

FEATURES:
DISPLACEMENT: 2550 tons full load
LENGTH: 357.6 ft (109 m)
BEAM: 44 ft (13.4 m)
DRAUGHT: 12.5 ft (3.8 m)
SPEED: 27 kts

ARMAMENT:
MISSILES: SSM – eight McDonnell
Douglas Harpoon (2 quad)
launchers; A/S – Honeywell
ASROC Mk 112 octuple launcher;
payload – Mk 46 Mod 5 Neartip
torpedoes
GUNS: One OTOBreda 3 in
(76 mm)/62 Compact; one GE/GD
20 mm Phalanx CIWS Mk 15
TORPEDOES: Six 324 mm Type 68
(2 triple) tubes; Honeywell Mk 46
Mod 5 Neartip
DECOYS: Two Loral Hycor SRBOC
6-barrel Mk 36

ELECTRONICS:
RADARS: Air-search – Melco
OPS-14C; surface search –
JRC OPS-28C/D; fire control –
Type 2-21
SONARS: Hitachi OQS-8;
hull-mounted
EW: Nec NOLR-8 ESM

Ishikari/Yuubari JAPAN

Yuubari

- Long forecastle with 3 in rounded gun turret in 'A' position and prominent A/S mortar at 'B' position
- Low forward supstructure with squat enclosed pylon supporting fire control radar
- Lattice mast at aft end of bridge superstructure with complex pole mast atop
- Squat tapered funnel with square exhaust on top well aft of midships
- Break down to long quarterdeck with two Harpoon quad launchers port and starboard at stern

NOTE: 'Yuubari' slightly longer version of 'Ishikari'

SPECIFICATION:

COUNTRY OF ORIGIN: Japan
CLASS: Ishikari/Yuubari (FFG/DE)
ACTIVE: 3
NAME (PENNANT NUMBER):
Ishikari (DE 226), Yuubari (DE 227),
Yuubetsu (DE 228)

FEATURES:

DISPLACEMENT: 1690 tons full
load; 1450 tons (DE 226)
LENGTH: 298.5 ft (91 m); 278.8 ft
(85 m) (DE 226)
BEAM: 35.4 ft (10.8 m)
DRAUGHT: 11.8 ft (3.6 m)
SPEED: 25 kts

ARMAMENT:

MISSILES: SSM – Harpoon
(2 quad)
GUNS: One OTO Melara 3 in (76
mm)/62 Compact; one GE/GD 20
mm Phalanx CIWS Mk 15
TORPEDOES: Six 324 mm Type 68
(2 triple) tubes; Honeywell Mk 46
Mod 5 Neartip
A/S MORTARS: One 375 mm
Bofors Type 41, 4-6-barrel
DECOYS: Two Loral Hycor SRBOC
6-barrel Mk 36 chaff

ELECTRONICS:

RADARS: Surface search – JRC
OPS-28B/28-1; navigation –
Fujitsu OPS-19B; fire control –
Type 2-21
SONARS: Nec SQS-36J; hull-
mounted, active/passive
EW: Nec NOLR-6B ESM

Soho KOREA (NORTH)

'Soho' class

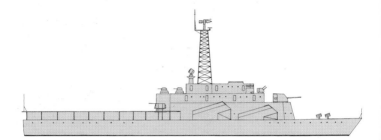

- Twin hull design
- Low freeboard, continuous maindeck from stem to stern
- Wide beam
- Clear forecastle with two A/s mortars only
- Slab-sided superstructure with two box launchers, port and starboard, on either side of superstructure
- Prominent 3.9 in gun turret on forward edge of superstructure, with two twin 25 mm mountings immediately above and just forward of bridge
- Very high lattice mast on superstructure just forward of midships
- Long platform aft for medium helicopter

SPECIFICATION:

COUNTRY OF ORIGIN: Korea (North)
CLASS: Soho (FFG)
ACTIVE: 1
NAME (PENNANT NUMBER): — (823)

FEATURES:

DISPLACEMENT: 1640 tons full load
LENGTH: 242.1 ft (73.8 m)
BEAM: 50.9 ft (15.5 m)
DRAUGHT: 12.5 ft (3.8 m)
SPEED: 23 kts

ARMAMENT:

MISSILES: SSM – four CSS-N-2
GUNS: One 3.9 in (100 mm)/56; four 37 mm/63 (2 twin); four 30 mm/66 (2 twin); four 25 mm/60 (2 twin)
A/S MORTARS: Two RBU 1200 5-tube fixed launchers

ELECTRONICS:

RADARS: Surface search – Square Tie; fire control – Drum Tilt
SONARS: Stag Horn; hull-mounted active search/attack
EW: China RW-23 Jug Pair (Watch Dog) ESM

AIR SUPPORT:

HELICOPTERS: Platform for medium helicopter

Najin KOREA (NORTH)

Najin 531

- High bows with sweeping, continuous maindeck from stem to stern
- Long forecastle with an array of weapons systems. From stem to bridge superstructure – two RBU A/S mortars, 3.9 in single gun turret, one twin 57 mm gun in open mounting, two twin 25 mm
- Tall bridge structure with box-like optical director atop with Square Tie air-search radar just aft
- High lattice mast, aft of bridge superstructure, just forward of midships
- Two funnels, one just aft of bridge, with 30 mm mounting aft; the other funnel well aft of midships
- SSM launchers between funnels to port and starboard
- Low lattice aft mast just forward of aft funnel
- 3.9 in gun turret in 'Y' position, 57 mm open mounting in 'X' position

NOTE: Some resemblance to the ex-Soviet 'Kola' class, now deleted

SPECIFICATION:

COUNTRY OF ORIGIN: Korea (North)
CLASS: Najin (FFG)
ACTIVE: 2
NAME (PENNANT NUMBER): (531), (591)

FEATURES:
DISPLACEMENT: 1500 tons full load
LENGTH: 334.6 ft (102 m)
BEAM: 32.8 ft (10 m)
DRAUGHT: 8.9 ft (2.7 m)
SPEED: 24 kts
RANGE: 4000 miles at 13 kts

ARMAMENT:
MISSILES: SSM – two CSS-N-1
GUNS: Two 3.9 in (100 mm)/56; four 57 mm/80 (2 twin); 12 or four 30 mm/66 (6 or 2 twin); 12 25 mm machine guns (6 twin)
A/S MORTARS: Two RBU 1200 5-tube fixed launchers
DEPTH CHARGES: Two projectors, two racks
MINES: 30
DECOYS: 6 chaff launchers

ELECTRONICS:
RADARS: Air-search – Square Tie; surface search – Pot Head; navigation – Pot Drum; fire control – Drum Tilt
SONARS: Stag Horn, hull-mounted active search/attack
EW: China RW-23 Jug Pair (Watch Dog) ESM

Ulsan KOREA (SOUTH)

Pusan

- High bows with continuous maindeck from stem to stern
- 3 in gun mounting in 'B' and 'Y' positions
- High superstructure at forward end with lower continuous superstructure to afterdeck
- Single sloping funnel aft of midships
- Large pyramid mainmast, supporting prominent spherical radome, at after end of bridge structure
- Slim, enclosed aftermast supporting DA05 air/surface search radar aerial
- Harpoon SSM angled twin launchers aft of funnel
- 40 mm sited one mount in front of bridge and two mounts to port and starboard at extreme end of raised after superstructure
- 30 mm sited two mountings in front of bridge and two mountings at extreme end of after superstructure
- A modified unit was delivered to Bangladesh in 2001, but has been decommissioned for design modification, warranty repairs and capability upgrades

NOTE: The first five ships are the same but *Kyong Buk* has the four Emerson Electric 30 mm guns replaced by three Breda 40 mm, and the last four of the class have a built-up gun platform aft

SPECIFICATION:

COUNTRY OF ORIGIN: Korea (South)
CLASS: Ulsan (FFG)
ACTIVE: 9
NAME (PENNANT NUMBER): Ulsan (FF 951), Seoul (FF 952), Chung Nam (FF 953), Masan (FF 955), Kyong Buk (FF 956), Chon Nam (FF 957), Che Ju (FF 958), Pusan (FF 959), Chung Ju (FF 961)

FEATURES:

DISPLACEMENT: 2180 tons full load; 2300 tons (FF 957 onwards)
LENGTH: 334.6 ft (102 m)
BEAM: 37.7 ft (11.5 m)
DRAUGHT: 11.5 ft (3.5 m)
SPEED: 34 kts
RANGE: 4000 miles at 15 kts

ARMAMENT:

MISSILES: SSM – eight McDonnell Douglas Harpoon (4 twin) launchers
GUNS: Two 3 in OTO Melara (76 mm)/62 Compact; eight Emerson Electric 30 mm (4 twin) (FF 951-955); six Breda 40 mm/70 (3 twin) (FF 956-961)
TORPEDOES: Six 324 mm Mk 32 (2 triple) tubes; Honeywell Mk 46 Mod 1
DEPTH CHARGES: 12
DECOYS: Four Loral Hycor SRBOC 6-barrel Mk 36; SLQ-25 Nixie towed torpedo decoy

ELECTRONICS:

RADARS: Air/surface search – Signaal DA05; surface search – Signaal ZW06 (FF 951-956), Marconi S 1810 (FF 957-961); fire control – Signaal WM28 (FF 951-956), Marconi ST 1802 (FF 957-961); navigation – Raytheon SPS-10C (FF 957-961)
SONARS: Raytheon DE 1167; hull-mounted active search and attack
EW: ULQ-11K ESM

Lekiu MALAYSIA

Jebat (*Michael Nitz*)

- High bow with straight leading edge sloping down towards bridge
- 57 mm gun mounting in 'A' position
- Seawolf VLS SAM launchers immediately forward of bridge in 'B' position
- Raised angular bridge structure with all-round windows
- Large enclosed main-mast amidships with sloping forward edge and vertical after edge
- Distinctive DA08 air-search radar aerial atop aftermast
- Very large square section funnel with shallow sloping after edge abaft aftermast
- Steeply sloping hangar doors down to large, low profile flight deck

SPECIFICATION:

COUNTRY OF ORIGIN: UK
CLASS: Lekiu (FFG)
ACTIVE: 2
NAME (PENNANT NUMBER): Lekiu (30), Jebat (29)

FEATURES:

DISPLACEMENT: 2390 tons full load
LENGTH: 346 ft (105.5 m) oa
BEAM: 42 ft (12.8 m)
DRAUGHT: 11.8 ft (3.6 m)
SPEED: 28 kts
RANGE: 5000 miles at 14 kts

ARMAMENT:

MISSILES: SSM – eight Aerospatiale MM 40 Exocet, Block 2; SAM – British Aerospace VLS Seawolf
GUNS: One Bofors 57 mm/70 SAK Mk 2; two MSI Defense Systems 30 mm/75 DS 30B
TORPEDOES: Six Whitehead B 515 324 mm (2 triple) tubes; Marconi Stingray
DECOYS: Two Super Barricade 12-barrel launchers; Graseby Sea Siren torpedo decoy

ELECTRONICS:

RADARS: Air-search – Signaal DA08; surface search – Ericsson Sea Giraffe 150HC; navigation – Racal Decca; fire control – two Marconi 1802
SONARS: Thomson-Sintra Spherion; hull-mounted, active search/attack
EW: AEG Telefunken/Marconi Mentor ESM, MEL Scimitar ECM

AIR SUPPORT:

HELICOPTERS: One Westland Super Lynx (ASW)

Bronstein MEXICO

Nicolas Bravo (old pennant number) (*Mexican Navy*)

- Sweeping continuous maindeck to break down to low freeboard quarterdeck
- Stem anchor and portside anchor (just forward of 3 in gun mounting) necessitated by large bow sonar dome
- Long forecastle with 3 in gun mounting on raised platform
- ASROC box launcher immediately aft with wide break before bridge superstructure
- Tall bridge structure with box above all-round windows
- Large enclosed mainmast/funnel combined amidships with v-shaped exhausts and complex array of radar aerials
- Torpedo tubes alongside superstructure just aft of midships
- Ship's boats on prominent davits at aft end of superstructure
- Short helicopter platform but no hangar facilities

SPECIFICATION:

COUNTRY OF ORIGIN: USA
CLASS: Bronstein (FF)
ACTIVE: 2
NAME (PENNANT NUMBER):
Hermengildo Galeana
(ex-*Bronstein*) (F202, ex-E 42, ex-FF 1037), Nicolas Bravo
(ex-*McCloy*) (F201, ex-E 40, ex-FF 1038)

FEATURES:

DISPLACEMENT: 2650 tons full load
LENGTH: 371.5 ft (113.2 m)
BEAM: 40.5 ft (12.3 m)
DRAUGHT: 13.5 ft (4.1 m)
SPEED: 24 kts
RANGE: 3924 miles at 15 kts

ARMAMENT:

MISSILES: A/S – Honeywell ASROC Mk 112 octuple launcher (non-operational)
GUNS: Two USN 3 in (76 mm)50 (twin) or one Bofors 57 mm/70 Mk2 SAK
TORPEDOES: Six 324 mm US Mk 32 Mod 7 (2 triple) tubes; Honeywell Mk 46
DECOYS: Two Loral Hycor 6-barrel Mk 33 fixed launchers; chaff/IR flares; T-Mk 6 Fanfare Torpedo decoy

ELECTRONICS:

RADARS: Air-search – Lockheed SPS-40D; surface search – Raytheon SPS-10F; navigation – Marconi LN66; fire control – General Electric Mk 35
SONARS: EDO/General Electric SQS-26 AXR bow-mounted, active search/attack

AIR SUPPORT:

HELICOPTERS: Platform only

Oslo NORWAY

Bergen

SPECIFICATION:

COUNTRY OF ORIGIN: Norway
CLASS: Oslo (FFG)
ACTIVE: 3
NAME (PENNANT NUMBER):
Bergen (F 301), Trondheim
(F 302), Narvik (F 304)

FEATURES:
DISPLACEMENT: 1950 tons
full load
LENGTH: 317 ft (96.6 m)
BEAM: 36.8 ft (11.2 m)
DRAUGHT: 18 ft (5.5 m) (screws)
SPEED: 25+ kts
RANGE: 4500 miles at 15 kts

ARMAMENT:
MISSILES: SSM – four Kongsberg
Penguin Mk 1; SAM – Raytheon
RIM-7M Sea Sparrow Mk 29
octuple launcher
GUNS: Two US 3 in (76 mm)/50
Mk 33 (twin); one Bofors
40 mm/70; two Rheinmetall
20 mm/20 (not in all)
TORPEDOES: Six 324 mm US
Mk 32 (2 triple) tubes;
Marconi Stingray
A/S MORTARS: Kongsberg Terne III
6-tubed trainable
MINES: Mine-laying capability
DECOYS: Two chaff launchers

ELECTRONICS:
RADARS: Air-search – Siemens/
Plessey AWS-9; surface search –
Racal Decca TM 1226; navigation
– Decca; fire control – NobelTech
9LV 218 Mk 2; Raytheon Mk 95
(Sea Sparrow)
SONARS: Thomson-Sintra/Simrad
TSM 2633; combined hull and
VDS; Simrad Terne III
EW: Argo AR 700 ESM

- High bow with continuous sweeping maindeck from stem to stern
- Long forecastle with 3 in gun twin mounting forward of Kongsburg Terne III 6-tube A/S mortar launchers
- High superstructure with large pedestal-mounted AWS-9 air-search radar aerial atop
- Unusual tripod/pole mainmast configuration at after end of forward superstructure sloping at an angle aft
- Low, slim, black-capped angled funnel below angled mainmast
- After superstructure has tall slim pedestal-mounted Mk 95 fire control radar aerial atop
- Sea Sparrow SAM box launcher at after end of after superstructure
- 40 mm/70 gun mounting in 'Y' position
- Penguin SSM launcher right aft on quarterdeck

Fridtjof Nansen NORWAY

Fridtjof Nansen (*Norwegian Navy*)

- Sharply raked bows with long foredeck, 3 in gun mounting midway between stem and bridge superstructure
- High, flush central superstructure with massive enclosed mast with SPY-1F phased array radar panels atop bridge superstructure
- Fire control radar immediately above bridge
- Kongsberg SSM launchers, angled port and starboard, on superstructure immediately aft of mainmast
- Slim tapered funnel with two low exhausts atop. Ship's boats alongside
- Aft superstructure with optronics director and fire control radar atop low deckhouse
- Short flightdeck aft
- Rounded surfaces to superstructure

NOTE: Design based on Spanish F-100

SPECIFICATION:

COUNTRY OF ORIGIN: Spain
CLASS: Fridtjof Nansen (Project
SMP 6088) (FFG)
BUILDING: 5
NAME (PENNANT NUMBER):
Fridtjof Nansen (F 310), Roald
Amundsen (F 311), Otto Sverdrup
(F 312), Helge Ingstad (F 313),
Thor Heyerdahl (F 314)

FEATURES:
DISPLACEMENT: 5290 tons full load
LENGTH: 433.1 ft (132 m)
BEAM: 55.1 ft (16.8 m)
DRAUGHT: 16.1 ft (4.9 m)
SPEED: 27 kts
RANGE: 4500 miles at 16 kts

ARMAMENT:
MISSILES: SSM – eight Kongsberg
NSM; SAM – Mk 41 with eight
cells for 32 Evolved Sea Sparrow
GUNS: One OTO Melara 3 in
(76 mm)/62 Super Rapid; four
12.7 mm machine guns; fitted for
one 40 mm/70 gun
TORPEDOES: Six 324 mm
(2 double) tubes; Marconi Stingray
DECOYS: Terma SKWS chaff,
IR/acoustic

ELECTRONICS:
RADARS: Air-search – Lockheed
Martin SPY-1F phased array;
surface search – Litton;
navigation – two Litton; fire
control – two Mk 82
SONARS: Thomson-Marconi
Spherion MRS 2000 and Mk 2
ATAS VDS
EW: Condor CS-3701 ESM

AIR SUPPORT:
HELICOPTERS: One NH 90

Amazon PAKISTAN

Badr

- Long forecastle with raised bows
- 4.5 in gun mounting in 'A' position
- China LY 60N sextuple SAM box launchers on raised platform immediately forward of bridge in D 181, D 183 and D 185. Harpoon SSM launchers in D 186, D 184 and D 182
- Low superstructure with tall enclosed mast aft of bridge, topped by Type 992R air/surface search radar in D 186; replaced by Signaal DA08 larger array in D 185, D 181 and D 183
- Low, squat funnel with sloping top from forward to aft
- Slim black-painted aftermast immediately forward of funnel
- Vulcan Phalanx CIWS aft end of hanger. D 182, D 184 and D 186 have Selenia Type 912 (RTN-10X) fire control radar atop hanger roof, forward of CIWS mounting, and torpedo tubes at break down to flight deck (latter, also D 184 and D 186)
- Short helicopter flight deck, with break down to very short quarterdeck

contd.

Amazon contd.

SPECIFICATION:

COUNTRY OF ORIGIN: UK
CLASS: Amazon (Tariq) (Type 21)
(DDG/DD/FFG/FF)
ACTIVE: 6
NAME (PENNANT NUMBER):
Tariq (ex-*Ambuscade*) (D 181,
ex-F 172), Babur (ex-*Amazon*)
(D 182, ex-F 169), Khaibar
(ex-*Arrow*) (D 183, ex-F 173), Badr
(ex-*Alacrity*) (D 184, ex-F 174),
Tippu Sultan (ex-*Avenger*) (D 185,
ex-F 185), Shahjahan (ex-*Active*)
(D 186, ex-F 171)

FEATURES:

DISPLACEMENT: 3700 tons
full load
LENGTH: 384 ft (117 m) oa
BEAM: 41.7 ft (12.7 m)
DRAUGHT: 19.5 ft (5.9 m) screws
SPEED: 30 kts
RANGE: 4000 miles at 17 kts

ARMAMENT:

MISSILES: SSM – four Harpoon 1C
in D 182, 184 and 186; SAM –
China LY 6ON sextuple launcher
in D 181, 183 and 185
GUNS: One Vickers 4.5 in
(114 mm)/55 Mk 8; one 20 mm
Vulcan Phalanx Mk 15 replacing
Seacat in D 183, 184 and 186;
two MSI DS 30B 30 mm/75
(D 182, 185, 186)
TORPEDOES: Six 324 mm Plessey
STWS Mk 2 (2 triple) tubes in
D 184 and 186; others with
Bofors Type 43X2 single
launchers
DECOYS: Two Vickers Corvus
8-tubed trainable launchers;
SRBOC Mk 36 launchers in
D 181, 182-183; Graseby
Type 182 towed torpedo decoy

ELECTRONICS:

RADARS: Air/surface search –
Marconi Type 992R, replaced by
Signaal DA08 in D 181, 183, 185;
surface search – Kelvin Hughes
Type 1006 in D 184, 186
(Type 1007 in remainder);
fire control – one Selenia Type
912 (RTN 10X) in D 182, 184, 186,
one China LL-1 in D 181, 183
and 185 (for LY 6ON)
SONARS: Graseby Type 184P
hull-mounted, active
search/attack; Kelvin Hughes
Type 162M, hull-mounted;
Thomson-Marconi ATAS, active
EW: Thomson-CSF DR-3000S ESM

AIR SUPPORT:

HELICOPTERS: One Westland Lynx
HAS 3 (ASW/ASV)

Cannon PHILIPPINES, THAILAND

Rajah Humabon

- Low freeboard, continuous maindeck from high, sharp bow to stern
- Open 3 in gun mountings in 'A' and 'B' positions
- High superstructure with open bridge forward
- Tall pole mainmast at after end of forward superstructure. Thai unit has large air/surface search radar array on gantry
- Tall, slender funnel with top angled to aft with ship's boats on davits either side

SPECIFICATION:

COUNTRY OF ORIGIN: USA
CLASS: Cannon (FF)
ACTIVE: 1 Philippines, 1 Thailand
NAME (PENNANT NUMBER):
PHILIPPINES – Rajah Humabon
(ex-*Hatsuhi*, ex-*Atherton*) (PF 11,
ex-PF 78, ex-DE 263, ex-DE 169)
THAILAND – Pin Klao
(ex-*Hemminger*) (413, ex-3, ex-1,
ex-DE 746)

FEATURES:

DISPLACEMENT: 1930 tons full
load (Thailand); 1750 tons
(Philippines)
LENGTH: 306 ft (93.3 m)
BEAM: 36.6 ft (11.2 m)
DRAUGHT: 14 ft (4.3 m)
SPEED: 18 kts
RANGE: 6700 miles at 19 kts

ARMAMENT:

GUNS: Three USN 3 in (76 mm)/50
Mk 22; six Bofors 40 mm/56
(3 twin)
TORPEDOES: Six 324 mm US
Mk 32 (not in Philippines)
A/S MORTARS: One Hedgehog
Mk 10 (not in Philippines)
DEPTH CHARGES: Eight projectors;
two racks (Thailand); eight K-gun
Mk 6 projectors; one rack
(Philippines)

ELECTRONICS:

RADARS: Air/surface search –
Raytheon SPS-5 (Thailand only);
surface search – Raytheon SPS-5
(Philippines); navigation –
Raytheon SPS-21 (Thailand),
RCA/GE Mk 26 (Philippines); fire
control – Western Electric Mk 34,
RCA/General Electric Mk 26
(Thailand)
SONARS: SQS-11 hull-mounted
active attack (Thailand); SQS-17B,
hull-mounted active search and
attack (Philippines)
EW: WLR-1 ESM (Thailand only)

Baptista de Andrade/João Coutinho   PORTUGAL

Honorio Barreto

- Stepped forecastle with 3.9 in gun mounting in 'A' position. 3 in twin mounting in 'João Coutinho' class
- Tall lattice mainmast just forward of midships with Kelvin Hughes radar
- Large, single, black-capped funnel with sloping after end
- 40 mm/70 mounting atop superstructure aft of funnel. Substituted with 40 mm/60 twin mountings in 'João Coutinho' class

NOTE: All ASW equipment removed in 1999/2000

SPECIFICATION:

COUNTRY OF ORIGIN: Spain
CLASS: Baptista de Andrade/
João Coutinho (FS)*
* Classified as corvettes
ACTIVE: 3 (Baptista de Andrade),
4 (João Coutinho)
NAME (PENNANT NUMBER):
BAPTISTA DE ANDRADE – Baptista
de Andrade (F 486), João Roby
(F 487), Afonso Cerqueira (F 488)
JOÃO COUTINHO – Antonio Enes
(F 471), João Coutinho (F 475),
Jacinto Candido (F 476), General
Pereira d'Eca (F 477)

FEATURES:
DISPLACEMENT: 1380 tons
full load
LENGTH: 277.5 ft (84.6 m)
BEAM: 33.8 ft (10.3 m)
DRAUGHT: 10.2 ft (3.1 m); 10.8 ft
(3.3 m) ('João Coutinho' class)
SPEED: 22 kts
RANGE: 5900 miles at 18 kts

ARMAMENT:
GUNS: Two Creusot-Loire 3.9 in
(100 mm)/55 Mod 1968 ('Baptista
de Andrade' class); two US 3 in
(76 mm)/50 (twin) Mk 33 in 'João
Coutinho' class; two Bofors
40 mm/70; two Bofors 40 mm/60
(twin) in 'João Coutinho' class

ELECTRONICS:
RADARS: Air/surface search –
Kelvin Hughes 1007 ('João
Coutinho' class); navigation –
Decca
RM 316P and one KH 5000
Nucleos 2; Racal Decca
RM 1226C ('João Coutinho' class)

AIR SUPPORT:
HELICOPTERS: Platform only for
one Westland Super Lynx Mk 95

Comandante João Belo   PORTUGAL, URUGUAY

Comandante Hermengildo Capelo (*J. Mortimer*)

- Long forecastle with high forward superstructure and high freeboard
- 3.9 in gun turret in 'A' position
- Mortier 305 mm 4 barrel A/S launcher on Uruguay ships in 'B' position
- Large lattice mainmast at after end of forward superstructure
- Single large, black-capped funnel well aft of midships
- DRBC 31D fire control director atop after superstructure
- 3.9 in gun mountings aft ('X' position, removed from Portuguese ships)

NOTE: SSM launchers removed from Uruguay units in 1999/2000

SPECIFICATION:

COUNTRY OF ORIGIN: France
CLASS: Comandante João Belo (FF), Commandant Rivière (FFG)
ACTIVE: 3 Portugal (Comandante João Belo), 3 Uruguay (Commandant Rivière)
NAME (PENNANT NUMBER):
PORTUGAL – Comandante João Belo (F 480), Comandante Hermengildo Capelo (F 481), Comandante Sacadura Cabral (F 483)
URUGUAY – Uruguay (ex-*Commandant Bourdais*) (1), General Artigas (ex-*Victor Schoelcher*) (2), Montevideo (ex-*Admiral Charner*) (3, ex-4)

FEATURES:

DISPLACEMENT: 2250 tons full load
LENGTH: 336.9 ft (102.7 m)
BEAM: 38.4 ft (11.7 m)
DRAUGHT: 14.4 ft (4.4 m) (Portugal); 14.1 ft (4.3 m) (Uruguay)
SPEED: 25 kts
RANGE: 7500 miles at 15 kts

ARMAMENT:

GUNS: Two (one in Portuguese ships) Creusot-Loire or DCN 3.9 in (100 mm)/55 Mod 1953; two Bofors 40 mm/60/70 (two Hispano-Suiza 30 mm Uruguay)
TORPEDOES: Six 324 mm Mk 32 Mod 5 (2 triple tubes); Honeywell Mk 46 Mod 5 (Portugal); six 21.7 mm (550 mm) (2 triple) tubes; ECAN L3 (Uruguay)
A/S MORTARS: One Mortier 305 mm 4-barrel launcher (Uruguay only)
DECOYS: Two Loral Hycor SRBOC 6-barrel Mk 36 SRBOC chaff launchers; SLQ-25 Nixie towed torpedo decoy (Portugal only)

ELECTRONICS:

RADARS: Air-search – Thomson-CSF DRBV 22A; surface search – Thomson-CSF DRBV 50 (Portugal only); navigation – Kelvin Hughes KH 1007 (Portugal), Racal Decca 1226 (Uruguay); fire control – Thomson-CSF DRBC 31D (Portugal), Thomson-CSF DRBC 32C (Uruguay)
SONARS: CDC SQS-510 hull-mounted active search/attack (Portugal); EDOM SQS-17, hull-mounted (Uruguay); Thomson-Sintra DUBA 3A, hull-mounted (both classes)

Marasesti ROMANIA

Marasesti (*H & L van Ginderen collection*)

- Continuous sweeping maindeck line from stem to stern with open quarterdeck below. Small break at forward SSM position
- 3 in gun mountings in 'A' and 'B' positions with Styx SS-N-2C SSM in box-like angled launchers alongside 'B' position and facing astern at aft end of superstructure
- Tall, box-like bridge superstructure topped by short lattice mast and, immediately above bridge, Hawk Screech fire control radar on raised platform
- Second lattice mast, aft, on raised platform, forward of square, tapering funnel

SPECIFICATION:

COUNTRY OF ORIGIN: Romania
CLASS: Marasesti (FFG)
ACTIVE: 1
NAME (PENNANT NUMBER):
Marasesti (ex-*Muntenia*) (111)

FEATURES:

DISPLACEMENT: 5790 tons full load
LENGTH: 474.4 ft (144.6 m)
BEAM: 48.6 ft (14.8 m)
DRAUGHT: 23 ft (7 m)
SPEED: 27 kts

ARMAMENT:

MISSILES: SSM – eight SS-N-2C Styx
GUNS: Four USSR 3 in (76 mm)/60
(2 twin); four 30 mm/65
6-barrelled
TORPEDOES: Six 21 in (533 mm)
(2 triple) tubes; Russian 53-65
A/S MORTARS: Two RBU 6000
12-tubed trainable launchers
DECOYS: Two PK 16 chaff
launchers

ELECTRONICS:

RADARS: Air/surface search – Strut
Curve; surface search – Plank
Shave; navigation – Nayada
(MR 212); fire control – two
Drum Tilt, Hawk Screech
SONARS: Hull-mounted, active
search/attack
EW: Two Watch Dog ESM, Bell
Clout and Bell Slam ECM

AIR SUPPORT:

HELICOPTERS: Two IAR-316B
Alouette III (ASW)

Tetal/Improved Tetal ROMANIA

Admiral Petre Barbuneanu

SPECIFICATION:

COUNTRY OF ORIGIN: Romania
CLASS: Tetal/Improved Tetal*
* Rated as corvettes
ACTIVE: 2 (Tetal), 2 (Improved Tetal)
NAME (PENNANT NUMBER):
TETAL – Admiral Petre Barbuneanu (260), Vice Admiral Eugeniu Rosca (263)
IMPROVED TETAL – Contre Admiral Eustatiu Sebastian (264), Admiral Horia Macelariu (265)

FEATURES:

DISPLACEMENT: 1440 tons full load; 1500 tons (Improved Tetal)
LENGTH: 303.1 ft (95.4 m)
BEAM: 38.4 ft (11.7 m)
DRAUGHT: 9.8 ft (3 m); 10 ft (3.1 m) (Improved Tetal)
SPEED: 24 kts

ARMAMENT:

GUNS: Four USSR 3 in (76 mm)/60 (2 twin) (Tetal); one USSR 3 in (76 mm)/60 (Improved Tetal); four USSR 30 mm/65 (2 twin) (Tetal); four 30 mm/65 AK 630 (Improved Tetal); two 14.5 mm machine guns (Tetal)
TORPEDOES: Four 21 in (533 mm) (twin) tubes; Russian Type 53-65
A/S MORTARS: Two RBU 2500 16-tubed trainable (Tetal); two RBU 6000 12-tubed trainable (Improved Tetal)
DECOYS: Two PK 16 chaff launchers

ELECTRONICS:

RADARS: Air/surface search – Strut Curve; navigation – Nayada; fire control – Drum Tilt, Hawk Screech (only in Tetal)
SONARS: Hercules (MG 322) hull-mounted, active search/attack
EW: Two Watch Dog ESM

AIR SUPPORT:

HELICOPTERS: One IAR 316B Alouette III (ASW) (Improved Tetal only)

- Regular profile hull with continuous maindeck from stem to stern
- Very long forecastle with 3 in gun mounting in 'A' position
- A/S mortar mounting in 'B' mounting position
- Long superstructure centred well aft of midships
- Large mainmast amidships, with enclosed bottom half and lattice top. (Lattice throughout in 'Improved Tetal')
- Hawk Screech fire control radar aerial atop after end of bridge structure in 'Tetal' class. Drum Tilt in 'Improved Tetal'
- Drum Tilt fire control radar aerial mounted atop tall pedestal towards after end of superstructure ('Tetal' class only)
- Short, squat black-capped funnel aft of mainmast and aft of superstructure in 'Improved Tetal'
- 30 mm/65 gun mountings at after end of after superstructure, one port one starboard
- 3 in gun mounting in 'Y' position in 'Tetal' class. Missing from 'Improved Tetal' – long helicopter deck substituted

NOTE: Heavily modified Soviet 'Koni' design

Grisha II/III/V RUSSIA, LITHUANIA, POLAND, UKRAINE
Aukstaitis (*Michael Nitz*)

- High bow with sweeping lines to stern
- SA-N-4 Gecko SAM launcher in 'A' mounting position. 57 mm/80 gun twin mounting in this position in 'Grisha II'
- Two A/S mortar launchers, port and starboard in 'B' mounting position
- Pyramid mainmast at after end of forward superstructure
- Small 'Y' shaped (in profile) lattice mast at top after end of mainmast (enclosed in 'Grisha II')
- Pop Group fire control radar aerial atop forward superstructure, forward of mainmast (except 'Grisha II')
- Single, low profile, square shaped funnel just aft of midships
- Small after superstructure with slender lattice mast at forward end, and Muff Cob fire control radar aerial atop after end. Bass Tilt in 'Grisha III/V' with 30 mm/65 mountings
- 57 mm/80 gun mounting in 'Y' position

NOTE: Most obvious identification of 'Grisha II' is 57 mm/80 gun mounting in 'A' position. 'Grisha III' same as 'Grisha I' except for raised after superstructure with Bass Tilt fire control radar aerial atop. 'Grisha V' is the only type with a

SPECIFICATION:

COUNTRY OF ORIGIN: Russia
CLASS: Grisha II (Type 1124P)
(Albatros) (FFL)
ACTIVE: 2 Ukraine
CLASS: Grisha III (Type 1124M)
(Albatros) (FFL)
ACTIVE: 2 Lithuania, 3 Russia,
one designated 'Grisha IV'
CLASS: Grisha V (Type 1124EM/P)
(Albatros) (FFL)
ACTIVE: 20 Russia, 1 Ukraine
BUILDING: 1 Ukraine
CLASS: Kaszub (Type 620) (FSG)
ACTIVE: 1 Poland
NAME (PENNANT NUMBER):
LITHUANIA – Zemaitis (F 11
ex-MPK 108), Aukstaitis
(F 12 ex-MPK 44)
UKRAINE – Grisha II – Chernigiv
(ex-Izmail) (U 205), Vinnitsa (ex-
Dnepr) (U 206); Grisha V – Lutsk
(U 200, ex-400), Ternopil (U 202)
POLAND – Kaszub (240)
RUSSIA – Grisha III – MPK 49, 127,
191; Grisha V – MPK 7, 14, 17, 28,
56, 59, 64, 82, 107, 113, 118, 130,
134, 139, 194, 199, 214, 217, 221, 222

Krivak I/II/III RUSSIA, UKRAINE

Neukrotimy, Russian Krivak II

'Krivak I':
- Long forecastle with, from forward, Raduga ss-n-14 Silex A/s curved missile launcher, SA-N-4 Gecko SAM launcher and ss-n-25 SSM launcher (latter not Ukraine)
- Forward superstructure with, at after end, complex of three lattice masts forming the mainmast structure with large air-search radar aerial atop
- Single, low profile funnel well aft of midships
- Pop Group and Owl Screech fire control radar aerials mounted on complex structure between mainmast and funnel
- 3 in gun mountings in 'Y' and 'X' positions

NOTE: Most obvious identification of 'Krivak II/III' is RBU 6000 A/s mortar mounting in place of SSM launcher on forecastle. 'Krivak III' has a 3.9 gun mounting in 'A' position and a flight deck over open quarterdeck, replacing

 Krivak III

gun mountings in 'x'
and 'y' positions
NOTE 2: See entry for
Indian 'Talwar' class –
dramatic development
of improved 'Krivak III'
NOTE 3: The Russian
Border Guard also
operates seven 'Krivak
III' units. These hulls
have diagonal
white/blue/red stripes
in all units except those
based in the Black Sea

SPECIFICATION:

COUNTRY OF ORIGIN: Russia
CLASS: Krivak I/II/III (Type
1135/1135m/1135MP) (FFG/FF/FFH)
ACTIVE: 15 Russia, 1 Ukraine
NAME (PENNANT NUMBER):
RUSSIA – TYPE I/TYPE I MOD:
Legky (ex-*Leningradsky
Komsomolets*) (930), Letuchy (661),
Pylky (702), Zadorny (955), Ladny
(801), Zharky (937)
RUSSIA – TYPE II: Neukrotimy
(731), Pytlivy (808)
RUSSIA – TYPE III: Menzhinsky
(113), Dzerzhinsky (057), Orel
(ex-*Imeni XXVII Sezda KPSS*) (156),
Pskov (ex-*Imeni LXX Letiya
VCHK-KGB*) (104), Anadyr (ex-*Imeni
LXX Letiya Pogramvoysk*) (060),
Kedrov (103), Vorovsky (052)
UKRAINE – TYPE III: Hetman
Sagaidachny (U 130, ex-201)

FEATURES:

DISPLACEMENT: 3650 tons full load
LENGTH: 405.2 ft (123.5 m)
BEAM: 46.9 ft (14.3 m)
DRAUGHT: 16.4 ft (5 m)
SPEED: 32 kts
RANGE: 4600 miles at 20 kts

ARMAMENT:

MISSILES: SSM – eight Zvezda
SS-N-25 Sapless (Kh 35 Uran)
(2 quad), (Krivak I after modernisation not Ukraine unit); SAM –
two SA-N-4 Gecko twin launchers
(one in Krivak III); A/S – Raduga
SS-N-14 Silex quad launcher (not
in Krivak III); payload – nuclear
or Type E53-72 torpedo
GUNS: Four 3 in (76 mm)/60 (2 twin)
(Krivak I); two 3.9 in (100 mm)/59
(Krivak II) (one in Krivak III); two
30 mm/65 (Krivak III)
TORPEDOES: Eight 21 in (533 mm)
(2 quad) tubes
MINES: Capacity for 16 (not
Ukraine)
A/S MORTARS: Two RBU 6000
12-tubed trainable (not
modernised Krivak I)
DECOYS: Four PK 16 or ten PK 10
chaff launchers; towed torpedo
decoy

ELECTRONICS:

RADARS: Air-search – Head Net
'c', 3D, or Half Plate (Krivak I) or
Top Plate (Krivak mod. I and
Krivak III); surface search – Don
Kay or Palm Frond or Don 2 or
Spin Trough and Peel Cone (Peel
Cone only in Russian Krivak III);
navigation – Kivach (Ukraine
only); fire control – two Eye Bowl
(not in Krivak III), two Pop Group
(one in Krivak III), Owl Screech
(Krivak I), Kite Screech (Krivak II
and III),
Bass Tilt (Krivak III)
SONARS: Bull Nose (MGK 335MS);
hull-mounted, active
search/attack; Mare Tail or Steer
Hide (some Krivak Is after
modernisation); VDS
EW: Two Bell Shroud, two Bell
Squat, Half Cup laser
intercept (in some but
not Ukraine)

AIR SUPPORT:

HELICOPTERS: One Kamov Ka-27
Helix (ASW) (Krivak III)

217

Neustrashimy RUSSIA

Neustrashimy

- Elegant profile with front of long forecastle slightly depressed
- 3.9 in gun mounting in 'A' position
- SA-N-9 Gauntlet (Klinok) SAM VLS tubes just aft of forward mounting
- RBU 12000 A/S mortar mounting in 'B' mounting position
- Forward superstructure has short forward mast at its after end supporting Cross Sword fire control radar aerial
- Twin funnels. Forward one aft of forward superstructure, after one aft of mainmast
- Large, pyramid mainmast well aft of midships with distinctive Top Plate air/surface radar aerial atop
- Two horizontal launchers at main deck level, alongside aft funnel, port and starboard, angled at 18° from forward that double for A/S missiles and torpedoes
- CADS-N-1 SAM/guns mounting at after end of after superstructure, just forward of flight deck
- VDS towing array right aft

NOTE: Class slightly larger than 'Krivak'. Helicopter deck extends across the full width of the ship
NOTE 2: After funnel is unusually flush decked, therefore not obvious in profile

SPECIFICATION:

COUNTRY OF ORIGIN: Russia
CLASS: Neustrashimy (Jastreb) (Type 1154) (FFG)
ACTIVE: 1
NAME (PENNANT NUMBER): Neustrashimy (712)

FEATURES:

DISPLACEMENT: 4250 tons full load
LENGTH: 430.4 ft (131.2 m) oa
BEAM: 50.9 ft (15.5 m)
DRAUGHT: 15.7 ft (4.8 m)
SPEED: 30 kts
RANGE: 4500 miles at 16 kts

ARMAMENT:

MISSILES: SSM – fitted for but not with eight SS-N-25 Sapless (Kh 35 Uran); SAM – four SA-N-9 Gauntlet (Klinok) octuple vertical launchers; SAM/guns – two CADS-N-1 (Kortik/Kashtan) – each has a twin 30 mm Gatling combined with eight SA-N-11 Grisson and Hot Flash/Hot Spot fire control radar/optronic director; A/S – SS-N-15/16, Type 40 torpedo or nuclear warhead fired from torpedo tubes
GUNS: One 3.9 in (100 mm)
TORPEDOES: Six 21 in (533 mm) tubes combined with a/s launcher; can fire SS-N-15/16 missiles or anti-submarine torpedoes
A/S MORTARS: One RBU 12000; 10-tubed, trainable
MINES: Two rails
DECOYS: Eight PK 10 and two PK 16 chaff launchers

ELECTRONICS:

RADARS: Air-search – Top Plate, 3D; air/surface search – Cross Dome; navigation – two Palm Frond; fire control – Cross Sword, (SAM) Kite Screech B (SSM/guns), two Salt Pot, four Box Bar
SONARS: Ox Yoke and Whale Tongue, hull-mounted; Ox Tail VDS or towed sonar array
EW: Two Foot Ball, two Half Hat, four Half Cup laser intercept

AIR SUPPORT:

HELICOPTERS: One Kamov Ka-27PL Helix (ASW)

Steregushchiy RUSSIA

Steregushchiy

- Multipurpose frigate to replace 'Grisha' class
- Incorporates features to reduce radar echo
- Gun in 'A' position with CADS-N-1 launcher behind in front of bridge
- Tall pyramid structure at aft end of bridge supporting enclosed mast
- Quad SS-N-25 launchers in gap between forward superstructure and very low, squat funnel
- Second CADS-N-1 launcher on top of aft superstructure

SPECIFICATION:

COUNTRY OF ORIGIN: Russia
CLASS: Steregushchiy
ACTIVE: 1
BUILDING: 2
PLANNED: 2
NAME (PENNANT NUMBER):
Steregushchiy (—),
Soobrazitelny (—)

FEATURES:
DISPLACEMENT: 1900 tons full load
LENGTH: 366.2 ft (111.6 m) oa
BEAM: 45.9 ft (14 m)
DRAUGHT: 12.1 ft (3.7 m)
SPEED: 26 kts
RANGE: 4000 miles at 14 kts

ARMAMENT:
MISSILES: SSM – eight Zvezda
SS-N-25 (Kh 35 Uran) (2 quad);
SAM/guns– two CADS-N-1
(Kashtan) combined with eight
SA-N-11 (Grisson);
A/S – Medvedka (SS-N-29)
GUNS: One 100 mm A-190;
two 14.5 mm machine guns

ELECTRONICS:
RADARS: Air/surface search –
Top Plate, 3D; fire control –
Plank Shave, Kite Screech
SONARS: Bow-mounted
EW: ESM/ECM

AIR SUPPORT:
HELICOPTERS: Platform aft for
one Ka-27 Helix

Madina SAUDI ARABIA

Abha

- Long forecastle. Continuous maindeck profile with break down to quarterdeck
- 3.9 in gun mounting in 'A' position
- Forward superstructure has slim tripod mainmast at after end
- Unusually large funnel with large black, wedge-shaped smoke deflector at after end, sited just aft of midships
- Otomat SSM launchers in break between funnel and forward superstructure
- Crotale SAM launcher atop after superstructure
- Small flight deck
- Short quarterdeck with VDS operating gear

SPECIFICATION:

COUNTRY OF ORIGIN: France
CLASS: Madina (Type F 2000S) (FFG)
ACTIVE: 4
NAME (PENNANT NUMBER):
Madina (702), Hofouf (704), Abha (706), Taif (708)

FEATURES:

DISPLACEMENT: 2870 tons full load
LENGTH: 377.3 ft (115 m)
BEAM: 41 ft (12.5 m)
DRAUGHT: 16 ft (4.9 m) (sonar)
SPEED: 30 kts
RANGE: 8000 miles at 15 kts; 6500 miles at 18 kts

ARMAMENT:

MISSILES: SSM – eight OTO Melara/Matra Otomat Mk 2 (2 quad); SAM – Thomson-CSF Crotale Naval octuple launcher
GUNS: One Creusot-Loire 3.9 in (100 mm)/55 compact Mk 2; four Breda 40 mm/70 (2 twin)
TORPEDOES: Four 21 in (533 mm) tubes; ECAN F17P
DECOYS: CSEE Dagaie double trainable mounting

ELECTRONICS:

RADARS: Air/surface search/IFF – Thomson-CSF Sea Tiger (DRBV 15); navigation – Racal Decca TM 1226; fire control – Thomson-CSF Castor IIB/C, Thomson-CSF DRBC 32
SONARS: Thomson-Sintra Diodon TSM 2630; hull-mounted, integrated Sorel VDS
EW: Thomson-CSF DR-4000 ESM; Thomson-CSF Janet ECM

AIR SUPPORT:

HELICOPTERS: One Aerospatiale SA 365F Dauphin 2 (SSM targeting)

Formidable SINGAPORE

Formidable

SPECIFICATION:

COUNTRY OF ORIGIN: France
CLASS: Formidable
ACTIVE: 2
BUILDING: 4
NAME (PENNANT NUMBER):
Formidable (68), Intrepid (69),
Steadfast (70), Tenacious (71),
Stalwart (72), Supreme (73)

FEATURES:

DISPLACEMENT: 3200 tons
full load
LENGTH: 374 ft (114 m)
BEAM: 52.5 ft (16 m)
DRAUGHT: 16.4 ft (5 m)
SPEED: 27 kts
RANGE: 4000 miles at 15 kts

ARMAMENT:

MISSILES: SSM – eight Boeing
Harpoon; SAM – Eurosaam SAAAM
4 octuple Sylver A43 VLS for
MBDA Aster 15
GUNS: One OTO Melara 3 in
(76 mm)/62 Super Rapid;
two 20 mm; two 12.7 mm
machine guns
TORPEDOES: Six 324 mm (2 triple
recessed); Eurotorp A 244/S
DECOYS: Three EADS NGDS
12-barrelled chaff launchers

ELECTRONICS:

RADARS: Air/surface search –
Thales Herakles 3D; surface
search/navigation – two Terma
Scanter 2001
SONARS: EDO 980 LF ALOFTS VDS
EW: Rafael C-Pearl-M ESM

- Derived from 'La Fayette' class (see separate entry on page 180)
- The major differences from 'La Fayette' are weapons and sensors
- Tall pyramid structure on top of bridge supporting large 3-D radar antenna
- Enclosed mast built into leading edge of aft superstructure
- Large helicopter platform aft with hangar in front
- All weapons and deck equipment enclosed or mounted low down to minimize radar echo
- All large flat surfaces sloped to reduce radar echo

Valour (Meko A-200) SOUTH AFRICA

Mendi (*Michael Nitz*)

- Long forecastle, angled main superstructure profile with break down to flight deck
- 3 in gun mounting in 'A' position
- Tall forward superstructure has large enclosed mainmast topped with air/surface search radar and thin pole mast at after end
- Break in superstrrructure with Exocet ssm angled launchers pointing port, starboard
- Squat funnel raised above aft superstructure, sited just aft of midships and topped by thin, tall pyramid mast at forward edge
- 'Window' in superstructure revealing ship's boat
- 35 mm twin cannon aft end of hangar
- Small flight deck

SPECIFICATION:

COUNTRY OF ORIGIN: Germany
CLASS: Valour (Meko A-200) (FSG)
PLANNED: 4
NAME (PENNANT NUMBER):
Amatola (F 145), Isandlwana
(F 146), Spioen Kop (F 147),
Mendi (F 148)

FEATURES:
DISPLACEMENT: 3590 tons full load
LENGTH: 397 ft (12.1 m)
BEAM: 53.8 ft (16.4 m)
DRAUGHT: 20.3 ft (6.2 m)
SPEED: 28 kts
RANGE: 7700 miles at 15 kts

ARMAMENT:
MISSILES: SSM – eight Exocet
MM 40 Block 2 (2 quad); SAM –
Umkhonto 32-cell VLS
GUNS: One OTOBreda 76 mm/62
Compact; two LIW DPG 35 mm
(twin); two Oerlikon 20 mm
TORPEDOES: Four 324 mm
(2 twin tubes)
DECOYS: Two Super Barricade
chaff launchers

ELECTRONICS:
RADARS: Air/surface search –
Thales MRR 3D; navigation –
two Racal Bridgemaster E; fire
control – two Reutech RTS 6400
SONARS: Thomson Marconi 4132
Kingklip, hull-mounted,
active search
EW: ESM and ECM

AIR SUPPORT:
HELICOPTERS: One Westland
Super Lynx (in due course)

Alvaro de Bazán SPAIN

Blas de Lezo (*Michael Nitz*)

- Long forecastle, with curving break down to slab-sided bridge superstructure
- 5 in gun mounting in 'A' position
- VLS SAM in forecastle at curving break in deckline
- Tall massive forward superstructure has Aegis SPY-1D panels above bridge
- Thin pyramid mainmast, sloping aft with forward gantries
- Two funnels, forward integrated into bridge superstructure, aft very low and squat and angled
- Break in superstructure with Harpoon SSM angled launchers pointing port and starboard. Cranes alongside aft funnel
- Fire control radar on large pyramid structure on hangar roof
- 20 mm cannon raised turret aft end of hangar
- Flight deck dropping down to very short quarterdeck
- Rounded surfaces for stealth

NOTE: Main gun, for gunfire support for land force, taken from US 'Tarawa' class

SPECIFICATION:

COUNTRY OF ORIGIN: Spain
CLASS: Alvaro de Bazán (FFG)
ACTIVE: 3
BUILDING: 4
PLANNED: 2
NAME (PENNANT NUMBER): Alvaro de Bazán (F 101), Almirante Don Juan de Borbón (F 102), Blas de Lezo (F 103), Mendez Nuñez (F 104)

FEATURES:
DISPLACEMENT: 5853 tons full load
LENGTH: 481.3 ft (141.7 m) oa
BEAM: 61 ft (18.6 m)
DRAUGHT: 16.1 ft (4.9 m)
SPEED: 28 kts
RANGE: 4500 miles at 18 kts

ARMAMENT:
MISSILES: SSM – eight Harpoon Block II (2 quad); SAM – Mk 41 48-cell VLS for Evolved Sea Sparrow and Standard SM-2MR Block IIIA
GUNS: One FMC 5 in (127 mm)/54 Mk 45 Mod 2; one Bazán 20 mm/120 Meroka 2B; two Oerlikon 20 mm
TORPEDOES: Four 324 mm (2 twin tubes); Mk 46 Mod 5
A/S MORTARS: Two ABCAS/SSTDS lauchers
DECOYS: Four SRBOC Mk 36 Mod 2 chaff launchers; SLQ-25A Nixie torpedo decoy

ELECTRONICS:
RADARS: Air/surface search – Aegis SPY-1D; surface search – DRS SPS-67 (RAN-12S); navigation – one Raytheon SPS-73(V); fire control – two Raytheon SPG-62 Mk 99 (for SAM)
SONARS: Raytheon DE 1160 F, hull-mounted, active search/attack
EW: Regulus Mk 9500 ESM, Ceselsa Aldebaran ECM

AIR SUPPORT:
HELICOPTERS: One SH-60B Seahawk LAMPS III

Chao Phraya THAILAND

Chao Phraya

- RBU 1200 A/S mortar mounting forward of 100 mm/56 gun twin mounting in 'A' position
- 37 mm/76 gun twin mounting in 'B' position
- High forward superstructure with distinctive domed Sun Visor fire control director atop
- Pyramid mainmast at after end of forward superstructure with slim lattice mast atop its after end
- YJ-1 SSM angled ribbed launchers forward and aft of funnel
- Single, angular low profile funnel well aft of midships
- Ship's boat on davits between funnel and mainmast
- Short lattice mast aft of after SSM launchers with Rice Lamp fire control. 37 mm/76 gun mounting immediately astern
- 100 mm/76 gun mounting in 'Y' position in 455 and 456. The other two have a raised flight deck over the open quarterdeck

SPECIFICATION:

COUNTRY OF ORIGIN: China
CLASS: Chao Phraya (Types 053 HT and 053 HT(H)) (modified Jianghu III) (FFG)
ACTIVE: 4
NAME (PENNANT NUMBER): Chao Phraya (455), Bangpakong (456), Kraburi (457), Saiburi (458)

FEATURES:

DISPLACEMENT: 1924 tons full load
LENGTH: 338.5 ft (103.2 m)
BEAM: 37.1 ft (11.3 m)
DRAUGHT: 10.2 ft (3.1 m)
SPEED: 30 kts
RANGE: 3500 miles at 18 kts

ARMAMENT:

MISSILES: SSM – eight YJ-1(C-801); SAM – HQ-61 launcher for PL-9 or Matra Sadral/Mistral to be fitted
GUNS: Two (457 and 458) or four China 100 mm/56 (1 or 2 twin); eight China 37 mm/76 (4 twin) H/PJ 76A
A/S MORTARS: Two RBU 1200 (China Type 86) 5-tubed fixed launchers
DEPTH CHARGES: Two BMB racks
DECOYS: Two China Type 945 GPJ 26-barrel chaff launchers

ELECTRONICS:

RADARS: Air/surface search – China Type 354 Eye Shield; surface search/fire control – China Type 352C Square Tie; navigation – Racal Decca 1290 A/D ARPA and Anritsu RA 71CA; fire control – China Type 343 Sun Visor, China Type 341 Rice Lamp
SONARS: China Type SJD-5A; hull-mounted, active search/attack
EW: China Type 923(1) ESM; China Type 981(3) ECM

AIR SUPPORT:

HELICOPTERS: Platform for one Bell 212 (Commando assault/ support) (457 and 458)

Makut Rajakumarin THAILAND

Makut Rajakumarin

- High bow, with continuous sweeping maindeck to very sharp break down to short quarterdeck
- 4.5 in gun turret just forward of bridge superstructure
- Low superstructure with enclosed mainmast forward of midships, with forward gantry and spherical fire control radar atop
- Low, angled funnel well aft of midships
- Short pedestal mast supporting prominent air/surface search radar aerial forward of funnel
- Ship's boat on davits just aft of funnel
- Twin 40 mm/70 gun turret aft end of superstructure
- 4.5 in gun turret in 'Y' position

NOTE: Lost flagship role, now a training ship

SPECIFICATION:

COUNTRY OF ORIGIN: UK
CLASS: Yarrow type (FF/AX)
ACTIVE: 1
NAME (PENNANT NUMBER):
Makut Rajakumarin (43, ex-7)

FEATURES:
DISPLACEMENT: 1900 tons full load
LENGTH: 320 ft (97.6 m)
BEAM: 36 ft (11 m)
DRAUGHT: 18.1 ft (5.5 m)
SPEED: 26 kts
RANGE: 5000 miles at 18 kts

ARMAMENT:
GUNS: Two Vickers 4.5 in
(114 mm)/55 Mk 8; two Bofors
40 mm/70 (twin); two Breda
40 mm/70 (twin); two Oerlikon
20 mm
TORPEDOES: Six Plessey PMW 49A
tubes; Honeywell Mk 46
A/S MORTARS: One Limbo
3-tube Mk 10
DEPTH CHARGES: One rack
DECOYS: Two Loral Mk 135
chaff launchers

ELECTRONICS:
RADARS: Air/surface search –
Signaal DA05; surface search
–Signaal ZW06; navigation –
Racal Decca; fire control –
Signaal WM22/61
SONARS: Atlas Elektronik
DSQS-21C; hull-mounted,
active search/attack
EW: Elettronica Newton
ESM/ECM, WLR-1 ESM

Naresuan THAILAND

Taksin (*Hachiro Nakai*)

- High bow, 5 in gun mounting in 'ᴀ' position
- Sea Sparrow sᴀᴍ vʟs launchers below maindeck level between forward mounting and bridge
- High, slab-sided forward superstructure with lattice mainmast atop at after end of bridge
- Harpoon ssᴍ launchers aft of forward superstructure
- Large platform amidships supporting Signaal ʟᴡo8 air-search radar aerial
- Square section funnel with wedge-shaped smoke deflector atop
- After superstructure has Signaal sᴛɪʀ fire control radar at forward end, China 374 ɢ fire control director on low enclosed pylon, and ᴊᴍ-83ʜ optical fire control director aft
- 37 mm/76 gun mountings, port and starboard, outboard of stir fire control radar and one deck level down
- Flight deck aft with open quarterdeck below

SPECIFICATION:

COUNTRY OF ORIGIN: China
CLASS: Naresuan (TYPE 25T) (FFG)
ACTIVE: 2
NAME (PENNANT NUMBER):
Naresuan (421, ex-621), Taksin (422, ex-622)

FEATURES:

DISPLACEMENT: 2980 tons full load
LENGTH: 393.7 ft (120 m)
BEAM: 42.7 ft (13 m)
DRAUGHT: 12.5 ft (3.8 m)
SPEED: 32 kts
RANGE: 4000 miles at 18 kts

ARMAMENT:

MISSILES: ssм – eight McDonnell Douglas Harpoon (2 quad) launchers; sᴀᴍ – Mk 41 ʟᴄʜʀ 8-cell vʟs launcher, Sea Sparrow
GUNS: One ꜰᴍᴄ 5 in (127 mm)/54 Mk 45 Mod 2; four China 37 mm/76 (2 twin) ʜ/ᴘᴊ 76ᴀ
TORPEDOES: Six 324 mm Mk 32 Mod 5 (2 triple) tubes; Honeywell Mk 46
DECOYS: 4 -China Type 945 ɢᴘ ᴊ 26-barrel chaff launchers

ELECTRONICS:

RADARS: Air-search – Signaal ʟᴡo8; surface search – China Type 360; navigation – two Raytheon sᴘs-64(ᴠ)5; fire control – two Signaal sᴛɪʀ (ssм and 5 in gun), China 374 ɢ, (37 mm gun)
SONARS: China sᴊᴅ-7; hull-mounted, active search/attack
EW: Elettronica Newton Beta

AIR SUPPORT:

HELICOPTERS: One Super Lynx or one Sikorsky s-70ʙ-7 Seahawk

Tapi/Bayandor THAILAND, IRAN

Tapi

- Unusual curved bow
- Long, sloping forecastle with open 3 in gun mounting in 'A' position. Not present in Thai units
- 20 mm gun mounting in 'B' position in Iranian units. Oto Melara 3 in, on bigger raised platform in Thai ships
- High, complex midships superstructure with sloping pole mainmast atop
- Large SPS-6C (LW04, Thailand) air/surface search radar aerial on forward platform halfway up mainmast
- Tall, sloping, black-capped funnel with curved after profile. Straight after end to funnel profile in Thai ships
- 3 in gun mounting in 'Y' position and 40 mm/60 mounting in 'X' position (Iranian ships). 40 mm/70 gun mounting in 'Y' position in Thai ships
- 20 mm mounting after end of quarterdeck in Iranian ships. Torpedo tubes on quarterdeck in Thai ships

SPECIFICATION:

COUNTRY OF ORIGIN: USA
CLASS: PF 103 (Tapi) (FF) (Bayandor) (FS)
ACTIVE: 2 Thailand, 2 Iran
NAME (PENNANT NUMBER):
THAILAND – Tapi (431, ex-5), Khirirat (432, ex-6)
IRAN – Bayandor (81, ex-US PF 103)*, Naghdi (82, ex-US PF 104)*
* Officially rated as corvettes

FEATURES:
DISPLACEMENT: 1135 tons full load (Iran); 1172 tons (Thailand)
LENGTH: 275.6 ft (84.0 m) (Iran); 275 ft (83.8 m) (Thailand)
BEAM: 33.1 ft (10.1 m) (Iran); 33 ft (10 m) (Thailand)
DRAUGHT: 10.2 ft (3.1 m) (Iran); 10 ft (3 m) (Thailand)
SPEED: 20 kts
RANGE: 2400 miles at 18 kts

ARMAMENT:
GUNS: Two US 3 in (76 mm)/50 Mk 3/4; one Bofors 40 mm/60 (twin); two Oerlikon GAM-BO1 20 mm; two 12.7 mm machine guns (Iran); one OTO Melara 3 in (76 mm)/62 Compact; one Bofors 40 mm/70; two Oerlikon 20 mm; two 12.7 mm machine guns (Thailand)
TORPEDOES: Six 324 mm UK Mk 32 (2 triple) tubes; Honeywell Mk 46 (Thailand only)
DEPTH CHARGES: One rack (Thailand only)

ELECTRONICS:
RADARS: Air/surface search – Westinghouse SPS-6C (Signaal LW04, Thailand); surface search – Racal Decca (Raytheon SPS-53E, Thailand); navigation – Raytheon 1650 (Iran); fire control – Western Electric Mk 36 (Iran), Signaal WM22-61 (Thailand)
SONARS: EDO SQS-17A; hull-mounted (Iran); Atlas Elektronik DSQS-21C, hull-mounted, active search/attack (Thailand)

Broadsword (Type 22, Batch 3) UK

Cornwall

Similar in profile to 'Broadsword' class Type 22 Batch 2. Major identification differences are as follows:

- Steeper angle stern profile
- 4.5 gun mounting in 'A' position
- Harpoon SSM angled launchers forward of mainmast
- Signaal/GE Goalkeeper CIWS immediately forward of mainmast

SPECIFICATION:

COUNTRY OF ORIGIN: UK
CLASS: Broadsword (Type 22) (Batch 3) (FFG)
ACTIVE: 4
NAME (PENNANT NUMBER): Cornwall (F 99), Cumberland (F 85), Campbeltown (F 86), Chatham (F 87)

FEATURES:

DISPLACEMENT: 4900 tons full load
LENGTH: 485.9 ft (148.1 m)
BEAM: 48.5 ft (14.8 m)
DRAUGHT: 21 ft (6.4 m)
SPEED: 30 kts
RANGE: 4500 miles at 18 kts

ARMAMENT:

MISSILES: SSM – eight McDonnell Douglas Harpoon Block 1C (2 quad) launchers; SAM – two British Aerospace Seawolf GWS 25 Mod 3
GUNS: One Vickers 4.5 in (114 mm)/55 Mk 8; one Signaal/General Electric 30 mm 7-barrel Goalkeeper; two GAM-BO1-1 20 mm
DECOYS: Outfit DLH; four Marconi Sea Gnat 6-barrel 130 mm/102 mm fixed launchers; Graseby Type 182 or SLQ-25A towed torpedo decoy
EW: Racal UAT ESM

ELECTRONICS:

RADARS: Air/surface search – Marconi Type 967/968; surface search – Racal Decca Type 2008; navigation – Kelvin Hughes Type 1007; fire control – two Marconi Type 911
SONARS: Ferranti/Thomson-Sintra Type 2050; hull-mounted, active search/attack

AIR SUPPORT:

HELICOPTERS: Two Westland Lynx HMA Mk 3/8

Duke (Type 23) UK

Iron Duke

- High bow with continuous maindeck through to stern
- Three major weapons sited on forecastle from the bow aft, 4.5 in gun mounting, Seawolf SAM VLS launchers, Harpoon SSM angled launchers
- Forward superstructure has large enclosed mainmast at after end with distinctive SATCOM domes, port and starboard, on wing platforms at its base
- Unusual square section funnel amidships with two large black exhausts protruding from the top forward edge
- Square profile after superstructure with short pyramid mast at forward edge
- Flight deck aft above open quarterdeck

NOTE: All vertical surfaces have a 7° slope and rounded edges to reduce IR emissions

SPECIFICATION:

COUNTRY OF ORIGIN: UK
CLASS: Duke (Type 23) (FFG)
ACTIVE: 13
NAME (PENNANT NUMBER):
Argyll (F 231), Lancaster (F 229, ex-F 232), Iron Duke (F 234), Monmouth (F 235), Montrose (F 236), Westminster (F 237), Northumberland (F 238), Richmond (F 239), Somerset (F 82), Sutherland (F 81), Kent (F 78), Portland (F 79), St Albans (F 83)

FEATURES:
DISPLACEMENT: 4200 tons full load
LENGTH: 436.2 ft (133 m)
BEAM: 52.8 ft (16.1 m)
DRAUGHT: 18 ft (5.5 m) (screws)
SPEED: 28 kts
RANGE: 7800 miles at 15 kts

ARMAMENT:
MISSILES: SSM – eight McDonnell Douglas Harpoon (2 quad) launchers; SAM – British Aerospace Seawolf GWS 26 Mod 1 VLS
GUNS: One Vickers 4.5 in (114 mm)/55 Mk 8; two DES/MSI DS 30B 30 mm/75
TORPEDOES: Four Cray Marine 324 mm (2 twin) tubes; Marconi Stingray
DECOYS: Outfit DLH; four Marconi Sea Gnat 6-barrel 130 mm/102 mm launchers; Type 2170 torpedo defence system
EW: Racal UAT ESM

ELECTRONICS:
RADARS: Air/surface search – Plessey Type 996(1), 3D; surface search – Racal Decca Type 1008; navigation – Kelvin Hughes Type 1007; fire control – two Marconi Type 911
SONARS: Ferranti/Thomson-Sintra Type 2050, bow-mounted, active search/attack; Dowty Type 2031Z; towed array (F 229, 231, 234-236, 238-239); to be replaced by Type 2087 from 2005

AIR SUPPORT:
HELICOPTERS: One Westland Lynx HMA 3/8 or EH Industries EH 101 Merlin HM 1 (ASV/ASW)

Corvettes

Djebel Chenoua   ALGERIA

El Chihab (without main armament) (*Diego Quevedo*)

- Continuous main deck from high, sharp bow, to low freeboard at stern
- 3 in gun mounting on forecastle immediately forward of bridge superstructure
- Steep fronted, high forward superstructure with all round bridge windows
- Tall pole mainmast at after end of forward superstructure
- 'Step down' in superstructure after of mainmast
- Very low after superstructure
- Long, low quarterdeck

NOTE: Hull size suggests association with Bazán 'Cormoran' class
NOTE 2: First two ships fitted with SSM and 76 mm guns as main armament

SPECIFICATION:

COUNTRY OF ORIGIN: Algeria
CLASS: Djebel Chenoua (C 58)
(Type 802) (FS)
ACTIVE: 3
NAME (PENNANT NUMBER):
Djebel Chenoua (351),
El Chihab (352), Al Kirch (353)

FEATURES:
DISPLACEMENT: 540 tons full load
LENGTH: 191.6 ft (58.4 m)
BEAM: 27.9 ft (8.5 m)
DRAUGHT: 8.5 ft (2.6 m)
SPEED: 31 kts

ARMAMENT:
MISSILES: SSM – four China C802
(2 twin) (CSS-N-8 Saccade)
GUNS: One Russian 3 in
(76 mm)/60; two 30 mm (twin)

ELECTRONICS:
RADARS: Surface search –
Racal Decca 1226

Nanuchka ALGERIA, LIBYA, RUSSIA

Salah Rais

- SA-N-4 Gecko SAM launcher in 'A' mounting position
- Large, distinctive Square Tie air/surface search radome atop bridge, forward of mainmast. Band Stand datalink for SS-N-9 in Russian units. Not in Algerian 802
- Styx/Siren SSM launchers on main deck adjacent to bridge, port and starboard. Two SS-N-25 launchers in Algerian 802

NOTE: 'Nanuchka IV' similar to III except she is trials vehicle for SS-NX-26

SPECIFICATION:

COUNTRY OF ORIGIN: Russia

CLASS: Nanuchka (Burya/Veter/Nakat) (Type 1234) (FSG)

ACTIVE: 3 Algeria ('Nanuchka II'/Burya), 1 Libya ('Nanuchka II'/Burya), 15 Russia (14 'Nanuchka III' (Veter) (Type 1234.1) and 1 'Nanuchka IV' (Nakat) (Type 1234.2))

NAME (PENNANT NUMBER):
ALGERIA – Rais Hamidou (801), Salah Rais (802), Rais Ali (803)
LIBYA – Tariq Ibn Ziyad (ex-Ean Mara) (416)
RUSSIA – Nanuchka III: Passat (570), Smerch (423), Razliv (450), Zyb (560), Liven (551), Geyzer (555), Rassvet (520), Mirazh (617), Moroz (409), Uragan (505), Tusha (553), Aysberg (535), Meteor (590), Shtyl (620)
RUSSIA – Nanuchka IV: Nakat (526)

FEATURES:

DISPLACEMENT: 660 tons full load
LENGTH: 194.5 ft (59.3 m)
BEAM: 38.7 ft (11.8 m)
DRAUGHT: 8.5 ft (2.6 m)
SPEED: 33 kts
RANGE: 2500 miles at 12 kts

ARMAMENT:

MISSILES: SSM – four SS-N-2C Styx ('Nanuchka II'), six Chelomey SS-N-9 Siren (Malakhit) (2 triple) launchers (Russia), 16 (4 quad) Zvezda SS-N-25 in Algerian hull 802; SAM – SA-N-4 Gecko twin launcher
GUNS: Two 57 mm/80 twin automatic ('Nanuchka II'); one 3 in (76 mm)/60 ('Nanuchka III/IV'); one 30 mm/65 ('Nanuchka III/IV' and Algeria)
DECOYS: Two PK 16 ('Nanuchka II') or four PK 10 ('Nanuchka III/IV') chaff launchers

ELECTRONICS:

RADARS: Air/surface search – Peel Pair (Plank Shave in later 'Nanuchka IIIs'); surface search – Square Tie ('Nanuchka II', Algeria 801, 803); navigation – Nayada (Russia), Don 2 ('Nanuchka II'); fire control – Pop Group (SA-N-4), Muff Cob ('Nanuchka II'), Bass Tilt ('Nanuchka III')
EW: Bell Tap ESM ('Nanuchka II'); Foot Ball and Half Hat (Russia); Half Cup laser warner (Russia)

Al Manama/Victory/Muray Jib   BAHRAIN, SINGAPORE,

Muray Jib (*Lürssen*)

- Continuous maindeck from stem to stern
- Low freeboard
- Forward superstructure has enclosed mainmast centrally sited atop. Singapore ships' mainmast bigger and taller with angled pole-mast atop. Upper portion of UAE ships' taller mast latticed
- 3 in gun mounting in 'A' position
- Flat-topped after superstructure with helicopter platform atop in Bahrain and UAE units
- No deck house with helicopter platform on Singapore ships. SATCOM dome atop short pole-mast aft of Harpoon SSM angled launchers with torpedo tubes outboard in these units
- 40 mm/70 mountings in 'Y' position (Bahrain ships)
- Goalkeeper CIWS immediately aft of mainmast in UAE ships
- Exocet SSM launchers between main superstructure and helicopter platform in Bahrain/UAE ships
- Crotale SAM launcher right aft in UAE ships
- Barak SAM launchers fitted either side of VDS in Singapore hulls

UNITED ARAB EMIRATES (UAE)

SPECIFICATION:

COUNTRY OF ORIGIN: Germany
CLASS: Al Manama/Victory/Muray
Jib (Lürssen MGB 62) (FSG)
ACTIVE: 2 Bahrain ('Al Manama'
class), 6 Singapore ('Victory'
class), 2 UAE ('Muray Jib' class)
NAME (PENNANT NUMBER):
BAHRAIN – Al Manama (50),
Al Muharraq (51)
SINGAPORE – Victory (P 88), Valour
(P 89), Vigilance (P 90), Valiant
(P 91), Vigour (P 92), Vengeance
(P 93)
UAE – Muray Jib (161, ex-CM 01,
ex-P 6501), Das (162, ex-CM 02,
ex-P 6502)

FEATURES:

DISPLACEMENT: 632 tons full load
(Bahrain); 630 tons (UAE); 595
tons (Singapore)
LENGTH: 206.7 ft (63 m) (Bahrain,
UAE); 204.7 ft (62.4 m) oa
(Singapore)
BEAM: 30.5 ft (9.3 m) (Bahrain,
UAE); 27.9 ft (8.5 m) (Singapore)
DRAUGHT: 9.5 ft (2.9 m) (Bahrain);
8.2 ft (2.5 m) (UAE); 10.2 ft (3.1 m)
(Singapore)
SPEED: 32 kts (Bahrain, UAE);
35 kts (Singapore)
RANGE: 4000 miles at 16 kts,
(Bahrain, UAE); 4000 miles at
18 kts (Singapore)

ARMAMENT:

MISSILES: SSM – eight
Aerospatiale MM 40 Exocet
Block II (2 twin) launchers
(Bahrain, UAE), eight McDonnell
Douglas Harpoon (Singapore
only); SAM – Thomson-CSF
modified Crotale Navale octuple
launcher (UAE), IAI/Rafael
Barak 1, two octuple launchers
(Singapore)
GUNS: One OTO Melara 3 in
(76 mm)/62 Compact (Super
Rapid, Singapore, UAE); two
Breda 40 mm/70 (twin) (Bahrain);
one Signaal Goalkeeper CIWS
30 mm (UAE); four CIS 50 12.7
mm machine guns (Singapore);
two 7.62 mm machine guns
(Bahrain, UAE)
TORPEDOES: Six 324 mm
Whitehead B 515 (2 triple tubes);
Whitehead A 244S (Singapore
only)
DECOYS: CSEE Dagaie (Bahrain
and UAE); two Plessey Shield
chaff launchers and four Rafael
long-range launchers (2 twin)
(Singapore)

ELECTRONICS:

RADARS: Air/surface search –
Ericsson Sea Giraffe 50/150HC;
navigation – Racal Decca 1226
(Bahrain, UAE), Kelvin Hughes
1007 (Singapore); fire control –
CelsiusTech 9LV 331 (gun and
SSM) (Bahrain), Bofors Electronic
9LV 223 (UAE), Thomson-CSF
DRBV 51C (Crotale, UAE), two Elta
EL/M-2221(X) (Singapore)
SONARS: Thomson-Sintra TSM
2064; VDS (Singapore only)
EW: Racal Decca Cutlass/Cygnus
ESM/ECM (Bahrain, UAE); Elisra
SEWS ESM; Rafael RAN 1101 ECM
(Singapore)

AIR SUPPORT:

HELICOPTERS: One Eurocopter
BO 105 (Bahrain); one
Aerospatiale SA 316 Alouette (UAE)

Barroso BRAZIL

Barroso

- Very sharp bow with forecastle sloping steeply down to slab-sided forward superstructure. 4.5 in gun mounting two-thirds from stem to bridge
- Steep fronted, high forward superstructure
- Short mast at after end of forward superstructure topped by pole mast. Forward edge sloping aft
- Break between forward and aft superstructures with angled Exocet launchers pointing port and starboard
- Large enclosed mainmast at forward edge of aft superstructure topped by surface search radar
- Squat, tapered, black-capped funnel aft of midships, atop after superstructure
- 40 mm/70 CIWS turret at after end of hangar
- Flight deck on main deck level forward of break down to open quarterdeck

SPECIFICATION:

COUNTRY OF ORIGIN: Brazil
CLASS: Barroso (FSG)
BUILDING: 1
NAME (PENNANT NUMBER): Barroso (V 34)

FEATURES:

DISPLACEMENT: 2350 tons full load
LENGTH: 328 ft (100 m)
BEAM: 37.4 ft (11.4 m)
DRAUGHT: 12.1 ft (5.3 m)
SPEED: 29 kts
RANGE: 4000 miles at 15 kts

ARMAMENT:

MISSILES: SSM – four Aerospatiale MM 40 Exocet
GUNS: One Vickers 4.5 in (115 mm) Mk 8; one Bofors SAK Sea Trinity CIWS 40 mm/70 Mk 3; two 12.7 mm machine guns
TORPEDOES: Six 324 mm Mk 32 (2 triple) tubes; Honeywell Mk 46 Mod 5 Neartip
DECOYS: Two IPQM chaff launchers

ELECTRONICS:

RADARS: Surface search – AESN RAN-20S; navigation – Terma Scanter; fire control – AESN RTN-30-X
SONARS: EDO 997(F); hull-mounted, active
EW: IPQM/Elebra ET/SLQ-1A ESM, IPQM/Elebra ET/SLQ-2 ECM

AIR SUPPORT:

HELICOPTERS: One Westland Super Lynx AH-11A (ASW/ASV)

Inhaúma BRAZIL

Inhaúma

SPECIFICATION:

COUNTRY OF ORIGIN: Brazil
CLASS: Inhaúma (FSG)
ACTIVE: 4
NAME (PENNANT NUMBER):
Inhaúma (V 30), Jaceguay (V 31),
Julio de Noronha (V 32),
Frontin (V 33)

FEATURES:

DISPLACEMENT: 1970 tons
full load
LENGTH: 314.2 ft (95.8 m)
BEAM: 37.4 ft (11.4 m)
DRAUGHT: 12.1 ft (5.3 m)
SPEED: 27 kts
RANGE: 4000 miles at 15 kts

ARMAMENT:

MISSILES: SSM – four Aerospatiale
MM 40 Exocet
GUNS: One Vickers 4.5 in
(115 mm) Mk 8; two Bofors
40 mm/70
TORPEDOES: Six 324 mm Mk 32
(2 triple) tubes; Honeywell
Mk 46 Mod 5 Neartip
DECOYS: Two Plessey Shield
chaff launchers

ELECTRONICS:

RADARS: Surface search – Plessey
AWS 4; navigation – Kelvin
Hughes Type 1007; fire control –
Selenia Orion RTN 10X
SONARS: Atlas Elektronik
DSQS-21C; hull-mounted, active
EW: Racal Cygnus B1 ESM;
IPqM SDR-7 or Elebra SLQ-1 ECM

AIR SUPPORT:

HELICOPTERS: One Westland
Super Lynx AH-11 (ASW/ASV) or
Aerospatiale UH-12/13 Ecureuil
(support)

- Apart from forecastle and quarterdeck, unusually high freeboard superstructure, flush with ship's side
- 4.5 in gun mounting in 'A' position
- Steep fronted, high forward superstructure
- Large enclosed mainmast at after end of forward superstructure topped by slender lattice mast
- Lattice aftermast atop forward end of after superstructure
- Squat, tapered, black-capped funnel aft of midships atop after superstructure
- 40 mm/70 gun mountings at after end of superstructure, port and starboard
- Flight deck on maindeck level forward of break down to quarterdeck

Brunei BRUNEI

Bendahara Sakam

- Scaled down version of Malaysian 'Lekiu' class frigates
- Continuous main deck sweeping from high sharply raked bows to low freeboard stern, over open quarterdeck
- 3 in gun turret mounting on raised platform immediately forward of VLS SAM and bridge
- Low superstructure with large enclosed angled mainmast at after end, topped by slender pole mast
- Clear break in superstructure with Exocet angled quad launchers, pointing port and starboard
- Squat, tapered, and very long black-capped funnel aft of midships
- Long flight deck on main deck level – platform only

SPECIFICATION:

COUNTRY OF ORIGIN: UK
CLASS: Brunei (FSG)
ACTIVE: 3
NAME (PENNANT NUMBER):
Nakhoda Ragham (28),
Bendahara Sakam (29),
Jerambak (30)

FEATURES:
DISPLACEMENT: 1940 tons
full load
LENGTH: 311.7 ft (95 m) oa
BEAM: 42 ft (12.8 m)
DRAUGHT: 11.8 ft (3.6 m)
SPEED: 30 kts
RANGE: 5000 miles at 12 kts

ARMAMENT:
MISSILES: SSM – eight Aero-
spatiale MM 40 Exocet Block II;
SAM – BAE 16-cell VLS Seawolf
GUNS: One OTOBreda 3 in
(76 mm) Super Rapid; two
MSI 30 mm/75
TORPEDOES: Six 324 mm Marconi
(2 triple) tubes
DECOYS: Two Super Barricade
chaff launchers

ELECTRONICS:
RADARS: Air/surface search –
Plessey AWS 9; navigation –
Kelvin Hughes Type 1007; fire
control – two Marconi 1802
SONARS: Thomson Marconi;
4130CI hull-mounted
EW: Thales Cutlass ESM;
Thales Scorpion ECM

AIR SUPPORT:
HELICOPTERS: Platform for one
medium

Tarantul I/II/III
Nipat (*Michael Nitz*)

BULGARIA, INDIA, POLAND, ROMANIA, RUSSIA, UKRAINE, VIETNAM, YEMEN

- Continuous maindeck from stem to stern with sweeping lines down from high bow to midships, then gently sloping up to slightly higher stern
- 3 in gun mounting mid-forecastle
- High central superstructure with mainmast atop. Some Russian 'Tarantul II/III' units have radomes atop bridge and/or mainmast
- Distinctive, forward pointing Styx ssm tubular launchers (two port, two starboard) on maindeck adjacent mainmast
- 30 mm/65 mountings, port and starboard, on after end of after superstructure

NOTE: The above features generally apply to all three types
NOTE 2: Former East German 'Tarantul I' now undergoing trials with us Navy

contd.

Tarantul I/II/III contd.

SPECIFICATION:

COUNTRY OF ORIGIN: Russia
CLASS: Tarantul I (Type 1241.1)
(Zborul, Gornik, Veer, Type
1241 RE); Tarantul II (Type
1241.1M) (Veer, Type 1241 RE);
Tarantul III (Type 1241.1 MP)
(Molnya) (FSG)
ACTIVE: 1 Bulgaria (Tarantul II),
13 India (Tarantul I/'Veer' class),
4 Poland (Tarantul I/'Gornik'
class), 3 Romania (Tarantul
I/'Zborul' class), 24 Russia
(4 Tarantul II; 20 Tarantul III),
1 Ukraine (Tarantul II), 4 Vietnam
(Tarantul I), 1 Yemen (Tarantul I)
BUILDING: 10 Vietnam
NAME (PENNANT NUMBER):
BULGARIA – Mulniya (101)
INDIA – Veer (K 40), Nirbhik
(K 41), Nipat (K 42), Nishank
(K 43), Nirghat (K 44), Vibhuti
(K 45), Vipul (K 46), Vinash (K 47),
Vidyut (K 48), Nashak (K 83),
Prahar (K 98) Prabal (K 99),
Pralaya (K 91)
POLAND – Gornik (434), Hutnik
(435), Metalowiec (436),
Rolnik (437)
ROMANIA – Zborul (188),
Pescarusul (189), Lastunul (190)
RUSSIA – TARANTUL II: (R 255),
(R 125), (R 29), (R 71)
RUSSIA – TARANTUL III: (R 42),
(R 291), (R 129), (R 187), (R 2),
(R 293), (R 271), (R 20), (R 14),
(R 18), (R 24), (R 297), (R 109),
(R 239), (R 60), (R 298), (R 19),
(R 261), (R 5), (R 442),
UKRAINE – Pridneprovye
(ex-Nicopol) (U 155, ex-R 54)
VIETNAM – HQ 371, HQ 372,
HQ 373, HQ 374
YEMEN – 124 (ex-971)

FEATURES:

DISPLACEMENT: 455 tons full load;
450 tons (Vietnam); 580 tons
(Yemen); 477 tons (India K 91,
K 92)
LENGTH: 184.1 ft (56.1 m)
BEAM: 37.7 ft (11.5 m)
DRAUGHT: 8.2 ft (2.5 m)
SPEED: 36 kts
RANGE: 1650 miles at 14 kts

ARMAMENT:

MISSILES: SSM – four (2 twin)
Raduga SS-N-2C/D Mod 1 Styx
launchers (16 (4 quad) SS-N-25,
India K 91, K 92), SS-N-22
Sunburn (3M-82 Moskit) (2 twin)
launchers ('Tarantul III'); SAM –
SA-N-5 Grail quad launcher
(Bulgaria, India, Poland, Russia,
Ukraine, Vietnam, Yemen)
GUNS: One 3 in (76 mm)/60;
(one OTO Melara 3 in 76 mm/60
Super Rapid in India K 91, K 92);
two 30 mm/65 AK 630
DECOYS: Two PK 16 or four PK 10
('Tarantul III') chaff launchers;
PK 16 chaff launchers
(India, Poland)

ELECTRONICS:

RADARS: Air/surface search –
Plank Shave ('Tarantul I'), Cross
Dome (India K 91, K 92), Band
Stand (with Plank Shave)
('Tarantul II' and III); navigation –
Spin Trough or Kivach II (Mius,
India), Perchora 436, 437
(Vietnam), Racal Decca
Bridgemaster (Poland); fire
control – Bass Tilt
SONARS: Foal Tail; VDS; active
(Poland, Russia, Vietnam)
EW: Bharat Ajanta P Mk II
(Indian); two Half Hat (Bulgaria)

Pauk I/II BULGARIA, CUBA, INDIA, RUSSIA, UKRAINE, VIETNAM

Bodri (below); Ajay, India (overleaf)

- High angled bow with long forecastle
- 3 in gun mounting in 'A' position
- Large, central, stepped superstructure extending from forecastle to afterdeck
- Prominent raised pedestal supporting fire control radar aerial sited amidships atop superstructure
- Tall lattice mainmast well aft of midships with small lattice mast atop at after end
- Torpedo tubes mounted on maindeck (two port, two starboard). One pair adjacent bridge, second pair adjacent mainmast (not Cuban ship)
- A/S mortars on maindeck, either side of forward superstructure
- 30 mm/65 AK 630 gun mounting right aft in 'x' position

NOTE: This appears to be an ASW version of the 'Tarantul' class
NOTE 2: First three of Russian 'Pauk I' have a lower bridge than successors
NOTE 3: Indian Pauk IIs have longer superstructure than 'Pauk I'
NOTE 4: All Russian Border Guard hulls have white, blue and red diagonal stripes painted on hulls
NOTE 5: Ukrainian Border Guard hulls are black painted with blue and yellow diagonal stripes. Upper works are painted white
NOTE 6: Vietnam's Improved 'Pauk' superstructure is set back well aft, with a lattice mast supporting a Cross Dome radome, aft of midships with SSM angled launchers outboard

contd.   Pauk I

Pauk I/II contd.

SPECIFICATION:

COUNTRY OF ORIGIN: Russia

CLASS: Pauk I (Type 1241P) (Reshitelni), Pauk II (Type 1241PE) (Abhay), Improved Pauk ('Ho-a') (FS/FSG/PCF)

ACTIVE: 2 Bulgaria (Pauk I 'Reshitelni' class FS/PCF), 1 Cuba (Pauk II FS), 4 India (Pauk II 'Abhay' class FS), 20 Russia (18 Pauk I Border Guard and 2 Pauk II, Border Guard), 1 Ukraine (Pauk I) (plus 3, Border Guard), 2 Improved Pauk, Vietnam

NAME (PENNANT NUMBER):
BULGARIA – Reshitelni (13), Bodri (14)
CUBA – 321
INDIA – Abhay (P 33), Ajay (P 34), Akshay (P 35), Agray (P 36)
RUSSIA – Pskr 800-812, Pskr 814-818, Novorossiysk (043), Kuban (149)
UKRAINE – Khmelnitsky (U 208); Border Guard – Grigory Kuropiatnikov (BG 50, ex-Pskr 817), Poltava (BG 51, ex-Pskr 813), Grigory Gnatenko (BG 52, ex-Pskr 815)
VIETNAM – HQ 381, ?

FEATURES:

DISPLACEMENT: 440 tons full load; 485 tons (India); 495 tons (Russia 'Pauk II' Border Guard); 517 tons (Vietnam)

LENGTH: 195.2 ft (59.5 m) (Bulgaria); 189 ft (57.5 m) (Russia, Ukraine); 191.9 ft (58.5 m) (Cuba, India, Russia 'Pauk II'); 195.2 ft (59.5 m) (Bulgaria); 203.4 ft (62 m) (Vietnam)

BEAM: 33.5 ft (10.2 m); 36.1 ft (11 m) (Vietnam)

DRAUGHT: 8.2 ft (2.5 m) (Vietnam); 10.8 ft (3.3 m); 11.2 ft (3.4 m) (Cuba)

SPEED: 32 kts

RANGE: 2200 miles at 14 kts

ARMAMENT:

MISSILES: SAM – SA-N-5 Grail quad launcher (no SAM launchers in Ukrainian Border Guard ships); eight Zvezda SS-N-25 (2 quad) (Vietnam)

GUNS: One 3 in (76 mm)/60; one 30 mm/65 AK 630; four 25 mm (2 twin) fitted on stern of Cuban ship

TORPEDOES: Four 16 in (406 mm) tubes; Type 40 ('Pauk I', not Cuba) or four 21 in (533 mm) ('Pauk II'); SET-65E (India); none in Vietnam ships

A/S MORTARS: Two RBU 1200 5-tubed fixed launcher; not in Vietnam

MINES: Rails only fitted in Vietnam

DEPTH CHARGES: Two racks; 12 mines (not Cuba, India or Russian 'Pauk II')

DECOYS: Two PK 16 or PK 10 chaff launchers

ELECTRONICS:

RADARS: Air/surface search – Peel Cone ('Pauk I'), Positive E ('Pauk II'), Cross Dome (India, Russia 'Pauk II'); surface search – Kivach, Pechora or SRN 207 (Russia, Ukraine), Spin Trough (Bulgaria); navigation – Pechora (Cuba, India); fire control – Bass Tilt

SONARS: Rat Tail; VDS (mounted on transom) (Cuba, India); Foal Tail VDS (Bulgaria, Russia, Ukraine)

EW: Three Brick Plug (Bulgaria, Russia, Ukraine) ESM; two Half Hat (Russia 'Pauk I', Ukraine) ESM

Pauk II

Kralj CROATIA

Kralj Petar Kresimir

- Smooth, rounded hull with low forecastle and continuous maindeck from stem to stern
- 57 mm/70 gun mounting in 'A' position
- Long, central superstructure, raised in bridge area and at aft end
- Pyramid shaped, lattice mainmast aft of bridge
- 30 mm/65 ak 630 mounting on raised platform at aft end of superstructure
- Saab RBS 15 SSM angled box launchers on afterdeck, port and starboard, trained forward

NOTE: Derived from the 'Koncar' fast attack (missile) class with a stretched hull and a new superstructure. Mine rails may be removed in favour of increasing SSM capability

SPECIFICATION:

COUNTRY OF ORIGIN: Croatia
CLASS: Kralj (Type R-03) (FSG)
ACTIVE: 2
NAME (PENNANT NUMBER): Kralj Petar Kresimir IV (ex-*Sergej Masera*) (Rtop 11), Kralj Dmitar Zvonimir (Rtop 12)

FEATURES:

DISPLACEMENT: 385 tons full load; 401 tons (Rtop 12)
LENGTH: 175.9 ft (53.6 m)
BEAM: 27.9 ft (8.5 m)
DRAUGHT: 7.5 ft (2.3 m)
SPEED: 36 kts
RANGE: 1700 miles at 18 kts

ARMAMENT:

MISSILES: SSM – four or eight Saab RBS 15B (2 or 4 twin)
GUNS: One Bofors 57 mm/70 (launchers for illuminants on side of mounting); one 30 mm/65 AK 630
MINES: Four AIM-70 magnetic or six SAG-1 acoustic in lieu of SSMs
DECOYS: Two Wallop Barricade chaff/IR launchers

ELECTRONICS:

RADARS: Surface search – Racal BT 502; navigation – Racal 1290A; fire control – PEAB 9LV 249 Mk 2
SONARS: RIZ PP 10M; hull-mounted, active search

Assad ECUADOR, IRAQ, MALAYSIA

Laksamana Tun Abdul Jamil (AMS)

- High bow with sweeping continuous main deck aft to stern
- 3 in gun mounting in 'A' position
- Square profile main superstructure with raised bridge area (Ecuador only).
  Iraqi and Malaysian ships have flatter roofs to bridge with slight slope in line
  with superstructure
- Pyramid mainmast atop centre of main superstructure
- Prominent Aspide SAM Albatros box launcher atop after end of main
  superstructure
- Two Exocet SSM launchers immediately aft of forward superstructure and
  40 mm/70 gun turret in 'Y' position (Ecuador)
- 40 mm/70 gun turret mounting on superstructure, just aft of midships, with
  angled Otomat Teseo SSM launchers, facing port and starboard, on main deck
  after of superstructure (Malaysian ships)

• Raised helicopter
landing platform aft of
ssm launchers (Ecuador
and Iraq, not Malaysian
ships); telescopic
hangar (Iraqi ships)

SPECIFICATION:

COUNTRY OF ORIGIN: Italy
CLASS: Assad/Esmeraldas/
Laksamana (FSG)
ACTIVE: 6 Ecuador (Esmeraldas
class), 2 Iraq (Assad class)*,
4 Malaysia (Laksamana class)
* Iraqi ships moored in Italian
ports because of UN sanctions;
Malaysian ships formerly built
for Iraq
NAME (PENNANT NUMBER):
ECUADOR – Esmeraldas (CM 11),
Manabi (CM 12), Los Rios (CM 13),
El Oro (CM 14), Los Galapagos
(CM 15), Loja (CM 16)
IRAQ – Mussa Ben Nussair
(F 210), Tariq Ibn Ziad (F 212)
MALAYSIA – Laksamana Hang
Nadim (ex-*Khalid Ibn Al Walid*)
(F 134, ex-F 216), Laksamana Tun
Abdul Jamil (ex-*Saad Ibn Abi
Waccade*) (F 135, ex-F 218),
Laksamana Muhammad Amin
(ex-*Abdulla Ben Abi Sarh*) (F 136,
ex-F 214), Laksamana Tan
Pushmah (ex-*Salahi Ad Deen
Alayoori*) (F 137, ex-F 220)

FEATURES:

DISPLACEMENT: 685 tons full load
(Ecuador, Iraq); 705 tons
(Malaysia)
LENGTH: 204.4 ft (62.3 m)
BEAM: 30.5 ft (9.3 m)
DRAUGHT: 8 ft (2.5 m)
SPEED: 36 kts
RANGE: 2300 miles at 18 kts
(Malaysia); 4000 miles at 18 kts
(Iraq); 4400 miles at 14 kts
(Ecuador)

ARMAMENT:

MISSILES: SSM – six Aerospatiale
MM 40 Exocet (2 triple) launchers
(Ecuador), six OTO Melara/Matra
Otomat Teseo Mk 2 (TG 2)
(3 twin) (Iraq, Malaysia); SAM –
Selenia Elsag Albatros quad
launcher, Aspide
GUNS: One OTO Melara 3 in
(76 mm)/62 Compact (Ecuador,
Iraq), Super Rapid (Malaysia); two
Breda 40 mm/70 (twin) (not Iraq)
TORPEDOES: Six 324 mm ILAS-3
(2 triple) tubes; Whitehead
Motofides A244S (not Iraq)
DECOYS: One or two Breda
105 mm SCLAR chaff/
illuminants launchers

ELECTRONICS:

RADARS: Air/surface search –
Selenia RAN-10S (Ecuador),
RAN 12L/X (Iraq, Malaysia);
navigation – SMA SPN-703
(3 RM 20) (Ecuador, Iraq), Kelvin
Hughes 1007 (Malaysia); fire
control – two Selenia Orion 10X
SONARS: Thomson Sintra Diodon;
hull-mounted (Ecuador); Atlas
Elektronik ASO 84-41, hull-
mounted (Iraq, Malaysia)
EW: Selenia INS-3 ESM, Selenia
TQN-2 ECM (Iraq, Malaysia);
Elettronica Gamma ED ESM/ECM
(Ecuador)

AIR SUPPORT:

HELICOPTERS: One Bell 206B
(platform only) (Ecuador); one
Agusta AB 212 (Iraq)

Braunschweig (K 130) GERMANY

Braunschweig (forepart under construction) (*Michael Nitz*)

- High forecastle with central superstructure flush with ship's side
- Long, low freeboard flight deck
- 76 mm gun on forecastle immediately forward of raised platform with RAM launcher
- Tall enclosed, chunky pyramidal mast at aft end of bridge superstructure, with air search radar atop
- Tall slender funnel aft of midships
- Second RAM launcher aft end of superstructure

SPECIFICATION:

COUNTRY OF ORIGIN: Germany
CLASS: Braunschweig (K 130) (FSG)
ORDERED: 5
NAME (PENNANT NUMBER): Braunschweig (F 260), Magdeburg (F 261), Erfurt (F 262), Oldenburg (F 263), Ludwigshafen (F 264)

FEATURES:

DISPLACEMENT: 1662 tons full load
LENGTH: 289.8 ft (88.3 m)
BEAM: 43.4 ft (13.2 m)
DRAUGHT: 15.7 ft (4.8 m)
SPEED: 26 kts
RANGE: 2500 miles at 15 kts

ARMAMENT:

MISSILES: SSM – four Saab RBS-15; SAM – two RAM 21-cell Mk 49 launchers
GUNS: One OTOBreda 76 mm/62; two Mauser 27 mm
DECOYS: Two chaff launchers

ELECTRONICS:

RADARS: Air/surface search – DASA TRS-3D
EW: EADS SPS-N-5000 ESM, DASA SPN/KJS 5000 ECM

AIR SUPPORT:

HELICOPTERS: One medium NH 90; two VTOL drones

Niki GREECE

Niki

- 40 mm/70 gun twin mounting in 'A' position
- High, smooth, forward superstructure with tripod mainmast at after end
- Black-capped, sloping-topped funnel amidships
- Torpedo tubes, port and starboard, on maindeck outboard of after superstructure
- 40 mm/70 gun twin mounting at after end of after superstructure

NOTE: *Doxa* has a deckhouse before bridge for sick bay

SPECIFICATION:

COUNTRY OF ORIGIN: Germany
CLASS: Niki (Thetis) (Type 420) (FS/PG)
ACTIVE: 4
NAME (PENNANT NUMBER):
Niki (ex-*Thetis*) (P 62, ex-P 6052), Doxa (ex-*Najade*) (P 63, ex-P 6054), Eleftheria (ex-*Triton*) (P 64, ex-P 6055), Agon (ex-*Andreia*, ex-*Theseus*) (P 66, ex-P 6056)

FEATURES:

DISPLACEMENT: 732 tons full load
LENGTH: 229.7 ft (70 m)
BEAM: 26.9 ft (8.2 m)
DRAUGHT: 8.6 ft (2.7 m)
SPEED: 19.5 kts
RANGE: 2760 miles at 15 kts

ARMAMENT:

GUNS: Four Breda 40 mm/70 (2 twin); two 12.7 mm machine guns
TORPEDOES: Six 324 mm single tubes; four Honeywell Mk 46 Mod 5 Neartip
DEPTH CHARGES: Two rails

ELECTRONICS:

RADARS: Surface search – Thomson-CSF TRS 3001; navigation – Decca BM-E
SONARS: Atlas Elektronik ELAC 1 BV; hull-mounted, active search/attack
EW: Thomson-CSF DR 2000S ESM

Khukri/Kora INDIA

Khukri

- High bow with steep sloping forecastle
- 3 in gun mounting mid-forecastle
- SS-N-2D Mod 1 Styx SSM box launchers forward of bridge, port and starboard in 'Khukri' class
- SS-N-25 Sapless tubular SSM launchers in same position in 'Kora' class
- Unusual curved sloping front up to bridge windows ('Khukri' class only)

Both classes share the following recognition features:
- Midships superstructure has large lattice mainmast at after end
- Distinctive Positive E/Cross Dome air-search radome atop mainmast
- Low funnel, with three pipe exhausts, aft of mainmast
- 30 mm/65 gun mountings on platforms, port and starboard, immediately aft of funnel
- Raised flight deck forward of short quarterdeck

SPECIFICATION:

COUNTRY OF ORIGIN: India
CLASS: Khukri/Kora (Projects 25 and 25A) (FSG)
ACTIVE: 4 ('Khukri' class), 4 ('Kora' class)
NAME (PENNANT NUMBER):
KHUKRI – Khukri (P 49), Kuthar (P 46), Kirpan (P 44), Khanjar (P 47)
KORA – Kora (P 61), Kirch (P 62), Kulish (P 63), Karmukh (P 64)

FEATURES:
DISPLACEMENT: 1423 tons full load; 1460 tons ('Kora')
LENGTH: 298.9 ft (91.1 m)
BEAM: 34.4 ft (10.5 m)
DRAUGHT: 13.1 ft (4 m) ('Khukri'); 14.8 ft (4.5 m) ('Kora')
SPEED: 24/25 kts
RANGE: 4000 miles at 16 kts

ARMAMENT:
MISSILES: SSM – four SS-N-2D Styx (2 twin) launchers ('Khukri' class); Zvezda SS-N-25 (Kh 35 Uran) Sapless (2 quad) ('Kora' class); SAM – SA-N-5 Grail
GUNS: One USSR 3 in (76 mm)/60 AK 176; two 30 mm/65 (twin) AK 630
DECOYS: Two PK 16 chaff launchers ('Khukri' class); four PK 10 ('Kora'); BEL TOTED towed torpedo decoy

ELECTRONICS:
RADARS: Air-search – Cross Dome; air/surface search – Plank Shave; navigation – Bharat 1245; fire control – Bass Tilt
EW: BEL Lynx (P 62-P 64)

AIR SUPPORT:
HELICOPTERS: Platform only for HAL SA 319B Chetak (Alouette III)

Eilat (Saar 5) ISRAEL

Eilat

- High bow, short sloping forecastle
- 3 in gun mounting or Vulcan Phalanx CIWS on raised forecastle position
- Barak I SAM in vertical launch tubes immediately forward of bridge superstructure
- Pair of decoy launchers, port and starboard, atop bridge
- High, bulky forward slab-sided superstructure with tall pole mainmast atop
- Harpoon SSM angled launchers immediately aft of forward superstructure
- Squat, square black-capped funnel with unusual sloping forward edge
- Barak I SAM VLS launcher immediately aft of funnel
- Substantial angular after superstructure with after pole mast atop
- Large Elta EL/M-2218s air-search radar aerial atop after superstructure
- Flight deck right aft with low freeboard

SPECIFICATION:

COUNTRY OF ORIGIN: Israel
CLASS: Eilat (Saar 5) (FSG)
ACTIVE: 3
NAME (PENNANT NUMBER): Eilat (501), Lahav (502), Hanit (503)

FEATURES:
DISPLACEMENT: 1295 tons full load
LENGTH: 283.5 ft (86.4 m) oa
BEAM: 39 ft (11.9 m)
DRAUGHT: 10.5 ft (3.2 m)
SPEED: 33 kts
RANGE: 3500 miles at 17 kts

ARMAMENT:
MISSILES: SSM – McDonnell Douglas Harpoon (2 quad) launchers; SAM – two Israeli Industries Barak I (vertical launch)
GUNS: One OTO Melara 3 in (76 mm)/62 Compact (interchangeable with a Bofors 57 mm gun or Vulcan Phalanx CIWS); two Sea Vulcan 25 mm CIWS
TORPEDOES: Six 324 mm Mk 32 (2 triple) tubes; Honeywell Mk 46
DECOYS: Three Elbit/Deseaver chaff launchers; Rafael ATC-1 towed torpedo decoy

ELECTRONICS:
RADARS: Air-search – Elta EL/M-2218s; surface search – Cardion SPS-55; fire control – three Elta EL/M-2221 GM STGR
SONARS: EDO Type 796 Mod 1, hull-mounted; Rafael towed array (fitted but not with)
EW: Elisra NS 9003 ESM; two Rafael 1010; Elisra NS 9005 ECM

AIR SUPPORT:
HELICOPTERS: One Aerospatiale SA 366G Dauphin or Sea Panther

Minerva ITALY

Sfinge

- Continuous maindeck from bow to break down to quarterdeck
- Long forecastle with 3 in gun mounting at mid-point
- Isolated forward superstructure with short pole mast at after end
- Midships enclosed mainmast supporting distinctive SPS-774 air/surface search radar aerial
- Tapered black-capped funnel atop central after superstructure with unusual forward sloping top and black smoke deflectors
- Aspide SAM Albatros box launcher at after end of after superstructure
- Low freeboard quarterdeck

SPECIFICATION:

COUNTRY OF ORIGIN: Italy
CLASS: Minerva (FS)
ACTIVE: 8
NAME (PENNANT NUMBER):
Minerva (F 551), Urania (F 552),
Danaide (F 553), Sfinge (F 554),
Driade (F 555), Chimera (F 556),
Fenice (F 557), Sibilla (F 558)

FEATURES:

DISPLACEMENT: 1285 tons full load
LENGTH: 284.1 ft (86.6 m)
BEAM: 34.5 ft (10.5 m)
DRAUGHT: 10.5 ft (3.2 m)
SPEED: 24 kts
RANGE: 3500 miles at 18 kts

ARMAMENT:

MISSILES: SSM – fitted for but not
with four or six Teseo Otomat
between the masts; SAM –
Selenia Elsag Albatros octuple
launcher, Aspide
GUNS: One OTO Melara 3 in
(76 mm)/62 Compact
TORPEDOES: Six 324 mm
Whitehead B 515 (2 triple) tubes;
Honeywell Mk 46
DECOYS: Two Wallop Barricade
double layer launchers; SLQ-25
Nixie towed torpedo decoy

ELECTRONICS:

RADARS: Air/surface search –
Selenia SPS-774 (RAN 10S);
navigation – SMA SPN-728(v)2;
fire control – Selenia SPG-76
(RTN 30X)
SONARS: Raytheon/Elsag DE 1167;
hull-mounted
EW: Selenia SLQ-747 ESM/ECM

Sariwon KOREA (NORTH)

Tral 671

- Very high forecastle, with sharp break at aft end of superstructure to very low freeboard
- 'Tral' class has 85 mm gun in tank turret, raised, on forecastle
- Unusual slanting stern
- Short bridge superstructure topped by pedestal mast with tall pole mast atop
- Ship's boat on davits in break between superstructure
- Narrow angled funnel on low superstructure amidships
- Minelaying rails visible along whole of upper deck after of bridge superstructure
- 'Sariwon' design based on original Soviet 'Tral' fleet minelayer design of mid-1930s

NOTE: Three 'Sariwon' built in North Korea in mid-1960s

SPECIFICATION:

COUNTRY OF ORIGIN:
Korea (North)/Russia
CLASS: Sariwon (FS)
ACTIVE: 5
NAME (PENNANT NUMBER):
611, 612, 613, 614, 671

FEATURES:
DISPLACEMENT: 650 tons full load
LENGTH: 203.7 ft (62.1 m)
BEAM: 23.9 ft (7.3 m)
DRAUGHT: 7.8 ft (2.4 m)
SPEED: 16 kts
RANGE: 2700 miles at 16 kts

ARMAMENT:
GUNS: Four 57 mm/80 (2 twin);
four 37 mm/6 (2 twin); 16
14.5 mm machine guns (4 quad)
DEPTH CHARGES: Two rails,
30 mines
MINES: Two rails

ELECTRONICS:
RADARS: Surface search – Pot
Head or Don 2; navigation –
Model 351

Dong Hae KOREA (SOUTH)

Dong Hae

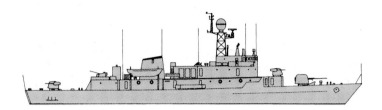

- Continuous maindeck sweeping from high bow to lower freeboard stern
- 3 in gun mounting in 'A' position. Emmerson Electric 30 mm twin gun mounting in 'B' position
- High forward superstructure with tall lattice mainmast at after end with distinctive WM28 spherical radome atop
- Large funnel well aft of midships, with torpedo tubes immediately forward
- Ship's boats outboard in davits at funnel level
- Twin 30 mm gun mounting on afterdeck

SPECIFICATION:

COUNTRY OF ORIGIN:
Korea (South)
CLASS: Dong Hae (FS)
ACTIVE: 4
NAME (PENNANT NUMBER):
Dong Hae (751), Su Won (752), Kang Reung (753), An Yang (755)

FEATURES:
DISPLACEMENT: 1076 tons full load
LENGTH: 256.2 ft (78.1 m)
BEAM: 31.5 ft (9.6 m)
DRAUGHT: 8.5 ft (2.6 m)
SPEED: 31 kts
RANGE: 4000 miles at 15 kts

ARMAMENT:
GUNS: One OTO Melara 3 in (76 mm)/62 Compact; four Emerson Electric 30 mm (2 twin); two Bofors 40 mm/60 (twin)
TORPEDOES: Six 324 mm Mk 32 (2 triple) tubes; Honeywell Mk 46
DEPTH CHARGES: 12
DECOYS: Four MEL Protean fixed launchers

ELECTRONICS:
RADARS: Surface search – Raytheon SPS-64; fire control – Signaal WM28
SONARS: Signaal PHS-32 hull-mounted, active search and attack

Po Hang KOREA (SOUTH)

Nam Won

- 3 in gun mounting in 'A' position. Breda 40 mm/70 twin gun mounting in 'B' position (761 onwards); Emerson Electric 30 mm twin mounting in 'B' position (756-759)
- High forward superstructure with enclosed mainmast at after end
- WM28 fire control radome atop mainmast
- Large funnel well aft of midships with gas turbine air intakes immediately forward
- Ship's boats in davits at funnel level outboard of air intakes
- Exocet SSM box launchers at after end of after superstructure (756-759). Replaced by 40 mm/70 gun turret mounting (761 onwards)
- Twin 30 mm or OTO Melara 3 in gun mounting on afterdeck

SPECIFICATION:

COUNTRY OF ORIGIN: South Korea
CLASS: Po Hang (FS/FSG)
ACTIVE: 24
NAME (PENNANT NUMBER):
Po Hang (756), Kun San (757), Kyong Ju (758), Mok Po (759), Kim Chon (761), Chung Ju (762), Jin Ju (763), Yo Su (765), Jin Hae (766), Sun Chon (767), Yee Ree (768), Won Ju (769), An Dong (771), Chon An (772), Song Nam (773), Bu Chon (775), Jae Chon (776), Dae Chon (777), Sok Cho (778), Yong Ju (779), Nam Won (781), Kwan Myong (782), Sin Hung (783), Kong Ju (785)

FEATURES:

DISPLACEMENT: 1220 tons full load
LENGTH: 289.7 ft (88.3 m)
BEAM: 32.8 ft (10 m)
DRAUGHT: 9.5 ft (2.9 m)
SPEED: 32 kts
RANGE: 4000 miles at 15 kts

ARMAMENT:

MISSILES: SSM – two Aerospatiale MM 38 Exocet (756-759 only); four McDonnell Douglas Harpoon (2 twin)
GUNS: One or two OTO Melara 3 in (76 mm)/62 Compact; four Emerson Electric 30 mm (2 twin) (756-759); four Breda 40 mm/70 (2 twin) (761 onwards)
TORPEDOES: Six 324 mm Mk 32 (2 triple) tubes; Honeywell Mk 46 (756-759 only)
DEPTH CHARGES: 12 (761 onwards)
DECOYS: Four MEL Protean fixed launchers; two Loral Hycor SRBOC 6-barrel Mk 36 (in some)

ELECTRONICS:

RADARS: Surface search – Marconi 1810 and/or Raytheon SPS-64; fire control – Signaal WM28 or Marconi 1802
SONARS: Signaal PHS-32 hull-mounted active search and attack

Kedah (Meko A100) MALAYSIA

Pahang (*Michael Nitz*)

- Space available within hull for future weapons and sensors, possibly including SSM, SAM, sonar and EW
- 3 in gun in 'A' position well forward on long forecastle
- Large space between gun and bridge to accommodate future weapons fit
- Large midships structure with bridge topped by small, squat pyramid mast carrying optronic weapon control system
- Large pyramid mast behind supporting air/surface seach radar
- Large space between mast and low squat funnel available for future possible SSM fit
- 30 mm mount sited on top of rear end of superstructure
- Large platform aft capable of being used for medium sized helicopter

SPECIFICATION:

COUNTRY OF ORIGIN: Germany
CLASS: Kedah
ACTIVE: 3
BUILDING: 3
NAME (PENNANT NUMBER):
Kedah (171), Pahang (172),
Perak (173), Terengganu (174),
Kelantan (175), Selangor (176)

FEATURES:
DISPLACEMENT: 1650 tons full load
LENGTH: 298.9 ft (91.1 m)
BEAM: 39.4 ft (12 m)
DRAUGHT: 9.8 ft (3 m)
SPEED: 22 kts
RANGE: 6050 miles at 12 kts

ARMAMENT:
MISSILES: SSM – fitted for but
not with Exocet MM40; SAM –
fitted for but not with RAM CIWS
GUNS: One OTOBreda 3 in
(76 mm)/62 Super Rapid; one
30 mm OTOBreda/Mauser; two
12.7 mm machine guns
DECOYS: RBOC chaff launcher

ELECTRONICS:
RADARS: Surface search –
TRS-3D/16ES; navigation – to be
announced; fire control – to be
announced
SONARS: Fitted for but not with
EW: To be announced

Mk 9 Vosper Thornycroft Type NIGERIA

Erinomi

- Sharp bow, short forecastle with 3 in gun immediately forward of bridge
- Tall bridge structure with all-round windows
- Long central superstructure with short lattice mainmast immediately aft of bridge with spherical fire control radome atop
- Very large and prominent angled and tapered funnel amidships
- Break in main deck immediately aft of funnel
- Very short quarterdeck

SPECIFICATION:

COUNTRY OF ORIGIN: UK
CLASS: Mk 9 Vosper Thornycroft type (FS)
ACTIVE: 1
NAME (PENNANT NUMBER): Enymiri (F 84)

FEATURES:

DISPLACEMENT: 780 tons full load
LENGTH: 226 ft (69 m)
BEAM: 31.5 ft (9.8 m)
DRAUGHT: 9.8 ft (3 m)
SPEED: 27 kts
RANGE: 2200 miles at 14 kts

ARMAMENT:

MISSILES: SAM – Short Brothers Seacat triple launcher (non-operational)
GUNS: One OTO Melara 76 mm/62 Mod 6 Compact; one Breda Bofors 40 mm/70 Type 350; two Oerlikon 20 mm
A/S MORTARS: One Bofors 375 mm twin launcher

ELECTRONICS:

RADARS: Air/surface search – Plessey AWS 2; navigation – Racal Decca TM 1226; fire control – Signaal WM24
SONARS: Plessey PMS 26 hull-mounted, active attack
EW: Decca Cutlass ESM

Qahir OMAN

Qahir Al Amwaj

- Sloping straight-edged bow with long, gently sloping forecastle
- Two Exocet SSM launchers immediately forward of bridge, after one trained to port, forward one to starboard
- 3 in gun mounting forward of SSM launchers
- Large, smooth midships superstructure with angled surfaces for low reflective radar signature
- Squat black-capped funnel immediately abaft mainmast
- Crotale NG SAM box launcher at after end of superstructure immediately forward of flight deck
- Long flight deck

SPECIFICATION:

COUNTRY OF ORIGIN: UK
CLASS: Qahir (FSG)
ACTIVE: 2
NAME (PENNANT NUMBER):
Qahir Al Amwaj (Q 31),
Al Mua'zzer (Q 32)

FEATURES:
DISPLACEMENT: 1450 tons full load
LENGTH: 274.6 ft (83.7 m) oa
BEAM: 37.7 ft (11.5 m)
DRAUGHT: 11.8 ft (3.6 m)
SPEED: 28 kts
RANGE: 4000 miles at 10 kts

ARMAMENT:
MISSILES: SSM – eight
Aerospatiale MM 40 Block II
Exocet; SAM – Thomson-CSF
Crotale NG, octuple launcher
GUNS: One OTO Melara 3 in
(76 mm)/62 Super Rapid; two
Oerlikon/Royal Ordnance
20 mm GAM-B01; two 7.62 mm
machine guns
TORPEDOES: Six 324 mm (2 triple
tubes) may be fitted
DECOYS: Two Barricade 12-barrel
chaff launchers

ELECTRONICS:
RADARS: Air/surface search –
Signaal MW08; navigation – Kelvin
Hughes 1007; fire control – Signaal
Sting, Thomson-CSF DRBV 51C
SONARS: Thomson-Sintra/
BAeSEMA ATAS towed array
EW: Thomson-CSF DR 3000 ESM

AIR SUPPORT:
HELICOPTERS: Platform for one
Super Lynx type

Orkan (Sassnitz) POLAND, GERMANY

Orkan (*Michael Nitz*)

- Continuous main deck lines from stem to stern
- One USSR 3 in gun mounting ('A' position) (Polish ships only)
- Low bridge structure with prominent wings
- Long central super-structure with, midships, large lattice mainmast atop
- Tall square funnel just aft of midships (German hulls)
- 30 mm/65 ak 630 gun mounting on afterdeck (Polish ships only)
- German coast guard ships have blue hulls, yellow, orange and black diagonal stripes, and white and light blue upper works. 'Kustenwache' is painted in white letters on hull

SPECIFICATION:

COUNTRY OF ORIGIN:
East Germany

CLASS: Orkan (Sassnitz) (Type 660, ex-151) (FSG)

ACTIVE: 3 Poland, 2 Germany (Coast Guard)

NAME (PENNANT NUMBER):
POLAND – Orkan (421), Piorun (422), Grom (ex-*Huragan*) (423)
GERMANY – Neustrelitz (ex-*Sassnitz*) (BG 22, ex-P 6165, ex-591), Bad Düben (ex-*Binz*) (BG 23, ex-593)

FEATURES:

DISPLACEMENT: 326 tons full load (Poland); 369 tons (Germany)

LENGTH: 163.4 ft (49.8 m) (Poland); 160.4 ft (48.9 m) (Germany)

BEAM: 28.5 ft (8.7 m)

DRAUGHT: 7.2 ft (2.2 m)

SPEED: 38 kts (Poland); 25 kts (Germany)

RANGE: 1600 miles at 14 kts

ARMAMENT:

MISSILES: SSM – Eight Saab RBS 15 Mk 3 (2 quad) launchers;
SAM – SA-N-5 Grail quad launcher (Poland only, no missiles in German hulls)

GUNS: One USSR 3 in (76 mm)/66 AK 176; one 30 mm/65 AK 630 (Poland only); two 7.62 mm machine guns (German ships' only armament)

DECOYS: Jastrzab 81 mm and one 10-barrel Jastrzab 122 mm chaff launcher (Poland only)

ELECTRONICS:

RADARS: Surface search –AMB Sea Giraffe (Poland), Racal AC 2690 BT (Germany); navigation – PIT (Poland), Racal ARPA (Germany); fire control – Bass Tilt MR-123 (Poland only)

EW: PIT ESM (Poland)

Badr SAUDI ARABIA

Hitteen

- Long forecastle with 3 in gun mounting midpoint between bows and bridge
- Centrally sited superstructure with fat central lattice mainmast with SPS-40B air-search radar and tall pole mast above
- Sperry Mk 92 fire control spherical radome atop bridge roof
- Short, black-capped funnel at after end of superstructure
- Torpedo tubes on maindeck level at after end of superstructure
- Harpoon SSM angled launchers on long afterdeck
- CIWS mounting right aft

SPECIFICATION:

COUNTRY OF ORIGIN: USA
CLASS: Badr (FSG)
ACTIVE: 4
NAME (PENNANT NUMBER):
Badr (612), Al Yarmook (614),
Hitteen (616), Tabuk (618)

FEATURES:
DISPLACEMENT: 1038 tons
full load
LENGTH: 245 ft (74.7 m)
BEAM: 31.5 ft (9.6 m)
DRAUGHT: 8.9 ft (2.7 m)
SPEED: 30 kts
RANGE: 4000 miles at 20 kts

ARMAMENT:
MISSILES: SSM – eight McDonnell
Douglas Harpoon (2 quad)
launchers
GUNS: One FMC/OTO Melara
3 in (76 mm)/62 Mk 75 Mod 0;
one GE/GD 20 mm 6-barrel
Vulcan Phalanx; two Oerlikon
20 mm/80; one 81 mm mortar;
one 40 mm Mk 19 grenade
launcher
TORPEDOES: Six 324 mm US Mk
32 (2 triple) tubes; Honeywell
Mk 46
DECOYS: Two Loral Hycor SRBOC
6-barrel Mk 36 fixed launchers

ELECTRONICS:
RADARS: Air-search – Lockheed
SPS-40B; surface search – ISC
Cardion SPS-55; fire control –
Sperry Mk 92
SONARS: Raytheon SQS-56
(DE 1164); hull-mounted
EW: SLQ-32(V)1 ESM

Göteborg SWEDEN

Gälve

- Continuous maindeck lines from stem to stern
- 57 mm/70 gun mounting in 'A' position
- Saab Elma A/S mortar launchers in 'B' mounting position
- Long central superstructure with, midships, large pyramid enclosed mainmast atop. Topmast modified in *Sundsvall* with IRST detector fitted aft of mast
- Torpedo tubes on maindeck outboard of bridge
- Saab RBS 15 SSM angled twin box launchers, two port, two starboard, on maindeck at after end of superstructure. Aft pair outboard of low enclosed mast with fire control radar atop
- 40 mm/70 gun mounting on afterdeck. Turret in K 22 stealth-adapted, producing angled, sloping profile
- VDS towing equipment right aft

SPECIFICATION:

COUNTRY OF ORIGIN: Sweden
CLASS: Göteborg (FSG)
ACTIVE: 4
NAME (PENNANT NUMBER):
Göteborg (K 21), Gälve (K 22),
Kalmar (K 23), Sundsvall (K 24)

FEATURES:
DISPLACEMENT: 399 tons full load
LENGTH: 187 ft (57 m)
BEAM: 26.2 ft (8 m)
DRAUGHT: 6.6 ft (2 m)
SPEED: 30 kts

ARMAMENT:
MISSILES: SSM – eight Saab RBS 15
(4 twin) launchers
GUNS: One Bofors 57 mm/70
Mk 2; one Bofors 40 mm/70
TORPEDOES: Four 15.75 in (400 mm)
tubes; Swedish Ordnance Type
43/45 can be fitted
A/S MORTARS: Four Saab Elma
601 9-tubed launchers
DEPTH CHARGES: On mine rails
DECOYS: Four Philips Philax
launchers (A/S mortars adapted
to fire IR/chaff decoys)

ELECTRONICS:
RADARS: Air/surface search –
Ericsson Sea Giraffe 150HC;
navigation – Terma PN 612; fire
control – two Bofors Electronics
9GR 400
SONARS: Thomson-Sintra
TSM 2643 Salmon, VDS; Simrad
SA 950, hull-mounted, active
attack; Hydra multi-sonar;
STN Atlas passive towed array
EW: Condor ESM

Stockholm SWEDEN

Malmö

- Long forecastle with Saab Elma LLS-920 A/S mortar launcher at forward end and 57 mm/70 gun mounting midpoint between bows and bridge
- Short, high, slab-sided central superstructure with lattice mainmast at after end
- Fire control radar atop bridge
- Distinctive RBS 15 SSM angled twin box launchers; two port, two starboard, on maindeck at after end of superstructure
- Short, slim lattice aftermast isolated, aft of SSM launchers
- 40 mm/70 gun mounting right aft, forward of VDS

NOTE: Developed from 'Spica II' class

SPECIFICATION:

COUNTRY OF ORIGIN: Sweden
CLASS: Stockholm (FSG)
ACTIVE: 2
NAME (PENNANT NUMBER): Stockholm (K 11), Malmö (K 12)

FEATURES:
DISPLACEMENT: 372 tons full load
LENGTH: 164 ft (50 m)
BEAM: 24.6 ft (7.5 m)
DRAUGHT: 6.9 ft (2.1 m)
SPEED: 32 kts

ARMAMENT:
MISSILES: SSM – eight Saab RBS 15 Mk II (4 twin) launchers
GUNS: One Bofors 57 mm/70 Mk 2; one Bofors 40 mm/70
TORPEDOES: Four 15.75 in (400 mm) tubes; Swedish Ordnance Type 43 can be fitted
A/S MORTARS: Four Saab Elma LLS-920 9-tubed launchers

ELECTRONICS:
RADARS: Air/surface search – Ericsson Sea Giraffe 50HC; navigation – Terma PN 612; fire control – Philips 9LV 200 Mk 3
SONARS: Simrad SA 950, hull-mounted, active attack; Thomson-Sintra TSM 2642 Salmon, VDS
EW: Condor CS 5460 ESM

Visby SWEDEN

Visby (*Michael Nitz*)

- Continuous maindeck lines from stem to stern with sharp bows
- Angular 57 mm/70 gun mounting in 'A' position
- Short, central 'swept back' slab-sided angled superstructure with high bridge amidships
- Low pyramid enclosed mast atop bridge
- Helicopter flight deck aft, occupying 40% of overall length

NOTE: MCMV can carry STN Atlas Seafox mine disposal vehicle

SPECIFICATION:

COUNTRY OF ORIGIN: Sweden
CLASS: Visby (FSG)
ACTIVE: 1
BUILDING: 4
NAME (PENNANT NUMBER):
Visby (K 31), Helsingborg (K 32), Härnösand (K 33), Nyköping (K 34), Karlstad (K 35)

FEATURES:

DISPLACEMENT: 620 tons full load
LENGTH: 236.2 ft (72 m)
BEAM: 34.1 ft (10.4 m)
DRAUGHT: 8.2 ft (2.5 m)
SPEED: 35 kts

ARMAMENT:

MISSILES: SSM – 8 Saab RBS 15 Mk II (Batch 2)
GUNS: One Bofors 57 mm/70 SAK Mk 3
TORPEDOES: Four 15.75 in (400 mm) fixed tubes; Swedish Ordnance Type 43/45
A/S MORTARS: Saab Alecto 601 127 mm launchers
DECOYS: Chaff launchers (A/S mortars adapted to fire IR/chaff decoys)

ELECTRONICS:

RADARS: Air/surface search – Ericsson Sea Giraffe AMB 3D; surface search – Celsiustech Pilot; fire control – CEROS 200 Mk 3
SONARS: CDC Hydra bow-mounted active, plus passive towed array and VDS
EW: Condor CS 701 ESM/ECM

AIR SUPPORT:

HELICOPTERS: One Agusta A109M (ASW) or UAV

Khamronsin THAILAND

Thayanchon

- Short forecastle with 76 mm/62 gun mounting in 'A' position
- High freeboard, slab-sided superstructure running from forecastle to afterdeck
- Lattice mainmast amidships, atop central superstructure
- Squat, black-capped funnel with sloping top aft of mainmast
- 30 mm/70 gun mounting in 'x' position
- Break down from maindeck to short quarterdeck

NOTE: Based on a Vosper Thornycroft 'Province' class 56 M design, stretched by increasing the frame spacing along the whole length of the hull
NOTE 2: Fourth of class, lightly armed with different superstructure, active with marine police

SPECIFICATION:

COUNTRY OF ORIGIN: UK
CLASS: Khamronsin (FS)
ACTIVE: 3
NAME (PENNANT NUMBER):
Khamronsin (531, ex-1),
Thayanchon (532, ex-2),
Longlom (533, ex-3)

FEATURES:
DISPLACEMENT: 630 tons full load
LENGTH: 203.4 ft (62 m) oa
BEAM: 26.9 ft (8.2 m)
DRAUGHT: 8.2 ft (2.5 m)
SPEED: 25 kts
RANGE: 2500 miles at 15 kts

ARMAMENT:
GUNS: One OTO Melara
76 mm/62 Mod 7; two Breda
30 mm/70 (twin); two 12.7 mm
machine guns
TORPEDOES: Six Plessey PMW 49A
(2 triple) launchers; Marconi
Stingray

ELECTRONICS:
RADARS: Air/surface search –
Plessey AWS 4; navigation –
Racal Decca 1226
SONARS: Atlas Elektronik
DSQS-21C; hull-mounted, active
search/attack

Rattanakosin THAILAND

Rattanakosin

- High bow, short forecastle
- 3 in gun mounting in 'A' position
- 40 mm/70 gun twin mounting in 'B' position
- Slab-sided high superstructure running from forecastle to afterdeck
- Large, solid pyramid mainmast atop forward superstructure supporting spherical WM 25/41 fire control radome
- Low, tapered funnel well aft of midships with curved after profile and twin exhaust protruding from top
- Short, enclosed aftermast, immediately aft of funnel, supporting DA05 air/surface search radar aerial
- Harpoon SSM angled launchers atop after end of superstructure
- Aspide SAM Albatros launcher right aft on quarterdeck

SPECIFICATION:

COUNTRY OF ORIGIN: USA
CLASS: Rattanakosin (FSG)
ACTIVE: 2
NAME (PENNANT NUMBER):
Rattanakosin (441, ex-1),
Sukhothai (442, ex-2)

FEATURES:
DISPLACEMENT: 960 tons full load
LENGTH: 252 ft (76.8 m)
BEAM: 31.5 ft (9.6 m)
DRAUGHT: 8 ft (2.4 m)
SPEED: 26 kts
RANGE: 3000 miles at 16 kts

ARMAMENT:
MISSILES: SSM – eight McDonnell
Douglas Harpoon (2 quad)
launchers; SAM – Selenia Elsag
Albatros octuple launcher, Aspide
GUNS: One OTO Melara 3 in
(76 mm)/62 Compact; two
Breda 40 mm/70 (twin); two
Rheinmetall 20 mm
TORPEDOES: Six 324 mm US Mk 32
(2 triple) tubes; Marconi Stingray
DECOYS: CSEE Dagaie 6- or
10-tubed trainable launchers

ELECTRONICS:
RADARS: Air/surface search –
Signaal DA05; surface search –
Signaal ZW06; navigation – Decca
1226; fire control – Signaal WM 25/41
SONARS: Atlas Elektronik
DSQS-21C; hull-mounted, active
search/attack
EW: Elettronica ESM

Patrol
Forces

Osa ALGERIA, BULGARIA, CROATIA, CUBA, EGYPT, ERITREA, KOREA (NORTH), LIBYA, POLAND, SYRIA, VIETNAM

Dubrovnik (Croatia) Modified OSA I without Styx missile

- 30 mm/65 gun mounting in 'A' position
- Low profile rounded superstructure running from the forecastle almost to the stern
- Pole mainmast just forward of midships with surface search radar aerial atop
- Prominent raised pedestal aft supporting fire control radar aerial
- Four large distinctive Styx SSM launchers to port and starboard, two outboard of mainmast and two outboard of fire control director (aft)
- 30 mm/65 mounting right aft

NOTE: Similar 'Huangfen' class also operated by China (14), Bangladesh ('Durdharsha' class) (4), North Korea (4), Pakistan (1) and Yemen (3)

NOTE 2: Croatian unit converted to a minelayer in 1995. Distinctive low ribbed superstructure extended aft in Croatian unit

NOTE 3: 'Matka' class hydrofoil PHGS, with similar hulls to 'Osa' operated by Russia (2), Georgia (1) and Ukraine (2, as 'Vekhr' class)

SPECIFICATION:

COUNTRY OF ORIGIN: Russia
CLASS: Osa I (Type 205) (Puck), Osa II (Type 205M) (PCFG)
ACTIVE: 9 Algeria ('Osa II'; 5 Bulgaria (2 'Osa I', 3 'Osa II'); 1 Croatia (modified 'Osa I') (PCF/ML); 6 Cuba ('Osa II'); 3 Egypt ('Osa I'); 3 Bulgaria ('Osa II'); 1 Eritrea ('Osa II'); 8 Korea (North) ('Osa I'); 5 Libya ('Osa II'); 2 Poland ('Osa I') ('Puck' class); 10 Syria (2 'Osa I', 8 'Osa II'); 8 Vietnam ('Osa II')
NAME (PENNANT NUMBER):
ALGERIA – 644-652
BULGARIA – Osa I: Burya (103), Typhoon (112); Osa II: Uragon (102), Svetkavitsa (111), Smerch (113), Gram (104)
CROATIA – Dubrovnik (ex-*Mitar Aceu*) (OBM 41, ex-310)
CUBA – 261, 262, 267, 268, 271, 274
EGYPT – 631, 633, 643
ERITREA – FMB 161
LIBYA – Al Zuara (513), Al Ruha (515), Al Fikah (523), Al Mathur (525), Al Bitar (531)
POLAND – Swinoujscie (431), Wladyslawowo (433)
SYRIA – Osa I: 31-32; Osa II: 33-40
VIETNAM – HQ 354-361

FEATURES:
DISPLACEMENT: 210 tons full load ('Osa I'); 245 tons ('Osa II')
LENGTH: 126.6 ft (38.6 m)
BEAM: 24.9 ft (7.6 m)
DRAUGHT: 8.9 ft (2.7 m)
SPEED: 35 kts ('Osa I'); 37 kts ('Osa II')
RANGE: 400 miles at 34 kts ('Osa I'); 500 miles at 35 kts ('Osa II')

ARMAMENT:
MISSILES: SSM – four SS-N-2A Styx ('Osa I'), four SS-N-2B/C Styx ('Osa II') (not Croatia, Cuba), SA-N-5 Grail quad launcher (Egypt, Poland)
GUNS: Four 30 mm/65 (2 twin)
DECOYS: PK 16 chaff launcher (Syria, 'Osa II')

ELECTRONICS:
RADARS: Air/surface search – Kelvin Hughes (Egypt only); surface search/fire control – Square Tie (not Egypt); navigation – Racal Decca 916 (Egypt), SRN 207M (Poland); fire control – Drum Tilt
EW: China BM/HZ 8610 ESM (Korea (North))

Kebir ALGERIA, BARBADOS
Trident

- Continuous maindeck from stem to stern
- 76 mm/62 Compact gun mounting in 'A' position in some Algerian hulls. Others have 25 mm gun. Machine gun mounting in Barbados unit
- Stepped, central superstructure
- Open bridge atop enclosed bridge with all round windows
- Large whip aerial either side of forward end of superstructure
- Tripod mainmast amidships with small pole structure
- Small ship's boat stowed at after end of superstructure with small crane

SPECIFICATION:

COUNTRY OF ORIGIN: UK
CLASS: Kebir (PC)
ACTIVE: 13 Algeria, 1 Barbados
NAME (PENNANT NUMBER):
ALGERIA — El Yadekh (341),
El Mourakeb (342), El Kechef
(343), El Moutarid (344), El Rassed
(345), El Djari (346), El Saher (347),
El Moukadem (348), — (349),
El Kanass (350), — (356), — (357),
— (358)
BARBADOS — Trident (P0 1)

FEATURES:

DISPLACEMENT: 200 tons full load
(Algeria); 190 tons (Barbados)
LENGTH: 123 ft (37.5 m)
BEAM: 22.6 ft (6.9 m)
DRAUGHT: 5.6 ft (1.7 m)
SPEED: 27 kts
RANGE: 3300 miles at 15 kts

ARMAMENT:

GUNS: One OTO Melara 76 mm/62
Compact (Algeria 341, 342); four
USSR 25 mm/60 (2 twin)
(remainder, Algeria); two USSR
14.5 mm (twin) in first five
Algerian units; four 12.7 mm
machine guns (Barbados)

ELECTRONICS:

RADARS: Surface search – Racal
Decca 1226 (Algeria); Racal Decca
Bridgemaster (Barbados)

TNC 45 ARGENTINA, BAHRAIN, ECUADOR, GHANA, KUWAIT, MALAYSIA,
Al Taweelah

- Sweeping bow, low freeboard. Continuous main deck from stem to stern
- 3 in gun mounting in 'A' position, except Ghana (Bofors 40 mm/70), Malaysia, Singapore and Thailand (Bofors 57 mm/70)
- High superstructure forward of midships (deckhouse extended aft, Ghana)
- Open bridge atop enclosed bridge
- Lattice mainmast aft of bridge with short pole mast at after end
- Large spherical fire control radome with two smaller radomes on short mast atop bridge (Singapore)
- Four Exocet SSM launchers, two trained to port, two to starboard in crossover configuration aft of superstructure (MM 38 Exocet fitted in one Argentine ship 1997/98). No missiles, Ghana or Malaysia
- Harpoon SSM in crossover configuration aft of superstructure in Singapore units
- 40 mm/70 mounting right aft (two in 'Intrepida' class). One Oerlikon 35 mm/90 twin mounting in 'Y' position in Ecuador ships; Breda 40 mm/70 twin mounting in 'Y' position (Bahrain, Kuwait and UAE units)

NOTE: Argentine hulls painted in brown/green camouflage
NOTE 2: Only second pair of Bahrain units (22-23) have communications radome on after superstructure

SINGAPORE, THAILAND, UNITED ARAB EMIRATES (UAE)

Baung (3509), Pari (3510)
SINGAPORE – Sea Wolf (P 76), Sea
Lion (P 77), Sea Dragon (P 78),
Sea Tiger (P 79), Sea Hawk (P 80),
Sea Scorpion (P 81)
THAILAND – Prabparapak (311,
ex-1), Hanhak Sattru (312, ex-2),
Suphairin (313, ex-3)
UAE – Ban Yas (P 151, ex-P 4501),
Marban (P 152, ex-P 4502),
Rodqm (P 153, ex-P 4503),
Shaheen (P 154, ex-P 4504), Sagar
(P 155, ex-P 4505), Tarif (P 156,
ex-P 4506)

FEATURES:

DISPLACEMENT: 259 tons full load
(Bahrain); 268 tons (Argentina,
Thailand); 269 tons (Ghana); 255
tons (Ecuador, Kuwait); 244 tons
(Malaysia); 254 tons (Singapore);
260 tons (UAE)
LENGTH: 147.3 ft (44.9 m); 147.6 ft
(45 m) (Ecuador); 149 ft (45.4 m)
(Thailand)
BEAM: 22.9 ft (7 m) (Bahrain);
24.3 ft (7.4 m) (Argentina,
Thailand); 23 ft (7 m) (Ecuador,
Ghana, Kuwait, Malaysia,
Singapore, UAE)
DRAUGHT: 8.2 ft (2.5 m); 7.5 ft
(2.3 m) (Kuwait, Thailand); 8.9 ft
(2.7 m) (Ghana); 7.9 ft (2.4 m)
(Argentina)
SPEED: 38 kts; 32 kts (Malaysia)
35 kts (Singapore); 27 kts (Ghana);
41 kts (Kuwait); 40 kts (Bahrain,
Ecuador, Thailand, UAE)
RANGE: 1800 miles at 16 kts;
1600 miles at 16 kts (Bahrain)

ARMAMENT:

MISSILES: SSM – four Aerospatiale
MM 40 Exocet (2 twin) launchers
(MM 38 in Argentine Intrepida
only and Ecuador; no missiles
in Ghana, Malaysia), four
McDonnell Douglas Harpoon
(2 twin) (Singapore), four IAI
Gabriel I launchers (Singapore),
5 IAI Gabriel (1 triple, 2 single)
(Thailand); SAM – Matra Simbad
twin launcher, Mistral
(Singapore only)
GUNS: One OTO Melara 3 in
(76 mm)/62 Compact (all, except
Ghana, Malaysia, Singapore and
Thailand); two Bofors 40 mm/70
(Ghana); one Bofors 57 mm/70
(Malaysia); one Bofors 40 mm/70
(Malaysia, Thailand); one Bofors
40 mm/70 (Malaysia,
Thailand); one or two Bofors

SPECIFICATION:

COUNTRY OF ORIGIN: Germany
CLASS: Intrepida, Ahmad El Fateh,
Quito, Jerong, Sea Wolf,
Prabparapak, Ban Yas (TNC 45)
(PCF/PCFG)
ACTIVE: 2 Argentina ('Intrepida'
class), 4 Bahrain ('Ahmad el
Fateh' class), 3 Ecuador ('Quito'
class), 2 Ghana, 1 Kuwait,
6 Malaysia ('Jerong' class),
6 Singapore ('Sea Wolf' class),
3 Thailand ('Prabparapak' class),
6 UAE ('Ban Yas' class)
NAME (PENNANT NUMBER):
ARGENTINA – Intrepida (P 85),
Indomita (P 86)
BAHRAIN – Ahmad El Fateh (20),
Al Jabiri (21), Abdul Rahman Al
Fadel (22), Al Taweelah (23)
ECUADOR – Quito (LM 21),
Guayaquil (LM 23), Cuenca
(LM 24)
GHANA – Dzata (P 26), Sebo (P 27)
KUWAIT – Al Sanbouk (P 4505)*
*survivor of a class of 6;
remainder casualties in 1991
Gulf War
MALAYSIA – Jerong (3505), Todak
(3506), Paus (3507), Yu (3508),

40 mm/70 in (Argentina); two
Oerlikon 35 mm/90 (twin)
(Ecuador); two Breda 40 mm/70
(Bahrain, Kuwait, UAE); three
7.62 mm machine guns
(Bahrain); two 7.62 mm machine
guns (UAE)
DECOYS: CSEE Dagaie launcher
(Bahrain, Kuwait, UAE); two Hycor
Mk 137 sextuple RBOC chaff
launchers; four Rafael (2 twin)
long-range chaff launchers
(Singapore)
TORPEDOES: Two 21 in (533 mm)
tubes; AEG SST-4 (Argentina only)

ELECTRONICS:

RADARS: Air/surface search –
Ericsson Sea Giraffe 50 HC
(Bahrain, Kuwait, UAE), Thomson-
CSF Triton (Ecuador), Racal Decca
1226 (Singapore); surface search
– Kelvin Hughes Type 17
(Thailand), Decca 626 (Argentina),
Kelvin Hughes 1007 (Malaysia),
Decca TM 1226c, (Ghana),
navigation – Racal Decca 1226,
(Bahrain, Ecuador, Kuwait,
Malaysia), Signaal Scout (UAE);
fire control – CelsiusTech 9LV
226/231 (Bahrain), CelsiusTech
9LV 200 MK 2/3 (Kuwait, UAE),
Signaal WM22 (guns/missiles),
Signaal Mk 11 (torpedo guidance)
(Argentina), Thomson-CSF Pollux
(Ecuador), Signaal WM28/5
(Singapore, Thailand)
EW: Racal RDL-1/2 ESM
(Argentina, Thailand); Racal
Cutlass ESM (Kuwait, UAE); Thales
Sealion ESM; Racal Cygnus
(not in 20 or 21) ECM (Bahrain);
Elisra NS-9010 ESM (Ecuador);
Thales DR 3000 ESM (Malaysia);
RQN-3B (INS-3) ESM/ECM
(Singapore)

269

Dabur ARGENTINA, CHILE, FIJI, ISRAEL, NICARAGUA

Baradero

- Low, sleek hull
- Low compact superstructure with open bridge and slim enclosed mast aft of bridge
- Guns forward and aft of superstructure

NOTE: Similar in profile to 'Dvora/Super Dvora' classes, which are derived from 'Dabur' class. 'Dabur' class has shorter deck aft of superstructure

SPECIFICATIONS:

COUNTRY OF ORIGIN: Israel
CLASS: Dabur (Baradero), (Grumete Diaz), (Vai), (PC)
ACTIVE: 4 Argentina ('Baradero' class), 10 Chile ('Grumete Diaz' class), 2 Fiji ('Vai' class), 15 Israel, 3 Nicaragua
NAME (PENNANT NUMBER):
ARGENTINA – Baradero (P 61), Barranqueras (P 62), Clorinda (P 63), Concepción del Uruguay (P 64)
CHILE – Diaz (1814), Bolados (1815), Salinas (1816), Tellez (1817), Bravo (1818), Campos (1819), Machado (1820), Johnson (1821), Troncoso (1822), Hudson (1823)
FIJI – Saku (303), Saqa (304)
ISRAEL – 860-920 series
NICARAGUA – G.C. (201), G.C. (203), G.C. (205)

FEATURES:

DISPLACEMENT: 39 tons full load
LENGTH: 64.9 ft (19.8 m)
BEAM: 18 ft (5.5 m)
DRAUGHT: 5.8 ft (1.8 m)
SPEED: 19 kts
RANGE: 450 miles at 13 kts

ARMAMENT:

GUNS: Two Oerlikon 20 mm; two 12.7 mm machine guns; Carl Gustav 84 mm portable rocket launchers (Israel); two Oerlikon 20 mm (Chile); two Oerlikon 20 mm; four 12.7 mm machine guns (Argentina); two Oerlikon 20 mm; two 7.62 mm machine guns (Fiji); two Oerlikon 25 mm (twin); two 12.7 mm machine guns (Nicaragua)
TORPEDOES: Two 324 mm tubes, Honeywell Mk 46 (Israel only)
DEPTH CHARGES: Two racks (Argentina and Israel only)

ELECTRONICS:

RADARS: Surface search – Decca 101 (Argentina, Nicaragua); Racal Decca Super 101 Mk 3 (Chile, Fiji, Israel)
SONARS: Active search/attack, (Israel only)

Armidale AUSTRALIA

Armidale (*Rafael*)

- 25 mm gun in 'A' position
- Main deck continuous to end of superstructure then sharp break down to quarterdeck
- Streamlined sloping top to forward part of superstructure with enclosed bridge set back
- Large whip aerial either side of forward part of superstructure
- Small mast on top of bridge supporting large round antenna
- Large partial lattice mast carrying navigation radar extending up from engine exhausts which connect into rear of bridge

SPECIFICATIONS:

COUNTRY OF ORIGIN: Australia
CLASS: Armidale
ACTIVE: 1
BUILDING: 11
NAME (PENNANT NUMBER):
Armidale (83), Bathurst (—),
Bundaberg (—), Albany (—), Pirie
(—), Maitland (—), Ararat (—),
Launceston (—), Larrakia (—),
Wollongong (—), Childers, (—),
Broome (—)

FEATURES:

DISPLACEMENT: 270 tons full load
LENGTH: 184.6 ft (56.8 m)
BEAM: 29.5 ft (9 m)
DRAUGHT: 10 ft (3 m)
SPEED: 25 kts
RANGE: 3000 miles at 12 kts

ARMAMENT:

GUNS: One 25 mm Rafael M242Q
Bushmaster; two 12.7 mm
machine guns

ELECTRONICS:

RADARS: Surface search

Fremantle AUSTRALIA

Gawler

- Continuous maindeck from stem to stern
- 40 mm/60 open gun mounting in 'A' position
- Stepped, central superstructure
- Sloping top to forward end of superstructure with bridge set back
- Open bridge atop after end of enclosed bridge
- Large whip aerial either side of forward end of superstructure
- Pole mainmast amidships with small lattice structure supporting navigation radar just forward
- Small ship's boat stowed at after end of superstructure

SPECIFICATIONS:

COUNTRY OF ORIGIN: UK
CLASS: Fremantle (PC)
ACTIVE: 15
NAME (PENNANT NUMBER):
Fremantle (203), Warrnambool (204), Townsville (205), Wollongong (206), Launceston (207), Whyalla (208), Ipswich (209), Cessnock (210), Bendigo (211), Gawler (212), Geraldton (213), Dubbo (214), Geelong (215), Gladstone (216), Bunbury (217)

FEATURES:
DISPLACEMENT: 245 tons full load
LENGTH: 137.1 ft (41.8 m)
BEAM: 23.3 ft (7.1 m)
DRAUGHT: 5.9 ft (1.8 m)
SPEED: 30 kts
RANGE: 1450 miles at 30 kts

ARMAMENT:
GUNS: One Bofors
AN 4-40 mm/60; one 81 mm mortar; three 12.7 mm machine guns

ELECTRONICS:
RADARS: Navigation – Kelvin Hughes Type 1006
EW: AWADI Type 133 Prism

Stenka AZERBAIJAN, CAMBODIA, CUBA, GEORGIA, RUSSIA, UKRAINE

Stenka

FEATURES:

DISPLACEMENT: 253 tons full load
LENGTH: 129.3 ft (39.4 m)
BEAM: 25.9 ft (7.9 m)
DRAUGHT: 8.2 ft (2.5 m)
SPEED: 37 kts; 34 kts (Cuba)
RANGE: 800 miles at 24 kts

ARMAMENT:

GUNS: Four 30 mm/65 AK 230
(2 twin); two 37 mm/68
(Cambodia, Georgia); one
Bofors 40 mm/70 (Cambodia)
TORPEDOES: Four 16 in (406 mm)
tubes (not Azerbaijan, Cambodia,
Cuba or Georgian Coast Guard)
DEPTH CHARGES: Two racks (12)
(not Azerbaijan, Cambodia, Cuba
or Georgian Coast Guard)

ELECTRONICS:

RADARS: Surface search – Pot
Drum or Peel Cone (not
Georgian Coast Guard), Racal
Decca Bridgemaster (Cambodia);
navigation – Palm Frond, Racal
Decca (Cambodia); fire control –
Drum Tilt (not in Georgian Coast
Guard), (Muff Cobb, Cambodia
and Cuba)
SONARS: Stag Ear or Foal Tail VDS
(not Azerbaijan, Cambodia, Cuba
or Georgian Coast Guard)

- Short high freeboard forecastle with 30 mm/65 or 23 mm/87 gun mounting in 'A' position
- Large superstructure, higher at forward end, extending to quarterdeck. Superstructure has vertical ribbed appearance
- Complex tripod mainmast atop after end of bridge supporting surface search radar aerial
- Distinctive Drum Tilt fire control radar aerial on pedestal at after end of superstructure
- 30 mm/65 gun mounting on forecastle in 'A' position and on quarterdeck in 'X' position

SPECIFICATION:

COUNTRY OF ORIGIN: Russia
CLASS: Stenka (Type 205P) (PCF)
ACTIVE: 2 Azerbaijan, 2
Cambodia, 2 Cuba (Border
Guard), 2 Georgia (1 Coast
Guard), 15 Russia (Border Guard),
13 Ukraine (Border Guard)
NAME (PENNANT NUMBER):
AZERBAIJAN – — (ex-AK 234),
— (ex-AK 374)
CAMBODIA – Mondolkiri (1131),
Ratanakiri (1134)
CUBA – Border Guard 801, 816
GEORGIA – Batumi (ex-PSKR-638)
(301, ex-648), Coast Guard –
Giorgi Toreli (ex-Anastasiya,
ex-PSKR-631) (P 21)
RUSSIA – Border Guard –
PSKR-631, PSKR-641, PSKR-659-60,
PSKR-665, PSKR-657, PSKR-690,
PSKR-700, PSKR-712, PSKR-714-715,
PSKR-717-718, PSKR-723, PSKR-725
UKRAINE – Border Guard – Volin
(ex-020, ex-PSKR-637), Mikolaiv
(BG 57, ex-PSKR-722), Zakarpattiya
(ex-031, ex-PSKR-648), Pavel
Derzhavin (ex-037, ex-PSKR-720),
Zaporizkaya SEC (ex-032,
ex-PSKR-650), Odessa (ex-033,
ex-PSKR-652), Bukovina (ex-034,
ex-PSKR-702), Donbass (BG 32,
ex-035, ex-PSKR-705), Podilliya
(ex-036, ex-PSKR-709), Perekop
(BG 30), plus three more

Madhumati/Sea Dragon BANGLADESH, KOREA (SOUTH)

Madhumati

- Sweeping main deck from high sharp bow, with low break just forward of bridge, then smooth, uncluttered lines to low stern
- Tall, flat-fronted, central superstructure with prominent bridge wings
- 57 mm/70 gun mounting in 'A' position in Bangladesh unit
- 47 mm/70 gun open mounting in 'A' position in South Korean hulls
- Tall, lattice mainmast aft end of central superstructure in South Korean hulls. Thin enclosed mast in Bangladesh ship
- Distinctive black-topped rounded funnel aft of superstructure
- Ship's boat outboard of funnel on davits
- 40 mm/70 open mounting on quarterdeck in Bangladesh unit

NOTE: One 76 mm can be mounted on forecastle of South Korean units

SPECIFICATION:

COUNTRY OF ORIGIN:
Korea (South)
CLASS: Madhumati/Sea Dragon
(PC/OPV)
ACTIVE: 1 Bangladesh
('Madhumati' class), 6 South
Korea (operated by Maritime
Police)
NAME (PENNANT NUMBER):
BANGLADESH – Madhumati (P 911)
KOREA (SOUTH) – PC 501, 502, 503,
505, 506, 507

FEATURES:
DISPLACEMENT: 640 tons full
load (South Korea); 635 tons
(Bangladesh)
LENGTH: 199.5 ft (60.8 m)
BEAM: 26.2 ft (8 m)
DRAUGHT: 8.9 ft (2.7 m)
SPEED: 24 kts
RANGE: 6000 miles at 15 kts

ARMAMENT:
GUNS: One Bofors 57 mm/70
Mk 1; one Bofors 40 mm/70;
two Oerlikon 20 mm
(Bangladesh); one Bofors
40 mm/60; two Oerlikon 20 mm;
two Browning 12.7 mm machine
guns (Korea (South))

ELECTRONICS:
RADARS: Surface search – Kelvin
Hughes KH 1007 (Bangladesh);
navigation – GEM Electronics
SPN-753B (Bangladesh)

Meghna/Grajau BANGLADESH, BRAZIL
Gurupá

- Smooth, uncluttered lines from bow to stern
- Small, flat fronted, central superstructure stepped down at after end
- 40 mm/70 gun mounting in 'A' position, P 40-43, Brazilian units
- 57 mm/70 gun mounting in 'A' position, Bangladesh hulls
- Tall, lattice mainmast atop central superstructure
- 'Step down' at aft end of superstructure
- 20 mm gun mounting on afterdeck (Brazil) or 40 mm/70 open mounting (Bangladesh)

SPECIFICATION:

COUNTRY OF ORIGIN: UK
CLASS: Megna/Grajaú (PG)
ACTIVE: 2 Bangladesh ('Meghna' class), 12 Brazil ('Grajaú' class)
NAME (PENNANT NUMBER):
BANGLADESH – Meghna (P 211), Jamuna (P 212)
BRAZIL – Grajaú (P 40), Guaiba (P 41), Graúna (P 42), Goiana (P 43), Guajará (P 44), Guaporé (P 45), Gurupá (P 46), Gurupi (P 47), Guanabara (P 48), Guaruja (P 49), Guaratuba (P 50), Gravataí (P 51)

FEATURES:
DISPLACEMENT: 263 tons full load (Brazil); 410 tons (Bangladesh)
LENGTH: 152.6 ft (46.5 m)
BEAM: 24.6 ft (7.5 m)
DRAUGHT: 7.5 ft (2.3 m)
SPEED: 22 kts
RANGE: 2000 miles at 12 kts

ARMAMENT:
GUNS: One Bofors 40 mm/70; two Oerlikon 20 mm (P 40-44, Brazil); two Oerlikon/BMARC 20 mm GAM-BO1 (P 45-51, Brazil); one Bofors 57 mm/70 Mk 1, one Bofors 40 mm/70 and two 7.62 mm machine guns (Bangladesh)

ELECTRONICS:
RADARS: Surface search – Racal Decca 1290A (Brazil); Decca 1229 (Bangladesh)

Hegu/Houku BANGLADESH, EGYPT, PAKISTAN

615 (Egypt) (A. *Sheldon Duplaix*)

- Low freeboard
- 23 mm/60 or 25 mm/60 gun twin mounting in 'A' position
- Very small and low central superstructure
- Stout, pole mainmast atop central superstructure
- Square Tie air/surface search radar aerial atop mainmast
- Two large, distinctive SSM launchers on quarterdeck, both raised at forward end and angled slightly outboard

NOTE: Chinese variant of the Russian 'Komar' class
NOTE 2: Chinese hydrofoil variant, 'Hema' class, has a semi-submerged foil forward and an extra 6 feet in length, allowing the mounting of a second twin 25 mm gun abaft the missile launchers

SPECIFICATION:

COUNTRY OF ORIGIN: China
CLASS: Hegu/Houku (Type 024) (Durbar) (PCFG)
ACTIVE: 5 Bangladesh ('Durbar' class), 4 Egypt, 4 Pakistan
NAME (PENNANT NUMBER):
BANGLADESH – Durbar (P 8111), Duranta (P 8112), Durvedya (P 8113), Durdam (P 8114), Uttal (P 8141)
EGYPT – (609), (611), (613), (615)
PAKISTAN – Haibut (P1021), Jalalat (P1022), Jurat (P1023), Shujaat (P1024)

FEATURES:
DISPLACEMENT: 79.2 tons full load
LENGTH: 88.6 ft (27 m)
BEAM: 20.7 ft (6.3 m)
DRAUGHT: 4.3 ft (1.3 m)
SPEED: 37.5 kts
RANGE: 400 miles at 30 kts

ARMAMENT:
MISSILES: SSM – two SY-1 (CSS-N-1 Scrubbrush)
GUNS: Two USSR 25 mm/60 (twin); two 23 mm (twin) (Egypt); two Norinco 25 mm/80 (twin) (Pakistan)

ELECTRONICS:
RADARS: Air/surface search – Square Tie

Hainan BANGLADESH, CHINA, EGYPT, KOREA (NORTH), MYANMAR, SRI LANKA

Hainan 643 – China

- High bow, long sloping forecastle, low freeboard
- RBU 1200 A/S mortars towards forward end of forecastle
- 57 mm/70 gun twin mounting in 'A' position
- 25 mm/60 gun twin mounting in 'B' position
- Tall, angular midships superstructure
- Small lattice mainmast atop after end of bridge
- 57 mm/70 gun twin mounting in 'Y' position
- 25 mm/60 gun twin mounting in 'X' position on raised platform

NOTE: A larger Chinese-built version of Soviet SO 1. North Korea also operates 19 of this class
NOTE 2: Missile launchers can be fitted in lieu of the after 57 mm mounting. Later Chinese ships have a tripod foremast and a short stub mainmast. First six Myanmar hulls are of this type
NOTE 3: 'Houxin' (Type 037/1G) class is a missile-armed version of the 'Hainan' class. See separate entry on page 285
NOTE 4: Seven modified units in service with Algerian Coast Guard

SPECIFICATION:

COUNTRY OF ORIGIN: China
CLASS: Hainan (Durjoy) (Type 037) (PC)
ACTIVE: 1 Bangladesh ('Durjoy' class), 98 China, 8 Egypt, 6 Korea (North), 10 Myanmar, 1 Sri Lanka
NAME (PENNANT NUMBER):
BANGLADESH – Nirbhoy (P 812)
CHINA – various numbers
EGYPT – Al Nour (430), Al Hady (433), Al Hakim (439), Al Wakil (436), Al Jabbar (445), Al Qader (448), Al Salam (442), Al Rafa (451)
KOREA (NORTH) – (201-204), (292-293)
MYANMAR – Yan Sit Aung (441), Yan Myat Aung (442), Yan Nyein Aung (443), Yan Khwin Aung (444), Yan Ye Aung (445), Yan Min Aung (446), Yan Paing Aung (447), Yan Win Aung (448), Yan Aye Aung (449), Yan Zwe Aung (450)
SRI LANKA – Parakramabahu

FEATURES:
DISPLACEMENT: 392 tons full load
LENGTH: 192.8 ft (58.8 m)
BEAM: 23.6 ft (7.2 m)
DRAUGHT: 7.2 ft (2.2 m)
SPEED: 30.5 kts
RANGE: 1300 miles at 15 kts

ARMAMENT:
MISSILES: Four YJ-1 (C-801) SSM launchers in lieu of after 57 mm gun (China, optional)
GUNS: Four China 57 mm/70 (2 twin); four USSR 25 mm /60 (2 twin) (23 mm (2 twin), Egypt)
TORPEDOES: Six (322 mm) (2 triple) tubes in two of Egyptian class; Mk 44 or Marconi Stingray
DEPTH CHARGES: Two BMB-2 projectors; two racks
DECOYS: Two PK 16 chaff launchers (Korea (North))

ELECTRONICS:
RADARS: Surface search – Pot Head or Skin Head; navigation – Pathfinder (Myanmar), Decca (Egypt)
SONARS: Stag Ear (SS 12 VDS in some, China); Tamir II, hull-mounted (Bangladesh)
EW: China BM/HZ 8610 ESM (China, Korea (North))

Island BANGLADESH, TRINIDAD & TOBAGO

Nelson

- High bow profile with break down to lower level forward of bridge, high freeboard
- Tall, substantial superstructure just aft of midships
- 40 mm gun mounting on unusual raised barbette at after end of forecastle in 'B' mounting position
- Short, tripod mainmast atop mid-superstructure
- Prominent funnel, with sloping after end, atop superstructure aft of mainmast
- Two small crane jibs at after end of superstructure, port and starboard

NOTE: *Shaheed Ruhul Amin* is operated by Bangladesh as a training ship
NOTE 2: Scottish Fisheries Protection Agency operates the unarmed OPV *Westra*, similar to 'Island' class

SPECIFICATION:

COUNTRY OF ORIGIN: UK
CLASS: Island (OPV)
ACTIVE: 6 Bangladesh, 1 Trinidad & Tobago
NAME (PENNANT NUMBER):
BANGLADESH – Shaheed Ruhul Amin (ex-*Jersey*) (A 511, ex-P 295), Kapatakhaya (ex-*Shetland*) (P 912, ex-P 298), Karatoa (ex-*Alderney*) (P 913, ex-P 278), Gomati (ex-*Anglesey*) (P 914, ex-P 277), Sangu (ex-*Guernsey*) (P 713, ex-P 297), Turag (ex-*Lindisfarne*) (P 713, ex-P 300)
TRINIDAD & TOBAGO – Nelson (ex-*Orkney*) (CG 20, ex-P 299)

FEATURES:
DISPLACEMENT: 1260 tons full load
LENGTH: 195.3 ft (59.5 m) oa
BEAM: 36 ft (11 m)
DRAUGHT: 15 ft (4.5 m)
SPEED: 16.5 kts
RANGE: 7000 miles at 12 kts

ARMAMENT:
GUNS: One Bofors 40 mm/60, two 7.62 mm machine guns

ELECTRONICS:
RADARS: Navigation – Kelvin Hughes Type 1006
EW: Orange Crop ESM (Bangladesh)

Bizerte CAMEROON, SENEGAL, TUNISIA

Bizerte (A *Companera i Rovira*)

- Continuous deck sweeping down from high bow
- 37 mm/63 gun twin open mounting in 'A' position (Tunisia); vice, 40 mm/70 (Senegal and Cameroon)
- Very small and low central superstructure with wide step up to bridge windows, with open bridge atop
- Lattice mainmast atop central superstructure
- Rounded aft edge of superstructure, outboard of funnel
- 37 mm/63 gun twin open mounting on quarterdeck (Tunisia); vice 40 mm/70 (Senegal and Cameroon)

SPECIFICATION:

COUNTRY OF ORIGIN: France
CLASS: Bizerte (Type PR 48) (PC)
ACTIVE: 1 Cameroon, 2 Senegal, 3 Tunisia
NAME (PENNANT NUMBER):
CAMEROON – L'Audacieux (P 103)
SENEGAL – Popenguine, Podor
TUNISIA – Bizerte (P 301), Horria (ex-*Liberté*) (P 302), Monastir (P 304)

FEATURES:

DISPLACEMENT: 250 tons full load
LENGTH: 157.5 ft (48 m) (Tunisia, Cameroon); 156 ft (47.5 m) (Senegal)
BEAM: 23.3 ft (7.1 m)
DRAUGHT: 7.5 ft (2.3 m) (Tunisia, Cameroon); 8.1 ft (2.5 m) (Senegal)
SPEED: 20 kts
RANGE: 2000 miles at 16 kts

ARMAMENT:

MISSILES: SSM – eight Aerospatiale SS 12M (Tunisia only)
GUNS: Four 37 mm/63 (2 twin) (Tunisia); two Bofors 40 mm/70; two 7.62 mm machine guns (Senegal); two Bofors 40 mm/70 (Cameroon)

ELECTRONICS:

RADARS: Surface search – Thomson-CSF DRBN 31 (Tunisia); Racal Decca 1226 (Senegal)

La Combattante II/IIA CHILE, EGYPT, GEORGIA, GREECE, IRAN,

Fuchs (*Michael Nitz*)

- Small bridge superstructure forward of midships
- 35 mm/90 gun mounting in 'A' position, Georgian unit (57 mm/70 gun in Malaysian ships; OTO Melara 3 in, Chilean, Greek, Libyan and Iranian ships)
- Tall lattice mainmast at after end of superstructure (fire control radome atop in Iranian ships)
- Fire control radar aerial atop bridge roof, (not Iranian ships)
- SSM launchers aft of superstructure. Forward two immediately aft of superstructure trained forward and to starboard, after two trained forward and to port. (Two Exocet launchers only in Malaysian ships, two twin Harpoon or four C-802 SSM in Iranian ships)
- 35 mm/90 gun mounting aft in 'Y' position (Georgian unit). 40 mm/70 in same position in Malaysian ships and in some Iranian units (some with 20 mm). (Chilean, Egyptian, Greek and Libyans have 40 mm/70 turret mounting)

NOTE: See 'Combattante III' entry, page 296, in service with Greece, Nigeria, Qatar and Tunisia

SPECIFICATION:

COUNTRY OF ORIGIN: France
CLASS: La Combattante II/IIA
(Riquelme, Votsis, Kaman,
Perdana) (PGF/PCFG)
ACTIVE: 4 Chile ('Riquelme'
class, Type 148), 5 Egypt,
1 Georgia (Combattante II),
6 Greece (Combattante IIA)
('Votsis' class), 11 Iran ('Kaman'
class), 8 Libya, 4 Malaysia
('Perdana' class)
NAME (PENNANT NUMBER):
CHILE – Riquelme (ex-Wolf)
(LM 36, ex-P 6149), Orella
(ex-Elster) (LM 37, ex-P 6154),
Serrano (ex-Tiger) (LM 38,
ex-P 6141), Uribe (ex-Luchs)
(LM 39, ex-P 6143)
EGYPT – 23 of July (ex-Alk) (601,
ex-P 6155), 6 of October
(ex-Fuchs) (602, ex-P 6146),
21 of October (ex-Löwe)
(603 ex-P 6148), 18 of June
(ex-Dommel) (604 ex-P 6156),
25 of April (ex-Weihe) (605
ex-P 6157)
GEORGIA – —— (ex-Ypoploiarchos
Batsis, ex-Calypso) (—, ex-P 17)

GREECE – 'Votsis' class –
Ypoploiarchos Votsis (ex-Iltis)
(P 72, ex-P 51), Anthypoploiarchos
Pezopoulos (ex-Storch) (P 73,
ex-P 30), Plotarchis Vlahavas
(ex-Marder) (P 74), Plotarchis
Maridakis (ex-Häher) (P 75),
Ypoploiarchos Tournas (ex-
Leopard) (P 76), Plotarchis
Sakipis (ex-Jaguar) (P 77)
IRAN – Kaman (P 221), Zoubin
(P 222), Khadang (P 223), Peykan
(P 224), Falakhon (P 226),
Shamshir (P 227), Gorz (P 228),
Gardouneh (P 229), Khanjar
(P 230), Neyzeh (P 231),
Tarbarzin (P 232)
LIBYA – Sharaba (ex-Beir Grassa)
(518), Wahag (ex-Beir Gzir) (522),
Shehab (ex-Beir Gtifa) (524),
Shouaia (ex-Beir Algandula) (528),
Shoula (ex-Beir Ktitat) (532),
Shafak (ex-Beir Alkrarim) (534),
Rad (ex-Beir Alkur) (538), Laheeb
(ex-Beir Alkuefat) (542)
MALAYSIA – Perdana (3501),
Serang (3502), Ganas (3503),
Ganyang (3504)

FEATURES:

DISPLACEMENT: 255 tons full load
(Georgia); 311 tons (Libya); 265
tons (Chile, Egpyt, Greece,
Malaysia); 275 tons (Iran)
LENGTH: 154.2 ft (47 m); 160.7 ft
(49 m) (Libya)
BEAM: 23.3 ft (7.1 m); 23.1 ft (7 m)
(Chile, Egypt, Greece, Malaysia)
DRAUGHT: 8.2 ft (2.5 m) (Georgia);
6.2 ft (1.9 m) (Iran); 6.6 ft (2 m)
(Libya); 12.8 ft (3.9 m) (Malaysia);
8.9 ft (2.7 m) (Chile, Egypt,
Greece)
SPEED: 36.5 kts; 31 kts (Chile);
39 kts (Libya)
RANGE: 1600 miles at 15 kts;
1800 at 15 kts (Malaysia)

ARMAMENT:

MISSILES: SSM – four Aerospatiale
MM 38 Exocet (Chile, Egypt,
Greece P 72-73, two only in
Malaysian ships), four McDonnell
Douglas Harpoon
(2 twin) (Greece P 74-75), four
OTO Melara/Matra Otomat Mk 2
(TG 1) (Libya), two or four
Chinese C-802 (1 or 2 twin) or
four Harpoon (2 twin) (Iran)

GUNS: Four Oerlikon 35 mm/90
(2 twin) (Georgia); one OTO
Melara 3 in (76 mm)/62 Compact;
one Breda/Bofors 40 mm/70
(some have 20 mm or 23 mm
gun vice 40 mm) and two
12.7 machine guns (Iran); one
OTO Melara 3 in (76 mm)/62
Compact; one Bofors 40 mm/70
(twin) (Chile, Egypt, Greece,
Libya); one Bofors 57 mm/70;
one Bofors 40 mm/70 (Malaysia)
TORPEDOES: Two 21 in (533 mm)
tubes AEG SST-4 (Georgia only)
DECOYS: Wolke chaff launcher;
Hot Dog IR launcher (Egypt)

ELECTRONICS:

RADARS: Surface search –
Thomson-CSF Triton (Chile,
Egypt, Greece, Libya, Malaysia);
surface search/fire control –
Signaal WM28 (Iran); navigation –
Racal Decca 1226C (Georgia,
Iran), Kelvin Hughes 1007
(Malaysia), SMA 3 RM 20 (Chile,
Egypt, Greece); fire control -
Thomson-CSF Pollux (Georgia,
Malaysia), Thomson-CSF Castor
IIB (Chile, Egypt, Greece, Libya)
EW: Thomson-CSF DR 2000S
(Georgia, Greece); Thomson-
CSF TMV 433 Dalia ESM (Iran);
Thomson-CSF DR 3000 ESM
(Malaysia)

Reshef (Saar 4) CHILE, GREECE, ISRAEL, SOUTH AFRICA, SRI LANKA

René Sethren (now decommissioned)

- Long sleek hull, high bows, low freeboard
- CIWS mounting in 'A' position (Israeli ships). 3 in gun mounting (Chile, South Africa)
- Short superstructure well forward of midships
- Large lattice mainmast aft of superstructure
- Air/surface search radar aerial atop mainmast
- Combination of Harpoon and Gabriel SSM launchers aft of superstructure (Israeli ships). Gabriel/Skerpioen SSM launchers (Chile, South Africa)
- 3 in gun mounting in 'Y' position

NOTE: Easily confused with the 'Saar 4.5' class

SPECIFICATION:

COUNTRY OF ORIGIN: Israel
CLASS: Reshef (Saar 4), (Casma, Warrior (ex-Minister) (PCFG)
ACTIVE: 3 Chile ('Casma' class), 3 Greece (Coast Guard), 2 Israel ('Reshef' class), 3 South Africa ('Warrior,' ex-'Minister' class), 2 Sri Lanka
NAME (PENNANT NUMBER):
CHILE – Casma (ex-*Romah*) (LM 30), Chipana (ex-*Keshet*) (LM 31), Angamos (ex-*Reshef*) (LM 34)
GREECE – Coast Guard – Fournoi (LS 060), Ro (LS 070), A.G. Efstratios (LS 080)
ISRAEL – Nitzhon, Atsmout
SOUTH AFRICA – Isaac Dyobha (ex-*Frans Erasmus*) (P 1565), Galeshewe (ex-*Hendrik Mentz*) (P 1567), Makhanda (ex-*Magnus Malan*) (P 1569)
SRI LANKA – Nandimithra (ex-*Moledt*) (P 701), Suranimala (ex-*Komemiut*) (P 702)

FEATURES:

DISPLACEMENT: 450 tons full load (Chile, Greece, Israel, Sri Lanka); 430 tons (South Africa)
LENGTH: 190.6 ft (58 m); 204 ft (62.2 m) (South Africa)
BEAM: 25 ft (7.8 m)
DRAUGHT: 8 ft (2.4 m)
SPEED: 32 kts
RANGE: 4000 at 17.5 kts

ARMAMENT:

MISSILES: SSM – Harpoon (twin or quad) launchers; four to six IAI Gabriel II (Israel), four Gabriel I or II (Chile), three Gabriel II (Sri Lanka), six Skerpioen (South Africa)
GUNS: One or two OTO Melara 3 in (76 mm)/62 Compact; two Oerlikon 20 mm; one GE/GD Vulcan Phalanx Mk 15; two 12.7 mm machine guns (Israel); two OTO Melara 3 in (76 mm)/62 Compact (Chile, South Africa); one OTO Melara 3 in (76 mm)/62, one 40 mm and two Rafael Typhoon 20 mm (Sri Lanka); two Oerlikon 20 mm (Chile, Sri Lanka); two LIW Vektor 35 mm (twin) may replace one 76 mm gun in one South African hull for trials, plus two LIW Mk 1 20 mm and two 12.7 mm machine guns (South Africa); one 30 mm, two 12.7 mm machine guns (Greece)
DECOYS: One 45-tube, four or six 24-tube, four single tube chaff launchers (Israel); four Rafael LRCR decoy launchers (Chile); four ACDS chaff launchers (South Africa); not fitted in Sri Lankan units

ELECTRONICS:

RADARS: Air/surface search – Thomson-CSF TH-D 1040 Neptune (Israel, Sri Lanka); Elta EL/M 2208 (Chile, South Africa), Signaal variant (Greece); navigation – Raytheon 20X (Chile), Bridgemaster (Greece); fire control – Selenia Orion RTN 10X or Elta M-2221 (in some, Chile and Sri Lanka, none in Greece)
SONARS: EDO 780; VDS; occasionally fitted in some of the Israeli ships
EW: Elisra NS 9003/5 ESM (Israel); Elta MN-53 ESM; Elta Rattler ECM (Chile); Delcon ESM; Elta Rattler ECM (South Africa)

Israel

Fast Attack Craft Missile CHINA

2208

- Wave-piercing catamaran hull with centre bow
- Features radar cross section reduction measures
- Distinguished by two very large exhausts aft
- Central bridge set well forward with sharply rear sloping enclosed mast at rear

NOTE: Details are speculative

SPECIFICATION:

COUNTRY OF ORIGIN: France
CLASS: To be announced
ACTIVE: 3
NAME (PENNANT NUMBER):
— (2208), — (2209), — (2210)

FEATURES:

DISPLACEMENT: 220 tons full load
LENGTH: 139.8 ft (42.6 m)
BEAM: 40 ft (12.2 m)
DRAUGHT: 4.9 ft (1.5 m)
SPEED: 36 kts
RANGE: To be announced

ARMAMENT:

MISSILES: SSM – four
GUNS: One 30 mm/65 AK 630

ELECTRONICS:

RADARS: Surface search – Type 362; navigation – to be announced

Houjian/Huang CHINA

Panyu

- High bow, sloping forecastle
- 37 mm/63 gun twin mounting in 'A' position
- Main superstructure stepped down at after end
- Tall, lattice mainmast at after end of bridge superstructure
- Distinctive Rice Lamp fire control director atop bridge roof
- Boxlike C-801 SSM launchers aft of forward superstructure, port and starboard, trained forward and slightly outboard
- Two 30 mm/65 gun mountings in 'Y' and 'X' positions

SPECIFICATION:

COUNTRY OF ORIGIN: China
CLASS: Houjian/Huang
(Type 037/2) (PGG)
ACTIVE: 7
NAME (PENNANT NUMBER):
Yangjiang (770), Shunde (771),
Nanhai (772), Panyu (773),
— (774), — (775), — (776)

FEATURES:

DISPLACEMENT: 520 tons standard
LENGTH: 214.6 ft (65.4 m)
BEAM: 27.6 ft (8.4 m)
DRAUGHT: 7.9 ft (2.4 m)
SPEED: 32 kts
RANGE: 1800 miles at 18 kts

ARMAMENT:

MISSILES: SSM – six YJ-1 (Eagle
Strike) (C-801) (C SS-B-4 Sardine)
(2 triple)
GUNS: Two 37 mm/63 (twin)
Type 76A; four 30 mm/65 (2 twin)
Type 69
DECOYS: Two Type 945G
26-barrelled launcher

ELECTRONICS:

RADARS: Surface search – Type 381
Rice Shield; navigation – Type
765; fire control – Type 347 G
Rice Lamp
EW: Type 928 ESM

Houxin CHINA, MYANMAR, SRI LANKA

Houxin (China)

- High bow, long forecastle
- 37 mm/63 gun twin open mounting in 'A' position
- Sri Lankan unit has two A/S mortars forward of gun mounting
- Long, central superstructure stepped down at after end
- Two 14.5 mm machine-gun mountings, port and starboard, in 'B' mounting position
- Large lattice mainmast amidships with Square Tie surface search radar aerial atop
- Small gap between forward and low after superstructure
- 37 mm/63 gun twin mounting atop after superstructure in 'x' position, in Chinese and Myanmar units
- Two forward pointing (twin) SSM launchers, port and starboard, on quarterdeck. Both launchers angled up and slightly outboard

NOTE: Missile armed version of 'Hainan' class. Some variations in the bridge superstructure of later Chinese ships

SPECIFICATION:

COUNTRY OF ORIGIN: China
CLASS: Houxin (Type 037/1G)
ACTIVE: 16 China, 6 Myanmar, 1 Sri Lanka
NAME (PENNANT NUMBER):
CHINA – (751-760), (764-769)
MYANMAR – Maga (471), Saittra (472), Duwa (473), Zedya (474), (475-476)
SRI LANKA – Parakramabahu (P 351)

FEATURES:
DISPLACEMENT: 478 tons full load
LENGTH: 203.4 ft (62.8 m)
BEAM: 23.6 ft (7.2 m)
DRAUGHT: 7.5 ft (2.4 m)
SPEED: 28 kts
RANGE: 1300 miles at 15 kts

ARMAMENT:
MISSILES: SSM – four YJ-1 (Eagle Strike) (C-801) (2 twin), not Sri Lanka
GUNS: Four 37 mm/63 Type 76A (2 twin); four 14.5 mm machine guns Type 69 (2 twin)
A/S MORTARS: Two Type 87 6-tube launchers (Sri Lanka only)

ELECTRONICS:
RADARS: Surface search – Square Tie, (Myanmar, China); navigation – Anritsu RA 723 (China, Sri Lanka); fire control – Rice Lamp
SONARS: Stag Ear, hull-mounted active (Sri Lanka only)

Flyvefisken DENMARK

Ravnen (H.M. *Steele*)

- 3 in gun mounting in 'A' position
- High freeboard with break down to afterdeck adjacent to funnel
- High, angular central superstructure flush with ship's side
- Tall enclosed mainmast amidships with AWS 6 or TRS-3D (P 557-563) air/surface search radar aerial atop
- Very low profile, black-capped funnel aft of mainmast with sloping after end
- Two Harpoon SSM angled launchers, athwartships in crossover configuration, aft of funnel adjacent to break in maindeck
- Two torpedo tubes (one port, one starboard) outboard of SSM launchers

NOTE: The overall design allows ships to change as required to the attack, patrol, MCMV or minelayer roles. Requirement is to be able to change within 48 hours

SPECIFICATION:

COUNTRY OF ORIGIN: Denmark
CLASS: Flyvefisken (PG/MHC/MLC/AGSC)
ACTIVE: 14
NAME (PENNANT NUMBER):
Flyvefisken (P 550), Hajen (P 551), Havkatten (P 552), Laxen (P 553), Makrelen (P 554), Støren (P 555), Svaerdfisken (P 556), Glenten (P 557), Gribben (P 558), Lommen (P 559), Ravnen (P 560), Skaden (P 561), Viben (P 562), Søløven (P 563)

FEATURES:
DISPLACEMENT: 480 tons full load
LENGTH: 177.2 ft (54 m)
BEAM: 29.5 ft (9 m)
DRAUGHT: 8.2 ft (2.5 m)
SPEED: 30 kts
RANGE: 2400 miles at 18 kts

ARMAMENT:
MISSILES: SSM – eight McDonnell Douglas Harpoon; SAM – three Mk 48 Mod 3 twin launchers, Sea Sparrow (fitted for attack/MCM/minelaying roles)
GUNS: One OTO Melara 3 in (76 mm)/62 Super Rapid; two 12.7 mm machine guns
TORPEDOES: Two 21 in (533 mm) tubes; Eurotorp MU90 Impact
MINES: 60 (minelaying role only)
DECOYS: Two Sea Gnat 130 mm DL-6T 6-barrel chaff launchers

ELECTRONICS:
RADARS: Air/surface search – AWS 6 (P 550-P 556); TRS-3D (P 557-P 563); surface search – Terma Scanter Mil; navigation – Furuno; fire control – 9LV 200 Mk 3
SONARS: Thomson-Sintra TSM 2640 Salmon, VDS; CTS-36/39 hull-mounted (for ASW only)

Ramadan EGYPT

El Kadessaya (*H & L van Ginderen collection*)

- Very short forecastle with 3 in gun mounting in 'A' position
- Main superstructure well forward of midships
- Large, pyramid mainmast at after end of superstructure with pole mast atop after end
- Distinctive Marconi S 820 air/surface search radome atop mainmast
- Small after superstructure supporting short enclosed mast with radome atop
- Otomat SSM launchers sited between superstructures. Forward two trained to port, after two starboard. All launchers angled towards the bow
- 40 mm/70 gun mounting in 'Y' position

NOTE: US Navy's 'Cyclone' PCFS based on 'Ramadan' design but of markedly different appearance. See separate entry on page 316

See separate entry on page 316

SPECIFICATION:

COUNTRY OF ORIGIN: UK
CLASS: Ramadan (PCFG)
ACTIVE: 6
NAME (PENNANT NUMBER):
Ramadan (670), Khyber (672), El Kadessaya (674), El Yarmouk (676), Badr (678), Hettein (680)

FEATURES:
DISPLACEMENT: 307 tons full load
LENGTH: 170.6 ft (52 m)
BEAM: 25 ft (7.6 m)
DRAUGHT: 7.5 ft (2.3 m)
SPEED: 40 kts
RANGE: 1600 miles at 18 kts

ARMAMENT:
MISSILES: SSM – four OTO Melara/Matra Otomat Mk 2; SAM – Portable SA-N-5 sometimes carried
GUNS: One OTO Melara 3 in (76 mm)/62 Compact; two Breda 40 mm/70 (twin)
DECOYS: Four Protean fixed chaff launchers

ELECTRONICS:
RADARS: Air/surface search – Marconi S 820; navigation – Marconi S 810; fire control – two Marconi ST 802
EW: Racal Cutlass ESM, Racal Cygnus ECM

Storm ESTONIA, LATVIA, LITHUANIA

Bulta

- Low profile, compact craft
- Long clear forecastle on Latvian hull
- 40 mm open mounting immediately forward of bridge on Lithuanian hull
- Twin 25 mm/80 on raised platform, immediately forward of bridge, in Estonian boat
- Low, rounded central superstructure
- Central tripod mainmast
- Twin 14.5 mm MG on raised platform on quarterdeck, Estonian unit
- 40 mm gun mounting on quarterdeck, Latvian craft

SPECIFICATION:

COUNTRY OF ORIGIN: Norway
CLASS: Storm (PCF)
ACTIVE: 1 Estonia (Border Guard), 4 Latvia, 3 Lithuania
NAME (PENNANT NUMBER):
ESTONIA – Torm (ex-*Arg*) (PVL 105, ex-P 968)
LATVIA – Bulta (ex-*Traust*) (P 04, ex-P 973), Lode (ex-*Hvass*) (P 02), Linga (ex-*Gnist*) (P 03), Zibens (ex-*Djerv*) (P 01, ex-P 966)
LITHUANIA – Dzūkas (ex-*Kjekk*) (P 31, ex-P 965), Selis (ex-*Skuud*) (P 32, ex-P 967), Skalvis (ex-*Steil*) (P 33, ex-P 969)

FEATURES:

DISPLACEMENT: 135 tons full load
LENGTH: 120 ft (36.5 m)
BEAM: 20 ft (6.1 m)
DRAUGHT: 5 ft (1.5 m)
SPEED: 32 kts
RANGE: 800 miles at 25 kts

ARMAMENT:

GUNS: One Bofors 40 mm/60 (Latvia, Lithuania); one Bofors 3 in (76 mm)/50 (Lithuania); two 25 mm/80 (twin); two 14.5 mm (twin) machine guns (Estonia)

ELECTRONICS:

RADARS: Surface search – Racal Decca TM 1226; Furuno (Lithuania)

Missiles now deleted from quarterdeck

Super Dvora/Super Dvora Mk II/III

ERITREA, INDIA, ISRAEL, SLOVENIA, SRI LANKA

Super Dvora Mk III (*Israeli Aircraft Industries*)

- Low profile, compact craft
- Slightly raised bow with continuous maindeck from stem to stern. Low freeboard
- Low profile superstructure with slim enclosed mast aft of open bridge
- Gun mountings forward of bridge and right aft

SPECIFICATION:

COUNTRY OF ORIGIN: Israel
CLASS: Super Dvora/Super Dvora Mk II, Mk III (PCF)
ACTIVE: 4 Eritrea (Mk II), 5 India (Mk II), 14 Israel (9 Mk I, 4 Mk II, 1 Mk III), 1 Slovenia (Mk II), 9 Sri Lanka (4 Mk I, 5 Mk II)
BUILDING: 2 (India), 5 (Israel, Mk III)
PLANNED: 4 (Israel, Mk III)
NAME (PENNANT NUMBER):
ERITREA – (P 101), (P 102), (P 103), (P 104)
INDIA – T 80-T 86
ISRAEL – 811-819 (Mk I), 820-823 (Mk II)
SLOVENIA – Ankaran (HPL 21)
SRI LANKA – Mk I: P 440-443 (ex-P 465-468); Mk II: P 460 (ex-P 441), P 461 (ex-P 496), P 462 (ex-P 497), P 464, P 465

FEATURES:

DISPLACEMENT: 54 tons full load; 60 tons (India); 58 tons (Slovenia, Eritrea); 64 tons (Sri Lanka, Mk II); 72 tons (Israel, Mk III)
LENGTH: 71 ft (21.6 m), Mk I; 82 ft (25 m), Mk II; 73.5 ft (22.4 m) (Sri Lanka, Mk I); 89.9 ft (27.4 m) (Israel, Mk III)
BEAM: 18 ft (5.5 m) (Mk I); 18.4 ft (5.6 m) (Mk II); 18.7 ft (5.7 m) (Israel, Mk III)
DRAUGHT: 5.9 ft (1.8 m) (Mk I); 3.6 ft (1.1 m) (Mk II)
SPEED: 36 kts (Mk I); 46 kts (Mk III)
RANGE: 1200 miles at 17 kts

ARMAMENT:

MISSILES: SSM – Hellfire (sometimes carried, Israel only)
GUNS: Two Oerlikon 20 mm/80 or Bushmaster 25 mm/87 Mk 96 or three Rafael Typhoon 12.7 mm (triple machine guns); two 12.7 mm or 7.62 mm machine guns; one 84 mm rocket launcher (Israel); one Bushmaster 25 mm M242; one 20 mm; two 7.62 mm (Israel, Mk III); two 23 mm (twin); two 12 mm machine guns (Eritrea); one Oerlikon 20 mm; two 12.7 mm machine guns (India); two Oerlikon 20 mm; two 12.7 mm machine guns (Sri Lanka, Mk I); one Rafael Typhoon 20 mm or two Royal Ordnance GCM-A03 30 mm (twin); two Oerlikon 20 mm; four 12.7 mm machine guns; six 7.62 mm machine guns (Sri Lanka, Mk II); two 12.7 mm machine guns (Slovenia)

ELECTRONICS:

RADARS: Surface search – Raytheon (Eritrea, Israel), Koden MD 3220 (India, Slovenia, Sri Lanka, Mk II), Decca 926 (Sri Lanka, Mk I)

Hamina FINLAND

Hamina

- High, sharply raked bow with maindeck sweeping down to low stern
- 40 mm/70 gun turret mounting mid-forecastle
- Central, angular, stepped superstructure, with bridge set back
- Short, robust enclosed mainmast amidships
- RBS 15F SSM angled box launchers aft of superstructure on very short quarterdeck

NOTE: SAM and 23 mm guns are interchangeable within the same barbette
NOTE 2: Continuation of the 'Rauma' class design

SPECIFICATION:

COUNTRY OF ORIGIN: Finland
CLASS: Hamina (PCFG)
ACTIVE: 2
BUILDING: 2
NAME (PENNANT NUMBER):
Hamina (80, ex-74) Tornis (81),
— (82), — (83)

FEATURES:
DISPLACEMENT: 270 tons full load
LENGTH: 164 ft (50.8 m)
BEAM: 26.2 ft (8.3 m)
DRAUGHT: 6.2 ft (2 m)
SPEED: 32 kts
RANGE: 500 miles at 30 kts

ARMAMENT:
MISSILES: SSM – six Saab RBS 15SF;
SAM – Matra Sadral sextuple
launcher, Mistral
GUNS: Bofors 40 mm/70; (six
103 mm rails for rocket
illuminants); two Sako 23 mm/87
(twin) can be fitted instead of
Sadral; two 12.7 mm machine guns
A/S MORTARS: Four Saab Elma
LLS-920 9-tubed launchers
DEPTH CHARGES: One rail
DECOYS: Philax chaff launcher

ELECTRONICS:
RADARS: Air-search – DASA
TRS-3D; surface search – Signaal
Scout; navigation – Raytheon
ARPA; fire control – Bofors
Electronic 9LV 225
SONARS: Simrad Subsea Toadfish
sonar, search and attack;
Finnyards Sonac/PTA towed array
EW: MEL Matilda ESM

Helsinki FINLAND

Turku

- Short forecastle with 57 mm/70 gun mounting in 'A' position
- High rounded superstructure forward of midships
- Tall, slender, enclosed mainmast atop superstructure aft of bridge
- Two 23 mm/87 gun mountings on wings at after end of superstructure (can be replaced by Sadral/Mistral SAM launcher)
- Four twin RBS 15 SSM launchers on afterdeck; two port, two starboard, trained forward and angled outboard

NOTE: See also Rauma class which was developed from this design

SPECIFICATION:

COUNTRY OF ORIGIN: Finland
CLASS: Helsinki (PCFG)
ACTIVE: 4
NAME (PENNANT NUMBER):
Helsinki (60), Turku (61), Oulu (62), Kotka (63)

FEATURES:
DISPLACEMENT: 300 tons full load
LENGTH: 147.6 ft (45 m)
BEAM: 29.2 ft (8.9 m)
DRAUGHT: 9.9 ft (3 m)
SPEED: 30 kts

ARMAMENT:
MISSILES: SSM – eight Saab RBS 15; SAM – two sextuple Sadral launchers, Mistral
GUNS: One Bofors 57 mm/70; four Sako 23 mm/87 (2 twin) (in place of Sadral launcher)
DEPTH CHARGES: Two rails
DECOYS: Philax chaff launcher

ELECTRONICS:
RADARS: Surface search – 9GA 208; navigation – Raytheon ARPA; fire control – CelsiusTech 9LV 225
SONARS: Simrad Marine SS 304; Finnyards Sonac/PTA towed array
EW: Argo ESM

Rauma FINLAND

Porvoo

- High bow with long forecastle
- 40 mm/70 gun mounting mid-forecastle
- Saab Elma LLS-920 A/S mortar between mounting and forward superstructure
- Central, angular, stepped superstructure
- 9LV 225 fire control radar aerial atop bridge roof
- Short, robust pole mainmast amidships
- 9GA 208 surface search radar aerial atop mainmast
- Two RBS 15 SSM launchers outboard of after end of superstructure with second two right aft on the port and starboard quarter

NOTE: SAM and 23 mm guns are interchangeable within the same barbette

SPECIFICATION:

COUNTRY OF ORIGIN: Finland
CLASS: Rauma (PCFG)
ACTIVE: 4
NAME (PENNANT NUMBER):
Rauma (70), Raahe (71),
Porvoo (72), Naantali (73)

FEATURES:

DISPLACEMENT: 248 tons full load
LENGTH: 157.5 ft (48 m)
BEAM: 26.2 ft (8 m)
DRAUGHT: 4.5 ft (1.5 m)
SPEED: 30 kts

ARMAMENT:

MISSILES: SSM – six Saab RBS 15SF;
SAM – Matra Sadral sextuple
launcher, Mistral
GUNS: One Bofors 40 mm/70;
(six 103 mm rails for rocket
illuminants); two Sako 23 mm/87
(twin) can be fitted instead of
Sadral
A/S MORTARS: Four Saab Elma
LLS-920 9-tubed launchers
DEPTH CHARGES: One rail
DECOYS: Philax chaff launcher

ELECTRONICS:

RADARS: Surface search – 9GA
208; navigation – Raytheon ARPA;
fire control – CelsiusTech 9LV 225
SONARS: Simrad Subsea Toadfish
sonar; Finnyards Sonac/PTA
towed array
EW: MEL Matilda ESM

P 400 FRANCE, GABON, OMAN

La Tapageuse

- 40 mm/60 gun mounting in 'A' position (Oto Melara 76 mm/62 Super Rapid fitted in Omani units from 1998)
- High, angular, midships superstructure
- Pole mainmast, angled aft, atop superstructure amidships (lattice mast in Omani ships)
- Very unusual twin funnels aft of superstructure at outboard extremities of hull. Funnels are of square section, black-capped, and angled aft
- Omani ships have single tapered funnel with tall whip aerial at forward end

SPECIFICATION:

COUNTRY OF ORIGIN: France
CLASS: P 400 (Patra/Al Bushra) (PC/OPV)
ACTIVE: 10 France, 2 Gabon ('Patra' class), 3 Oman ('Al Bushra' class OPV)
NAME (PENNANT NUMBER):
FRANCE – L'Audacieuse (P 682), La Boudeuse (P 683), La Capricieuse (P 684), La Fougueuse (P 685), La Glorieuse (P 686), La Gracieuse (P 687), La Moqueuse (P 688), La Railleuse (P 689), La Rieuse (P 690), La Tapageuse (P 691)
GABON – Général d'Armée Ba-Oumar (P 07), Colonel Djoue-Dabany (P 08)
OMAN – Al Bushra (B 1), Al Mansoor (B 2), Al Najah (B 3)

FEATURES:

DISPLACEMENT: 477 tons full load; 475 tons (Oman); 446 tons (Gabon)
LENGTH: 178.6 ft (54.5 m); 179 ft (54.6 m) (Gabon)
BEAM: 26.2 ft (8 m)
DRAUGHT: 8.5 ft (2.5 m); 8.9 ft (2.7 m) (Oman)
SPEED: 24.5 kts
RANGE: 4200 miles at 15 kts

ARMAMENT:

GUNS: One Bofors 40 mm/60; one Giat 20F2 20 mm; two 12.7 mm machine guns (France); one Bofors 57 mm/70 SAK 57 Mk 2 (P 07); two Giat 20F2 20 mm (twin) (P 08 which also has an Oerlikon 20 mm) (Gabon); one OTO Melara 76 mm/62 Compact; two Oerlikon/Royal Ordnance 20 mm GAM-BO1 20 mm and two 12.7 mm machine guns (Oman)

ELECTRONICS:

RADARS: Surface search – Racal Decca 1226 (France, Gabon), Kelvin Hughes 1007 ARPA (Oman)
EW: Thomson-CSF DR 3000 ESM (Oman)

Albatros GERMANY, TUNISIA

Geier (*Michael Nitz*)

- Long forecastle, prominent breakwater forward of 3 in gun mounting in 'A' position
- Narrow, long central superstructure, stepped down aft of bridge
- Lattice structure aft of bridge supporting distinctive WM 27 surface search/fire control radome
- Tall tripod pole mainmast at after end of superstructure
- Exocet SSM ribbed launchers aft of superstructure, trained forward and to port and immediately aft, trained forward and to starboard
- 3 in gun mounting aft of SSM launchers in 'Y' position
- Two torpedo tubes outboard of after gun mounting, trained aft

NOTE: Decommissioned German units being transferred to Tunisia

SPECIFICATION:

COUNTRY OF ORIGIN: Germany
CLASS: Albatros (Type 143B) (PCFG)
ACTIVE: 4 Germany, 6 Tunisia
NAME (PENNANT NUMBER):
GERMANY – Geier (P 6113), Seeadler (P 6118), Habicht (P 6119), Kormoran (P 6120)
TUNISIA – — (ex-*Geier*) (ex-P 6113), — (ex-*Sperber*) (ex-P 6115), — (ex-*Greif*) (ex-P 6116), — (ex-*Seeadler*) (ex-P 6118), — (ex-*Habicht*) (ex-P 6119), — (ex-*Kormoran*) (ex-P 6120)

FEATURES:
DISPLACEMENT: 398 tons full load
LENGTH: 189 ft (57.6 m)
BEAM: 25.6 ft (7.8 m)
DRAUGHT: 8.5 ft (2.6 m)
SPEED: 40 kts
RANGE: 1300 miles at 30 kts

ARMAMENT:
MISSILES: SSM – four Aerospatiale MM 38 Exocet (2 twin) launchers (not Tunisia)
GUNS: Two OTO Melara 3 in (76 mm)/62 Compact; two 12.7 mm machine guns may be fitted
TORPEDOES: Two 21 in (533 mm) aft tubes; AEG Seeal
DECOYS: Buck-Wegmann Hot Dog/ Silver Dog chaff/IR flare dispenser

ELECTRONICS:
RADARS: Surface search/fire control – Signaal WM 27; navigation – SMA 3 RM 20
EW: Racal Octopus ESM/ECM (integrated Cutlass and Scorpion)

Gepard GERMANY

Hermelin (*Michael Nitz*)

- Long forecastle with 3 in gun mounting in 'A' position
- Central superstructure with high forward end, stepped down aft of bridge
- Distinctive surface WM 27 search/fire control radome atop short lattice mast after end of bridge
- Tall tripod pole mainmast at after end of superstructure
- Two Exocet SSM launchers aft of superstructure trained forward and to port and two further aft trained forward and to starboard
- RAM SAM box launcher right aft

SPECIFICATION:

COUNTRY OF ORIGIN: Germany
CLASS: Gepard (Type 143 A) (PCFG)
ACTIVE: 10
NAME (PENNANT NUMBER):
Gepard (P 6121), Puma (P 6122),
Hermelin (P 6123), Nerz (P 6124),
Zobel (P 6125), Frettchen (P 6126),
Dachs (P 6127), Ozelot (P 6128),
Wiesel (P 6129), Hyäne (P 6130)

FEATURES:
DISPLACEMENT: 391 tons full load
LENGTH: 190 ft (57.6 m)
BEAM: 25.6 ft (7.8 m)
DRAUGHT: 8.5 ft (2.6 m)
SPEED: 40 kts
RANGE: 2600 miles at 16 kts

ARMAMENT:
MISSILES: SSM – four Aerospatiale
MM 38 Exocet; SAM – GDC RAM
21- cell point defence system
GUNS: One OTO Melara 3 in
(76 mm)/62 Compact
DECOYS: Buck-Wegmann Hot
Dog/Silver Dog chaff/IR flare
dispenser

ELECTRONICS:
RADARS: Surface search/fire
control – Signaal WM 27;
navigation – SMA 3 RM 20
EW: DASA FL 1800 Mk 2 ESM/ECM

La Combattante III/IIIB/IIIM GREECE, NIGERIA, QATAR, TUNISIA

Plotarchis Blessas

- Low freeboard craft with 3 in gun mounting in 'A' position
- Long, low profile, rounded superstructure well forward of midships
- Fire control radar aerial mounted on lattice structure atop bridge roof
- Tall lattice mainmast atop mid-superstructure
- Surface search radar aerial atop mainmast
- Two 30 mm gun mountings (one port, one starboard) atop after end of superstructure
- Low profile after superstructure forward of 3 in gun mounting in 'Y' position (Greek ships only). 40 mm/70 twin mounting in Nigerian, Qatar and Tunisian units
- SSM ribbed launchers between forward and after superstructures. Tube launchers, port and starboard, in Qatar ships
- Two single torpedo tubes trained aft and sited outboard either side of after mounting (Greek ships only)

NOTE: See entry on 'Combattante II' class in service with Chile, Germany, Greece, Iran, Libya and Malaysia on page 280

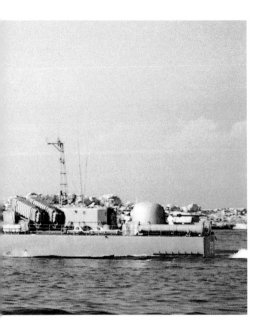

SPECIFICATION:

COUNTRY OF ORIGIN: France
CLASS: La Combattante
III/IIIB/IIIM (Anthypoploiarchos
Laskos, Damsah) (PCFG)
ACTIVE: 9 Greece
('Anthypoploiarchos Laskos'
class), 1 Nigeria (Combattante
IIIB), 1 Qatar ('Damsah'
Combattante IIIM class), 3 Tunisia
(Combattante IIIM class)
NAME (PENNANT NUMBER):
GREECE – Anthypoploiarchos
Laskos (P 20), Plotarchis Blessas
(P 21), Ypoploiarchos Mikonios
(P 22), Ypoploiarchos Troupakis
(P 23), Simeoforos Kavaloudis
(P 24), Ypoploiarchos Degiannis
(P 26), Simeoforos Xenos (P 27),
Simeoforos Simitzopoulos (P 28),
Simeoforos Starakis (P 29)
NIGERIA – Ayam (P 182)
QATAR – Damsah (Q 01),
Al Ghariyah (Q 02), Rbigah (Q 03)
TUNISIA – La Galité (501), Tunis
(502), Carthage (503)

FEATURES:

DISPLACEMENT: 425 tons full load
(Greece P 20-23, Tunisia); 429
tons (Greece, P 24-29); 395 tons
(Qatar); 430 tons (Nigeria)
LENGTH: 184 ft (56.2 m) (Greece,
Nigeria); 183.7 ft (56 m) (Qatar,
Tunisia)
BEAM: 26.2 ft (8 m) (Greece);
26.9 ft (8.2 m) (Qatar, Tunisia);
24.9 ft (7.6 m) (Nigeria)
DRAUGHT: 7 ft (2.1 m) (Greece,
Nigeria); 7.2 ft (2.2 m) (Qatar,
Tunisia)
SPEED: 36 kts (Greece, P 20-23);
32.5 kts (Greece, P 24-29); 38 kts
(Nigeria, Qatar, Tunisia)
RANGE: 2700 miles at 15 kts
(Greece); 2000 miles at 15 kts
(remainder)

ARMAMENT:

MISSILES: SSM – four Aerospatiale
MM 38 Exocet (Greece P 20-23,
Nigeria), eight MM 40 Exocet
(2 quad) (Qatar, Tunisia), six
Kongsberg Penguin Mk 2
(Greece, P 24-29)
GUNS: Two OTO Melara 3 in
(76 mm)/62 Compact; four
Emerson Electric 30 mm (2 twin)
(Greece); one OTO Melara 3 in
(76 mm)/62; two Breda
40 mm/70 (twin) (Nigeria, Qatar,
Tunisia); four Emerson Electric
30 mm (2 twin) (Nigeria); four
Oerlikon 30 mm/75 (2 twin)
(Qatar, Tunisia)
TORPEDOES: Two 21 in (533 mm)
aft tubes; AEG SST-4 (Greece only)
DECOYS: Buck-Wegmann
launchers (Greece); CSEE Dagaie
single trainable launcher (Qatar,
Tunisia)

ELECTRONICS:

RADARS: Air/surface search –
Thomson-CSF Triton; navigation
– Racal Decca 1226C (Greece,
Qatar), Racal Decca TM 1226
(Nigeria); fire control –
Thomson-CSF Castor II/
Thomson-CSF Pollux
EW: Thomson-CSF DR 2000 ESM
(Greece, Tunisia); Decca RDL ESM
(Nigeria); Racal Cutlass/Cygnus
ESM/ECM (Qatar)

Greece

Lürssen FPB 57 GHANA, INDONESIA, KUWAIT, NIGERIA, TURKEY

Singa

- Long forecastle with 3 in or Bofors SAK 57 mm/70 gun mounting or Bofors 40 mm/60 in 'A' position
- Low freeboard
- Rounded, short superstructure forward of midships stepped down at after end (longer superstructure in Ghanaian and Kuwait units)
- Raised helicopter platform extending aft from superstructure in Indonesia 'Kakap' class
- Short, square profile lattice mainmast at after end of superstructure
- Surface search radome atop mainmast (not Ghanaian, Kuwaiti or Indonesian 'Kakap' units)
- SSM launchers in 'V' formation on afterdeck (no missiles, Ghana, Indonesia, Nigeria)
- 35 mm/70 mounting right aft in 'Y' position (40 mm/70, Ghana and Indonesian 'Singa' class but absent in Indonesian 'Kakap' class). Twin Breda 40 mm/70 turret in this position in Kuwaiti and Nigerian units

NOTE: The Turkish 'Yildiz' class is based on the 'Dogan' class hull. Turkish 'Kiliç' class is a variant of 'Yildiz', with very tall and solid enclosed mast at aft end of bridge superstructure with angled step down to long quarterdeck

SPECIFICATION:

COUNTRY OF ORIGIN: Germany
CLASS: Lürssen FPB 57 (Singa), (Kakap) (Ekpe) (Dogan) (PC/PCF/PCFG)
ACTIVE: 2 Ghana, 8 Indonesia (4 'Singa' class (PC), 4 'Kakap' class (PC)) , 1 Kuwait, 3 Nigeria ('Ekpe' class), 8 Turkey ('Dogan' class PCFG)
NAME (PENNANT NUMBER):
GHANA – Achimota (P 28), Yogaga (P 29)
INDONESIA – 'Singa' class: Singa (651), Ajak (653), Pandrong (801), Sura (802)
'Kakap' class: Kakap (811), Kerapu (812), Tongkol (813), Barakuda (ex-Bervang) (814)
KUWAIT – Istiqlal (P 5702)
NIGERIA – Ekpe (P 178), Damisa (P 179), Agu (P 180)
TURKEY – Dogan (P 340), Marti (P 341), Tayfun (P 342), Volkan (P 343), Rüzgar (P 344), Poyraz (P 345), Gurbet (P 346), Firtina (P 347)

FEATURES:

DISPLACEMENT: 389 tons full load (Ghana); 410 tons (Kuwait); 423 tons (Indonesian 'Kakap' class); 428 tons (Indonesian 'Singa' class); 436 tons (Turkey); 444 tons (Nigeria)
LENGTH: 190.6 ft (58.1 m)
BEAM: 25 ft (7.6 m); 24.9 (7.6) (Kuwait, Nigeria)
DRAUGHT: 8.8 ft (2.7 m) (Turkey); 8.9 ft (2.7 m) (Kuwait); 9.2 ft (2.8 m) (Ghana, Indonesia); 10.2 ft (3.1 m) (Nigeria)
SPEED: 42 kts (Nigeria); 38 kts (Turkey); 30 kts (Ghana); 27 kts (Indonesia)

ARMAMENT:

MISSILES: SSM – eight McDonnell Douglas Harpoon (2 quad) launchers (Turkey); four Exocet MM 40 (Kuwait) (no missiles Ghana, Indonesia, Nigeria)
GUNS: One OTO Melara 3 in (76 mm)/62 Compact; two Oerlikon 35 mm/90 (twin) (Turkey); one OTO Melara 3 in (76 mm)/62 Compact; two Breda 40 mm/70 (twin) (Ghana, Kuwait, Nigeria); one Bofors SAK 57 mm/70 Mk 2; one Bofors SAK 40 mm/70; two Rheinmetall 20 mm (Indonesian 'Singa' class); one Bofors 40 mm/70; two 12.7 mm machine guns (Indonesian 'Kakap' class)
TORPEDOES: Two 21 in (533 mm) Toro tubes, AEG SUT (Indonesian 'Singa' units 651, 653)
MINES: Fitted for minelaying (Kuwait only)
DECOYS: Two multi-barrelled launchers (not Ghana or Nigeria); CSEE Dagaie training mounting (Kuwait); two Mk 36 SRBOC chaff launchers (Turkey)

ELECTRONICS:

RADARS: Surface search – Racal Decca 1226 (Turkey, Nigeria), Thomson-CSF Canopus A (Ghana), Racal Decca 2459 (Indonesia), Marconi S 810 (Kuwait), Signaal Scout (Indonesian 'Singa' class); navigation – Decca TM 1226C (Ghana, Kuwait), Kelvin Hughes 1007 (Indonesian 'Kakap' class); fire control – Signaal WM28/41 (Turkey, Nigeria), Signaal WM22 (Indonesian 'Singa' class), Philips 9LV 200 (Kuwait)
SONARS: Signaal PMS 32 (some Indonesian 'Singa' units)
EW: Thomson-CSF DR 3000 ESM (Indonesia); MEL Susie ESM (Turkey 344-347); Racal Cutlass ESM; Racal Cygnus ECM (Kuwait)

AIR SUPPORT:

Helicopters: Platform for Nurtanio NBO 105C (Indonesian 'Kakap' class only)

Indonesia, *Sura*

Sukanya INDIA, SRI LANKA
Sujata

- High maindeck dropping down to low freeboard, midships
- Raised platform immediately forward of bridge
- High main superstructure, with prominent bridge wings, forward of midships
- Massive tall enclosed mainmast atop central superstructure
- Prominent tall rounded funnel midships
- Large, square helicopter hangar with, aft, very long helicopter landing area over open quarterdeck

NOTE: Based on 'Ulsan' class frigate design

NOTE 2: One unit transferred by India to Sri Lankan service and recommissioned on December 9, 2000

NOTE 3: Four units of this class operated by Indian coastguard – *Samar* (42), *Sangram* (43), *Sarang* (44) and *Sagar* (45). More heavily armed and with one OTO Melara 3 in (76 mm)/62 and a telescopic hangar

SPECIFICATION:

COUNTRY OF ORIGIN:
Korea (South)
CLASS: Sukanya (OPV)
ACTIVE: 6 India, 1 Sri Lanka
NAME (PENNANT NUMBER):
INDIA – Sukanya (P 50), Subhadra (P 51), Suvarna (P 52), Savitri (P 53), Sharada (P 55), Sujata (P 56)
SRI LANKA – Sayura (ex-*Saryu*) (P 620, ex-P 54)

FEATURES:
DISPLACEMENT: 1890 tons full load
LENGTH: 331.7 ft (101.1 m) oa
BEAM: 37.4 ft (11.5 m)
DRAUGHT: 14.4 ft (4.4 m)
SPEED: 21 kts
RANGE: 5800 miles at 15 kts

ARMAMENT:
GUNS: One Bofors 40 mm/60; four 12.7 mm machine guns (not Sri Lanka); two China 14.5 mm (twin) (Sri Lanka)
A/S MORTARS: Four RBU 2500 16-tube trainable launchers

ELECTRONICS:
RADARS: Surface search – Racal Decca 2459; navigation – Bharat 1245

AIR SUPPORT:
HELICOPTERS: 1 HAL SA 319B Chetak (Alouette III) (ASW) (India only)

Sibarau INDONESIA

Siliman

- Sweeping low freeboard maindeck from stem to stern
- 40 mm gun open mounting on forecastle
- Bridge superstructure steps up from forecastle and is angled down aft
- Short pole mainmast at aft end of superstructure
- Tall angled funnel immediately aft of mainmast

SPECIFICATION:

COUNTRY OF ORIGIN: Australia
CLASS: Sibarau (Attack) (PC)
ACTIVE: 8
NAME (PENNANT NUMBER):
Sibarau (ex-*Bandolier*) (847),
Siliman (ex-*Archer*) (848), Sigalu
(ex-*Barricade*) (857), Silea (ex-*Acute*) (858), Siribua (ex-*Bombard*)
(859), Siada (ex-*Barbette*) (862),
Sikuda (ex-*Attack*) (863), Sigurot
(ex-*Assail*) (864)

FEATURES:
DISPLACEMENT: 146 tons full load
LENGTH: 107.5 ft (32.8 m)
BEAM: 20 ft (6.1 m)
DRAUGHT: 6.1 ft (2.2 m)
SPEED: 21 kts
RANGE: 1200 miles at 13 kts

ARMAMENT:
GUNS: One Bofors 40 mm/60;
one 12.5 mm machine gun

ELECTRONICS:
RADARS: Surface search – Decca 916
EW: DASA Telegon VIII ESM

Eithne IRISH REPUBLIC

Eithne

- High freeboard with high central superstructure
- Short forecastle with 57 mm/70 gun mounting in 'B' position
- Large, solid-based lattice mainmast atop superstructure just aft of bridge
- Tall, tapered funnels at after end of superstructure
- Long flight deck with break down to short quarterdeck
- Distinctive flight deck overhang
- Ship's boats in davits high up superstructure, amidships

SPECIFICATION:
COUNTRY OF ORIGIN: Irish Republic
CLASS: Eithne (OPV)
ACTIVE: 1
NAME (PENNANT NUMBER): Eithne (P 31)

FEATURES:
DISPLACEMENT: 1910 tons full load
LENGTH: 265 ft (80.8 m)
BEAM: 39.4 ft (12 m)
DRAUGHT: 14.1 ft (4.3 m)
SPEED: 20+ kts
RANGE: 7000 miles at 15 kts

ARMAMENT:
GUNS: One Bofors 57 mm/70 Mk 1; two Rheinmetall 20 mm/20; two Wallop 57 mm launchers for illuminants

ELECTRONICS:
RADARS: Air/surface search – Signaal DA05 Mk 4; navigation – two Kelvin Hughes 6000A

AIR SUPPORT:
HELICOPTERS: Platform only

Peacock/Jacinto IRISH REPUBLIC, PHILIPPINES

Emilio Jacinto

- Low bow, low freeboard
- 3 in gun mounting in 'A' position
- Superstructure amidships, stepped down aft of bridge
- Lattice mainmast atop mid-superstructure
- Squat, square-section funnel with sloping top atop after end of superstructure
- Slender crane jib aft of funnel

SPECIFICATION:

COUNTRY OF ORIGIN: UK
CLASS: Peacock/P 41/Jacinto (PG/FS)
ACTIVE: 2 Irish Republic (PG), 3 Philippines (FS)
NAME (PENNANT NUMBER):
IRISH REPUBLIC – Orla (ex-*Swift*) (P 41), Ciara (ex-*Swallow*) (P 42)
PHILIPPINES – Emilio Jacinto (ex-*Peacock*) (PS 35, ex-P 239), Apolinario Mabini (ex-*Plover*) (PS 36, ex-P 240), Artemio Ricarte (ex-*Starling*) (PS 37, ex-P 241)

FEATURES:

DISPLACEMENT: 712 tons full load (Irish Republic); 763 tons (Philippines)
LENGTH: 204.1 ft (62.6 m)
BEAM: 32.8 ft (10 m)
DRAUGHT: 8.9 ft (2.7 m)
SPEED: 25 kts
RANGE: 2500 miles at 17 kts

ARMAMENT:

GUNS: One OTO Melara 3 in (76 mm)/62 Compact; four FN 7.62 mm machine guns (plus two 12.7 mm machine guns in Irish ships)

ELECTRONICS:

RADARS: Surface search – Kelvin Hughes Mk IV (Irish Republic); navigation – Kelvin Hughes Type 1006 (Philippines), Kelvin Hughes 5000A (Irish Republic)

Hetz (Saar 4.5) ISRAEL
Hetz class

- Long sleek hull, low freeboard
- Vulcan Phalanx CIWS mounting in 'A' position with distinctive domed top
- Short superstructure well forward of midships
- Massive enclosed angled mainmast at after end of superstructure
- Neptune air/surface search radar aerial atop mainmast
- Harpoon SSM tubular launchers aft of superstructure and forward of after mounting. Gabriel II box launchers immediately aft
- 3 in gun mounting right aft

NOTE: Easily confused with the 'Saar 4' class. *Hetz* upgrade continues on 'Saar 4' to convert into 'Saar 4.5'. *Yaffo* latest conversion in July, 1998
NOTE 2: Two 'Aliya' Class ('Saar 4.5'), *Aliya* and *Geoula*, operated by Israel. Of same basic hull design with substantially different weapons fits (CIWS in the eyes of the ships) and substantial slab-side superstructure aft

SPECIFICATION:

COUNTRY OF ORIGIN: Israel
CLASS: Hetz (Saar 4.5) (PGF)
ACTIVE: 8
NAME (PENNANT NUMBER):
Romat, Keshet, Hetz (ex-*Nirit*), Kidon, Tarshish, Yaffo, Herev, Sufa

FEATURES:
DISPLACEMENT: 488 tons full load
LENGTH: 202.4 ft (61.7 m)
BEAM: 24.9 ft (7.6 m)
DRAUGHT: 8.2 ft (2.5 m)
SPEED: 31 kts
RANGE: 3000 miles at 17 kts

ARMAMENT:
MISSILES: SSM – four Harpoon plus six IAI Gabriel II; SAM – Israeli Industries Barak I (vertical launch or pack launchers)
GUNS: One OTO Melara 3 in (76 mm)/62 Compact; two Oerlikon 20 mm; one Rafael Typhoon 25 mm (Herev); one GE/GD Vulcan Phalanx; two or four 12.7 mm (twin or quad) machine guns
DECOYS: Elbit Deseaver 72-barrel chaff/IR launchers

ELECTRONICS:
RADARS: Air/surface search – Thomson-CSF TH-D 1040 Neptune; fire control – Elta EL/M-222 1 GM STGR
EW: Elisra NS 9003/5 ESM/ECM

Cassiopea ITALY

Cassiopea

- Raked bows with continuous maindeck line from stem to helicopter deck above quarterdeck
- 3 in gun mounting on raised platform in 'A' position
- High square super-structure midships
- Large enclosed mainmast atop central superstructure supporting surface search radar aerial
- Angled funnel with two black exhausts side by side atop
- Thin pole mast aft of funnel with ship's boat on davits outboard

SPECIFICATION:

COUNTRY OF ORIGIN: Italy
CLASS: Cassiopea (OPV)
ACTIVE: 4
NAME (PENNANT NUMBER):
Cassiopea (P 401), Libra (P 402),
Spica (P 403), Vega (P 404)

FEATURES:
DISPLACEMENT: 1475 tons full load
LENGTH: 261.8 ft (79.8 m)
BEAM: 28.7 ft (11.8 m)
DRAUGHT: 11.5 ft (3.5 m)
SPEED: 20 kts
RANGE: 3300 miles at 17 kts

ARMAMENT:
GUNS: One OTO Melara 3 in
(76 mm)/62; one Breda Oerlikon
25 mm/90; two 12.7 mm
machine guns

ELECTRONICS:
RADARS: Surface search – SMA
SPS-702(V)2; navigation – SMA
SPN-748(V)2; fire control – Selenia
SPG-70 (RTN 10X)

AIR SUPPORT:
HELICOPTERS: One Agusta-Bell
AB 212 (ASW)

Comandante ITALY

Commandante Cigala Fulgosi (AMS)

- High forecastle with raked bows.
- 3 in gun mounting on raised platform in 'A' position
- High stealthy square main superstructure midships with square funnel at forward end of helicopter hangar
- Squat enclosed mainmast atop central superstructure supporting surface search radar aerial
- Short helicopter operating platform aft

NOTE: Two of class built for Transport Ministry, but operated by Navy. No helicopter hangar in these hulls

SPECIFICATION:

COUNTRY OF ORIGIN: Italy
CLASS: 1500 (OPV)
ACTIVE: 6
NAME (PENNANT NUMBER):
Comandante Cigala Fulgosi
(P 490), Comandante Borsini
(P 491), Comandante Bettica
(P 492), Comandante Foscari
(P 493), Sirio (P 409), Orione
(P 410)

FEATURES:
DISPLACEMENT: 1520 tons
full load
LENGTH: 290 ft (88.4 m)
BEAM: 40 ft (12.2 m)
DRAUGHT: 15.1 ft (4.6 m)
SPEED: 26 kts
RANGE: 3500 miles at 14 kts

ARMAMENT:
GUNS: One OTOBreda 3 in
(76 mm)/62 Compact (P 490-493);
two OTOBreda 25 mm/90

ELECTRONICS:
RADARS: Surface search – SPS-703;
navigation – SPS-753; fire control
– SPG-76 (RTN 30X)
EW: Selenia SLQ-747 ESM/ECM

AIR SUPPORT:
HELICOPTERS: One Agusta-Bell
AB 212 (ASW) or NH 90 in
due course

Province (Nyayo/Dhofar) KENYA, OMAN

Nyayo

- Short forecastle, 3 in gun mounting in 'A' position
- High superstructure forward of midships. Superstructure is flush with craft's sides
- Lattice mainmast centrally sited atop superstructure supporting AWS 4/6 air/surface search radar aerial
- Two quadruple Exocet SSM launchers on maindeck aft of superstructure. Both launchers angled slightly forward. Forward launcher port side and after one starboard (Oman). Four Otomat box launchers aft of superstructure in Kenyan units
- 40 mm/70 gun mounting right aft (Oman). Twin 30 mm gun in same position in Kenyan boats

NOTE: Mast structures in Omani ships are different, dependent on radars fitted

SPECIFICATION:

COUNTRY OF ORIGIN: UK
CLASS: Province (Nyayo, Dhofar) (PCFG)
ACTIVE: 2 Kenya ('Nyayo' class), 4 Oman ('Dhofar' class)
NAME (PENNANT NUMBER):
KENYA – Nyayo (P 3126), Umoja (P 3127)
OMAN – Dhofar (B 10), Al Sharqiyah (B 11), Al Bat'nah (B 12), Mussandam (B 14)

FEATURES:
DISPLACEMENT: 394 tons full load (Oman); 430 tons (Kenya)
LENGTH: 186 ft (56.7 m)
BEAM: 26.9 ft (8.2 m)
DRAUGHT: 7.9 ft (2.4 m)
SPEED: 40 kts
RANGE: 2000 miles at 18 kts

ARMAMENT:
MISSILES: SSM – eight Aerospatiale MM 40 Exocet (Oman); four OTO Melara/Matra Otomat Mk 2 (2 twin) (Kenya)
GUNS: One OTO Melara 3 in (76 mm)/62 Compact; two Breda 40 mm/70 (twin); two 20 mm machine guns (Oman); one OTO Melara 3 in (76 mm)/62 Compact; two Oerlikon/BMARC 30 mm GCM-A02 (twin); two Oerlikon/BMARC 20 mm A41A (Kenya)
DECOYS: Two Wallop Barricade 3-barrel launchers (Oman); two Wallop Barricade 18-barrel launchers (Kenya)

ELECTRONICS:
RADARS: Air/surface search – Plessey AWS 4 or AWS 6; navigation – Kelvin Hughes 1007 (Oman), Decca AC 1226 (Kenya); fire control – Philips 9LV 307 (Oman), Marconi/Ericsson ST802 (Kenya)
EW: Racal Cutlass ESM; Racal Scorpion (ECM)

Oman

La Combattante I   KUWAIT
Alfahaheel

- Continuous maindeck from stem to stern
- Angled, slab-sided superstructure with very tall sturdy enclosed mast with tall, slim pole atop, aft of midships. Whip aerial above bridge
- 40 mm/70 gun mounting immediately forward of bridge superstructure
- Sadral/Mistral SAM sextuple launcher atop superstructure immediately aft of mast
- Sea Skua SSM box launchers right aft

SPECIFICATION:

COUNTRY OF ORIGIN: France
CLASS: La Combattante I (Um Almaradim) (PCFG)
ACTIVE: 8
NAME (PENNANT NUMBER): Um Almaradim (P 3711), Ouha (P 3713), Failaka (P 3715), Maskan (P 3717), Al-Ahmadi (P 3719), Alfahaheel (P 3721), Al Yarmouk (P 3723), Garoh (P 3725)

FEATURES:

DISPLACEMENT: 245 tons full load
LENGTH: 137.8 ft (42 m) oa
BEAM: 26.9 ft (8.2 m)
DRAUGHT: 5.9 ft (1.8 m)
SPEED: 30 kts
RANGE: 1350 miles at 14 kts

ARMAMENT:

MISSILES: SSM – BAe Sea Skua (2 twin); SAM – Sadral sextuple launcher, Mistral
GUNS: One OTOBreda 40 mm/70; one Giat 20 mm M 621; two 12.7 mm machine guns
DECOYS: Two Dagaie Mk 2 chaff launchers

ELECTRONICS:

RADARS: Air/surface search – Thomson-CSF MRR; navigation – Litton Marine 20V90; fire control – BAe Seaspray Mk 3
EW: Thomson-CSF DR 3000 ESM

Spica-M/Handalan MALAYSIA

Gempita

- 57 mm/70 gun mounting in 'A' position
- Main superstructure just forward of midships with tall lattice mainmast at after end
- 9LV 212 fire control radar aerial atop bridge
- 9GR 600 surface search radar aerial atop mainmast
- Two twin Exocet SSM launchers aft of bridge, pointing forward and outboard in crossover formation, forward pair to port after pair to starboard
- 40 mm/70 gun mounting aft of SSM launchers on afterdeck

NOTE: Bridge further forward than in the original Swedish design to accommodate Exocet SSMs

NOTE 2: Croatian and Yugoslav navies operate 'Koncar' class PCFGs, designed by the Naval Institute in Zagreb and based on the 'Spica I' design. Bridge amidships like the Malaysian boats

NOTE 3: The Swedish Navy's 'Norrköping' class PCFGs were developed from the original 'Spica' class. See separate entry on page 323

NOTE 4: Trinidad and Tobago operates two Type CG 40 PCs, with similar hulls to the 'Spica' design, but with the bridge amidships

SPECIFICATION:

COUNTRY OF ORIGIN: Sweden
CLASS: Spica-M (Handalan) (PCFG)
ACTIVE: 4
NAME (PENNANT NUMBER):
Handalan (3511), Perkasa (3512),
Pendekar (3513), Gempita (3514)

FEATURES:

DISPLACEMENT: 240 tons full load
LENGTH: 142.6 ft (43.6 m)
BEAM: 23.3 ft (7.1 m)
DRAUGHT: 7.4 ft (2.4 m) (screws)
SPEED: 34.5 kts
RANGE: 1850 miles at 14 kts

ARMAMENT:

MISSILES: SSM– four Aerospatiale
MM 38 Exocet
GUNS: One Bofors 57 mm/70;
one Bofors 40 mm/70

ELECTRONICS:

RADARS: Surface search – Philips
9GR 600; navigation – Kelvin
Hughes 1007; fire control –
Philips 9LV 212
EW: Thales DR 3000 ESM

Musytari MALAYSIA

Marikh

- Sharp bows with continuous maindeck to just aft of midships, then sharp break down to helicopter flight deck
- 3.9 in gun mounting in 'A' position
- Main superstructure with prominent bridge wings, deck atop
- Two lattice masts, larger atop bridge superstructure
- 30 mm gun mounting at aft end of superstructure
- Ship's boat on davits at break in maindeck

SPECIFICATION:

COUNTRY OF ORIGIN:
Korea (South)
CLASS: Musytari (OPV)
ACTIVE: 2
NAME (PENNANT NUMBER):
Musytari (160), Marikh (161)

FEATURES:
DISPLACEMENT: 1300 tons full load
LENGTH: 246 ft (75 m)
BEAM: 35.4 ft (10.8 m)
DRAUGHT: 12.1 ft (3.7 m)
SPEED: 22 kts
RANGE: 5000 miles at 15 kts

ARMAMENT:
GUNS: One Cruesot-Loire 3.9 in (100 mm)/55 Mk 2 compact; two Emerson Electric 30 mm (twin)

ELECTRONICS:
RADARS: Air/surface search – Signaal DA05; navigation – Kelvin Hughes 1007; fire control – Philips 9LV
EW: Thales DR 3000 ESM

AIR SUPPORT:
HELICOPTERS: Platform for one medium helicopter – suitable for Sikorsky S-61A Nuri army support helicopter

Azteca MEXICO

Ignacio Zaragoza (now decommissioned)

- Continuous maindeck from stem to stern, high freeboard
- 40 mm/70 gun mounting in 'A' position
- Rounded, low profile central superstructure
- Small rounded mast and funnel combined at after end of superstructure with radar aerial at its forward end
- 20 mm gun mounting on afterdeck

SPECIFICATION:

COUNTRY OF ORIGIN: UK
CLASS: Azteca (PC)
ACTIVE: 19
NAME (PENNANT NUMBER):
Matias de Cordova (ex-Guaycura)
(PC 202, ex-P02), Ignacio López
Rayón (ex-Tarahumara) (PC 206,
ex-P06), Manuel Crescencio
Rejon (ex-Tepehuan) (PC 207,
ex-P07), Juan Antonio de la
Fuente (ex-Mexica) (PC 208,
ex-P08), Leon Guzman
(ex-Zapoteca) (PC 209, ex-209),
Ignacio Ramirez (ex-Haustela)
(PC 210, ex-210), Heriberto Jara
Corona (ex-Huichol) (PC 212,
ex-P12), Colima (ex-Yacqui)
(PC 214, ex-P14), Jose Joaquin
Fernandez de Lizardi
(ex-Tiapaneco) (PC 215, ex-P15),
Francisco J. Mugica (ex-Tarasco)
(PC 216, ex-P16), Jose Maria del
Castillo Velasco (ex-Otomi)
(PC 218, ex-P18), Jose Natividad
Macias (ex-Pimas) (PC 220,
ex-P20), Tamaulipas (ex-Mazateco)

(PC 223, ex-P23), Yucatan
(ex-Tolteca) (PC 224, ex-P24),
Tabasco (ex-Maya) (PC 225,
ex-P25), Cochimie (ex-Veracruz)
(PC 226, ex-P26), Puebla
(ex-Totonaca) (PC 228, ex-P28),
Leona Vicario (ex-Olmeca)
(PC 230, ex-P30), Josefa Oritz
de Dominguez (ex-Tiahuica)
(PC 231, ex-P31)

FEATURES:

DISPLACEMENT: 148 tons full load
LENGTH: 112.7 ft (34.4 m)
BEAM: 28.3 ft (8.7 m)
DRAUGHT: 7.2 ft (2.2 m)
SPEED: 24 kts
RANGE: 1500 miles at 14 kts

ARMAMENT:

GUNS: One Bofors 40 mm/70;
one Oerlikon 20 mm or one
7.62 mm machine gun

ELECTRONICS:

RADARS: Surface search –
Kelvin Hughes

311

Hauk NORWAY

'Hauk' class patrol boats

- Low profile, compact craft
- 40 mm/70 gun open mounting in 'A' position
- Low superstructure centred just forward of midships
- Forward pointing single torpedo tubes outboard of 'A' mounting, port and starboard
- Short lattice mainmast atop after end of superstructure
- 20 mm/20 gun mounting immediately aft of superstructure surrounded by high circular armoured breakwater
- Distinctive Penguin SSM launchers mounted on afterdeck, two port, two starboard, angled outboard

NOTE: Swedish 'Kaparen' class similar to 'Hauk' class. See separate entry on page 322

NOTE 2: Penguin SSM sometimes not embarked

SPECIFICATION:

COUNTRY OF ORIGIN: Norway
CLASS: Hauk (PCFG)
ACTIVE: 14
NAME (PENNANT NUMBER): Hauk (P 986), Ørn (P 987), Terne (P 988), Tjeld (P 989), Skarv (P 990), Teist (P 991), Jo (P 992), Lom (P 993), Stegg (P 994), Falk (P 995), Ravn (P 996), Gribb (P 997), Geir (P 998), Erle (P 999)

FEATURES:

DISPLACEMENT: 160 tons full load
LENGTH: 120 ft (36.5 m)
BEAM: 20.3 ft (6.2 m)
DRAUGHT: 5.9 ft (1.8 m)
SPEED: 32 kts
RANGE: 440 miles at 30 kts

ARMAMENT:

MISSILES: SSM – six Kongsberg Penguin Mk 2 Mod 5; SAM – twin Simbad launcher for Matra Sadral
GUNS: One Bofors 40 mm/70
TORPEDOES: Two 21 in (533 mm) tubes; FFV Type 613
DECOYS: Chaff launcher

ELECTRONICS:

RADARS: Surface search/navigation – two Litton
EW: Argo ESM

Skjold NORWAY

Skjold (*Michael Nitz*)

- SES hull with advanced stealth features including anechoic coatings
- Following trials, 'Skjold' has been fitted with a more raked bow to improve seaworthiness
- Two quad SSM mountings to be carried in recessed mounting aft of bridge
- Midships superstructure with sloping face topped by small bridge with fire control unit on top
- Sharply raked mast structure behind bridge
- All deck equipment recessed into hull
- 76 mm gun in 'A' position

SPECIFICATION:

COUNTRY OF ORIGIN: Norway
CLASS: Skjold
ACTIVE: 1
BUILDING: 5
NAME (PENNANT NUMBER): Skjold
(P 960), Storm (P 961), Skudd
(P 962), Steil (P 963), Glimt
(P 964), Gnist (P 965)

FEATURES:

DISPLACEMENT: 260 tons full load
LENGTH: 153.5 ft (46.8 m)
BEAM: 44.3 ft (13.5 m)
DRAUGHT: 7.5 ft (2.3 m); 2.6 ft
(0.8 m) (on cushion)
SPEED: 57 kts
RANGE: 800 miles at 40 kts

ARMAMENT:

MISSILES: SSM – eight Kongsberg
NSM; SAM – Mistral
GUNS: One OTOBreda 76 mm/62
Super Rapid
DECOYS: Buck Neue MASS decoys

ELECTRONICS:

RADARS: Air/surface search –
Thales MRR 3D; navigation – to be
announced; fire control – Celsius
Tech Ceros 2000

Dvora/Hai Ou PARAGUAY, SRI LANKA, TAIWAN

Taiwan Hai Ou

- Low, rounded bridge structure with square profile lattice mainmast at after end (Paraguay boats have tall, slim enclosed mast)
- Surface search and fire control radar aerials atop mainmast
- SSM launcher athwartships immediately aft of mainmast (Taiwan units only)
- 20 mm gun mounting forward of bridge (Sri Lanka)
- 20 mm gun mounting right aft (Sri Lanka, Taiwan)

NOTE: The first Taiwanese series had an enclosed mainmast and the missiles were nearer the stern. Second Taiwanese series changed to a lattice mainmast and moved the missiles further forward allowing room for 20 mm gun mounting

NOTE 2: See 'Super Dvora' entry on page 289

NOTE 2: See 'Super Dvora' entry on page 289

SPECIFICATION:

COUNTRY OF ORIGIN: Israel
CLASS: Dvora (Hai Ou) (PCFG)
ACTIVE: 2 Paraguay ('Modified Hai Ou' class), 3 Sri Lanka ('Dvora' class), 47 Taiwan ('Hai Ou' class)
PLANNED: 4 Paraguay
NAME (PENNANT NUMBER):
PARAGUAY – Capitan Ortiz (P 06), Teniente Robles (P 07)
SRI LANKA – P 401 (ex-P 260, ex-P 420, ex-P 453), P 402 (ex-P 261, ex-P 421, ex-P 454), P 403 (ex-P 262, ex-P 422, ex-P 455)
TAIWAN – FABG 7-12, FABG 14-21, FABG 23-30, FABG 32-39, FABG 41-45, FABG 47-57, FABG 59

FEATURES:
DISPLACEMENT: 47 tons full load
LENGTH: 70.8 ft (21.6 m)
BEAM: 18 ft (5.5 m)
DRAUGHT: 3.3 ft (1 m); 5.8 (1.8) (Sri Lanka)
SPEED: 36 kts
RANGE: 700 miles at 32 kts

ARMAMENT:
MISSILES: SSM – two Hsiung Feng I (Taiwan only)
GUNS: One CS 20 mm Type 75; two 12.7 mm machine guns (Paraguay, Taiwan); two Oerlikon 20 mm and two 12.7 mm machine guns (Sri Lanka)
DECOYS: Four Israeli AV2 chaff launchers (Taiwan only)

ELECTRONICS:
RADARS: Surface search – Marconi LN 66 (Taiwan), Anritsu 72 1UA (Sri Lanka); fire control – RCA R76 C5 (Taiwan)
EW: WD-2A ESM (Taiwan)

Taiwan

Velarde PERU

Santillana (*Peruvian Navy*)

- Unusual, downturned forward end of forecastle
- 3 in gun mounting in 'A' position
- High rounded main superstructure forward of midships
- Large lattice mainmast atop central superstructure supporting Triton surface search radar aerial
- Castor II fire control radar aerial atop bridge
- Four Exocet SSM launchers aft of superstructure. Forward pair angled to starboard, after pair to port
- 40 mm/70 gun twin mounting right aft

NOTE: Morocco operates two PR 72 class ('Okba') PCs and Senegal one PR 72M PC, which are similar in appearance, although smaller in dimensions and displacement

SPECIFICATION:

COUNTRY OF ORIGIN: France
CLASS: Velarde (PR-72P) (CM/PCFG)
ACTIVE: 6
NAME (PENNANT NUMBER):
Velarde (CM 21), Santillana
(CM 22), De Los Heros (CM 23),
Herrera (CM 24), Larrea (CM 25),
Sanchez Carrillon (CM 26)

FEATURES:

DISPLACEMENT: 560 tons full load
LENGTH: 210 ft (64 m)
BEAM: 27.4 ft (8.4 m)
DRAUGHT: 5.2 ft (2.6 m)
SPEED: 37 kts
RANGE: 2500 miles at 16 kts

ARMAMENT:

MISSILES: SSM – four Aerospatiale
MM 38 Exocet; SAM – SA-N-10
launcher may be fitted on the
stern
GUNS: One OTO Melara 3 in
(76 mm)/62 Compact; two
Breda 40 mm/70 (twin)

ELECTRONICS:

RADARS: Surface search –
Thomson-CSF Triton; navigation
– Racal Decca 1226; fire control –
Thomson-CSF Castor II
EW: Thomson-CSF DR 2000 ESM

Cyclone PHILIPPINES, USA

Chinook (now decommissioned)

- Short forecastle with sloping forward edge to main superstructure
- 25 mm gun mounting in 'A' position
- Raised bridge, with all round windows, set well aft from bows
- Continuous maindeck from stem to stern
- Superstructure built in three distinct sections with catwalks between the tops of each section
- Large lattice mainmast at after end of bridge supporting Rascar surface search radar aerial atop
- 25 mm gun mounting atop after section of superstructure in 'X' position

NOTE: The design is based on the Vosper Thornycroft 'Ramadan' class, modified to meet US Navy requirements, with one inch thick armour on the superstructure

NOTE 2: US boats operated by USCG

SPECIFICATION:

COUNTRY OF ORIGIN: USA
CLASS: Cyclone (PCF)
ACTIVE: 1 Philippines, 5 USA
NAME (PENNANT NUMBER):
PHILIPPINES – General Mariano Alvares (ex-*Cyclone*) (PS 38, ex-PC 1)
USA – Tempest (WPB 2, ex-PC 2), Monsoon (WPB 4, ex-PC 4), Zephyr (WPB 8, ex-PC 8), Shamal (WPC 13, ex-PC 13), Tornado (WPC 14, ex-PC 14)

FEATURES:

DISPLACEMENT: 334 tons full load; 360 tons (PC 2, 8, 13, 14)
LENGTH: 170.3 ft (51.9 m); 179 ft (54.6 ft) (PC 2, 8, 13, 14)
BEAM: 25.9 ft (7.9 m)
DRAUGHT: 7.9 ft (2.4 m)
SPEED: 35 kts
RANGE: 2500 miles at 12 kts

ARMAMENT:

GUNS: Two McDonnell Douglas 25 mm/87 MG 38; four 12.7 mm machine guns

ELECTRONICS:

RADARS: Navigation – Hughes/ Furuno SPS-73

Barzan (Vita/Super Vita) QATAR, GREECE

Huwar

- Low bow, low freeboard with slope down to afterdeck
- 3 in gun mounting in 'A' position
- Low superstructure amidships, stepped down aft of bridge (Greek units will have bridge raised above superstructure)
- Bridge with prominent all-round windows
- Squat, chunky enclosed mainmast with complex aerials atop mid-superstructure, with angled tall polemast at aft
- Four Exocet SSM launchers aft of superstructure. Forward pair angled to starboard, after pair to port
- Separate deck house with chaff launcher atop, aft of SSM launchers in Qatar ships. No chaff launcher in Greek hulls
- Goalkeeper CIWS right aft in Qatar units
- RAM box launcher right aft in Greek units

SPECIFICATION:

COUNTRY OF ORIGIN: UK
CLASS: Barzan (Vita), Super Vita (PGFG)
ACTIVE: 4 Qatar ('Vita' class), 1 Greece
BUILDING: 4 Greece ('Super Vita' class)
NAME (PENNANT NUMBER):
QATAR – Barzan (Q04), Huwar (Q05), Al Udeid (Q06), Al Deebel (Q07)
GREECE – Ypoploiarchos Roussen (P67), Ypoploiarchos Daniolos (P68), Ypoploiarchos Kristallides (P69), Ypoploiarchos Grigoro Poulos (P70), Anthypoploiarchos Ritsos (P71)

FEATURES:

DISPLACEMENT: 376 tons full load (Qatar); 580 tons (Greece)
LENGTH: 185.7 ft (56.3 m) (Qatar); 203.1 ft (61.9 m) (Greece)
BEAM: 29.5 ft (9 m) (Qatar); 31.2 ft (9.5 m) (Greece)
DRAUGHT: 8.2 ft (2.5 m) (Qatar); 8.5 ft (2.6 m) (Greece)
SPEED: 35 kts
RANGE: 1800 miles at 12 kts

ARMAMENT:

MISSILES: SSM – eight Exocet MM 40 Block II; SAM – Matra Sadral sextuple launcher for Mistral (Qatar), RAM Mk 31 Mod 1 (Greece)
GUNS: One OTO Melara 3 in (76 mm)/62 Super Rapid; one Signaal Goalkeeper 30 mm CIWS; two 12.7 mm machine guns (Qatar); two OTOBreda 30 mm (Greece)
DECOYS: CSEE Dagaie Mk 2 chaff/IR flares (Qatar); two Loral Hycor Mk 36 SRBOC (Greece)

ELECTRONICS:

RADARS: Air/surface search – Thomson-CSF MRR (Qatar), Thomson-CSF MW 08 (Greece); surface search – Signaal Scout Mk 2 (Greece); navigation – Kelvin Hughes 1007 (Qatar), Litton Marine Bridgemaster (Greece); fire control – Signaal Sting
EW: Thomson-CSF DR 3000S ESM; Dassault Salamandre ARB 33 ECM (Qatar); Argo AR-900 ESM (Greece)

Turya RUSSIA, VIETNAM

Turya (Russia)

- Blunt bow, short forecastle with 25 mm/80 gun twin mounting in 'A' position
- Angular central superstructure with raised open bridge just aft of enclosed bridge
- Lattice mainmast aft of bridge with surface search radar aerial atop
- Two torpedo tubes on maindeck each side of central superstructure, angled outboard (not in all Vietnamese units)
- Pedestal supporting Muff Cob fire control radar aerial atop after end of superstructure
- Prominent 57 mm/80 gun mounting right aft in 'Y' position

NOTE: Superstructure has similar 'ribbed' appearance as 'Stenka' class. Hull is derived from 'Osa' class

SPECIFICATION:

COUNTRY OF ORIGIN: Russia
CLASS: Turya (Type 206M) (PC/PTH)
ACTIVE: 2 Russia, 5 Vietnam
NAME (PENNANT NUMBER):
RUSSIA – 300, 373
VIETNAM – HQ 331-332, HQ 334-335, HQ 321

FEATURES:
DISPLACEMENT: 250 tons full load
LENGTH: 129.9 ft (39.6 m)
BEAM: 24.9 ft (7.6 m); 41 ft (12.5 m) (over foils)
DRAUGHT: 5.9 ft (1.8 m); 13.1 ft (4 m) (over foils)
SPEED: 40 kts (foilborne)
RANGE: 600 miles at 35 kts (foilborne); 1450 miles at 14 kts (hullborne)

ARMAMENT:
GUNS: Two USSR 57 mm/80 (twin, aft); two USSR 25 mm/80 (twin, fwd); one 14.5 mm machine gun in Russian hulls
TORPEDOES: Four 21 in (533 mm) tubes; Type 53 (not in all Vietnamese units)
DEPTH CHARGES: Two racks (one rack in Russian hulls)

ELECTRONICS:
RADARS: Surface search – Pot Drum; navigation – SRN 207 (Russia); fire control – Muff Cob
SONARS: Foal Tail VDS (not in all Vietnamese units)
EW: Brick Plug ESM (Russia)

Al Siddiq SAUDI ARABIA

Oqbah (*H & L van Ginderen collection*)

- High bow with sloping forecastle
- 3 in gun mounting in 'A' position
- High central superstructure flush with ship's side
- Large distinctive radome atop bridge roof
- Slim tripod mainmast amidships
- Angular, black-capped funnel with exhausts protruding at top aft of mainmast
- Whip aerials above bridge and at aft end of superstructure
- Crossover Harpoon SSM tubular launchers on afterdeck, after two trained to port, forward two to starboard
- Vulcan Phalanx CIWS mounting with distinctive white dome right aft

SPECIFICATION:

COUNTRY OF ORIGIN: USA
CLASS: Al Siddiq (PCFG)
ACTIVE: 9
NAME (PENNANT NUMBER):
Al Siddiq (511), Al Farouq (513),
Abdul Aziz (515), Faisal (517),
Khalid (519), Amyr (521), Tariq
(523), Oqbah (525), Abu Obaidah
(527)

FEATURES:
DISPLACEMENT: 495 tons full load
LENGTH: 190.5 ft (58.1 m)
BEAM: 26.5 ft (8.1 m)
DRAUGHT: 6.6 ft (2 m)
SPEED: 38 kts
RANGE: 2900 miles at 14 kts

ARMAMENT:
MISSILES: SSM – four McDonnell
Douglas Harpoon (2 twin)
launchers
GUNS: One FMC/OTO Melara 3 in
(76 mm)/62 Mk 75 Mod 0; one
GE/GD 20 mm 6-barrel Vulcan
Phalanx CIWS; two Oerlikon 20 mm/
80; two 81 mm mortars; two
40 mm Mk 19 grenade launchers
DECOYS: Two Loral Hycor SRBOC
6-barrel Mk 36 fixed chaff/IR
launchers

ELECTRONICS:
RADARS: Surface search – ISC
Cardion SPS 55; fire control –
Sperry Mk 92
EW: SLQ-32(V)1 ESM

Fearless SINGAPORE

Dauntless (*Sattler/Steele*)

- High bow with sloping forecastle, with low flush-sided superstructure, low freeboard afterdeck
- 3 in gun mounting in 'A' position
- Enclosed mainmast amidships with tall pole mast atop
- Prominent white radome at aft end of superstructure
- Simbad twin launcher right aft

NOTE: Simbad SAM launcher replaced by towed array in *Brave* and by 25 mm Bushmaster in *Resilience*

NOTE 2: *Sovereignty* has deck crane to facilitate special forces operations

NOTE 3: *Fearless* has new EW radome on mainmast

SPECIFICATION:

COUNTRY OF ORIGIN: Singapore
CLASS: Fearless (OPV)
ACTIVE: 11
NAME (PENNANT NUMBER):
Fearless (94), Brave (95),
Gallant (97), Daring (98),
Dauntless (99), Resilience (82),
Unity (83), Sovereignty (84),
Justice (85), Freedom (86),
Independence (87)

FEATURES:
DISPLACEMENT: 500 tons full load
LENGTH: 180.4 ft (55 m)
BEAM: 28.2 ft (8.6 m)
DRAUGHT: 8.9 ft (2.7 m)
SPEED: 20 kts

ARMAMENT:
MISSILES: SAM – Matra Simbad
twin launchers for Mistral
GUNS: One OTO Melara 3 in
(76 mm)/62 Super Rapid; four
CIS 50 12.7 mm machine guns
TORPEDOES: Six 324 mm
Whitehead B 515 (Triple);
Whitehead A244S
DECOYS: Two GEC Marine Shield
III sextuple fixed chaff launchers

ELECTRONICS:
RADARS: Surface search and fire
control – Elta EL/M-2228(X);
navigation – Kelvin Hughes 1007
SONARS: Thomson Sintra TSM
2362 Gudgeon hull-mounted,
active attack; towed array in *Brave*
EW: Elisra NS-9010C ESM

Serviola SPAIN

Vigía (Çamil Busquests I Vilanova)

- High bow with break in profile forward of superstructure
- High central freeboard adjacent to superstructure
- 3 in gun mounting in 'B' position
- Tall, angular central superstructure
- High, wide bridge set well aft from forward end of superstructure
- Lattice mainmast atop after end of bridge
- Large angular funnel at after end of superstructure, with wedge-shaped, black smoke deflector atop
- Large flight deck aft of superstructure

NOTE: Mexico operates six 'Uribe' class PGS, ordered to a 'Halcón' design with twin funnels and lengthy open quarterdeck beneath a helicopter deck – similar ships to the five operated by the Argentine Prefectura Naval. Mexico also operates four larger 'Holzinger' class which is a modified 'Halcón' design

NOTE 2: Other 'Serviola' equipment fits could include four Harpoon SSM, Meroka CIWS, Sea Sparrow SAM or a Bofors 375 mm ASW rocket launcher

SPECIFICATION:

COUNTRY OF ORIGIN: Spain
CLASS: Serviola (OPV)
ACTIVE: 4
NAME (PENNANT NUMBER):
Serviola (P 71), Centinela (P 72), Vigía (P 73), Atalaya (P 74)

FEATURES:
DISPLACEMENT: 1147 tons full load
LENGTH: 225.4 ft (68.7 m)
BEAM: 34 ft (10.4 m)
DRAUGHT: 11 ft (3.4 m)
SPEED: 19 kts
RANGE: 8000 miles at 12 kts

ARMAMENT:
GUNS: One US 3 in (76 mm)/50 Mk 27; two 12.7 mm machine guns

ELECTRONICS:
RADARS: Surface search – Racal Decca 2459; navigation – Racal Decca ARPA 2690 BT
EW: ULQ-13 ESM (in P 71)

AIR SUPPORT:
HELICOPTERS: Platform for one Agusta AB 212 (surface search)

Kaparen SWEDEN

Spejaran

- Long forecastle with 57 mm/70 gun mounting in 'A' position
- Low profile, rounded midships superstructure
- Short, tripod mainmast aft of bridge
- Surface search radar aerial atop mainmast
- 9LV 200 fire control radar aerial atop after end of bridge
- Forward pointing SSM launchers on afterdeck, angled outboard, port and starboard
- Short lattice aftermast with pole mast atop. Mine rails running from after end of bridge superstructure with an extension over the stern (cannot be used with missiles in place)

NOTE: Norwegian 'Hauk' class similar. See separate entry on page 312

See separate entry on page 312

SPECIFICATION:

COUNTRY OF ORIGIN: Norway
CLASS: Kaparen (PCFG)
ACTIVE: 2
NAME (PENNANT NUMBER):
Spejaren (P 162), Tirfing (P 166)

FEATURES:

DISPLACEMENT: 170 tons full load
LENGTH: 120 ft (36.6 m)
BEAM: 20.7 ft (6.3 m)
DRAUGHT: 5.6 ft (1.7 m)
SPEED: 36 kts

ARMAMENT:

MISSILES: SSM – six Kongsberg Penguin Mk 2
GUNS: One Bofors 57 mm/70 Mk 1; 57 mm illuminant launchers on either side of mounting
TORPEDOES: Four 15.75 in (400 mm); Swedish Ordnance Type 43/45 ASW
A/S MORTARS: Four Saab Elma 9-tube launchers
DEPTH CHARGES: Two racks
MINES: 24

ELECTRONICS:

RADARS: Surface search – Skanter 16 in Mk 009; fire control – Philips 9LV 200 Mk 2
SONARS: Simrad SA 950, hull-mounted; Simrad ST 570 VDS
EW: Saab Scania EWS 905 ESM

Norrköping SWEDEN

Norrköping

- Exceptionally long forecastle with 57 mm/70 gun mounting just aft of midway between bows and bridge
- Narrow superstructure centred well aft of midships
- Complex lattice mainmast atop mid-superstructure
- Sea Giraffe air/surface search radar aerial atop mainmast
- 9LV 200 fire control radar aerial atop bridge roof
- Single torpedo tubes outboard of gun mounting, port and starboard
- Afterdeck can be fitted with any one of several combinations of torpedo tubes and ssm launchers

NOTE: Similar to the original 'Spica' class from which they were developed. See separate entry on page 309

See separate entry on page 309

SPECIFICATION:

COUNTRY OF ORIGIN: Sweden
CLASS: Norrköping (PCFG)
ACTIVE: 2
NAME (PENNANT NUMBER):
Norrköping (R 131), Ystad (R 142)

FEATURES:

DISPLACEMENT: 230 tons full load
LENGTH: 143 ft (43.6 m)
BEAM: 23.3 ft (7.1 m)
DRAUGHT: 7.4 ft (2.4 m)
SPEED: 40.5 kts
RANGE: 500 miles at 40 kts

ARMAMENT:

MISSILES: SSM – eight Saab RBS 15
GUNS: One Bofors 57 mm/70
Mk 1; launchers for 57 mm
illuminants on side of mounting
TORPEDOES: Six 21 in (533 mm)
tubes (2-6 can be fitted at the
expense of missile armament);
Swedish Ordnance Type 613
MINES: Minelaying capability
DECOYS: Two Philips Philax fixed
chaff/IR launchers

ELECTRONICS:

RADARS: Air/surface search –
Ericsson Sea Giraffe 50HC; fire
control – Philips 9LV 200 Mk 1
EW: Argo AR-700 ESM

Jin Chiang TAIWAN

Jin Chiang

- High bows, angled forecastle, with superstructure flush with ship's side; low freeboard afterdeck
- 40 mm/70 gun mounting forward of bridge
- Prominent, angular superstructure, midships, with large square funnel aft
- Substantial lattice mainmast, topped by pole mast, aft of bridge, supporting air/surface search and navigation radar aerials

NOTE: Looks like enlarged version of Taiwanese 'Sui Chiang' class

SPECIFICATION:

COUNTRY OF ORIGIN: Taiwan
CLASS: Jin Chiang (PGG)
ACTIVE: 12
PLANNED: 12
NAME (PENNANT NUMBER): Jin Chiang (603), Tan Chiang (605), Hsin Chiang (606), Feng Chiang (607), Tseng Chiang (608), Kao Chiang (609), Jing Chiang (610), Hsian Chiang (611), Tsi Chiang (612) Po Chiang (614), Chan Chiang (615), Chu Chiang (617)

FEATURES:
DISPLACEMENT: 680 tons full load
LENGTH: 201.4 ft (61.4 m)
BEAM: 31.2 ft (9.5 m)
DRAUGHT: 9.5 ft (2.9 m)
SPEED: 25 kts
RANGE: 4150 miles at 15 kts

ARMAMENT:
MISSILES: Four Hsiung Feng 1
GUNS: One Bofors 40 mm/70; one CS 20 mm Type 75; two 12.7 mm machine guns
DEPTH CHARGES: Two racks
MINES: Two rails for Mk 6

ELECTRONICS:
RADARS: Air/surface search – Marconi LN66; navigation – Racal Decca Bridgemaster; fire control – Hughes HR-76C5
SONARS: Simrad, search/attack

Hua Hin THAILAND

Klaeng (*Royal Thai Navy*)

- Continuous main deck lines from stem to stern with sharp bows
- 76 mm/62 Compact gun mounting immediately forward of slope-sided bridge with all-round windows
- Lattice mast after of bridge on superstructure with pole mast aft
- Long central superstructure with long angled funnel aft of midships
- 40 mm/70 gun mounting on short quarterdeck

NOTE: Derived from the 'Khamronsin' design

SPECIFICATION:
COUNTRY OF ORIGIN: Thailand
CLASS: Hua Hin (FS)
ACTIVE: 3
NAME (PENNANT NUMBER): Hua Hin (541), Klaeng (542), Si Racha (543)

FEATURES:
DISPLACEMENT: 645 tons full load
LENGTH: 203.4 ft (62 m)
BEAM: 29.2 ft (8.9 m)
DRAUGHT: 8.9 ft (2.7 m)
SPEED: 25 kts
RANGE: 2500 miles at 15 kts

ARMAMENT:
GUNS: One 3 in (76 mm)/50; one Bofors 40 mm/70; two Oerlikon 20 mm GAM-B01; two 12.7 mm machine guns

ELECTRONICS:
RADARS: Surface search – Sperry Rascar; navigation – Sperry APAR

Castle UK

Dumbarton Castle

- High bow, long sweeping forecastle, high freeboard
- 30 mm/75 gun mounting forward of bridge in 'B' position
- Prominent, angular midships superstructure, lower at forward end
- High bridge set well aft from bows
- Substantial enclosed mainmast, topped by pole mast, amidships, supporting surface search and navigation radar aerials
- Large flight deck aft

SPECIFICATION:

COUNTRY OF ORIGIN: UK
CLASS: Castle (OPV)
ACTIVE: 2
NAME (PENNANT NUMBER):
Leeds Castle (P 258),
Dumbarton Castle (P 265)

FEATURES:
DISPLACEMENT: 1427 tons full load
LENGTH: 265.7 ft (81 m)
BEAM: 37.7 ft (11.5 m)
DRAUGHT: 11.8 ft (3.6 m)
SPEED: 19.5 kts
RANGE: 10,000 miles at 12 kts

ARMAMENT:
GUNS: One DES/MSI DS 30B
30 mm/75
DECOYS: Two or four Plessey
Shield 102 mm 6-tube chaff
launchers

ELECTRONICS:
RADARS: Surface search – Plessey
Type 944; navigation – Kelvin
Hughes Type 1006
EW: Orange Crop ESM

AIR SUPPORT:
HELICOPTERS: Platform for
operating Westland Sea King
or Lynx

River UK

Tyne

- High bow with main deck running back to behind superstructure, it then drops down to large clear quarterdeck
- Midships superstructure with platform for 20 mm in front of bridge
- Superstructure rises behind bridge and leads into large funnel
- Solid mast built into forward part of funnel
- Large 3-tonne crane at rear of superstructure for handling semi-rigid inflatable

SPECIFICATION:

COUNTRY OF ORIGIN: UK
CLASS: River
ACTIVE: 3
BUILDING: 1
NAME (PENNANT NUMBER):
Tyne (P 281), Severn (P 282),
Mersey (P 283), Clyde (P 284)

FEATURES:
DISPLACEMENT: 1700 tons full load
LENGTH: 261.7 ft (79.75 m)
BEAM: 44.6 ft (13.6 m)
DRAUGHT: 12.5 ft (3.8 m)
SPEED: 20 kts
RANGE: 5500 miles at 15 kts

ARMAMENT:
GUNS: One 20 mm
Oerlikon/BMARC; two 7.72 mm
machine guns

ELECTRONICS:
RADARS: Surface search – Kelvin
Hughes Nucleus; navigation –
Kelvin Hughes Nucleus

AIR SUPPORT:
HELICOPTERS: Vertrep only

Amphibious
Forces

Polnochny ALGERIA, AZERBAIJAN, BULGARIA, EGYPT, INDIA, RUSSIA,

Polnochny

This class varies in appearance to quite a large degree between groups and countries. Below are general common features:

• High bow with long deck aft to superstructure well aft of midships
• Squared profile lower superstructure with bridge superstructure atop
• Mainmast (lattice or tripod) at central superstructure
• Low profile funnel aft of mainmast
• Step down at after end of superstructure to short afterdeck
• Have bow ramps only
• Group D has a helicopter landing platform amidships

NOTE: Poland operates one modified Polnochny C, *Grunwald* (811), converted into an amphibious command vessel

FEATURES:

DISPLACEMENT: 800 tons full load (Group A); 834 tons (Group B); 1150 tons (Group C); 1253 tons (modified Group C); 1190 tons (Group D)

LENGTH: 239.5 ft (73 m) (Group A); 246.1 ft (75 m) (Group B); 266.7 ft (81.3 m) (Group C, Mod C and D); 275.3 ft (83.9 m) (Group D)

BEAM: 27.9 ft (8.5 m) (Group A); 31.5 ft (9.6 m) (Group B); 31.8 ft (9.7 m) (Group C/D)

DRAUGHT: 5.8 ft (1.8 m) (Group A); 7.5 ft (2.3 m) (Group B); 7.9 ft (2.4 m) (Group C/D)

SPEED: 19 kts (Group A); 18 kts (Group B/C); 16 kts (Group D)

RANGE: 1000 miles at 18 kts (Group A/B); 2000 miles at 12 kts (Group C/D)

ARMAMENT:

MISSILES: SAM – four SA-N-5 Grail quad launchers (Group B/C, Russia and Ukraine only); two Fasta 4M quad launchers for SA-N-5 (Poland)

GUNS: Two 30 mm/65 (twin) AK 230 (Group A); two or four 30 mm/65 (1 or 2 twin) AK 230 (Group B); four 30 mm/65 (2 twin) AK 230 (Group C/D); two 140 mm 18-barrel rocket launchers

ELECTRONICS:

RADARS: Surface search – Spin Trough (Bulgaria, Russia, Syria, Vietnam, Ukraine), Decca (Azerbaijan Group A, Egypt); navigation – Don 2 (Algeria, Azerbaijan Group B) or Don 2 or Krivach (SRN 745) (India Group C), SRN 7453 Nogat (Poland); fire control – Drum Tilt (not Bulgaria)

AIR SUPPORT:

HELICOPTERS: Platform only in Group D

SPECIFICATION:

COUNTRY OF ORIGIN: Russia

CLASS: Polnochny Group A (Type 770) (LSM)

ACTIVE: 2 Azerbaijan, 2 Bulgaria, 3 Egypt

NAME (PENNANT NUMBER):
AZERBAIJAN – 291 (ex-MDK 36), 380 (ex-MDC 37)
BULGARIA – Sirius (ex-*Ivan Zagubanski*) (701), Antares (702)
EGYPT – 301, 303, 305

CLASS: Polnochny Group B (Type 771) (LSM)

ACTIVE: 1 Algeria, 1 Azerbaijan, 6 Russia, 3 Syria, 3 Vietnam

NAME (PENNANT NUMBER):
ALGERIA – 471
AZERBAIJAN – D431 (ex-MDK 107)
RUSSIA – 578 +
SYRIA – 1-114, 2-114, 3-114
VIETNAM – HQ 511, HQ 513, HQ 512

CLASS: Polnochny Group C (Type 773) (LSM)

ACTIVE: 1 India, 1 Poland, 1 Ukraine

NAME (PENNANT NUMBER):
INDIA – Sharbah (L 17)

CLASS: Modified Polnochny Group C (Type 776) (LST)
POLAND – Grunwald (811)
UKRAINE – Kirovograd (ex-SDK 137) U 401

CLASS: Polnochny Group D (Type 773U) (LSM)

ACTIVE: 4 India

NAME (PENNANT NUMBER):
INDIA – Cheetah (L 18), Mahish (L 19), Guldar (L 21), Kumbhir (L 22)

Newport AUSTRALIA, BRAZIL, CHILE, MALAYSIA, MEXICO, MOROCCO,
Chung Ho SPAIN, TAIWAN

- Long forecastle with high, distinctive superstructure set well aft
- Distinctive twin derrick arms supporting bow ramp (absent, Australia)
- Australian ships have high forecastle dropping to long flight deck forward of bridge superstructure, with flight deck right aft
- Vulcan Phalanx atop bridge in other hulls
- Tall pole mainmast atop main superstructure supporting radar antennae
- Short lattice platform forward of tall rounded funnel
- Large crane derrick aft of funnel

SPECIFICATION:

COUNTRY OF ORIGIN: USA
CLASS: Newport class (LPA/LST)
ACTIVE: 2 Australia, 1 Brazil, 1 Chile, 1 Malaysia, 2 Mexico, 1 Morocco, 2 Spain, 2 Taiwan
NAME (PENNANT NUMBER):
AUSTRALIA – Kanimbla (ex-Saginaw) (L 51, ex-LST 1188), Manoora (ex-Fairfax County) (L 52, ex-LST 1193)
BRAZIL – Mattoso Maia (ex-Cayuga) (G 28, ex-LST 1186)
CHILE – Valdivia (ex-San Bernardino) (93, ex-LST 1189)
MALAYSIA – Sri Inderapura (ex-Spartanburg County) (1505, ex-LST 1192)
MEXICO – Rio Papaloapan (ex-Sonora, ex-Newport) (A 411, ex-A-04, ex-LST 1179), Usumacinta (ex-Frederick (A 412, ex-LST 1184)
MOROCCO – Sidi Mohammed ben Abdallah (ex-Bristol County) (407, ex-LST 1198)
SPAIN – Hernán Cortés (ex-Barnstaple County) (L 41, ex-LST 1197), Pizarro (ex-Harlan County) (L 42, ex-LST 1196)
TAIWAN – Chung Ho (ex-Manitowic) (232, ex-LST 1180), Chung Ping (ex-Sumter) (233, ex-LST 1181)

FEATURES:

DISPLACEMENT: 8450 tons full load; 8750 tons (Chile); 8550 tons (Spain)
LENGTH: 552.3 ft (168.2 m)
BEAM: 69.5 ft (21.2 m)

DRAUGHT: 17.5 ft (5.3 m)
SPEED: 20 kts
RANGE, MILES: 14,250 miles at 14/15 kts (Australia); 14,000 miles at 15 kts

ARMAMENT:

GUNS: Four USN 3 in (76 mm) (Mexico); one GE/GD 20 mm Vulcan Phalanx Mk 15 can be fitted in Australian hulls; four 12.7 mm machine guns; two Typhoon 25 mm (Australia); four 40 mm/ 60 (2 twin) (Taiwan); one Vulcan Phalanx CIWS (remainder) and eight 12.7 mm machine guns (Brazil); additionally, two Oerlikon 20 mm/85 and four 12.7 mm machine guns (Spain)
DECOYS: Two SRBOC Mk 36 chaff/IR launchers (Australia)
NOTE: No armament in Chilean vessels

ELECTRONICS:

RADARS: Surface search – Kelvin Hughes 1007 (Australia, Malaysia), Raytheon SPS-10F (Brazil, Mexico, Spain), Raytheon SPS-67 (Chile, Malaysia, Morocco, Taiwan); navigation – Kelvin Hughes (Australia), Raytheon SPS-64(v)6 and Furuno FR 2120 (Brazil), Marconi LN66 (Chile, Malaysia, Morocco, Spain, Taiwan), Raytheon SPS-64 (Mexico)
EW: Chong Feng III ESM/ECM (Taiwan); Celesa Deneb (Spain)

AIR SUPPORT:

HELICOPTERS: Four Black Hawk or three Sea Kings or one Chinook (Australia); platform only on remainder

 Not Australia

Ceará BRAZIL

Rio de Janeiro

- Long forecastle, stepped up to high, distinctive superstructure. Tall communications mast half way on forecastle
- High freeboard. Superstructure flush with ship's sides
- Tall pole mainmast atop main superstructure supporting air/surface search and surface search radar aerials with full pole mast at aft end
- Two large 50-ton capacity crane derricks aft of midships
- Tall thin rounded funnels

NOTE: Well dock 391 x 48 ft (119.2 x 14.6 m)

SPECIFICATION:

COUNTRY OF ORIGIN: France
CLASS: Ceará (Thomaston) (LSD)
ACTIVE: 2
NAME (PENNANT NUMBER):
Ceará (ex-*Hermitage*) (G 30,
ex-LSD 34), Rio de Janeiro
(ex-*Alamo*) (G 31,ex-LSD 33)

FEATURES:
DISPLACEMENT: 12,150 tons
full load
LENGTH: 510 ft (155.5 m)
BEAM: 84 ft (25.6 m)
DRAUGHT: 19 ft (5.8 m)
SPEED: 22.5 kts
RANGE: 10,000 miles at 18 kts

ARMAMENT:
GUNS: Six USN 3 in (76 mm)/50
(3 twin) Mk 33; four 12.7 mm
machine guns

ELECTRONICS:
RADARS: Air/surface search –
Plessey AWS-2; surface search –
Raytheon SPS-10FF; navigation –
Raytheon CRP 3100

AIR SUPPORT:
HELICOPTERS: Platform for
Super Puma

Foudre FRANCE

Foudre

- Short forecastle with high, distinctive superstructure set well forward
- High freeboard
- 40 mm/60 gun mounting immediately forward of bridge (*Foudre*) or 30 mm/70 (*Siroco*)
- Large complex lattice mainmast atop main superstructure supporting air/surface search and surface search radar aerials
- Two Syracuse SATCOM domes, on pedestals, on after outboard edges of superstructure
- Two Simbad/Mistral SAM launchers at base of mainmast
- Long flight deck aft of superstructure
- Large crane derrick at after end of well deck
- Two 20 mm gun mountings, port and starboard, aft of crane

NOTE: Designed to take a mechanised regiment of the Rapid Action Force and act as a logistic support ship

NOTE 2: Well dock 400.26 x 45.93 ft (122 x 14 m), can dock a 400-ton ship

SPECIFICATION:

COUNTRY OF ORIGIN: France
CLASS: Foudre (Type TCD 90/LSD)
ACTIVE: 2
NAME (PENNANT NUMBER):
Foudre (L 9011), Siroco (L 9012)

FEATURES:

DISPLACEMENT: 12,400 tons full load; 17,200 tons flooded
LENGTH: 551 ft (168 m)
BEAM: 77.1 ft (23.5 m)
DRAUGHT: 17 ft (5.2 m); 30.2 ft (9.2 m) flooded
SPEED: 21 kts
RANGE: 11,000 miles at 15 kts

ARMAMENT:

MISSILES: SAM – two Matra Simbad twin launchers, Mistral
GUNS: One Bofors 40 mm/60 (*Foudre*); two Giat 20F2 20 mm; three Breda/Mauser 30 mm/70 (*Siroco*)
DECOYS: SLQ-25 Nixie anti-torpedo decoy

ELECTRONICS:

RADARS: Air/surface search – Thomson-CSF DRBV 21A Mars; surface search – Racal Decca 2459 (*Foudre*); navigation – two Racal Decca RM DRBN 34A (L 9012) or Racal Decca 1229 (L 9011)
EW: Two Thales ARBB 36 ECM

AIR SUPPORT:

HELICOPTERS: Four Aerospatiale AS 332F Super Puma or two Aerospatiale SA 321G Super Frelon

Mistral FRANCE

Mistral (DCN)

- Blunt bows, with continuous deck from stem to stern
- High distinctive bridge structure offset on starboard side of ship, aft of midships
- Two large enclosed masts atop superstructure, with angled funnel integral part of aft mast
- Flight deck length of ship
- Two medium-sized crane derricks aft at well deck

NOTE: Two LCACs or four of a new class of LCU can be carried

NOTE 2: Flight deck 653 x 105 ft (199 x 32 m)

SPECIFICATION:

COUNTRY OF ORIGIN: France
CLASS: Mistral (LHD/NTCD)
ACTIVE: 0
BUILDING: 2
NAME (PENNANT NUMBER):
Mistral (L 9013), Tonnerre (L 9014)

FEATURES:

DISPLACEMENT: 21,500 tons full load; 32,300 tons flooded
LENGTH: 653 ft (199 m)
BEAM: 105 ft (32 m)
DRAUGHT: 20.3 ft (6.2 m)
SPEED: 19 kts
RANGE: 11,000 miles at 15 kts

ARMAMENT:

MISSILES: SAM – two Matra Simbad sextuple launchers, Mistral
GUNS: Two 30 mm; four 12.7 mm machine guns

ELECTRONICS:

RADARS: Air/surface search – Thomson-CSF MMR 3D; navigation – two Racal Decca Bridgemaster DRBN 38A
EW: ARBR 21 ESM

AIR SUPPORT:

HELICOPTERS: 16 NH 90 or Eurocopter Super Puma/Cougar tactical trooplift or Eurocopter Tigre attack helicopters

Ouragan FRANCE

Ouragan

- Very high freeboard section forward of midships
- High distinctive bridge structure offset on starboard side of ship, well forward of midships
- Large pole mainmast supporting radar aerials atop bridge roof
- Flight deck aft of bridge
- Two medium-sized crane derricks aft at well deck
- Small, black-capped funnel adjacent forward crane

NOTE: Three LCVPs can be carried
NOTE 2: Typical loads: 18 Super Frelon or 80 Alouette III helicopters or 120 AMX 13 tanks or 84 DUKWs or 340 vehicles or 12 50-ton barges. 400-ton ship can be docked

SPECIFICATION:

COUNTRY OF ORIGIN: France
CLASS: Ouragan (TCD/LSD)
ACTIVE: 2
NAME (PENNANT NUMBER):
Ouragan (L 9021), Orage (L 9022)

FEATURES:

DISPLACEMENT: 8500 tons full load; 14,400 tons flooded
LENGTH: 488.9 ft (149 m)
BEAM: 75.4 ft (23 m)
DRAUGHT: 17.7 ft (5.4 m); 28.5 ft (8.7 m) flooded
SPEED: 17 kts
RANGE: 9000 miles at 15 kts

ARMAMENT:

MISSILES: SAM – two Matra Simbad twin launchers, Mistral
GUNS: Two Breda/Mauser 30 mm/70; four 12.7 mm machine guns

ELECTRONICS:

RADARS: Air/surface search – Thomson-CSF DRBV 51A; navigation – two Racal Decca DRBN 34A

AIR SUPPORT:

HELICOPTERS: Four Aerospatiale SA 321G Super Frelon or 10 Aerospatiale SA 319B Alouette III

Jason GREECE

Ikaria (*Hellenic Navy*)

- High forecastle with 76 mm/62 gun mounting at mid-point on raised platform
- Break, down from forecastle to extensive well deck
- High superstructure aft of well deck
- Large tripod mainmast atop bridge roof supporting radar aerials
- Distinctive twin funnels, side-by-side, at after end of superstructure. Funnels of square section, black-capped, with sloping tops
- Large raised helicopter platform aft with stern overhang

NOTE: Bow and stern ramps, drive-through design

SPECIFICATION:

COUNTRY OF ORIGIN: Greece
CLASS: Jason (LST)
ACTIVE: 5
NAME (PENNANT NUMBER): Chios (L 173), Samos (L 174), Lesbos (L 176), Ikaria (L 175), Rodos (L 177)

FEATURES:

DISPLACEMENT: 4400 tons full load
LENGTH: 380.5 ft (116 m)
BEAM: 50.2 ft (15.3 m)
DRAUGHT: 11.3 ft (3.4 m)
SPEED: 16 kts

ARMAMENT:

GUNS: One OTO Melara 76 mm/62 Mod 9 Compact; two Breda 40 mm/70 (2 twin) Compact; four Rheinmetall 20 mm (2 twin)

ELECTRONICS:

RADARS: Surface search – Thomson-CSF Triton; navigation – Kelvin Hughes Type 1007; fire control – Thomson-CSF Pollux

AIR SUPPORT:

HELICOPTERS: Platform for one medium

Frosch I INDONESIA

Teluk Berau

- Wide bow ramp at forward end of forecastle with very distinctive wide, flat-topped bows
- Crane at mid-foredeck
- Large, stepped, slab-sided superstructure well aft of midships giving very high freeboard
- Distinctive vertical-ribbed appearance to main superstructure
- Large double-pole mainmast atop mid-superstructure supporting air/surface search and navigation radar aerials

NOTE: Former East German Navy ships transferred, unarmed, from Germany in August 1993

NOTE 2: Two 'Frosch II' class (*Teluk Cirebon*, ex-*Nordperd*, and *Teluk Sabang*, ex-*Südperd*, serve with the Indonesian Navy as support ships (AK/AR))

SPECIFICATION:

COUNTRY OF ORIGIN: former East Germany
CLASS: Frosch I (Type 108) (LSM)
ACTIVE: 12
NAME (PENNANT NUMBER): Teluk Gilimanuk (ex-*Hoyerswerda*) (531, ex-611), Teluk Celukan Bawang (ex-*Hagenow*) (532, ex-632), Teluk Cendrawasih (ex-*Frankfurt/Oder*) (533, ex-613), Teluk Berau (ex-*Eberswalde-Finow*) (534, ex-634), Teluk Peleng (ex-*Lübben*) (535, ex-631), Teluk Sibolga (ex-*Schwerin*) (536, ex-612), Teluk Manado (ex-*Neubrandenburg*) (537, ex-633), Teluk Hading (ex-*Cottbus*) (538, ex-614), Teluk Parigi (ex-*Anklam*) (539, ex-635), Teluk Lampung (ex-*Schwedt*) (540, ex-636), Teluk Jakarta (ex-*Eisenhüttenstadt*) (541, ex-615), Teluk Sangkulirang (ex-*Grimmen*) (542, ex-616)

FEATURES:

DISPLACEMENT: 1950 tons full load
LENGTH: 321.5 ft (98 m)
BEAM: 36.4 ft (11.1 m)
DRAUGHT: 9.2 ft (2.8 m)
SPEED: 18 kts

ARMAMENT:

GUNS: One 40 mm/60; two 37 mm (one twin); four 25 mm (2 twin)
MINES: Can lay 40 mines
DECOYS: Two PK 16 chaff launchers

ELECTRONICS:

RADARS: Air/surface search – Strut Curve; navigation – TSR 333

San Giorgio ITALY

San Giusto

- Short forecastle with break up to aircraft carrier type flight deck, which continues to stern
- Clean profile, high freeboard
- 3 in gun mounting in 'B' position
- High, angular, square profile island superstructure sited starboard side, midships
- Pole mainmast atop central island superstructure
- Three LCVPs carried in davits, two port side opposite island superstructure, the third starboard side forward of island superstructure
- Small, square profile, raked funnel atop island superstructure

NOTE: Bow ramp (except for amphibious landings). Stern docking well 67.25 x 22.96 ft (20.5 x 7 m). Fitted with a 30 ton lift and two 40-ton travelling cranes for LCMS

NOTE 2: *San Giusto* is of similar design except for a slightly longer island and different LCVP davit arrangement. Also, no bow doors and therefore no beaching capability

SPECIFICATION:

COUNTRY OF ORIGIN: Italy
CLASS: San Giorgio (LPDs)
ACTIVE: 3
NAME (PENNANT NUMBER): San Giorgio (L 9892), San Marco (L 9893), San Giusto (L 9894)

FEATURES:
DISPLACEMENT: 7960 tons full load; 8000 tons (*San Giusto*)
LENGTH: 437.2 ft (133.3 m); 449.5 ft (137 m) (*San Giusto*)
BEAM: 67.3 ft (20.5 m)
DRAUGHT: 17.4 ft (5.3 m)
FLIGHT DECK: 328.1 x 67.3 ft (100 x 20.5 m)
SPEED: 21 kts
RANGE: 7500 miles at 16 kts

ARMAMENT:
GUNS: One OTO Melara 3 in (76 mm)/62 (Compact *San Giusto*); two Breda/Oerlikon 25 mm; two 12.7 mm machine guns

ELECTRONICS:
RADARS: Surface search – SMA SPS-702; navigation – SMA SPN-748; fire control – Selenia SPG-70 (RTN 10X)
EW: SLQ-747 ESM/ECM (*San Giusto*)

AIR SUPPORT:
HELICOPTERS: Three Agusta-Sikorsky SH-3D Sea King or EH 101 Merlin, or five Agusta-Bell AB 212

Oosumi JAPAN

Oosumi

- Short forecastle with sharp break up to aircraft carrier style flight deck, continuous to stern
- Angular island sited starboard side, amidships
- Enclosed pyramid mainmast with OPS-14C air-search radar on projecting gantry forward
- Square black funnel at aft end of superstructure with projecting exhausts and pole aerials
- Large crane immediately aft of funnel
- Vulcan Phalanx CIWS on platforms forward and aft of superstructure

NOTE: Through deck and stern docking. Military lift: 330 troops, two LCAC, ten Type 90 tanks or 1400 tons cargo

SPECIFICATION:

COUNTRY OF ORIGIN: Japan
CLASS: Oosumi (LPD/LST)
ACTIVE: 2
BUILDING: 1
NAME (PENNANT NUMBER):
Oosumi (LST 4001), Shimokita
(LST 4002), Kunisaki (LST 4003)

FEATURES:
DISPLACEMENT: 8900 tons standard
LENGTH: 584 ft (178 m)
BEAM: 84.6 ft (25.8 m)
DRAUGHT: 19.7 ft (6 m)
FLIGHT DECK: 426.5 x 75.5 ft (130 x 23 m)
SPEED: 22 kts

ARMAMENT:
GUNS: Two GE/GD Vulcan Phalanx Mk 15 CIWS

ELECTRONICS:
RADARS: Air-search – Mitsubishi OPS-14C; surface search – JRC OPS-28D; navigation – JRC OPS-20

AIR SUPPORT:
HELICOPTERS: Platform for two Kawasaki/Boeing CH-47J Chinook

Rotterdam/Galicia NETHERLANDS, SPAIN

Rotterdam (*Michael Nitz*)

- Very short forecastle with sharp break up to very tall superstructure, slab-sided and flush with ship's sides
- Goalkeeper CIWS mounted on forecastle immediately forward of superstructure (Netherlands only)
- Bridge projects forward of superstructure
- Two thin rectangular funnels atop superstructure, port and starboard, midships, with pole aerials
- Large enclosed mainmast above bridge, with air/surface search radar atop. Two spherical SATCOM domes outboard of this mast
- Second enclosed mast between funnels
- Second Goalkeeper CIWS mounted on aft edge of superstructure. In Spanish ships, 20 mm Meroka
- Curved section 'cut out' of aft superstructure to accommodate ship's boats and crane derrick
- Long flight deck aft over dock

NOTE: The UK is building two 16,160-ton LSLS, *Lyme Bay* and *Largs Bay* based on the Rotterdam design

SPECIFICATION:

COUNTRY OF ORIGIN: Netherlands
CLASS: Rotterdam/Galicia (LPD/ATS)
ACTIVE: 1 Netherlands, 2 Spain
PLANNED: 1 Netherlands
NAME (PENNANT NUMBER):
NETHERLANDS – Rotterdam
(L 800), Johan de Zwitt (L 801)
SPAIN – Galicia (L 51), Castilla
(L 52)

FEATURES:

DISPLACEMENT: 12,750 tons full load (Netherlands); 16,680 tons (Netherlands L 802); 13,815 tons (Spain)
LENGTH: 544.6 ft (166 m); 557.5 ft (176 m) (L 801) (Netherlands); 524.9 ft (160 m) (Spain)
BEAM: 82 ft (25 m) (Spain); 95.8 ft (29.2 m) (Netherlands L 802)
DRAUGHT: 19.3 ft (5.9 m)
FLIGHT DECK: 183.7 x 82 ft (56 x 25 m) (Netherlands); 196.9 x 82 ft (60 x 25 m) (Spain)
SPEED: 19 kts
RANGE: 6000 miles at 12 kts

ARMAMENT:

GUNS: Two Signaal Goalkeeper 30 mm CIWS; eight 12.7 mm machine guns (Netherlands); one Bazán 20 mm/120 12-barrel Meroka; two Oerlikon 20 mm (Spain)
DECOYS: Four SRBOC chaff launchers

ELECTRONICS:

RADARS: Air/surface search – Signaal DA08 (Netherlands); surface search – Signaal Scout/Kelvin Hughes ARPA; TRS 3D/16 in L 52 in addition; navigation – two sets

AIR SUPPORT:

HELICOPTERS: Six NH 90 or four EH 101 Merlin or Sea King (Netherlands); six AB 212 or four SH-3D Sea Kings or four Eurocopter Tigre (Spain)

Ropucha RUSSIA, UKRAINE

Ropucha II

- Unusual squared-off forward end to forecastle
- 57 mm/80 ('Ropucha I') or 76 mm/60 gun mounting ('Ropucha II') at forward end of superstructure
- Large superstructure centred aft of midships
- Pole mast atop bridge roof
- Large lattice mainmast atop mid-superstructure
- Very wide square section funnels aft of mainmast

NOTE: A 'roll-on-roll-off' design with a tank deck running the whole length of the ship

NOTE 2: All have very minor differences in appearance (see 'Guns' and 'Missiles' sections)

NOTE 3: At least five Russian ships have rocket launchers at the after end of the forecastle

NOTE 4: One 'Ropucha II' has a masthead radar dome

SPECIFICATION:

COUNTRY OF ORIGIN: Russia
CLASS: Ropucha I (Type 775), Ropucha II (Type 775M) (LST)
ACTIVE: 14 Ropucha I, 3 Ropucha II (Russia), 1 Ropucha I (Ukraine)
NAME (PENNANT NUMBER):
RUSSIA – Ropucha I: 012, 016, 027, 031, 142, 156, 158, 102, 110, 125, 127, 055, 066, 070; Ropucha II: 130, 151, 077
UKRAINE – Konstantin Olshansky (ex-BDK 56) (U 402)

FEATURES:
DISPLACEMENT: 4400 tons full load
LENGTH: 369.1 ft (112.5 m); 370.7 ft (113 m) (Ukraine)
BEAM: 49.2 ft (15.9 m); 47.6 ft (14.5 m) (Ukraine)
DRAUGHT: 12.1 ft (3.7 m); 11.5 ft (3.6 m) (Ukraine)
SPEED: 17.5 kts
RANGE: 6000 miles at 12 kts

ARMAMENT:
MISSILES: SAM – four SA-N-5 Grail quad launchers (in at least two Russian ships and Ukraine unit)
GUNS: Four 57 mm/80 (2 twin) (Ropucha I); one 76 mm/60 (Ropucha II); two 30 mm/65 AK 630 (Ropucha II); two 122 mm UMS-73 Grad-M (naval) (in some); two 20-barrel rocket launchers
MINES: 92 contact type (Russia only)

ELECTRONICS:
RADARS: Air/surface search – Strut Curve (Ropucha I) or Cross Dome (Ropucha II); navigation – Don 2 or Nayada; fire control – Muff Cob (Ropucha I); Bass Tilt (Ropucha II)
SONARS: Mouse Tail VDS can be carried in Russian ships

Endurance SINGAPORE

Endurance (*Michael Nitz*)

- High forecastle with sharp drop down, forward of 'A' mounting, continuous to very long flight deck, over short open quarterdeck
- 76 mm gun on raised platform immediately forward of bridge
- Thin angled funnels, port and starboard, at aft end of bridge, supporting catwalks
- Fat pyramidal platform supporting radar aerial atop bridge
- Tall pyramidal enclosed mast aft end of superstructure
- Two large cranes immediately aft of funnels

NOTE: Through deck and stern docking. Military lift: 350 troops, 18 tanks, 20 vehicles, four LCVP

SPECIFICATION:

COUNTRY OF ORIGIN: Singapore
CLASS: Endurance (LPD/LST)
ACTIVE: 4
NAME (PENNANT NUMBER):
Endurance (L 207), Resolution
(L 208), Persistence (L 209),
Endeavour (L 210)

FEATURES:

DISPLACEMENT: 8500 tons full load
LENGTH: 462.6 ft (141 m)
BEAM: 68.9 ft (21 m)
DRAUGHT: 16.4 ft (5 m)
SPEED: 15 kts
RANGE: 10,400 miles at 12 kts

ARMAMENT:

MISSILES: Two Matra Simbad twin
launchers for Mistral
GUNS: One OTOBreda 76 mm/62
Super Rapid; five 12.7 mm
machine guns
DECOYS: Two GEC Marine
Shield III 102 mm sextuple fixed
chaff launchers

ELECTRONICS:

RADARS: Air/surface search – Elta
EL/M-2238; navigation – Kelvin
Hughes Type 1007
EW: Rafael RAN 1101 ESM/ECM

AIR SUPPORT:

HELICOPTERS: Two Super Pumas

Albion UK

Albion

- Short forecastle with angular raised platform with Goalkeeper CIWS atop
- Vertical forward face to bridge superstructure. Open walkway around bridge
- Pyramid enclosed foremast with air/surface search radar atop and navigation/aircraft control radar on projecting gantry forward
- Two square funnels on starboard side of superstructure with projecting exhausts
- Massive enclosed mainmast with air/surface search radar atop and SATCOM domes on gantries on either side
- Third enclosed pyramid mast at aft end of superstructure
- Large crane immediately aft of superstructure
- Flight deck over short open quarterdeck

NOTE: Well docks and stern gates, and side ramp access

SPECIFICATION:

COUNTRY OF ORIGIN: UK
CLASS: Albion (LPD)
ACTIVE: 2
NAME (PENNANT NUMBER):
Albion (L 14), Bulwark (L 15)

FEATURES:
DISPLACEMENT: 18,500 tons full load
LENGTH: 577.4 ft (176 m)
BEAM: 94.8 ft (28.9 m)
DRAUGHT: 23.3 ft (7.1 m)
SPEED: 18 kts
RANGE: 8000 miles at 15 kts

ARMAMENT:
GUNS: Two 20 mm (twin); two Goalkeeper CIWS
DECOYS: Eight Sea Gnat launchers and DLH offboard decoys

ELECTRONICS:
RADARS: Air/surface search – Siemens Plessey Type 996; surface search – Racal Decca 1008; navigation – two Racal Marine Type 1007
EW: Racal Thorn UAT 1/4

AIR SUPPORT:
HELICOPTERS: Platform for three EH Industries EH 101 Merlin; Chinook capable

Ocean UK

Ocean

- Aircraft carrier style flight deck, continuous to stern
- Vulcan Phalanx CIWS positioned in eyes of ship and on sponsons projecting, port and starboard, at stern
- Thin, angular island sited starboard side, amidships
- Prominent bridge angled out over flight deck
- Enclosed pyramid foremast atop bridge, with surface search radar on projecting gantry forward
- Square angled black funnel midway atop superstructure, with projecting exhausts and pole aerials
- Massive enclosed pyramidal mainmast at aft end of superstructure with air/surface radar atop. SATCOM dome on gantries projecting inboard and forward
- Large crane aft of superstructure on starboard side

NOTE: Based on *Invincible* CVS hull design. Military lift: four LCVP Mk 5 on davits, two Griffon hovercraft, 40 vehicles and equipment for most of a marine commando unit

SPECIFICATION:

COUNTRY OF ORIGIN: UK
CLASS: Ocean (LPH)
ACTIVE: 1
NAME (PENNANT NUMBER):
Ocean (L 12)

FEATURES:
DISPLACEMENT: 21,758 tons full load
LENGTH: 667.3 ft (203.4 m) oa
BEAM: 112.9 ft (34.4 m)
DRAUGHT: 21.3 ft (6.6 m)
FLIGHT DECK: 557.7 x 104 ft (170 x 31.7 m)
SPEED: 19 kts
RANGE: 8000 miles at 15 kts

ARMAMENT:
GUNS: Three Vulcan Phalanx Mk 15 CIWS; eight 20 mm GAM-B03 (4 twin)
DECOYS: Eight Sea Gnat 130 mm/102 mm launchers and DLH offboard decoys

ELECTRONICS:
RADARS: Air/surface search – AMS Type 996; surface search – Type 1008; surface search/aircraft control – two Type 1007
EW: Racal UAT ESM

AIR SUPPORT:
HELICOPTERS: 12 Sea King HC Mk 4/EH 101 Merlin plus six Lynx (or Apache)

Austin USA

Ogden

- High bow with wire aerial structure on forecastle
- Large superstructure forward of midships creating very high freeboard
- Two Vulcan Phalanx CIWS mountings, one forward end of main superstructure, the other atop superstructure, immediately aft of mainmast
- Large tripod mainmast atop mid-superstructure
- Unusual tall, slim twin funnels. Starboard funnel well forward of port one
- Crane derrick between funnels
- Long flight deck aft with telescopic hangar (no hangar in LPD 4)

NOTE: Enlarged version of 'Raleigh' class, now paid off

NOTE 2: There are structural variations in the positions of guns and electronic equipment in different ships of the class

NOTE 3: LPD 7-13 have an additional bridge and are fitted as flagships

NOTE 4: Coronado (AGF 11, ex-LPD 11) former class member, converted into command ship role

SPECIFICATION:

COUNTRY OF ORIGIN: USA
CLASS: Austin (LPD)
ACTIVE: 11
NAME (PENNANT NUMBER): Austin (LPD 4), Ogden (LPD 5), Duluth (LPD 6), Cleveland (LPD 7), Dubuque (LPD 8), Denver (LPD 9), Juneau (LPD 10), Shreveport (LPD 12), Nashville (LPD 13), Trenton (LPD 14), Ponce (LPD 15)

FEATURES:
DISPLACEMENT: 17,244 tons full load
LENGTH: 570 ft (173.8 m)
BEAM: 100 ft (30.5 m)
DRAUGHT: 23. ft (7 m)
SPEED: 21 kts
RANGE: 7700 miles at 20 kts

ARMAMENT:
GUNS: Two GE/GD 20 mm/76 Vulcan Phalanx Mk 15; two 25 mm Mk 38; eight 12.7 mm machine guns
DECOYS: Four Loral Hycor SRBOC 6-barrel Mk 36

ELECTRONICS:
RADARS: Air-search – Lockheed SPS-40E; surface search – Norden SPS-67; navigation – Raytheon SPS-73(V)12
EW: SLQ-32(V)1 ESM

AIR SUPPORT:
HELICOPTERS: Up to six Boeing CH-46D/E Sea Knight can be carried; hangar for only one light (not in LPD 4)

Blue Ridge USA

Blue Ridge

- Vulcan Phalanx CIWS mountings in eyes of the ship and right aft on specially built platform
- Numerous communications aerials and masts along length of maindeck, including tall lattice mast midway between bows and superstructure
- Small superstructure amidships
- Pole mainmast atop superstructure
- Twin, angled exhausts at top after end of superstructure
- Very unusual flared hull midships section to protect stowages for LCPS and LCVPS
- Large communications aerial mast mid-afterdeck
- Tall, enclosed pyramid structure topped by white dome, further aft

NOTE: Hull design similar to 'Iwo Jima' class

SPECIFICATION:

COUNTRY OF ORIGIN: USA
CLASS: Blue Ridge (LCC)
ACTIVE: 2
NAME (PENNANT NUMBER):
Blue Ridge (LCC 19), Mount
Whitney (LCC 20)

FEATURES:
DISPLACEMENT: 19,648 tons full
load (LCC 19); 19,760 tons (LCC 20)
LENGTH: 636.5 ft (194 m)
BEAM: 107.9 ft (32.9 m)
DRAUGHT: 28.9 ft (8.8 m)
SPEED: 23 kts
RANGE: 13,000 miles at 16 kts

ARMAMENT:
GUNS: Two GE/GD 20 mm/76
Vulcan Phalanx Mk 15
DECOYS: Four Loral Hycor SRBOC
6-barrel Mk 36; SLQ-25 Nixie
torpedo decoy

ELECTRONICS:
RADARS: Air-search – ITT SPS-48C,
Lockheed SPS-40E; surface search
– Raytheon SPS-65(V)1; navigation
– Marconi LN66; Raytheon
SPS-64(V)9
EW: SLQ-32(V)3 ESM/ECM

AIR SUPPORT:
HELICOPTERS: One Sikorsky
SH-3H Sea King

Tarawa USA

Pelelui

- Similar outline to 'Wasp' class but higher profile island with prominent crane aft of superstructure
- Vulcan Phalanx CIWS mounting on platform at forward end of island
- Two masts atop island, slightly taller lattice mast forward and complex pole mast aft
- SPS-52D air-search 3D radar aerial atop after end of island (forward end of island in 'Wasp' class)
- One RAM SAM launcher on platform, below flight deck at stern, starboard side; second above bridge offset to port
- Second CIWS mounting, below flight deck, at stern, port side

NOTE: Floodable docking well, 268 x 78 ft (81.68 x 23.77 m), beneath the after elevator capable of taking four LCUS

SPECIFICATION:

COUNTRY OF ORIGIN: USA
CLASS: Tarawa (LHA)
ACTIVE: 5
NAME (PENNANT NUMBER):
Tarawa (LHA 1), Saipan (LHA 2), Belleau Wood (LHA 3), Nassau (LHA 4), Peleliu (ex-*Da Nang*) (LHA 5)

FEATURES:
DISPLACEMENT: 39,967 tons full load
LENGTH: 834 ft (254.2 m)
BEAM: 131.9 ft (40.2 m)
DRAUGHT: 25.9 ft (7.9 m)
FLIGHT DECK: 820 x 118.1 ft (250 x 36 m)
SPEED: 24 kts
RANGE: 10,000 miles at 20 kts

ARMAMENT:
MISSILES: SAM – two GDC Mk 49 RAM
GUNS: Six Mk 242 25 mm automatic cannons; two GE/GD 20 mm/76 Vulcan Phalanx Mk 15; eight 12.7 mm machine guns; six Mk 242 25 mm automatic cannon
DECOYS: Four Loral Hycor SRBOC 6-barrel Mk 36; SLQ-25 Nixie torpedo decoy; NATO Sea Gnat; SLQ-49 chaff buoys

ELECTRONICS:
RADARS: Air-search – ITT SPS-48E, Lockheed SPS-40E, Hughes Mk 23 TAS; surface search – Raytheon SPS-67(v)3; navigation – Raytheon SPS-73
EW: SLQ-23(v)3 ESM/ECM

AIR SUPPORT:
FIXED WING AIRCRAFT: Harrier AV-8B VSTOL aircraft in place of helicopters as required
HELICOPTERS: 19 Sikorsky CH-53D Sea Stallion or 26 Boeing CH-46D/E Sea Knight (in due course)

San Antonio USA

San Antonio (*Northrop Grumman*)

- Short forecastle with VLS SAM forward of bridge
- Massive tall 'stealthy' superstructure, flush with ship's sides
- Two black-capped funnels with four black exhausts, offset port and starboard atop island
- Two massive pyramidal Advanced Enclosed Mast Systems atop superstructure
- Crane between funnels
- Flight deck aft with two hangars

NOTE: Well deck and stern gate arrangements similar to 'Wasp' class

SPECIFICATION:

COUNTRY OF ORIGIN: USA
CLASS: San Antonio (LPD)
ACTIVE: 1
BUILDING: 8
PLANNED: 3
NAME (PENNANT NUMBER): San Antonio (LPD 17), New Orleans (LPD 18), Mesa Verde (LPD 19), Green Bay (LPD 20), New York (LPD 21), San Diego (LPD 22), Anchorage (LPD 23), Arlington (LPD 24), Somerset (LPD 25)

FEATURES:

DISPLACEMENT: 25,300 tons full load
LENGTH: 683.7 ft (208.4 m)
BEAM: 104.7 ft (31.9 m)
DRAUGHT: 23 ft (7 m)
SPEED: 22 kts

ARMAMENT:

MISSILES: SAM – Mk 41 VLS for two octuple cell Evolved Sea Sparrow; two GDC Mk 31 Mod 1 RAM
GUNS: Two 30 mm Mk 46; four 12.7 mm machine guns
DECOYS: Six Mk 53 Mod 4 Nulka and chaff launchers; SLQ-25A Nixie torpedo decoy

ELECTRONICS:

RADARS: Air-search – ITT SPS-48E; surface search/navigation – Raytheon SPS-73(v)13; fire control – Lockheed SPQ-9B
EW: SLQ-32A(v)2 ESM/ECM

AIR SUPPORT:

HELICOPTERS: One Sikorsky CH-53E Sea Stallion or two CH-46E Sea Knight or one MV-22 Osprey or four UH-1

Wasp USA

Essex

- Effectively aircraft carrier style with continuous flight deck
- Large starboard side island amidships
- Two black-capped funnels, fore and aft atop island
- Two Sea Sparrow SAM box launchers, one at forward end of island, the other right aft on overhanging transom. RAM SAM also fitted forward of Sea Sparrow on superstructure and at stern
- Two similar pole masts atop island, after one slightly the taller of the two
- Vulcan Phalanx CIWS mountings, one atop bridge, one other on each quarter
- Two aircraft elevators, one to starboard and aft of the island and one to port amidships

NOTE: Stern doors with well deck of 267 x 50 ft (181.38 x 15.24 m)to accommodate up to three LCACS

NOTE 2: Vehicle storage is available for five M1A1 main battle tanks, 25 LAV-25 APCs, eight M 198 155 mm howitzers, 68 trucks, 10 logistic vehicles and several service vehicles

SPECIFICATION:

COUNTRY OF ORIGIN: USA
CLASS: Wasp (LHD)
ACTIVE: 7
BUILDING: 1
NAME (PENNANT NUMBER):
Wasp (LHD 1), Essex (LHD 2), Kearsarge (LHD 3), Boxer (LHD 4), Bataan (LHD 5), Bonhomme Richard (LHD 6), Iwo Jima (LHD 7), Makin Island (LHD 8)

FEATURES:

DISPLACEMENT: 40,650 tons full load (LHD 1-4); 40,358 tons (LHD 5-7); 41,772 tons (LHD 8)
LENGTH: 844 ft (257.3 m) oa
BEAM: 140.1 ft (42.7 m) oa
DRAUGHT: 26.6 ft (8.1 m)
FLIGHT DECK: 819 x 106 ft (249.6 x 32.3 m)
SPEED: 22 kts
RANGE: 9500 miles at 18 kts

ARMAMENT:

MISSILES: SAM – two Raytheon GMLS Mk 29 octuple launchers; Sea Sparrow; two GDC Mk 49 RAM GUNS: Two or three GE/GD 20 mm Vulcan Phalanx Mk 15; three Boeing Bushmaster 25 mm Mk 38; four 12.7 mm machine guns
DECOYS: Four or six Loral Hycor SRBOC 6-barrel Mk 36; SLQ-25 Nixie torpedo decoy; NATO Sea Gnat; SLQ-49 chaff buoys

ELECTRONICS:

RADARS: Air-search – ITT SPS-48E, Raytheon SPS-49(v)9, Hughes Mk 23 TAS; surface search – Norden SPS-67; navigation – SPS-73; fire control – two Mk 95
EW: SLQ-32(v)4/SLY-2 ESM/ECM; ULQ-20

AIR SUPPORT:

FIXED WING AIRCRAFT: Six to eight AV-8B Harriers or up to 20 in secondary role
HELICOPTERS: Capacity for 42 Boeing CH-46E Sea Knight; capability to support Bell AH-1W SuperCobra, Sikorsky CH-53E Super Stallion, Sikorsky CH-53D Sea Stallion, Bell UH-1N Twin Huey, AH-1T SeaCobra and Sikorsky SH-60B Seahawk

Whidbey Island/Harpers Ferry USA

Harpers Ferry

- Short forecastle with wire aerial structure on forecastle
- High superstructure well forward of midships
- Large lattice mainmast atop mid-superstructure
- Two Vulcan Phalanx CIWS mountings atop main superstructure, one on bridge roof, one immediately forward of funnel. (One CIWS immediately forward of bridge in 'Harpers Ferry' class)
- RAM SAM box launchers atop bridge and at aft end of superstructure in 'Harpers Ferry' class
- Large funnel with sloping after profile at after end of superstructure
- One or two large cranes aft of funnel
- Long afterdeck

NOTE: Based on the earlier 'Anchorage' class. 'Harpers Ferry' class cargo-carrying variants
NOTE 2: Well deck measures 440 x 50 ft (134.1 x 15.2 m) in the LSD but is shorter in the Cargo Variant (CV)
NOTE 3: Approximately 90% commonality between the two variants

SPECIFICATION:

COUNTRY OF ORIGIN: USA
CLASS: Whidbey Island (LSD)
ACTIVE: 8
NAME (PENNANT NUMBER):
Whidbey Island (LSD 41),
Germantown (LSD 42), Fort
McHenry (LSD 43), Gunston Hall
(LSD 44), Comstock (LSD 45),
Tortuga (LSD 46), Rushmore
(LSD 47), Ashland (LSD 48)
CLASS: Harpers Ferry (LSD-CV)
ACTIVE: 4
NAME (PENNANT NUMBER):
Harpers Ferry (LSD 49), Carter
Hall (LSD 50), Oak Hill (LSD 51),
Pearl Harbor (LSD 52)

FEATURES:

DISPLACEMENT: 15,939 tons full
load (LSD 41-48); 16,740 tons
(LSD 49 onwards)
LENGTH: 609.5 ft (185.8 m)
BEAM: 84 ft (25.6 m)
DRAUGHT: 20.5 ft (6.3 m)
SPEED: 22 kts
RANGE: 8000 miles at 18 kts

ARMAMENT:

MISSILES: SAM – one or two GDC
Mk 49 RAM
GUNS: Two GE/GD 20 mm/76
Vulcan Phalanx Mk 15; two
25 mm Mk 38; six 12.7 mm
machine guns
DECOYS: Four Loral Hycor
SRBOC 6-barrel Mk 36 and
Mk 50; SLQ-25 Nixie towed
torpedo decoy

ELECTRONICS:

RADARS: Air-search – Raytheon
SPS-49(V)5; surface search –
Norden SPS-67V; navigation –
Raytheon SPS-64(V)9 or
SPS-73(V)12
EW: SLQ-32(V)1 ESM

AIR SUPPORT:

HELICOPTERS: Platform only for
two Sikorsky CH-53D Sea Stallion

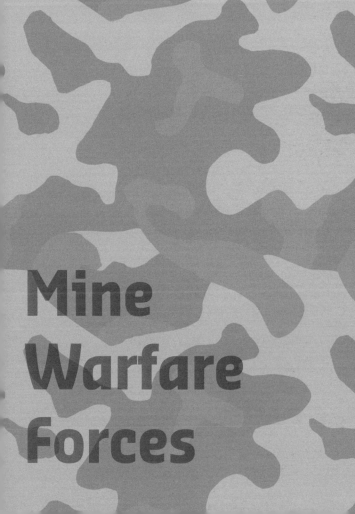

Mine
Warfare
Forces

Lerici/Gaeta   AUSTRALIA, ITALY, MALAYSIA, NIGERIA, THAILAND

Milazzo

- High bow, high freeboard. Sloping break, aft of funnel, down to sweep deck
- 20 mm/70 mounting in 'A' position. (40 mm/70 in Malaysian ships, 30 mm (twin) mounting in Nigerian ships. MSI DS 30B 30 mm in Australian and Thai ships)
- High bridge superstructure with forward sloping bridge windows
- SATCOM dome atop aft end of bridge in Australian ships
- Tapered funnel with unusual, wedge-shaped, smoke deflector atop

NOTE: Two types are easily distinguished by large pole mainmast sited immediately aft of bridge ('Lerici') and immediately forward of funnel ('Gaeta')
NOTE 2: Twelve of the much larger, modified Lerici design built by the USA as 'Osprey' class (see separate entry on page 373)
NOTE 3: South Korea's 'Swallow' class similar to 'Lerici'
NOTE 4: Italian ships fitted with telescopic crane for launching Callegari diver boats

SPECIFICATION:

COUNTRY OF ORIGIN: Italy
CLASS: Lerici (Mahamiru) (MHC/MSC)
ACTIVE: 4 Italy, 4 Malaysia
('Mahamiru' class), 2 Nigeria
NAME (PENNANT NUMBER):
ITALY – Lerici (M 5550), Sapri
(M 5551), Milazzo (M 5552), Vieste
(M 5553)
MALAYSIA – Mahamiru (11), Jerai
(12), Ledang (13), Kinabalu (14)
NIGERIA – Ohue (M 371), Maraba
(M 372)
CLASS: Gaeta (Huon), (Lat Ya)
(MHC/MSC)
ACTIVE: 6 Australia ('Huon' class),
8 Italy, 2 Thailand ('Lat Ya' class)
AUSTRALIA – Huon (82),
Hawkesbury (83), Norman (84),
Gascoyne (85), Diamantina (86),
Yarra (87)
ITALY – Gaeta (M 5554), Termoli
(M 5555), Alghero (M 5556),
Numana (M 5557), Crotone
(M 5558), Viareggio (M 5559),
Chioggia (M 5560), Rimini
(M 5561)
THAILAND – Lat Ya (633), Tha Din
Daeng (634)

FEATURES:

DISPLACEMENT: 620 tons full load;
697 tons ('Gaeta' onwards); 610
tons (Malaysia); 540 tons
(Nigeria); 680 tons (Thailand);
720 tons (Australia)
LENGTH: 164 ft (50 m); 172.1 ft
(52.5 m) ('Gaeta' class, Australia,
Thailand); 167.3 ft (51 m)
(Malaysia, Nigeria)
BEAM: 32.5 ft (9.9 m)
DRAUGHT: 8.6 ft (2.6 m); 9.2 ft
(2.8 m) (Malaysia); 9.8 ft
(3 m) (Australia); 9.4 ft (2.9 m)
(Thailand)
SPEED: 15 kts
RANGE: 1600 miles at 12 kts
(Australia); 2000 miles at 12 kts
(Malaysia, Thailand); 2500 miles
at 12 kts (Italy, Nigeria)

ARMAMENT:

GUNS: One Oerlikon 20 mm/70
(Italy); one MSI DS 30B 30 mm/75
(Australia, Thailand); one Bofors
40 mm/70 (Malaysia); two
Emerson Electric 30 mm (twin);
two Oerlikon 20 mm GAM-B01
(Nigeria)
COUNTERMEASURES: Minehunting
– one MIN Mk 2 ('Gaeta' class)
ROV, one Pluto mine destruction
system; minesweeping –
Oropesa Mk 4 wire sweep (Italy),
two Bofors SUTEC Double-Eagle
Mk 2 mine disposal vehicles,
ADI Oropesa mechanical sweep
(Australia), Thomson-CSF IBIS II
minehunting system, two
Improved PAP 104 ROVS,
Oropresa 'o' Mis-4 mechancial
sweep (Malaysia), two Pluto
systems, Oropesa 'o' Mis-4 and
IBIS V control system (Nigeria),
Atlas MWS 80-6 minehunting
system, magnetic and acoustic
and mechanical sweeps, two
Pluto Plus ROVS (Thailand)
DECOYS: Two Super Barricade
chaff launchers (Australia only)

ELECTRONICS:

RADARS: Navigation – SMA
SPN-728(v)3 (Italy); Kelvin Hughes
1007 (Australia); Racal Decca
1226; Thomson-CSF Tripartite III
(Malaysia); Racal Decca 1226
(Nigeria); Atlas Elektronik 9600M
(ARPA) (Thailand)
SONARS: FIAR SQQ-14(IT) VDS
(lowered from keel forward of
bridge) (Italy); Thomson-Sintra
TSM 2022, minehunting
(Malaysia, Nigeria); GEC Marconi
Type 2093 VDS (Australia);
Atlas Elektronik DSQS-11M,
hull-mounted, active (Thailand)

Tripartite BELGIUM, FRANCE, INDONESIA, NETHERLANDS, PAKISTAN

Crocus

- High bow and high freeboard
- Continuous maindeck aft to break down to low freeboard quarterdeck
- 20 mm/20 gun mounting in 'A' position
- Low superstructure from forecastle aft to quarterdeck
- Pole mainmast atop after end of bridge
- Squat, tapered, black-capped funnel with sloping top, atop superstructure
- Small crane on quarterdeck
- SATCOM on pole aft end of superstructure, (some Dutch ships)
- French ships being upgraded with TIUS 2022 Mk III sonar in hull-mounted and PVDS form on Double Eagle Mk II

NOTE: There are differences in design between Indonesian ships and the European Tripartite hulls. Deckhouses and general layout are different as the Indonesian units are required to act as minehunters, minesweepers and patrol ships

SPECIFICATION:

COUNTRY OF ORIGIN:
International
CLASS: Tripartite Minehunters
(Flower, Éridan, Pulau Rengat,
Alkmaar, Munsif) (MHC)
ACTIVE: 6 Belgium ('Flower' class)
13 France ('Éridan' class), 2
Indonesia ('Pulau Rengat' class),
10 Netherlands ('Alkmaar' class),
3 Pakistan ('Munsif' class)
NAME (PENNANT NUMBER):
BELGIUM – Aster (M 915),
Bellis (M 916), Crocus (M 917),
Lobelia (M 921), Narcis (M 923),
Primula (M 924)
FRANCE – Éridan (M 641),
Cassiopée (M 642), Andromède
(M 643), Pégase (M 644), Orion
(M 645), Croix du Sud (M 646),
Aigle (M 647), Lyre (M 648), Persée
(M 649), Sagittaire (M 650),
Verseau (ex-*Iris*) (M 651), Céphée
(ex-*Fuchsia*) (M 652), Capricorne
(ex-*Dianthus*) (M 653)

INDONESIA – Pulau Rengat (711),
Pulau Rupat (712)
NETHERLANDS – Haarlem (M 853),
Maassluis (M 856), Makkum
(M 857), Middelburg (M 858),
Hellevoetsluis (M 859), Schiedam
(M 860), Urk (M 861), Zierikzee
(M 862), Vlaardingen (M 863),
Willemstad (M 864)
PAKISTAN – Munsif (ex-*Sagittaire*)
(M 166), Muhafiz (M 163),
Mujahid (M 164)

FEATURES:

DISPLACEMENT: 595 tons full load;
605 tons (France); 568 tons
(Indonesia)
LENGTH: 168.9 ft (51.5 m)
BEAM: 29.2 ft (8.9 m)
DRAUGHT: 8.5 ft (2.6 m)
(Netherlands); 8.2 ft (2.5 m)
(Belgium, Indonesia, France);
9.5 ft (2.9 m) (Pakistan)
SPEED: 15 kts
RANGE: 3000 miles at 12 kts

ARMAMENT:

GUNS: One DCN 20 mm/20; one
12.7 machine gun (Belgium);
one Giat 20F2 20 mm (France,
Netherlands, Pakistan); one
12.7 mm machine gun (France,
Pakistan); one Rheinmetall
20 mm (Indonesia); Matra
Simbad/Mistral SAM launcher
may be added for patrol duties
or a third 20 mm gun)
COUNTERMEASURES: MCM – two
PAP 104 remote-controlled mine
locators; mechanical sweep gear
(medium depth); OD3 mechanical
sweep gear, AP-4 acoustic sweep,
Double Eagle ROV (France);
Elesco MKR 400 acoustic sweep,
MRK 960 magnetic sweep
(Pakistan); OD3 Oropesa
mechanical sweep, Fiskars F-82
magnetic sweep and SA Marine
AS 203 acoustic sweeps, two
PAP 104 Mk 4 ROV (Indonesia);
OD3 mechanical sweep
(Netherlands)

ELECTRONICS:

RADARS: Navigation – Racal
Decca 1229 (Belgium, France,
Pakistan M 166), Kelvin Hughes
1007 (Pakistan M 163-164), Racal
Decca TM 1229C (Indonesia,
Netherlands)
SONARS: Thomson-Sintra
DUBM 21A/B or 21D, hull-
mounted; Thomson-Sintra
TSM 2022 (Indonesia),
minehunting

357

Kingston CANADA

Kingston

- Long forecastle, with continuous maindeck to aft of stepped superstructure, then sharp drop down to sweep deck
- All round windows to bridge
- Thick pole mast atop bridge
- Two angled, thin funnels, port and starboard, aft of superstructure
- Crane derrick between funnels

SPECIFICATION:

COUNTRY OF ORIGIN: Canada
CLASS: Kingston (MCDV/MCM)
ACTIVE: 12
NAME (PENNANT NUMBER): Kingston (700), Glace Bay (701), Nanaimo (702), Edmonton (703), Shawinigan (704), Whitehorse (705), Yellowknife (706), Goose Bay (707), Moncton (708), Saskatoon (709), Brandon (710), Summerside (711)

FEATURES:

DISPLACEMENT: 962 tons full load
LENGTH: 181.4 ft (55.3 m)
BEAM: 37.1 ft (11.3 m)
DRAUGHT: 11.2 ft (3.4 m)
SPEED: 15 kts
RANGE: 5000 miles at 8 kts

ARMAMENT:

GUNS: One Bofors 40 mm/60 Mk 5C; two 12.7 mm machine guns
COUNTERMEASURES: MCM – one of three modular payloads, (a) Indal Technologies SLQ-38 (single and double Oropesa sweeps), (b) AN/SQS-511 route survey system, (c) Mine inspection, ISE TB 25 bottom inspection vehicle ROV

ELECTRONICS:

RADARS: Surface search – Kelvin Hughes 6000; naviagtion – Kelvin Hughes I-band
Sonars: MacDonald Dettwiler AN/SQS-511 towed side scan, active

Frankenthal GERMANY

Rottweil

- High freeboard forward with break down to maindeck level amidships
- 40 mm/70 gun mounting in 'A' position
- Tall, substantial superstructure stepped down aft of midships
- Small pole aerial atop bridge
- Tall, slim, tripod mainmast amidships
- Small crane on quarterdeck

NOTE: Same hull, similar superstructure as 'Ensdorf' class, Type 352

NOTE 2: Similar in appearance to five 'Kulmbach' class converted minehunters (M 1091, 1095, 1096, 1097, 1099) and five 'Ensdorf' converted minesweepers (M 1090, 1092, 1093, 1094, 1098)

NOTE 3: Equipped with two ATLAS Elektronik Pinguin-B3 drones with sonar and TV cameras

SPECIFICATION:

COUNTRY OF ORIGIN: Germany
CLASS: Frankenthal (Type 332) (MHC)
ACTIVE: 12
NAME (PENNANT NUMBER): Frankenthal (M 1066), Weiden (M 1060), Rottweil (M 1061), Bad Bevensen (M 1063), Bad Rappenau (M 1067), Grömitz (M 1064), Datteln (M 1068), Dillingen (M 1065), Homburg (M 1069), Sulzbach-Rosenberg (M 1062), Fulda (M 1058), Weilheim (M 1059)

FEATURES:
DISPLACEMENT: 650 tons full load
LENGTH: 178.8 ft (54.5 m)
BEAM: 30.2 ft (9.2 m)
DRAUGHT: 8.5 ft (2.6 m)
SPEED: 18 kts

ARMAMENT:
MISSILES: SAM – two Stinger quad launchers
GUNS: One Bofors 40 mm/70, (being replaced by Mauser 27 mm)

ELECTRONICS:
RADARS: Navigation – Raytheon SPS-64
SONARS: Atlas Elektronik DSQS-11M, hull-mounted

Ensdorf GERMANY

Ensdorf

Very similar profile to 'Frankenthal' class with main distinguishing differences as follows:

- Latticed, pyramid-shaped mainmast atop bridge roof supporting WM 20/2 surface search/fire control radome
- Mauser 27 mm turret mountings in 'A' and 'X' positions

NOTE: Five hulls of 'Hameln' class converted to minesweepers 2000-2001. Can control up to four remotely controlled minesweeping drones ('Seehund'). Sea Fox C ROV for mine disposal. Double Oropesa mechanical sweep. Very similar to 'Kulmbach' class (M 1091, 1095, 1096, 1097, 1099)

SPECIFICATION:

COUNTRY OF ORIGIN: Germany
CLASS: Ensdorf (Type 352) (MHC)
ACTIVE: 5
NAME (PENNANT NUMBER): Hameln (M 1092), Pegnitz (M 1090), Siegburg (M 1098), Ensdorf (M 1094), Auerbach (M 1093)

FEATURES:
DISPLACEMENT: 635 tons full load
LENGTH: 178.5 ft (54.4 m)
BEAM: 30.2 ft (9.2 m)
DRAUGHT: 8.2 ft (2.5 m)
SPEED: 18 kts

ARMAMENT:
MISSILES: SAM – two Stinger quad launchers
GUNS: Two Mauser 27 mm
MINES: 60
DECOYS: Two Silver Dog chaff rocket launchers

ELECTRONICS:
RADARS: Surface search/fire control – Signaal WM 20/2; navigation – Raytheon SPS-64
SONARS: STN ADS DSQS-15A mine avoidance, active
EW: Thomson-CSF DR 2000 ESM

Kulmbach GERMANY

Kulmbach

Very similar profile to 'Frankenthal' class with main distinguishing differences as follows:

- Latticed, pyramid-shaped mainmast atop bridge roof supporting WM 20/2 surface search/fire control radome
- Mauser 27 mm turret mounting forward of bridge
- Mauser 27 mm turret aft of superstructure

NOTE: Five hulls of 'Hameln' class converted to minehunters 1999-2001. Very similar to 'Ensdorf' class (M 1090, 1092, 1093, 1094, 1098). Disposal Sea Fox 1 used for inspection and Sea Fox c ROV for mine disposal

SPECIFICATION:

COUNTRY OF ORIGIN: Germany
CLASS: Kulmbach (Type 333) (MHC)
ACTIVE: 5
NAME (PENNANT NUMBER):
Überherrn (M 1095), Laboe
(M 1097), Kulmbach (M 1091),
Passau (M 1096), Herten (M 1099)

FEATURES:
DISPLACEMENT: 635 tons full load
LENGTH: 178.5 ft (54.4 m)
BEAM: 30.2 ft (9.2 m)
DRAUGHT: 8.2 ft (2.5 m)
SPEED: 18 kts

ARMAMENT:
MISSILES: SAM – two Stinger quad launchers
GUNS: Two Mauser 27 mm
MINES: 60
DECOYS: Two Silver Dog chaff rocket launchers

ELECTRONICS:
RADARS: Surface search/fire control – Signaal WM 20/2; navigation – Raytheon SPS-64
SONARS: Atlas Elektronik DSQS-11M, hull-mounted
EW: Thomson-CSF DR 2000 ESM

Natya I INDIA, LIBYA, RUSSIA, SYRIA, UKRAINE, YEMEN

Natya 1

- High bow, short forecastle with slender mast at forward end
- 30 mm/65 gun mounting in 'A' position
- Continuous maindeck aft to break down to sweep deck. Main superstructure well forward of midships
- Large lattice mainmast atop after end of superstructure supporting distinctive radar aerial
- Black-capped funnel with sloping top aft of midships
- Ship's boat in davits, starboard side just forward of funnel
- 30 mm/65 gun mounting in 'x' position
- Distinctive hydraulic gantries right aft (in some)

NOTE: Some have Gatling 30 mm guns
NOTE 2: At least one Libyan hull painted in green striped camouflage in 1991. Others may have blue hulls

SPECIFICATION:

COUNTRY OF ORIGIN: Russia
CLASS: Natya I (Type 266M)
(Pondicherry) (Akvamaren) (MSO)
ACTIVE: 12 India ('Pondicherry' class), 5 Libya, 10 Russia ('Akvameren' class), 1 Syria, 2 Ukraine, 1 Yemen
NAME (PENNANT NUMBER):
INDIA — Pondicherry (M 61), Porbandar (M 62), Bedi (M 63), Bhavnagar (M 64), Alleppey (M 65), Ratnagiri (M 66), Karwar (M 67), Cannanore (M 68) Cuddalore (M 69), Kakinada (M 70), Kozhikode (M 71), Konkan (M 72)
LIBYA — Al Isar (ex-Ras El Gelais) (113), Al Tiyar (ex-Ras Hadad) (111), Ras Al Fulaijah (117), Ras Al Massad (123), Ras Al Hani (125)
RUSSIA — Motorist (806), Valentine Pikul (770), Svyazist (610), Korovets (913), MT-265 (718), Kontradmiral Vlasov (855), MT-264 (738), Vitseadmiral Zacharin, Turbinist (912), Snayper (919)
SYRIA — (642)
UKRAINE — Zhovti Vody (ex-Zenitchik) (U310), Cherkasy (ex-Razvedchik) (U311)
YEMEN — (201)

FEATURES:

DISPLACEMENT: 804 tons full load
LENGTH: 200.1 ft (61 m)
BEAM: 33.5 ft (10.2 m)
DRAUGHT: 9.8 ft (3 m)
SPEED: 16 kts
RANGE: 3000 miles at 12 kts

ARMAMENT:

MISSILES: SAM — two SA-N-5/8 Grail quad launchers (in some, Russia)
GUNS: Four 30 mm/65 AK 230 (2 twin) or two 30 mm/65 AK 306; four 25 mm/80 (2 twin) (Russia, Ukraine); four 30 mm/65 (2 twin); four 25 mm/60 (2 twin) (India)
A/S MORTARS: Two RBU 1200 5-tubed fixed
COUNTERMEASURES: MCM—1 or two GKT-2 contact sweeps; one AT-2 acoustic; one TEM-3 magnetic sweep

ELECTRONICS:

RADARS: Surface search — Don 2 or Low Trough; fire control — Drum Tilt (not in all)
SONARS: MG 79/89 hull-mounted; minehunting (Russia, Ukraine); MG 69/79 remainder

Kondor II INDONESIA, LATVIA, URUGUAY

Fortuna

- Low freeboard with continuous maindeck from stem to stern
- 23/25 mm twin turret on barbette immediately forward of bridge (Indonesia and Latvia), 40 mm/70 in same position (Uruguay)
- High, stepped, smooth contoured superstructure centred well forward of midships
- Sturdy pole mainmast immediately aft of bridge, supporting radar aerials
- Squat, square sectioned funnel with sloping top sited midships
- Two 25 mm/80 twin gun mountings mounting on sponsons aft of funnel in Indonesian ships (absent in Uruguayan units). Latvia has two 20 mm cannon side by side in same position
- Small square structure on afterdeck
- Sweep gear right aft
- 'Kondor II' some 16 ft longer than 'Kondor I'
- 'Kondor I' has square profile funnel with sloping top. 'Kondor II' has rounded funnel with wedge-shaped smoke deflector at its after edge

NOTE: Malta operates three 'Kondor I' (P 30, P 31, P 29) as coastal patrol craft. Cape Verde operates one 'Kondor I' as a coastal patrol craft. Tunisian National Guard operates six 'Kondor I' class as patrol craft

SPECIFICATION:

COUNTRY OF ORIGIN: Germany
CLASS: Kondor II (Type 89) (MSC/PC)
ACTIVE: 9 Indonesia, 2 Latvia, 3 Uruguay
NAME (PENNANT NUMBER):
INDONESIA – Pulau Rote (ex-Wolgast) (721, ex-V 811), Pulau Raas (ex-Hettstedt) (722, ex-353), Pulau Romang (ex-Pritzwalk) (723, ex-325), Pulau Rimau (ex-Bitterfeld) (724, ex-332, ex-M 2672), Pulau Rondo (ex-Zerbst) (725, ex-335), Pulau Rusa (ex-Oranienburg) (726, ex-341), Pulau Rangsang (ex-Jüterbog) (727, ex-342), Pulau Raibu (ex-Sömmerda) (728, ex-311, ex-M 2670), Pulau Rempang (ex-Grimma) (729, ex-336)
LATVIA – Viesturs (ex-Kamenz) (M 01, ex-351), Imanta (ex-Röbel) (M 02, ex-324)
URUGUAY – Temerairo (ex-Riesa) (31), Fortuna (ex-Bernau) (33), Audaz (ex-Eisleben) (34)

FEATURES:

DISPLACEMENT: 310 tons full load; 410 tons (Latvia)
LENGTH: 186 ft (56.7 m)
BEAM: 24.6 ft (7.5 m)
DRAUGHT: 7.9 ft (2.4 m)
SPEED: 17 kts
RANGE: 2000 miles at 14 kts

ARMAMENT:

GUNS: Six 25 mm/80 (3 twin) (Indonesia); two Wrobel ZU 23-2MR 23 mm (twin); two FK20 20 mm (Latvia); one Hispano-Suiza 30 mm/70 (Uruguay)
MINES: Two rails (Indonesia, Uruguay only)

ELECTRONICS:

RADARS: Surface search – Racal Decca (Latvia); navigation – TSR 333 or Raytheon 1900
SONARS: Bendix AQS-17(V) VDS (Indonesia); Klein 2000 sidescan (Latvia)

Hatsushima/Uwajima JAPAN

'Hatsushima' class

- Continuous deck from bow aft to break adjacent to funnel, down to lower deck level
- Small bridge superstructure well forward of midships
- Tall tripod mainmast midships
- Tall, black-capped cylindrical funnel aft of mainmast at deck break
- Slender aftermast forward of sweep deck
- Sweeping gantries at after end of sweep deck

SPECIFICATION:

COUNTRY OF ORIGIN: Japan
CLASS: Hatsushima (MHC/MSC), Uwajima (MHC/MSC)
ACTIVE: 5 ('Hatsushima' class), 9 ('Uwajima' class)
NAME (PENNANT NUMBER):
HATSUSHIMA – Ogishima (MSC 666), Yurishima (MSC 668), Hikoshima (MSC 669), Awashima (MSC 670), Sakushima (MSC 671)
UWAJIMA – Uwajima (MSC 672), Eeshima (MSC 673), Tsukishima (MSC 674), Maejima (MSC 675), Kumejima (MSC 676), Makishima (MSC 677), Tobishima (MSC 678), Yugeshima (MSC 679), Nagashima (MSC 680)

FEATURES:

DISPLACEMENT: 510 tons full load
LENGTH: 180.4 ft (55 m); 190.3 ft (58 m) (MSC 670 on)
BEAM: 30.8 ft (9.4 m)
DRAUGHT: 7.9 ft (2.4 m)
SPEED: 14 kts

ARMAMENT:

GUNS: One JM-61 20 mm/76 Sea Vulcan 20

ELECTRONICS:

RADARS: Surface search – Fujitsu OPS-9 or OPDS-39 (MSC 674 onwards)
SONARS: Nec/Hitachi ZQS 2B or ZQS 3 (MSC 672 onwards), hull-mounted; minehunting

Sugashima JAPAN

Tsunoshima (*Michael Nitz*)

- Continuous deck from bow aft to curved break just aft of funnels, down to lower deck level
- Small bridge set well back from forward edge of superstructure
- Tall tripod mainmast midships
- Twin, tall, black-capped angled thin funnels, with pole aerials, aft of mainmast, just forward of deck break
- Sweeping gantries at after end of sweep deck

NOTE: Hull is similar to 'Uwajima' class, but upper deck is extended aft to provide greater stowage

NOTE 2: PAP 104 Mk 5 ROVS carried. ADI Dyad minesweeping gear fitted

SPECIFICATION:

COUNTRY OF ORIGIN: Japan
CLASS: Sugashima (MSC)
ACTIVE: 10
BUILDING: 2
NAME (PENNANT NUMBER):
Sugashima (MSC 681), Notojima (MSC 682), Tsunoshima (MSC 683), Naoshima (MSC 684), Toyoshima (MSC 685), Ukushima (MSC 686), Izushima (MSC 687), Aishima (MSC 688), Aoshima (MSC 689), Miyajima (MSC 690), Shishijima (MSC 691), — (MSC 692)

FEATURES:

DISPLACEMENT: 510 tons standard
LENGTH: 177.2 ft (54 m)
BEAM: 30.8 ft (9.4 m)
DRAUGHT: 9.8 ft (3 m)
SPEED: 14 kts

ARMAMENT:
GUNS: One JM-61 20 mm/76 Sea Vulcan 20

ELECTRONICS:
RADARS: Surface search – OPDS-39B
SONARS: Hitachi/Thomson/Marconi GEC Type 2093 VDS

Oksøy/Alta NORWAY

Karmøy

- Unusual blunt, flat-fronted bow
- Twin-hulled
- Flat forecastle forward of stepped, substantial superstructure
- Bridge just forward of midships set atop superstructure
- Lattice mainmast atop after end of bridge
- Unusual, square section twin funnels at after end of main superstructure
- Deck aft of funnels drops down to small sweep deck
- Modern design ship with clean lines and high freeboard

SPECIFICATION:

COUNTRY OF ORIGIN: Norway
CLASS: Oksøy/Alta (MHC/MSC)
ACTIVE: 6
NAME (PENNANT NUMBER):
MHC – Oksøy (M 340), Karmøy (M 341), Måløy (M 342), Hinnøy (M 343)
MSC – Alta (M 350), Otra (M 351)

FEATURES:

DISPLACEMENT: 375 tons full load
LENGTH: 181.1 ft (55.2 m)
BEAM: 44.6 ft (13.6 m)
DRAUGHT: 8.2 ft (2.5 m)
SPEED: 20.5 kts
RANGE: 1500 miles at 20 kts

ARMAMENT:

MISSILES: SAM – Matra Sadral, twin launcher, Mistral
GUNS: One or two Rheinmetall 20 mm; two 12.7 mm machine guns
COUNTERMEASURES: Minehunters – two Pluto submersibles; minesweepers – AGATE mechanical and Elma influence sweeping equipment

ELECTRONICS:

RADARS: Navigation – two Racal Decca
SONARS: Thomson Sintra/Simrad TSM 2023N, hull-mounted (minehunters); Simrad Subsea SA 950, hull-mounted (minesweepers)

Landsort SINGAPORE, SWEDEN

Katong

- High freeboard with continuous maindeck from stem to stern
- Main superstructure forward of midships with step down to sweep deck
- Bridge set atop mid-superstructure
- 40 mm/70 gun mounting in 'B' position
- Sturdy pole mainmast at after end of main superstructure with twin funnels at its base

NOTE: Bofors Sea Trinity CIWS trial in Sweden's *Vinga* in place of 40 mm/70

SPECIFICATION:

COUNTRY OF ORIGIN: Sweden
CLASS: Landsort (Bedok) (MHC)
ACTIVE: 4 Singapore ('Bedok' class), 7 Sweden
NAME (PENNANT NUMBER):
SINGAPORE – Bedok (M 105), Kallang (M 106), Katong (M 107), Punggol (M 108)
SWEDEN – Landsort (M 71), Arholma (M 72), Koster (M 73), Kullen (M 74), Vinga (M 75), Ven (M 76), Ulvön (M 77)

FEATURES:

DISPLACEMENT: 360 tons full load
LENGTH: 155.8 ft (47.5 m)
BEAM: 31.5 ft (9.6 m)
DRAUGHT: 7.3 ft (2.2 m)
SPEED: 15 kts
RANGE: 2000 miles at 12 kts

ARMAMENT:

MISSILES: SAM – Saab Manpads
GUNS: One Bofors 40 mm/70 Mod 48; two 7.62 mm machine guns (four 12.7 mm machine guns, Singapore)
A/S MORTARS: Four Saab Elma 9-tube launchers (Sweden only)
MINES: Two rails (Singapore only)
DECOYS: Two Philips Philax launchers can be carried (Sweden only)
COUNTERMEASURES: MCM – fitted for mechanical sweeps for moored mines, magnetic and acoustic sweeps; two PAP 1-4 Mk 5 ROVs embarked in Singapore ships (Sutec or Double Eagle ROV, possible to operate two unmanned magnetic and acoustic sweepers, Sweden)

ELECTRONICS:

RADARS: Navigation – Thomson-CSF Terma (Sweden); Norcontrol DB 2000 (Singapore)
SONARS: Thomson-CSF TSM-2022, hull-mounted; minehunting
EW: Matilda ESM

Hunt UK, GREECE

Evropi (Greece)

- High freeboard maindeck
- Continuous maindeck aft to sloping break down to sweep deck
- 30 mm/75 gun mounting mid-forecastle
- Midships super-structure has high bridge at forward end
- Tapered, enclosed mainmast amidships
- Navigation radar aerial atop bridge roof
- Large, black-capped funnel aft of mainmast
- Large structure on afterdeck housing various minehunting and minesweeping equipment

SPECIFICATION:

COUNTRY OF ORIGIN: UK
CLASS: Hunt (MSC/MHC)
ACTIVE: 11 UK, 2 Greece
NAME (PENNANT NUMBER):
UK – Brecon (M 29), Ledbury (M 30), Cattistock (M 31), Cottesmore (M 32), Brocklesby (M 33), Middleton (M 34), Dulverton (M 35), Chiddingfold (M 37), Atherstone (M 38), Hurworth (M 39), Quorn (M 41)
GREECE – Evropi (ex-*Bicester*) (M 62, ex-M 36), Kallisto (ex-*Berkeley*) (M 63, ex-M 40)

FEATURES:

DISPLACEMENT: 750 tons full load
LENGTH: 197 ft (60 m) oa
BEAM: 32.8 ft (10 m)
DRAUGHT: 9.5 ft (2.9 m) (keel)
SPEED: 15 kts
RANGE: 1500 miles at 12 kts

ARMAMENT:

GUNS: One DES/MSI DS 30B 30 mm/75; two Oerlikon/BMARC 20 mm GAM-CO1 (not Greece); two 7.62 mm machine guns
COUNTERMEASURES: Two PAP 104/105 remotely controlled submersibles; MS 14 magnetic loop; Sperry MSSA Mk 1 towed acoustic generator; conventional K 8 Oropesa sweeps

ELECTRONICS:

RADARS: Navigation – Kelvin Hughes Type 1007
SONARS: Thales Type 2193 (UK only); Plessey Type 193M Mod 1, hull-mounted, minehunting (Greece); Type 2059 to track PAP 104/105
EW: Matilda UAR 1 (Greece only)

Sandown   UK, SAUDI ARABIA

Shoreham (UK) (*Michael Nitz*)

- Short, sloping forecastle with 30 mm/75 gun mounting in 'A' position
- Long superstructure extending from forecastle to small quarterdeck
- Most of superstructure is flush with ship's side giving a slab-sided effect
- Bridge sited atop superstructure just forward of midships
- Navigation radar aerial atop bridge roof
- Tapered, enclosed mainmast amidships, with short pole mast atop
- Square profile, black-capped funnel with sloping top, aft of mainmast

NOTE: Spain operates five similar 'Segura' class minehunters

SPECIFICATION:

COUNTRY OF ORIGIN: UK
CLASS: Sandown (Al Jawf) (MHC)
ACTIVE: 3 Saudi Arabia ('Al Jawf' class), 8 UK
NAME (PENNANT NUMBER):
SAUDI ARABIA – Al Jawf (420), Shaqra (422), Al Kharj (424)
UNITED KINGDOM – Walney (M 104), Penzance (M 106), Pembroke (M 107), Grimsby (M 108), Bangor (M 109), Ramsey (M 110), Blythe (M 111), Shoreham (M 112)

FEATURES:

DISPLACEMENT: 484 tons full load; 480 tons (Saudi Arabia)
LENGTH: 172.2 ft (52.5 m); 172.9 ft (52.7 m) (Saudi Arabia)
BEAM: 34.4 ft (10.5 m)
DRAUGHT: 7.5 ft (2.3 m); 6.9 ft (2.1 m) (Saudi Arabia)
SPEED: 13 kts
RANGE: 2500 miles at 12 kts

ARMAMENT:

GUNS: One DES/MSI 30 mm/75 DS 30B (UK); two Electronics & Space Emerlec 30 mm (twin) (Saudi Arabia)
DECOYS: Two Loral Hycor SRBOC Mk 36 Mod 1 6-barrel chaff launcher (Saudi Arabia); two Barricade fitted for deployment in UK hulls
COUNTERMEASURES: ECA mine disposal system; two PAP 104 Mk 5

ELECTRONICS:

RADARS: Navigation – Kelvin Hughes Type 1007
SONARS: Marconi Type 2093 VDS; mine search and classification

369

Avenger USA

Chief

- High bow, sloping forecastle
- Continuous maindeck profile from bow aft, with two breaks down aft of main superstructure
- High superstructure extending from forecastle to sweep deck
- Large, distinctive tripod mainmast on bridge roof with short pole mast atop
- Very large tapered funnel aft of midships with sloping top and flat, sloping after end
- Sweep cable reels and floats on sweepdeck
- Unusually large for MCM craft

NOTE: Japan operates three 'Yaeyama' class MSOS (Yaeyama (MSO 301), Tsushima (MSO 302) and Hachijou (MSO 303)), which appear to be a derivative of the 'Avenger' class. Hulls are slightly smaller, with a full load displacement of 1275 tons. There is only one break in the maindeck down to the sweeping deck and the lattice mainmast is at the aft end of the superstructure. There is also a small radome atop the bridge roof in these vessels

SPECIFICATION:

COUNTRY OF ORIGIN: USA
CLASS: Avenger (MCM/MSO/MHO)
ACTIVE: 14
NAME (PENNANT NUMBER):
Avenger (MCM 1), Defender (MCM 2), Sentry (MCM 3), Champion (MCM 4), Guardian (MCM 5), Devastator (MCM 6), Patriot (MCM 7), Scout (MCM 8), Pioneer (MCM 9), Warrior (MCM 10), Gladiator (MCM 11), Ardent (MCM 12), Dextrous (MCM 13), Chief (MCM 14)

FEATURES:

DISPLACEMENT: 1379 tons full load
LENGTH: 224.3 ft (68.4 m)
BEAM: 38.9 ft (11.9 m)
DRAUGHT: 12.2 ft (3.7 m)
SPEED: 13.5 kts
RANGE: 2500 miles at 10 kts

ARMAMENT:

GUNS: Two 12.7 mm Mk 26 machine guns
COUNTERMEASURES: MCM – two SLQ-48; includes ROV mine neutralisation system; SLQ-37(V)3 magnetic/acoustic influence sweep; Oropesa SLQ-38 Type O Size 1; mechanical sweep

ELECTRONICS:

RADARS: Surface search – ISC Cardion SPS-55; navigation – ARPA 2525
SONARS: Raytheon/Thomson-Sintra SQQ-32 VDS; minehunting

Osprey USA

Heron

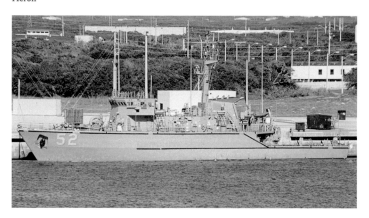

- Continuous maindeck from bow, aft, to break down to low freeboard afterdeck
- Main superstructure extending from forecastle to break
- High bridge at forward end of superstructure with unusual outward-sloping bridge windows
- Bulky, square section, tapered funnel at after end of superstructure with wedge shaped smoke deflector RAD-HAZ screen atop
- Narrow, square section enclosed mainmast immediately forward of funnel
- Large crane deck on afterdeck

NOTE: Modified design based on 'Lerici' class (see page 356), with much larger hull

SPECIFICATION:

COUNTRY OF ORIGIN: USA
CLASS: Osprey (MHC)
ACTIVE: 12
NAME (PENNANT NUMBER):
Osprey (MHC 51), Heron (MHC 52), Pelican (MHC 53), Robin (MHC 54), Oriole (MHC 55), Kingfisher (MHC 56), Cormorant (MHC 57), Black Hawk (MHC 58), Falcon (MHC 59), Cardinal (MHC 60), Raven (MHC 61), Shrike (MHC 62)

FEATURES:
DISPLACEMENT: 930 tons full load
LENGTH: 187.8 ft (57.2 m)
BEAM: 35.9 ft (11 m)
DRAUGHT: 9.5 ft (2.9 m)
SPEED: 10 kts
RANGE: 1500 miles at 10 kts

ARMAMENT:
GUNS: Two 12.7 mm machine guns
COUNTERMEASURES: MCM – Alliant SLQ-48 ROV mine neutralisation system ROV; Degaussing DGM-4

ELECTRONICS:
RADARS: Surface search – Raytheon SPS-64(V)9; navigation – R4 1XX
SONARS: Raytheon/Thomson-Sintra SQQ-32(V)3 VDS; minehunting

NATO STANAG Designators for Ships

AA	Auxiliary type ship, general	General designator for all naval auxiliary type ships
AH	Hospital ship	Ship 131.23 ft (40 m) or over, providing hospital services
AP	Personnel transport	Ship of 393.7 ft (120 m) or over, to transport troops and their supplies
CA	Cruiser, gun	A cruiser with 6 in guns or larger as main armament, carries no missiles
CC	Cruiser, general	Cruisers of 492.12 ft (150 m) and over
CG	Cruiser, guided missile	Cruiser having guided missiles as main armament
CGH	Cruiser, guided missile, helicopter	Guided missile cruiser with helicopter operational capability
CGN	Cruiser, guided missile, nuclear	As CG but with nuclear propulsion
CV	Aircraft carrier	Designator for aircraft carriers and multi-role aircraft carriers
CVG	Aircraft carrier, guided missile	Aircraft carrier fitted with surface-to-air guided missiles
CVH	Aircraft carrier, VSTOL/helicopter	Carrier not fitted with arrest gear/catapult, operating VSTOL and/or helicopters which is not an amphibious or mine warfare vessel
CVN	Aircraft carrier, nuclear	As CV but with nuclear propulsion
CVS	Aircraft carrier, ASW	Capable of operating VSTOL and/or helicopters in sustained ASW operations
DD	Destroyer, general	General designator for destroyer-type ships in range of c.311.67 to 459.31 ft (95 to 140 m)
DDE	Destroyer, escort	Canadian designator for destroyer type ships
DDG	Destroyer, guided missile	Destroyer fitted with surface-to-air guided missiles
DDH	Destroyer, helicopter	Canadian designator for destroyers with helicopter operating capability
FF	Frigate/corvette general	General designator for frigate. Ship of 246.06 to 492.12 ft (75 to 150 m). Generally lighter surface armament than DD
FFG	Frigate, guided missile	Frigate fitted with surface-to-air guided missiles
FFH	Frigate, helicopter	Frigate carrying helicopters
FFT	Frigate	Frigate that can be used as a training platform
FS	Corvette	Small escort of 196.84 to 328.08 ft (60 to 100 m)
FSG	Corvette (guided missile)	Small escort with missile capability
LCC	Amphibious command ship	Command ship for amphibious taskforce and landing assault operations
LCM	Landing craft, mechanised	Landing craft of 49.21 to 82.02 ft (15 to 25 m) capable of carrying one tank or 50–200 troops. Must have landing ramp
LCP	Landing craft, personnel	Landing craft of 24.6 to 98.42 ft (7.5 to 30 m) suitable for personnel only
LCU	Landing craft, utility	All purpose landing craft of 82.02 to 180.44 ft (25 to 55 m) capable of handling 2–3 tanks or 300–450 troops. Must have landing ramp
LCVP	Landing craft, vehicle, personnel	Similar to LCP but capable of carrying light vehicle in place of troops
LHA	Amphibious general assault ship	Large general purpose amphibious assault ship for landing an assault force from helicopters or landing craft. Must have internal stowage, ramp and flooded well
LHD	Amphibious assault ship	Large multi-purpose amphibious ship for landing an assault force from helicopters, multi-purpose landing craft and amphibious vehicles. Can also conduct missions with VSTOL aircraft and ASW helicopters
LL	Amphibious vessel, general	General designator for amphibious vessels
LPA	Amphibious transport, personnel	Ship capable of carrying 1300–1500 troops and landing them in its own landing craft
LPD	Amphibious transport, dock	Capable of carrying 1000 troops, up to 9 LCM. Must have helicopter platform
LPH	Amphibious assault ship	Large helicopter carrier for landing c. 1800 troops with its own aircraft
LSD	Landing ship, dock	Primarily tank and vehicle carrier, also capable of carrying 150–400 troops
LSM	Landing ship, medium	Of 147.63 to 278.86 ft (45 to 85 m) capable of beaching to land troops/tanks
LST	Landing ship, tank	Of 278.86 to 524.93 ft (85 to 160 m) to transport troops, vehicles and tanks for amphibious assault. Must have bow doors and/or ramps
MM	Mine warfare vessels, general	General designator for mine warfare vessels
MCM	Mine countermeasures vessel	Minehunter with mechanical and influence sweep capability
MH (I) (C) (O)	Minehunter, general	Fitted with equipment to hunt mines (Inshore) (Coastal) (Ocean). Ship of 82.02 to 196.84 ft (25 to 60 m) with enhanced minehunting capability. May also carry sweep gear and mine clearance divers
MHS	Minehunter and sweeper, general	Ship designed to sweep mines
MLC	Minelayer (coastal)	Small mine warfare ship capable of laying mines
MSC	Minesweeper, coastal	Of 131.23 to 196.84 ft (40 to 60 m)
MSO	Minesweeper, ocean	Of 150.91 ft (46 m) or more
OPV	Offshore patrol vessel	General purpose vessel used for fishery protection and light patrol duties
PC(F)	Patrol craft, general (fast)	General designator for patrol vessels
PG	Patrol ship, general	Of 147.63 to 278.86 ft (45 to 85 m) not designed to operate in open ocean. Must have at least 76 mm (3 in) armament
PG (F) (G)	Patrol or gunship (fast) (guided missile)	Patrol ship with missile capability
PHM	Patrol combatant, guided missile	High speed (hydrofoil) craft with SSM capability
PT (H)	Patrol/torpedo boat (hydrofoil)	High speed (35 kts) of 65.61 to 98.42 ft (20 to 30 m). Anti-surface torpedo equipped
SS	Submarine, general	General designator for submarines
SSA	Submarine, missile	Submarines fitted with underwater-to-surface guided missiles
SSBN	Submarine, ballistic missile, nuclear	Primary strategic nuclear submarine armed with ballistic missiles
SSGN	Submarine, attack, surface missile, nuclear	Nuclear submarine fitted with underwater or surface-to-surface missiles
SSK	Submarine, patrol	Non-nuclear long-range patrol submarine may have anti-surface or anti-submarine role
SSN	Submarine, attack, nuclear	Nuclear attack submarine with anti-submarine and anti-surface capability

It should be noted that not all countries conform to the NATO STANAG codings for their ships. There are a number of ships in this publication whose designations will not be found in the above list (e.g. France)

Glossary

AAW	Anti-air warfare
ACDS	Advanced combat direction system
ACV	Air cushion vehicle
AEW	Airborne early warning
AIP	Air independent propulsion
ANV	Advanced naval vehicle
ARM	Anti-radiation missile
A/S, ASW	Anti-submarine (warfare)
ASDS	Advanced Swimmer Delivery System
ASM	Air-to-surface missile
ASROC/SUBROC	Rocket-assisted torpedo
ASV	Anti-surface vessel
AUSS	Advanced Unmanned Search System
AUV	Autonomous Undersea Vehicle
AX/TD	Training ship
BPDMS	Base point defence missile system
Cal./Calibre	Diameter of a gun barrel; also used for measuring the length of the barrel
CIWS	Close-in weapons system
CH	Helicopter cruiser
COTS	Commercial off-the-shelf
cp	Controllable pitch propellers
DC	Depth charge
DCT	Depth charge thrower
DE	Destroyer escort (Japan)
DDK	Destroyer (Japan)
DDS	Dry Dock Shelter (mounted on aft casing of US SSNs for special forces operations)
DP	dual purpose
Displacement	The weight of water displaced by a ship's hull when floating. Standard: as defined by Washington Naval Conference 1922: fully manned and stored but without fuel or reserve feed-water Full load: fully laden with all stores, ammunition, fuel and water
DSV	Deep submergence vehicle
DSRV	Deep submergence recovery vehicle
ECM	Electronic countermeasures
ECCM	Electronic counter-countermeasures
EHF	Extremely high frequency
ELF	Extremely low frequency
ELINT	Electronic intelligence
ESM	Electronic support measures
ESSM	Evolved Sea Sparrow Missile
EW	Electronic warfare
FAC	Fast attack craft
FLIR	Forward looking infra-red radar
FRAM	Fleet rehabilitation and modernisation programme
fwd	forward
FY	fiscal year
GCCS	Global Command and Control System
GFCS	Gun fire control system
GMLS	Guided missile launch system
GPS	Global positioning system
GRP	Glass reinforced plastic
GWS	Guided weapons system
HE	High explosive
HF	High frequency
IFF	Identification friend/foe
IRST	Infra-red search and track
kT	Kiloton (explosive power equivalent to 1,000 tons of TNT)
kts	Knots (speed of 1 nautical mile per hour)
LAMPS	Light airborne multipurpose system (helicopter)
LAMS	Local area missile system
LCA	Landing craft – assault
LCAC	Landing craft – air cushion
LCL	Landing craft – logistic (UK)
LCM	Landing craft – mechanised load
LCP	Landing craft – personnel
LCT	Landing craft – tank
LCU	Landing craft – utility
LCVP	Landing craft – vehicles and personnel

LP	Low frequency
LMCR	Liquid metal cooled reactor
LRMP	Long-range maritime patrol
LSM	Landing ship, medium
MAD	Magnetic anomaly detector
MCM/MCMV	Mine countermeasures/mine countermeasures vessel
MF	Medium frequency
MFCS	Missile fire control system
MG	Machine gun
MIDAS	Mine and ice avoidance system
MIRV	Multiple, independently targetable re-entry vehicle (nuclear warhead)
MRV	Multiple re-entry vehicle (nuclear warhead)
MSC	US Military Sealift Command
MSC	Coastal minesweeper
MW	Megawatt
NBC	Nuclear, biological and chemical warfare
nm	Nautical miles
NMRS	Near-term Mine Reconnaissance System
NTDS	Naval tactical direction system
NTU	New threat upgrade
oa	Overall length between extremities
OPV	Offshore patrol vessel
OTH	Over the horizon
PAAMS	Principal anti-air missile system
PAN	Aircraft carrier, nuclear-powered (France)
PDMS	Point defence missile system
PWR	Pressurised water reactor
RAM	Rolling Airframe Missile
RAM	Radar absorbent material
RAS	Replenishment at sea
RBU	Russian anti-submarine rocket launcher
Ro-ro	Roll-on/roll-off
ROV	Remote operated vehicle
SAM	Surface-to-air missile
SAR	Search and rescue
SATCOM	Satellite communications
SAWCS	Submarine Acoustic Warfare Countermeasures System
SDV	Swimmer delivery vehicle
SES	Surface effect ships
SHF	Super high frequency
SINS	Ship's inertial navigation system
SLBM	Submarine-launched ballistic missile
SLCM	Ship (submarine)-launched cruise missile
SLEP	Service Life Extension Programme
SNLE/SNLE-NG	Sous-Marins Nucléaires Lanceurs d'Engins (French version of SSBN). NG stands for Nouvelle Génération
SRBOC	Super rapid blooming offboard chaff
SSDE/SSE	Submerged signal and decoy ejector
SSM	Surface-to-surface missile
SSTDS	Surface Ship Torpedo Defence System
STIR	Surveillance Target Indicator Radar
STOVL	Short Take-Off and Vertical Landing
SURTASS	Surface Towed Array Surveillance System
SUWN	Surface-to-underwater missile launcher
SWATH	Small waterplane area twin hull
TACAN	Tactical air navigation system
TACTASS	Tactical Towed-Acoustic Sensor System
TAS	Target Acquisition System
TASM	Tomahawk anti-ship missile
TASS	Towed Array Surveillance System
TBMD	Theatre ballistic missile defence
TCD	Landing ship, dock (France)
TLAM	Tomahawk Land Attack Missile with HE warhead
TLAM-N	Tomahawk Land Attack Missile – Nuclear
UAV	Unmanned Aerial Vehicle
UHF	Ultra-high frequency
UUV	Unmanned Undersea Vehicle
VDS	Variable depth sonar
Vertrep	Vertical replenishment
VLF	Very low frequency
VLS	Vertical launch system
VSTOL	Vertical or short take-off/landing (aircraft)
WIG	Wing-in-ground effect (aircraft)
wl	Water line (measurement of length between extremities on the water-line)

Index

Index

Index

Index

Index

Index

Index

Index

Index